Programming with Intel® Wireless MMX™ Technology

A Developer's Guide to Mobile Multimedia Applications

Nigel C. Paver
Bradley C. Aldrich
Moinul H. Khan

INTEL
PRESS

ISBN 0-9743649-1-6

This book is printed on acid-free paper. ∞

Publisher: Richard Bowles
Editor: David J. Clark
Managing Editor: David B. Spencer
Content Manager: Stuart Goldstein
Text Design and Composition: Wasser Studios
Graphic Art: Wasser Studios (illustrations), Ted Cyrek Designs (cover)

Library of Congress Cataloging in Publication Data:

Printed in the United States of America
    10 9 8 7 6 5 4 3 2 1
First printing, April 2004

Contents

Acknowledgments

Rarely is a book with this much information created by a small team. Fortunately, we had help from numerous experts within Intel Corporation and from many more throughout the industry.

Intel® Wireless MMX™ technology would not be possible without the dedication and hard work of the design team in Austin, Texas and Chandler, Arizona, including Bill Maghielse, Rupal Parikh, Murli Ganeshan, Jianwei Liu, David Deng, Wing Yu, Jayanti Gandhi, Manish Biyani, Mukesh Patel, and Kailesh Bavaria. The success of Intel Wireless MMX technology could not be possible without the support of the system software engineering group in Hudson, MA, including Mike Rosenzweig, Hiam Barad, Priya Vaidya, Jim Zhou, and the entire Intel Integrated Performance Primitives (Intel IPP) development team in Shanghai, China.

For the assistance on the tools chapter we would like to specifically thank Ramesh Peri, and Khem Raj, and for reviewing the vectorizer information we would like to thank Aart Bik. For help with the VTune™ analyzer and Intel IPP sections we acknowledge the assistance of James Reinders, Stewart Taylor, and Paul Guditz. We would also like to thank Sarita Maini and AG Ramesh for their support in arranging customer reviews of the manuscript and providing training collaterals. We would also like to thank the people at Intel Press for their support and encouragement; in particular we would like to thank Stuart Goldstein, David Spencer, and Matt Wangler.

We offer our appreciation to several Intel colleagues for their time, support, and expertise in reviewing early versions of the book: Bob Reese, Jeff McVeigh, Sarita Maini, AG Ramesh, Craig Spalding, Allen Hux, Peter Siljerud, Chris Emmons, and Sammy Tao. In addition, we give special thanks to reviewers David Brittain at Superscape; James Bruce, Vinayak Pore, and Niranjan Wartikar at PACE Soft Silicon; and Eric Hyche at RealNetworks, Inc. We would like to thank Melissa Moore for her assistance assembling the software tools for the CD-ROM and reviewing all the contents.

Numerous colleagues from Intel offered information, advice, and vision. Special thanks to Rami Sinno, Fares Bagh, David Borland, Tony Jebson, Mark Fullerton, Kyle Fox, Tom Yemington, Marty Pandola, David Rogers, Tom Adelmeyer, Steve Strazdus, Jay Heeb, and Gang Liang.

Finally, we would like to thank the patience of our families for enduring the many late nights working on this manuscript. Thank you Caroline, Oliver, and Shams.

Part I
What is Intel® Wireless MMX™ Technology?

Chapter 1

Introduction

Mobile multimedia is growing at a startling rate, fueling the trend toward rich multimedia and communications capabilities on mobile devices. End users in the handheld wireless market segment are demanding multimedia and communication experiences similar to those they enjoy on their desktop—but in a mobile setting. Video playback, multi-player gaming, and video conferencing are a few of the key applications driving the path to higher performance multimedia. The availability of more incoming multimedia data via wireless networks, camera sensors, and audio capture is feeding these ever-hungry multimedia applications

One of the biggest challenges for multimedia on mobile devices is to provide high performance with low power consumption. Playing a richly detailed 3D game on a mobile phone or personal digital assistant (PDA) can be highly enjoyable until the phone or PDA runs out of power. To address this challenge, Intel has introduced an extension of the Intel XScale® microarchitecture called Intel® Wireless MMX™ technology, which gives power-efficient acceleration to mobile multimedia applications.

This chapter provides an overview of the trends driving the increase in mobile multimedia, and it explains why Intel Wireless MMX technology is an important part of these trends. The rest of the book provides an introduction to Intel Wireless MMX technology and how it can be deployed to accelerate multimedia.

The Growing Need for Mobile Multimedia

As mobile users demand devices with more data functionality, such as access to services and applications, today's handheld devices and services are undergoing profound change. Historically, mobile phones were primarily a method of transferring voice traffic to the intended recipient. With the emergence of new cellular radio standards, the transmission of packetized data is also possible over the cellular network. Mobile phones are evolving from voice-centric devices to voice-plus-data devices. With the arrival of data, especially multimedia data, the application processing power of phones is increasing.

At the other end of the convergence spectrum are PDAs, where the focus is on providing the end user with a rich set of application services such as video and gaming. The growth of the Internet now allows for the integration of wireless radio communications into these products. In the case of PDAs, the data-centric device adds voice and radio technology. Figure 1.1 shows an example of how both the cellular and handheld PDA platforms are converging.

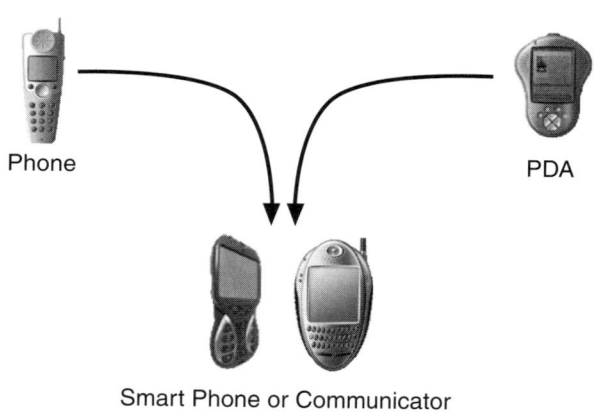

Phone

PDA

Smart Phone or Communicator

Figure 1.1   Convergence of Voice and Data

The converged devices are often known as smart phones or communicators. These devices provide content by means of a wireless connection to the Internet via either cellular or IEEE 802.11 connections. An applications subsystem running a full-featured operating system deals with the user interfaces and runs multimedia-rich user applications.

Technology Drivers

The growing demand for multimedia processing on the converged platforms is driven by two primary factors. The first factor is the growing capability and resolution of the display devices. The second factor is the increasing supply of multimedia data arriving over the network and through onboard sensors such as cameras.

Until recently, cellular phone handsets had very restricted display capabilities. The standard display was limited to a few lines of monochrome text on a small LCD panel. The recent evolution in both display technology and available computing power is producing more advanced products with higher resolution displays. Figure 1.2 shows that the trend toward increasing resolution follows two tracks, depending on the physical size, or form factor, of the product. The PDA form factor has historically been physically larger than a phone, so has supported bigger display resolutions. Today, quarter VGA (QVGA) displays (320×240 pixels) are common, and VGA displays (640×480 pixels) are emerging.

In the smaller physical form factor of the phone handset, the common display resolution is QCIF (176×144 pixels), with a trend toward QVGA—and ultimately VGA—as the data-processing capabilities of the phone increase.

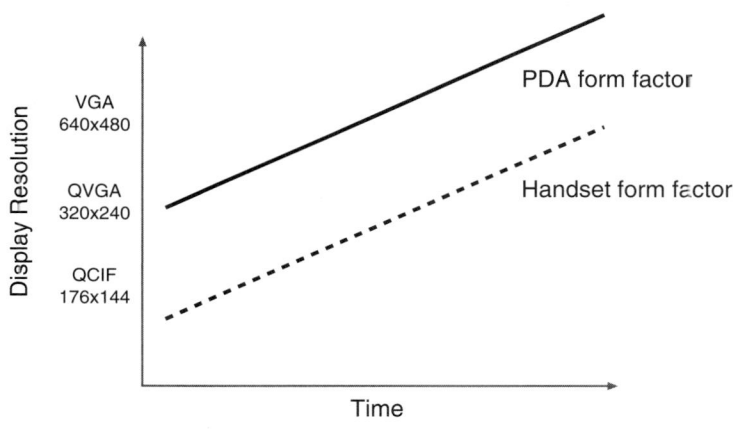

Figure 1.2   Evolution of Display Resolution

As the number of pixels in the display increases, so does the processing power needed to calculate each pixel value. For example, a VGA display typically takes four times the computation that a QVGA does to generate the content.

Intel Wireless MMX technology has been designed to accelerate this extra computation on multimedia workloads.

The early cellular standards were constrained to limited spectrum bandwidth and so could not provide substantial data transport capability. However, with the introduction of next generation 2.5G cellular radio standards such as General Packet Radio Service (GPRS) and Enhanced Data rates for Global Evolution (EDGE), the amount of data available increases up to 144 kilobits per second. This is a substantial improvement over the original 9.6 to 14 kilobits per second of the 2G standards. This evolution is set to continue with the introduction of 3G standards such as WCDMA and UMTS, where data rates of 384 kilobits per second are possible and likely to reach 2.048 megabits per second eventually. Figure 1.3 shows how the data transmission rates are increasing.

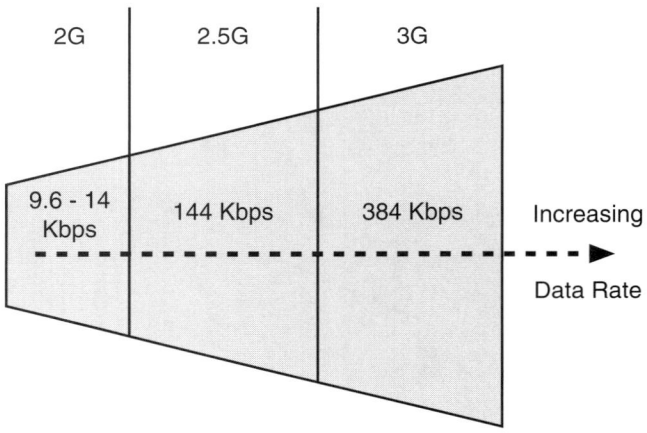

Figure 1.3   Evolution of Cellular Data Rates

The other primary source of multimedia content on handheld devices is from onboard interfaces such as camera interfaces, audio devices, and content stored on removable media such as flash memory cards. The resolution of camera sensors in handheld platforms is evolving rapidly from VGA still image capture to megapixel resolutions more typically seen in digital cameras. The resolution and frame rate for video captured from the same sensors is following a similar growth path; today video can be encoded at QCIF (176×144 pixels), with QGVA and VGA resolutions on the horizon for many product lines. The more pixels in an image or image sequence, the more computation power is required to process them.

The capacity of removable storage media is increasing. Today, 512-megabyte cards are available, and cards with capacity of 1-gigabyte and beyond are being introduced. With this amount of storage available, you can store many hours of VGA-resolution video content. This storage capability is driving the need for an increase in both the computing power to process the VGA content and the power efficiency to view many hours of video from a single battery charge. The increased capacity of the storage cards is also being used to store many hundreds of MP3 audio tracks. In this case, power efficiency becomes critical to ensure playback time meets user expectations.

Building the Application Base

A key aspect of any new platform is ensuring that sufficient applications and content are available to drive user demand. Easing the portability of applications from the desktop to the wireless handset is a key way to accelerate application deployment. Figure 1.4 shows how Intel Wireless MMX technology has been designed to make it easy to port from existing desktop applications that use the original MMX technology.

As Intel continues to develop new architectures to address the evolving demand for computing devices, the portability of applications between market segments becomes increasingly critical to the developer community to shorten time to market for new products. By using common cross-platform toolsets, optimized managed runtime environments (MRTE), and support for industry standards, software developers can accelerate their time to market.

To provide a framework for application development, the Intel Personal Internet Client Architecture (Intel PCA) was created to accelerate the development of data computing applications for handhelds such as phones and PDAs. Intel PCA provides the architectural framework for current and future generations of Internet-ready wireless devices. The architecture guides system implementations that promote a "rich handheld client," exploit client-side computing capabilities, and have predominantly cellular wireless access methods. Intel Wireless MMX technology is a key component in the Intel PCA framework for accelerating multimedia on mobile platforms.

Figure 1.4   Application Porting from the Desktop

Introducing Intel® Wireless MMX™ Technology

Intel Wireless MMX technology is a high-performance, low-power, seamless extension to Intel XScale microarchitecture. Intel Wireless MMX technology offers developers a powerful set of new instructions that should enhance the user's experience of multimedia mobile devices. Developed from a solid foundation of Intel® architecture (IA) technologies, Intel Wireless MMX technology combines the Intel MMX instruction set, the integer instructions from Streaming SIMD Extensions (SSE), and several new multimedia acceleration instructions unique to Intel XScale microarchitecture.

The powerful 64-bit single instruction multiple data (SIMD) architecture of Intel Wireless MMX technology gives a performance boost to many applications, including motion video, graphics combined with video, image processing, audio synthesis, speech synthesis and compression, telephony, conferencing, 2D graphics, and 3D graphics.

Intel Wireless MMX technology was defined to be simple. PC software developers who have already utilized Intel MMX technology and SSE should find a familiar programming environment in Intel Wireless MMX technology that helps speed the porting of existing code bases from the Intel Architecture to Intel PCA-based mobile devices. In addition, Intel Wireless MMX technology is designed to be general enough to address the needs of a large domain of mobile software applications built from current and future algorithms. Finally, Intel Wireless MMX instructions can be used in applications, codecs, algorithms, and drivers.

Intel has worked with industry-leading companies and has developed several Intel tool products to help ensure that Intel Wireless MMX technology is supported by an extensive development environment. Beyond the hardware, this environment includes compilers, vectorizing compilers, assemblers, debuggers, simulators, emulators, intrinsics functions, and the Intel Integrated Performance Primitives (Intel IPP). Together, these tools help enable optimizations so that developers using Intel Wireless MMX technology can begin developing more eficient multimedia products today.

Terminology

To simplify frequently used phrases in this book, the Intel XScale microarchitecture is referred to as either "the core" or "the main core." Similarly, the coprocessor unit supporting Intel Wireless MMX technology is referred to as either "the coprocessor" or "the SIMD coprocessor." For example, in place of the long-winded description, "Intel XScale microarchitecture registers," you will see the simpler phrase "the core registers."

Objectives of the Book

This book provides an introduction to Intel Wireless MMX technology as well as an overview of how to accelerate your application with Intel Wireless MMX technology. Case studies of multimedia algorithms show you how to get the best performance using Intel Wireless MMX technology. The book has three parts.

Part 1: Introduction to Intel® Wireless MMX™ Technology

The first four chapters provide the reader with an introduction to the basic concepts of Intel Wireless MMX technology.

Chapter 1—Introduction

This chapter introduces you to mobile multimedia development, the factors affecting the growth of that market segment, and how Intel Wireless MMX technology fits into the picture.

Chapter 2—Understanding SIMD Processing

This chapter describes the single instruction multiple data (SIMD) programming paradigm and explains how this paradigm applies to Intel Wireless MMX technology. It also provides insight and simple guidance on when SIMD techniques should be employed.

Chapter 3—The Big Picture

This chapter provides a detailed description of the programming model of Intel Wireless MMX technology. A description of the key instructions organized in the manner in which they are used is a key part of this chapter.

Chapter 4—Understanding the Hardware

This chapter describes implementation details of Intel Wireless MMX technology and how these details can affect performance. The chapter introduces the basic pipeline structure of the coprocessor and how this structure can lead to resource and data hazards. The chapter concludes with advice on how to understand hardware dependencies and how to avoid processor stalls in application code using Intel Wireless MMX technology.

Part 2: Optimization Techniques

Chapters 5 through 11 provide an overview of the tools and techniques you need to accelerate your application with Intel Wireless MMX technology. This overview includes descriptions of tools and libraries that you can use and explains how to schedule Intel Wireless MMX instructions and memory transactions for maximum performance.

Chapter 5—The Art of Optimization

This chapter introduces some of the key concepts and terminology you need to understand when optimizing your application.

Chapter 6—Finding the Bottlenecks

This chapter describes how to use the Intel VTune™ Performance Analyzer to find bottlenecks in your code that are candidates for optimization. The chapter provides background on the capabilities of the tool and describes how critical events in the system can be monitored and used to indicate performance issues.

Chapter 7—Intel® Integrated Performance Primitives

This chapter provides an introduction to the Intel® Integrated Performance Primitives (Intel® IPP). Intel IPP is a library of 2,000 multimedia and signal functions that can be used by developers to reduce application development time. The chapter also describes the naming convention used in the Intel IPP library to ease identification of library components.

Chapter 8—Embedded Software Development Tool Chain

This chapter introduces the basic capabilities available in the tool suite supporting Intel Wireless MMX technology. It includes a description of the compiler features that support Intel Wireless MMX technology, such as the vectorizer, inline assembly, and the C intrinsics. The chapter also contains an overview of the debugger environment available for code development with Intel Wireless MMX technology.

Chapter 9—Optimizing for Memory Subsystems

This chapter describes some of the common pitfalls of dealing with memory subsystems and describes techniques and optimizations to get the most out of the system.

Chapter 10—Optimizing for Pipelines

This chapter describes how to organize instruction sequences to maximize performance and reduce wasted stall cycles. It includes techniques that can be used on code that supports Intel Wireless MMX technology and code that supports Intel XScale technology.

Chapter 11—Porting Existing Code

This chapter provides guidance about how to port applications written for desktop applications that use standard MMX and SSE technology to Intel PCA platforms based on Intel XScale microarchitecture with Intel Wireless MMX technology. The chapter describes how the instructions map from one architecture to the other, compares the similarities and differences of the architectures, and provides some examples of porting code from one platform to another.

Part 3: Case Studies

The last four chapters pull together all the components of Intel Wireless MMX technology and apply them to common multimedia workloads so you can see these techniques in action.

Chapter 12—Accelerating Graphics Applications

This chapter provides an introduction to some common two-dimensional graphics techniques and shows how Intel Wireless MMX technology can be employed to improve performance. The chapter includes detailed code examples of how to achieve the best performance on common graphics routines.

Chapter 13—Digital Signal Processing

This chapter provides background and example implementations of some common digital signal processing functions such as finite impulse response filters (FIRs), infinite impulse response filters (IIRs), and FIR-LMS adaptive filters. Detailed code samples are provided.

Chapter 14—Digital Image Processing

This chapter provides an introduction to some of the basic image processing functions that are common in multimedia systems with integrated cameras. It includes descriptions of algorithms with detailed code examples.

Chapter 15—H.264 and MPEG-4 Video Compression

This chapter introduces some common video compression techniques and explains how deploying Intel Wireless MMX technology can accelerate video encoders and decoders. The chapter discusses detailed algorithms for speeding up critical inner loops and provides code samples of an optimal implementation using Intel Wireless MMX technology.

CD-ROM

The enclosed CD-ROM includes all code samples from the case study chapters of the book. In addition, PDF versions of the Intel Wireless MMX technology developer manual and Intel XScale microarchitecture developer manual are also provided. The CD-ROM also includes details of the first Intel PCA processor to contain Intel Wireless MMX technology. Finally, the CD also contains evaluation copies of some of the key Intel tools that are described in this book.

Chapter 2

Understanding SIMD Processing

An expert is someone who knows some of the worst mistakes that can be made in his subject and manages to avoid them.

—Werner Heisenberg

A common method of accelerating a task is to break it down into smaller parts, and then process the parts in parallel to reduce the overall elapsed time spent on the task. While you can subdivide a particular task and expose the parallelism through a variety of approaches, Intel® Wireless MMX™ technology employs a particular method of parallel processing called *single instruction multiple data,* commonly known by the acronym SIMD. This chapter reviews the fundamentals of SIMD processing and where it can be applied.

What is SIMD?

Single instruction multiple data, as the name suggests, takes an operation specified in one instruction and applies it to more than one set of data elements at the same time. For example, in a traditional scalar microprocessor, an add operation would add together a single pair of operands and produce a single result. In SIMD processing, a number of independent operand pairs are added together to produce the same number of independent sums. Figure 2.1 compares these two approaches.

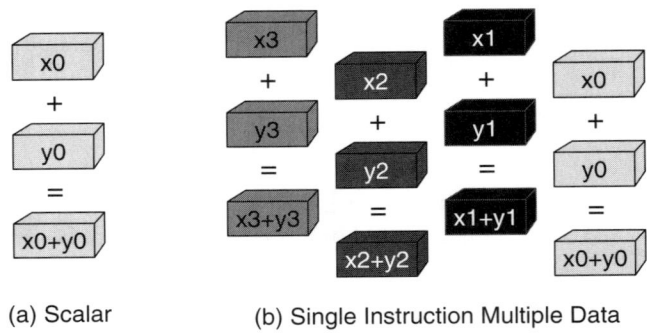

(a) Scalar   (b) Single Instruction Multiple Data

Figure 2.1   Comparison of Scalar and SIMD Processing

The number of parallel data elements processed at the same time is dependent on the size of the elements and the capacity of the data processing resources available. Usually the capacity of the data processing resources is fixed for a given architecture.

Packing Data

To make the handling of multiple data elements more convenient, they are packed together into a single register. An instruction then operates on the register's operands, which contain packed data elements, and produces a packed data result to store in the destination register. The number of data elements that can be packed into a single register is dependent on the size of the register. The number of elements per register is closely matched to the execution capability of the SIMD engine. In Intel Wireless MMX technology, the width of the registers and execution capability is 64 bits. This size register allows a packed add operation to operate on four 16-bit values at the same time, as shown in Figure 2.2.

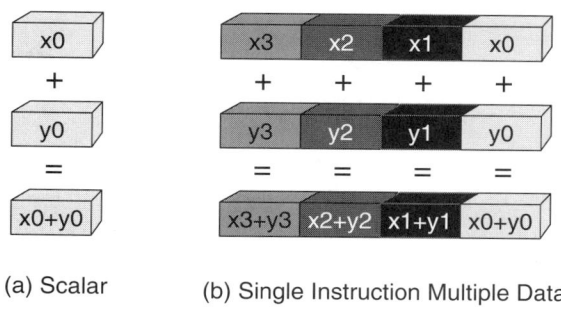

(a) Scalar   (b) Single Instruction Multiple Data

Figure 2.2   Four-Way Packed Add Operation

Data Types

The 64-bit register can be subdivided many ways, but four common formats are usually supported. Figure 2.3 shows the data formats supported for SIMD operations using Intel Wireless MMX instructions. A 64-bit register can contain eight 8-bit bytes, four 16-bit half-words, two 32-bit words, or a single 64-bit value.

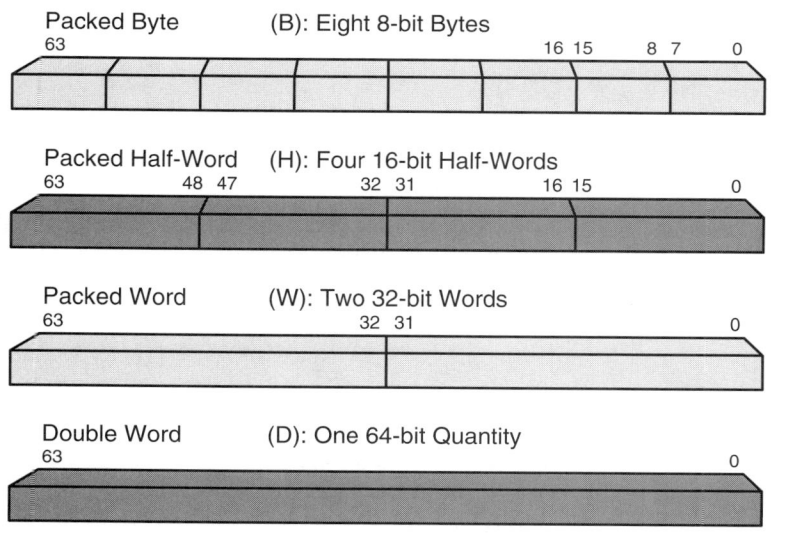

Figure 2.3   Packed Data Formats

For developers familiar with Intel MMX technology, the naming convention used for Intel Wireless MMX technology is slightly different. In the original Intel architecture, the size of a word was 16 bits. Although most modern microprocessors are now 32 bits and some are 64 bits, the definition of the word data type still remained 16 bits for reasons of backward compatibility. However, Intel Wireless MMX technology takes the definition of data type sizes from the baseline ARM[†] architecture where a word is defined to be 32 bits.

Fortunately, translation between the two different data type definitions is simple, as shown in Table 2.1. Developers who are familiar with the original MMX code need to be careful with data type naming.

Table 2.1   Translating Data Type Definitions

Quantity	Data type for Intel® Wireless MMX™ technology	Data type for Intel MMX technology
8 bits	Byte (B)	Byte (B)
16 bits	Half Word (H)	Word (W)
32 bits	Word (W)	Double Word (D)
64 bits	Double Word (D)	Quad Word (Q)

This book uses the data type naming convention for Intel Wireless MMX technology unless explicitly stated otherwise.

Operating on Packed Data

To allow you to operate on packed data, special instructions have been provided that take packed data types as operands. The instructions need to know what data types are stored in the 64-bit register. The programmer must determine how to interpret the data in the registers. To convey this information, you add a data type specifier as a suffix, as follows:

```
WADDB wR0, wR1, wR2
```

This line is the SIMD add instruction, WADD, with the byte data type specified by means of the B suffix. Thus, the data in the two source registers wR1 and wR2 are treated as eight independent byte operands in each register. Usually the data type of the result follows the data type of the input, as is the case with the add instruction. However, for some instructions you should either reduce or increase the precision of the result, as explained in the section on the pack and unpack instructions in Chapter 3.

Advantages of SIMD

The main advantage of SIMD is that processing multiple data elements at the same time, with a single instruction, can dramatically improve performance. For example, processing 12 data items could take 12 instructions for scalar processing, but would require only three instructions if four data elements are processed per instruction using SIMD. While the exact increase in code speed that you observe depends on many factors, you can achieve a dramatic performance boost if SIMD techniques can be utilized. Not everything is suitable for SIMD processing, and not all parts of an application need to be SIMD accelerated to realize significant improvements.

When Should SIMD Processing Be Used?

SIMD processing is most effective when the application contains a lot of data to be processed and data processing operations are independent. The benefit of SIMD processing is greatly enhanced if the data being processed is already in a format that can be easily mapped onto the packed data types. Identifying the data parallelism opportunities and the format of the incoming data are the two key aspects of deciding when to use Intel Wireless MMX technology.

Data Parallelism

To identify data parallelism in an application or some part of an application, look for the following characteristics:

- *Multiple*—The same operation must be applied to multiple data elements.

- *Independent*—The result of one operation must not depend on any other result in the same packed register.

- *Many*—The number of data elements should be greater than or equal to the number of the same data types that can be packed into a single register. The more data to be processed, the more efficient the technique becomes.

You can use SIMD techniques if the application does not exhibit these basic characteristics, but an assessment of these characteristics gives a good first simple indication of viability of SIMD processing for a given algorithm.

Some data parallelism can be easy to spot from the algorithm. For example, when processing image and video, the same operation is often applied to all the pixels in a particular region. An example might be comparing two 8×8 blocks in an image to see how well they match. Figure 2.4 shows the two 8×8 pixel blocks being compared.

The absolute differences between corresponding pixels in each block are calculated, and all the differences are then added together. A low value of the sum of absolute differences indicates that the two blocks are very similar; a high value for the sum of differences indicates a poor match between the two blocks. This operation is typical in a video compression algorithm. In this case, the same absolute difference operation is repeated for every pixel pair, and the results of these comparisons are then summed.

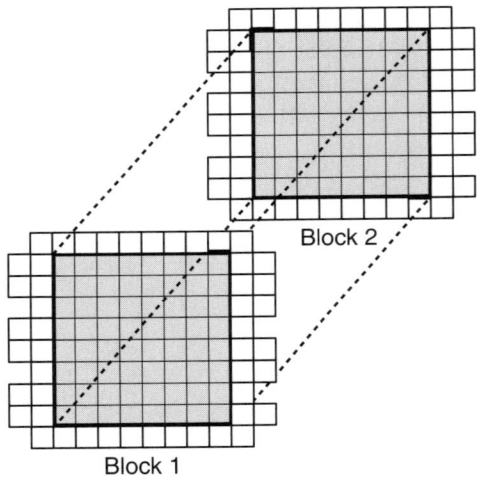

Figure 2.4   Comparing Two 8×8 Pixel Blocks

This example clearly exhibits the three data parallelism characteristics: it is multiple, independent, and repeated many times.

As you will see later, Intel Wireless MMX technology has explicit instruction set support for this operation in the form of the sum of absolute difference operation, or WSAD instruction. This instruction can perform eight byte-size absolute difference operations in parallel and sum the differences to a single result value, all in a single instruction.

Other forms of data parallelism may not be as easy to spot, but you can identify them by testing the three data parallelism characteristics. The example shown in Figure 2.5 is a simple loop where the elements of two arrays are added together and placed in a third array.

```
main() {

  unsigned char a1[8] = {1,1,1,1,1,1,1,1};
  unsigned char a2[8] = {1,1,1,1,1,1,1,1};
  unsigned char a3[8];

  for (i=0; i<8; i++) {
    a3[i] = a1[i] + a2[i];
  }
}
```

Figure 2.5   Identifying Data Parallelism in Loops

This code segment passes the *multiple* test because the same operation is repeated eight times: once in each iteration of the for loop. The code exhibits the *independent* characteristic because no particular output depends on the value of any other output; that is, a3[i] is a function only of the input arguments a1[i] and a2[i]. The *many* characteristic is present because the loop is repeated eight times. With an 8-bit char data type, eight such data elements would fit into a 64-bit packed register, which further satisfies the *many* criterion and ensures that a single instruction can operate on the maximum amount of data.

In this example, 8-byte (char) data elements are added together independently. Therefore, this entire for loop could be replaced with a single SIMD add instruction that processes eight bytes in parallel. Using Intel Wireless MMX instructions, this line would be written as:

```
WADDB wR0, wR1, wR2
```

where wR1 would be pre-loaded with the array a1[8] packed data, wR2 would be preloaded with the array a2[8] packed data, and wR0 would contain the a3[8] calculated result.

The parallelism can also be identified in the mathematical form of the algorithm. The equation below is typical example of the equation to calculate a single output of a finite impulse response (FIR) filter with N coefficients (C_i) operating on the source data X to produce the single output value Z.

$$Z = \sum_{i=0}^{i=N-1} Xi * Ci$$

The data parallelism in this algorithm is similar in style to the previous C code example. In this algorithm, the *multiple* requirement is satisfied by the fact that a multiplication operation is repeated for each corresponding coefficient and data pair. The *many* requirement is also easily satisfied by the fact the operation is repeated N times—at least 10 times, as most filters typically have 10 or more coefficients. The *independent* characteristic needs more investigation. The equation could be rewritten as:

```
Z=X0*C0+X1*C1+...Xn-1*Cn-1
```

In this form, you can see clearly that the calculation of the intermediate products still has independence, even though the final result is a function of these intermediate products. In this case, the calculations of the intermediate products are independent and suitable for SIMD processing. In fact, Intel Wireless MMX technology has instruction support for exactly this type of operation in the form of the multiply accumulate instruction, or WMAC. As you will see later, this takes four pairs of operands, performs the four independent multiplication operations, and then, as an added bonus, takes the four products and adds them together.

Data Formatting

To utilize SIMD techniques effectively, you must pack the incoming arguments efficiently into a format suitable for processing. If the source data is not in the correct format or needs reformatting, the computation required to reformat or repack the data could exceed the benefit of the SIMD processing. SIMD techniques work best when the arguments can be arranged in memory in the required packed format, so that only a single 64-bit load is required to bring the operands into a register for processing.

SIMD Data Organization

Data organization and layout play a critical role in the applicability of SIMD instructions. To show how data format can play a critical role in SIMD performance, consider an example where the dot product of eight vectors is calculated. Figure 2.6 shows the calculation that needs to be performed to achieve this result. Each output value in vector O is the dot product of the source vectors A, B, C, D, W, X, Y, and Z.

$$O[i] = A[i]W[i] + B[i]X[i] + C[i]Y[i] + D[i]Z[i]$$

Figure 2.6   Dot Product of Eight Matrices

At face value, this opportunity appears to be perfect for acceleration using SIMD techniques, and indeed it is, but you must pay special attention to the way the source data is arranged to gain optimum performance.

One typical way of representing this calculation in standard C code might look like the code segment shown in Figure 2.7.

```
Dotproduct () {

    struct {
        short   a[4],b[4],c[4],d[5];
    } op1;

    struct {
        short   w[4],x[4],y[4],z[4];
    } op2;

    for (i=0, i<4, i++) {
        DP[i] = op1.a[i]*op2.w[i] + op1.b[i]*op2.x[i] +
                op1.c[i]*op2.y[i] + op1.d[i]*op2.z[i];
    }
}
```

Figure 2.7   Vector Dot Product C Code Example 1

This example organizes the source data as a *structure of arrays* (SOA) and calculates the four outputs in the inner loop. One of the four output values is calculated during each inner-loop iteration.

An alternative method of organizing the data is as an *array of structures* (AOS) as shown below in Figure 2.8. Apart from the data organization, the functionality of the code remains the same.

```
Dotproduct2 () {

    typedef  struct {
        short  a, b, c, d;
    } op1type;

    typedef  struct {
        short  w,x,y,z;
    } op2type;

    op1type op1[4];
    op2type op2[4];

    for (i=0, i<4, i++) {
        O[i] = op1[i].a*op2[i].w + op1[i].b*op2[i].x +
               op1[i].c*op2[i].y + op1[i].d*op2[i].z;
    }
}
```

Figure 2.8   Vector Dot Product C Code Example 2

Although these examples look quite similar, the subtle difference lies in how the elements of the operands are stored in memory. Figure 2.9 shows how the two operands would be stored in memory for the structure of array format used in Figure 2.7. This storage is compared to the array of structure memory format used in Figure 2.8.

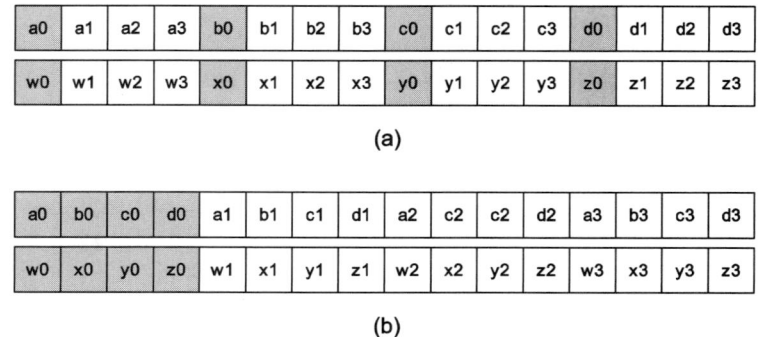

(a)

(b)

(a) Structure of Arrays Memory Layout

(b) Array of Structure Memory Layout

Figure 2.9   Memory Layout for Array Operands

In this example, the main difference between the two memory layouts is that, for structure of arrays, all the same elements of one array are stored together (a[0], a[1], a[2], a[3]), and in array of structures, all the elements of the structure are stored together (a[0], b[0], c[0], d[0]). The real impact appears when the inner loop calculation is performed. The gray shaded boxes indicate the operands required to calculate the first output:

```
O0 = a0*w0+b0*x0+c0*y0+d*z0
```

For the array of structures case (b) in Figure 2.9, all the elements of each operand are in consecutive memory, so they can be loaded with a single load-double operation for each operand. The format of the loaded data is exactly what is required for SIMD processing, and in the case of Intel Wireless MMX technology, the operation can be performed in a single instruction using the multiply accumulate instruction, or WMAC. The total cost for each output is only:

```
2 Loads + 1 WMAC = 3 instructions
```

However, for the structure of array memory organization, the elements of the two operands are not in consecutive memory locations. In this case, eight separate load operations are required to retrieve the data elements from memory. In addition, the data elements for each operand must be combined and packed into one register suitable for SIMD processing. This combining and packing takes a further six instructions—a combination of shift and or operations—to repack four elements into each source register. When the data is in the correct format, the same WMAC instruction can then be used to compute the result.

In this case, the instruction count is now:

```
8 Loads + 2*6 data repacking instructions + 1 WMAC = 21
```

This example demonstrates how the format of the source data can make a significant impact on the number of instructions required to do the operation. A factor of 7x difference in performance is shown for this particular SIMD code segment. The format of the source data is critical to potential use of SIMD techniques. If reformatting is required, as in the structure of arrays case, the cost of reformatting can quite easily cancel the benefits of SIMD processing, even costing more than processing the data in a scalar manner.

To achieve the maximum benefit from SIMD processing, you should carefully organize the data.

Inner Loops

Multimedia applications have a tendency to process lots of data in one form or another. This form could be pixels in an image or audio samples in a music clip. A profile of a typical video multimedia application reveals that the application spends a lot of time in a number of computationally intense inner loops that are repeated many times. In video decoders, the inner loops could be in a function like motion compensation. In addition, these inner loops usually have the correct *multiple, independent,* and *many* characteristics for SIMD acceleration. Therefore, inner loops of multimedia applications should be targeted for SIMD techniques.

Two steps are required to accelerate applications. First, identify the hotspot inner loops. Second, use SIMD techniques and optimizations to speed them up. In Chapter 7 you learn how to utilize tools such as the VTune™ Performance Analyzer to identify hotspots, and in Part 2 of the book we show you all the essential components of SIMD optimization.

The use of SIMD techniques should be focused on the inner loops where the advantages of data parallelism can be realized. SIMD should not be used where you have no data parallelism or the data cannot be stored in the right format. For example, general control code typically does not contain much data parallelism, so is not usually suitable for SIMD processing.

Key Points

The key points presented in this chapter are:

■ SIMD data-processing performs the same operation on multiple data elements packed into a single register.

■ SIMD data-processing is most efficient when the same operation is applied to many independent data elements repeatedly.

■ Arrange the format of the incoming data to eliminate or minimize any reformatting prior to SIMD processing.

■ Target multimedia application hotspots for SIMD data processing.

■ General control code is not a good candidate for SIMD acceleration.

Chapter 3

Intel® Wireless MMX™ Technology: The Big Picture

Architecture is the art of how to waste space.

—Philip Johnson

Intel® Wireless MMX™ technology is an instruction set extension of the Intel XScale® microarchitecture. The technology uses the ARM[†] architecture coprocessor model to add new SIMD instructions to the instruction set of the Intel XScale microarchitecture seamlessly. Intel Wireless MMX technology uses SIMD techniques to process many data elements in parallel. To facilitate this parallelism, the architecture provides extra registers to store packed data types before they are operated on by the new SIMD instructions. In common with the Intel XScale microarchitecture, the operation of the instructions strictly follows the load-store model. To put it another way, load-store models move data only between memory and the register file, and data processing instructions operate only on register operands.

The operation of a typical algorithm using Intel Wireless MMX technology has four basic steps:

1. Load the data into the packed register file.

2. Reorganize the data so that it is ready for SIMD processing. This step can be avoided by organizing the data memory in the correct format.

3. Perform the data processing operation on all elements in the packed data operands.

4. When the processing is complete, save the result back to memory.

The objective of this chapter is to introduce the instructions and programming model that you can use to construct efficient algorithms for Intel Wireless MMX technology. The chapter provides a description of the basic functionality and syntax of each instruction. This background information is essential for understanding the examples and case studies found later in the book.

Packed Data Storage

To provide storage space for the packed data operands, Intel Wireless MMX technology supports 16 64-bit registers. Each one of these registers can hold one of the following: eight byte operands (8-bit), four half-word operands (16-bit), two word operands (32-bit), or one double word operand (64-bit). The registers' operands are specified by a corresponding register identifier. Figure 3.1 shows the organization of the 16 64-bit registers and the wR prefix, a naming convention used for the packed data registers. The 16 registers are collectively known as the register file. A lowercase w is prefixed to all register identifiers that are part of Intel Wireless MMX technology.

An instruction can specify up to two source operands (wRn, wRm) and one destination operand (wRd), all of which may be different registers. This third register is different from the original Intel MMX technology, which has two source operands, one of which is also the destination register. A qualifier in the instruction specifies the way that the instruction interprets the 64-bit data or the source operands. The qualifier indicates the packed data type to be operated upon.

Intel Wireless MMX technology also provides four additional 32-bit registers, wCGR0–wCGR3, that are used primarily to store offsets for shift and alignment operations, but they also can be used as general-purpose storage. These four registers are part of the group of status and control registers, which use a prefix of wC to differentiate them from the packed data registers.

The control registers also include a coprocessor ID register that indicates type and revision of the coprocessor, a general control register that indicates whether any register contents have been updated, a set of SIMD saturation flags, and a set of SIMD arithmetic flags.

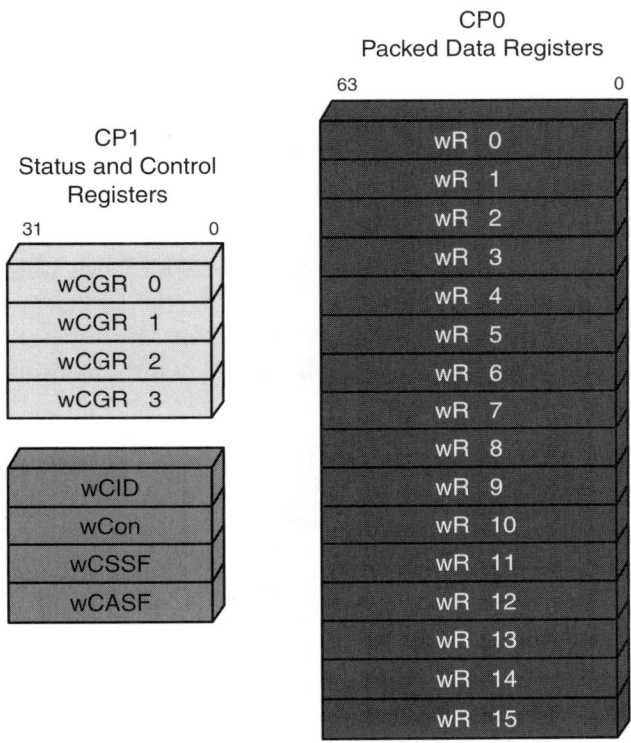

Figure 3.1 The Register File

Understanding Instruction Syntax

Intel Wireless MMX technology provides a rich set of data processing instructions that perform parallel operations on multiple data elements packed into 64-bit registers. In addition, the technology supports backward compatibility with the original accumulator instructions for Intel XScale microarchitecture, which operate on core registers, namely `TMIA`, `TMIAxy`, and `TMIAPH`.

In total, 43 instructions in the architecture are new. These instructions provide equivalent functionality to MMX technology and to integer Streaming SIMD Extensions (SSE) as a way to accelerate the porting of applications from desktop and mobile PC platforms to handheld and wireless systems.

Instruction Format

Intel Wireless MMX instructions follow the same assembler semantics as the baseline Intel XScale microarchitecture. In particular, they follow the format shown below:

```
OPERATION DEST, SRC1, SRC2
```

where `OPERATION` is the mnemonic of the instruction and `DEST`, `SRC1`, and `SRC2` are the register specifiers for the source and destination registers.

For example, the following instruction takes the contents of two source registers (`wR1`, `wR2`), adds them together, and places the result in `wR0`.

```
WADDB wR0, wR1, wR2
```

The three-operand instruction format also supports accumulating functions that were not possible in the original MMX instruction set. Intel Wireless MMX technology provides a single instruction multiply accumulate operation, or WMAC, that is useful for signal-processing operations. It also provides an accumulating version of sum of absolute differences named WSAD, which is used for video encode operations.

Instruction Prefix

Intel Wireless MMX instructions are prefixed with either the letter `W` or the letter `T`. The `W` prefix indicates that the instruction operates on co-processor data registers only, whereas a `T` prefix indicates that data is transferred between coprocessor registers and the core registers.

For example, WADD operates on coprocessor registers and writes the result back to another coprocessor register. However, the multiply implicit accumulate instruction TMIA takes values from a core register, performs the multiply accumulate operation, and writes the result to the coprocessor register file.

Qualifiers

You can add a suffix to the base mnemonic with qualifiers to indicate a particular variety of the selected operation or the type of data to be operated upon. When an instruction can operate on multiple data types, the data type qualifier is mandatory and it can be one of the letters shown in Table 3.1.

Table 3.1   Data Type Qualifiers

Data Size	Qualifier	Name
8 bits	B	Byte
16 bits	H	Half-Word
32 bits	W	Word
64 bits	D	Double Word

Instructions that support multiple data types usually support three out of the four quantities in the third column: B, H, and W, or H, W, and D. For example, WADDB specifies an addition of byte values, WADDH specifies an addition of half-word values, and WADDW specifies addition of word values.

Another example of a generic qualifier is the set of conditional execution predicates. These qualifiers are the same as the standard conditional execution qualifiers of the Intel XScale microarchitecture that determine whether a particular instruction is executed as a function of the arithmetic flags contained in the current program status register (CPSR) of the Intel XScale core.

For example, the following instruction executes a byte addition of the source operands in wR1 and wR2 if the zero flag is not set in the CPSR.

```
WADDBNE wR0, wR1, wR2
```

The condition predicate is always the last qualifier in the mnemonic and is optional. If no predicate is specified, the instruction is assumed always to execute regardless of the state of the arithmetic flags in the CPSR. Conditional execution and the relationship to packed data are discussed later in this chapter.

In addition to the generic data type qualifiers, the code might contain instruction-specific qualifiers that can be mandatory or optional, depending on the particular qualifier and instruction. For example, the byte addition example could specify that signed saturation, or SS qualifier, is also required:

```
WADDBUSS   wR0, wR1, wR2
```

With a basic understanding of register storage and instruction syntax, you're ready to begin the path to SIMD algorithm development. The first stop along the way is getting the data into the register file.

Getting the Data

The first step in developing an algorithm supporting Intel Wireless MMX technology is to get the data into the packed data register file. The data may reside in memory, or perhaps it is already in a core register. Load and store operations move operands from memory, whereas various forms of the transfer instructions move data back and forth to the core registers.

An important point to remember for memory transactions is that the Intel XScale core is responsible for communication with the data memories and the address calculations are based upon core registers, much like native data load and store operations.

Retrieving and Saving Data

Data is retrieved from memory using a load operation, or WLDR. The load operation supports all four types of data—byte, half-word, word, and double—with double being the most frequently used. For example, WLDRB loads a byte, WLDRH loads a half-word, WLDRW loads a word, and WLDRD loads the full 64-bit value. The WLDRD form of the instruction is used to load a complete set of packed data elements into a register, whereas the other forms of the instruction are used to load individual elements. The load instruction treats the word and smaller data types as unsigned operands, so that when they are loaded into the 64-bit destination register, they are zero-extended to the full precision. An example or the WLDRB instruction is shown in Figure 3.2(a).

The store instruction WSTR returns data to memory. If the data to be saved is less than 64 bits, then the data is selected from the least significant data element. To save individual elements from the packed data register, they must be shifted or rotated right—using WSRL or WROR, respectively—to the least significant position before the store instruction is executed.

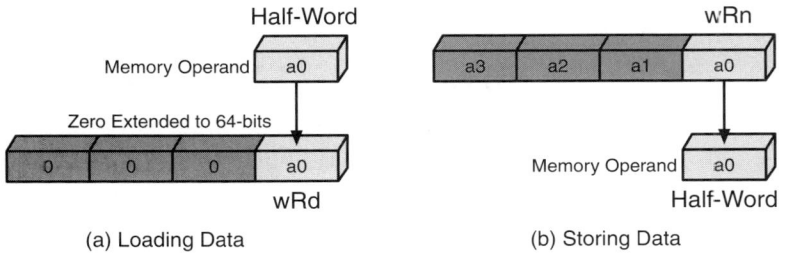

Figure 3.2   Loading and Storing Individual Elements

To calculate the memory access address, the load and store instructions support a number of indexing operations. The address is contained in a core base register, which can be modified by an immediate offset. The offset can either be added or subtracted from the base address. The adjustment using the offset can be applied before the memory operand is requested (pre-index) or after the memory operand has been requested (post-index). The post-index form is useful for modifying the memory pointer to prepare for the next operation.

For word and double-word data types, the valid range for the offset is 0 to 0x3FC. The offset is specified in bytes, but it must be a multiple of four. For byte and half-word data types, the offset is also specified in bytes, and this time it has a range of 0 to 0xFF with no restriction on four-byte multiple addresses. The multiple-of-four restriction on the word and the double-word data types allows these instructions to support a wider address range offset. If the multiple-of-four restrictions cannot be met, a separate address calculation using an addition or subtraction operation is required.

The syntax and semantics of the address modification specifiers are the same as those in a standard load instruction for the Intel XScale core. Sample usages for WLDR and WSTR are:

```
WLDRD   wR0, [R1], #-4    ;post-ndex
WSTRH   wR1, [R1,  #4]!   ;pre-index
```

The load performs a 64-bit memory load operation from the address contained in R1, and then the R1 register is modified by four bytes—one word—to point at the next operand. This post-index operation can prove useful for a typical stack operation. The WSTRH instruction stores the least-significant half-word from the wR1 register at the address specified by adding 4 to the contents of the R1 core register. The modified address is written back to R1. This example demonstrates use of the pre-index address mode.

As a feature of the overall architecture, all memory addresses that are used must be aligned to the boundary of the data type being loaded. For example, half-word loads must be aligned to a half-word boundary, word loads must be aligned to a word boundary, and double-word loads must be aligned to a double-word boundary of memory. You should be careful to meet these restrictions; as with all ARM unaligned memory accesses, an unaligned memory trap could result. To access words that do not align on the corresponding data type boundary, you can use the WALIGN instruction to extract the required unaligned double word from two adjacent boundary-aligned 64-bit values.

Aligning Data Elements

The WALIGN instruction is useful for handling double-word or packed data that is not stored in memory on a 64-bit boundary. The Intel Wireless MMX technology can load 64-bit, double-word data only from 64-bit aligned addresses. Therefore, when an unaligned value is required, the two 64-bit, aligned double words that the unaligned value straddles are loaded into the register file, and a WALIGN instruction extracts the exact 64 bits required. This technique saves time over the traditional approach of shifting and masking values to extract the correct alignment. The WALIGN instruction can extract any 64-bit value on a byte boundary from the two source registers.

Figure 3.3 shows how the WALIGN instruction adjusts the data. In this example, the required 64-bit value from address 0x103 is not a 64-bit aligned address. To get this value, the double-word data from address 0x100 is loaded into the right source register and double word data from address 0x108 is loaded into the left source register. The WALIGN instruction uses a specified offset of 3, causing the five bytes from the right register (bytes from addresses 0x103 to 0x107) to be extracted and combined with the lower three bytes of the left register (bytes from addresses 0x108 to 0x10A). Thus, after the WALIGN instruction executes, the destination contains the desired data from address 0x103 to 0x10A—that is, the 64-bit value at address 0x103.

The alignment offset can be specified as an immediate either by using the WALIGNI form of the instruction or the register WALIGNR format and placing the alignment offset in a wCGRx auxiliary register. The latter method is useful if the address offset is created by masking off the lower bits of the access address and then transferred to the wCGR registers using a TMCR instruction. A sample usage of the WALIGNI instruction is:

```
WALIGNI wR0,wR1,wR2,#3
```

Here the double word with an immediate byte offset of 3 is selected from the two source operands, and the result written back to the destination register, as shown in Figure 3.3.

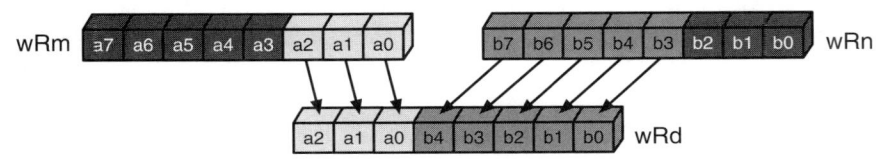

Figure 3.3   WALIGN Adjusting Data Alignment

Transferring a Whole Register to the Core

In addition to getting operands from the memory subsystem, applications may transfer data from a coprocessor register to a main core register and back again. The transfers can deal with 32-bit values to the control registers (TMCR and TMRC) and 64-bit values to the packed data registers (TMCRR and TMRRC). The TMCR operation is particularly useful for loading shift or alignment offsets that are derived from a memory address in the core registers to the wCGRn registers, making them ready for various alignment and shift operations that are common in multimedia operations.

Sample usages of these instructions are:

```
TMCR  wCGR0, R1            ; 32-bit transfer from the core
TMRC  R1,    wCGR0         ; 32-bit transfer to the core
TMCRR wR0,   R1,   R2      ; 64-bit transfer from the core
TMRRC R1,    R2,   wR0     ; 64-bit transfer to the core
```

For the TMCRR, the contents of R1 are placed in the lower 32 bits, and the contents of R2 are placed in the higher 32 bits. The TMRRC performs the opposite operation, in that it takes the contents of the coprocessor register wR0 and places the lower 32 bits into the core register R1 and the upper 32 bits in core register R2.

A useful tip for understanding the mnemonics is that the reverse order of the last letters indicates the direction of transfer. For example, TMCR means that a register (R) is transferred to the coprocessor (C). Similarly for 64-bit transfers the "CRR" ending of MCRR indicates that two registers (RR) are transferred to the coprocessor (C) and vice-versa for MRRC.

Transferring Elements to the Core

Instead of transferring a whole register to the core and back, you can transfer individual data elements to the core using the insert TINSTR and extract TEXTR instructions. It is also possible to transfer duplicates of a single element to all positions in a packed register using the broadcast TBCST instruction.

Inserting and Extracting a Particular Element

Figure 3.4 shows the TINSRH and TEXTRM instructions, which insert or extract the data element that is specified by the immediate value, in this case #1. Both instructions transfer the specified data element to or from the data element specified by the immediate operand. The valid ranges for immediate operands can be:

■ #0-7 for byte data types

■ #0-4 for half-word data types

■ #0-1 for word data types

For the extract operation, the data can be specified as signed or unsigned values, so that when the data is transferred to the core register, it is either sign extended for a signed data type, or zero extended for an unsigned data type.

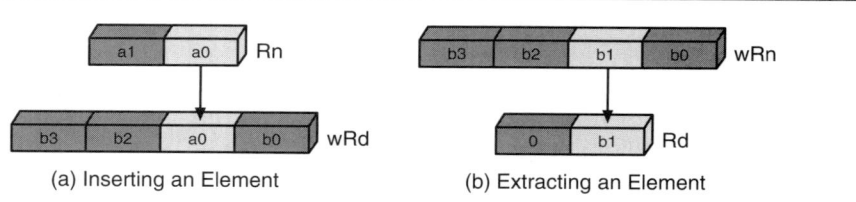

(a) Inserting an Element   (b) Extracting an Element

Figure 3.4   TINSTR/TEXTR Inserting and Extracting a Value into a Particular Element

Here are three examples of how these instructions might be used:

```
TINSRH    wR3, R2, #1
TEXTRMUH R1, wR8, #1    ; signed data
TEXTRMSH R1, wR8, #1    ; unsigned data
```

The insert instruction takes the least-significant half-word from the core R2 source register and writes it into element 1 of the wR3 destination register. The first extract instruction takes the unsigned data element at position 1 in the wR8 source register, zero-extends it to 32 bits, and writes the result into the R1 core destination register. The second extract instruction performs a similar operation but with signed data.

Broadcasting a Value

Another way of creating constant values in the packed data register is to repeat the same value in all elements. This replication is useful for creating a mask to use in SIMD processing. The TBCST instruction provides the ability to broadcast a data element from a core source register to all elements in the packed data destination register. Figure 3.5 shows the TBCSTH instruction where a half-word is transferred and inserted in all four data elements of the destination register.

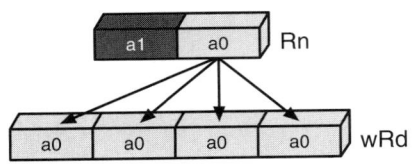

Figure 3.5   TBCST Broadcasting a Constant Value

An example usage of the instruction is:

```
TBCSTH wR5, R1
```

The instruction takes the least significant half-word from the core R1 register and broadcasts it to all elements in the wR5 destination register. The fact that the source for the TBCST instruction is a core register is useful, because the instruction set for the Intel XScale microarchitecture has better support for creating immediate values that may be used to create a mask.

Preparing the Data for Processing

The next step with the operand data is to be sure that its format is optimal for further processing using SIMD techniques. To verify that the format is optimal, you might increase or reduce the precision of the operands, either to make operands of an instruction match or to make sure that an instruction sequence does not overflow the precision of the original operands. For example, in video decode, the calculation of the residual error calculation involves adding 8-bit values to a higher precision 16-bit values. Usually the 8-bit values are extended to 16 bits, and after the addition is performed, the result is packed back into the reduced precision of eight bits to save memory storage space for the result.

Along with adjusting the precision of the data, you might have to rearrange the elements within the registers to use the computation resources most effectively.

Extending the Precision

Two main forms of the unpack instruction are:

■ WUNPCKE—unpacks and extends the precision

■ WUNPCKI—unpacks two registers and interleaves values

The latter is useful for rearranging data elements.

The WUNPCKE form of the instruction is used to increase the precision of half of the data elements in a single packed register. As each element is extended to twice the precision, only half the data can be accommodated at the new precision in the destination register. Thus, four single-byte data values can be extended to four half-words, two half-word values can be extended to two word values, and one word value can be extended to a double-word value. Either the low (L) or the high (H) part of the source can be selected for extension by using the H or L qualifiers.

You can choose between two ways to extend the precision, depending on whether the data is unsigned or signed. For unsigned data, Figure 3.6(a) shows how each of the most significant or least significant half-word elements are zero extended to word elements. To extend signed data to higher precision, each element selected is sign-extended to the higher precision, as shown in Figure 3.6(b).

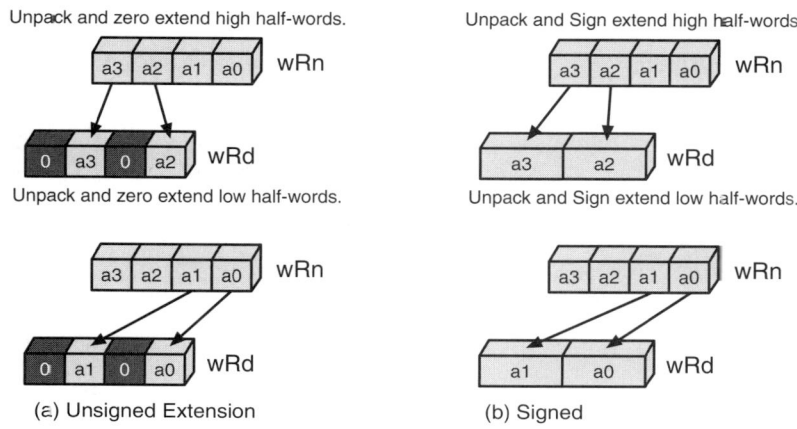

Figure 3.6   WUNPCKE Increasing the Precision of Unsigned Value

An example usage of the WUNPCKE instruction for unsigned and signed data is:

```
WUNCPKEHU  wR2, wR9    ;unsigned data
WUNPCKELS  wR11,wR15   ;signed data
```

In the first example, the two high-order, unsigned half-words of wR9 are each zero-extended to a word and placed in the wR2 destination register. In the second example, low-order, signed half-words in wR15 are each sign-extended to a word and placed in the destination register.

Reducing Precision

Reducing precision of operands is typically done at the end of a calculation to enable more efficient memory storage. The number of bits required to store the next lower precision value is half; for example, going from word to half-word reduces the required number of bits by 16. Another way of looking at this reduction is that the program can store twice as much data in the same memory space.

The WPACK instruction reduces the precision of the data from two registers and packs it into a single destination register. To do this, it converts the data elements from higher precision—such as 16 bits or 32 bits used for intermediate calculations—to lower-precision formats such as 8-bit color components or 16-bit audio samples. If the size of the result after packing would cause the register to overflow, this instruction also clips the result to the largest or smallest value that can be represented in the destination data type. This clipping is known as *saturation*. Figure 3.7 depicts the operation of packing eight half-word data values into eight bytes.

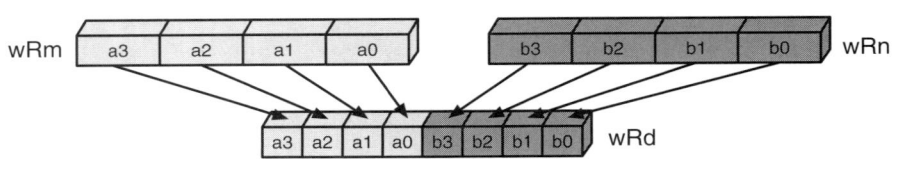

Figure 3.7   WPACK Packing Data from Higher Precision to Lower Precision

You can saturate the destination values using either signed or unsigned limits, as specified in the instruction mnemonic. If unsigned saturation is specified, as it is in Figure 3.7, the clipping limits are 0x00 and 0xFF, the minimum and maximum unsigned values. For signed saturation, the clipping limits are 0x80 and 0x7F, the minimum and maximum signed values for the destination byte data type. The incoming data type is always treated as signed, so the saturation qualifiers only refer to the output data type. For example, if a source data field contains 0x7FFF, with unsigned saturation the packed byte would contain 0xFF. With signed saturation, the packed data byte would contain 0x7F. Similarly, if the source data field contains 0x8000, with unsigned saturation the destination byte contains 0x00, and with signed saturation, the result would be 0x80.

You indicate the data type of the operands to be applied with instruction qualifiers. The saturation type is selected depending on whether the US, unsigned saturation, or SS, signed saturation, qualifier is specified.

Rearranging Data

SIMD processing works best when the program can process an entire row of data at the same time. If the data is arranged in another format, such as a column, you should rearrange it into a format that is more suitable for SIMD processing. The interleave form of the unpack instruction, WUNPCKI, is useful for rearranging data from columns to rows.

The WUNPCKI instruction takes the two source registers, interleaves either the lower or upper halves of the register, and places the result in the destination. The size of the data elements in the destination register remains the same. The size of the fields to interleave is determined by the data type qualifier selected for the instruction. As only half of each register is interleaved, a further qualifier determines whether the high (H) or low (L) half on the source registers should be interleaved. The WUNPCKILH instruction unpacks the four half-words in the lower part of the two source registers and places them in the destination. The WUNPCKIHH instruction unpacks the four data values from the upper part of the source registers. Figure 3.8 shows both of these cases. An example usage of the WUNPCKI instruction is:

```
WUNPCKILH    wR7, wR9, wR14
```

This instruction interleaves the upper half-words of registers wR14 and wR9 and places the result in the destination register wR7. The unpack with interleave is very useful for the matrix transpose operation common in graphics routines

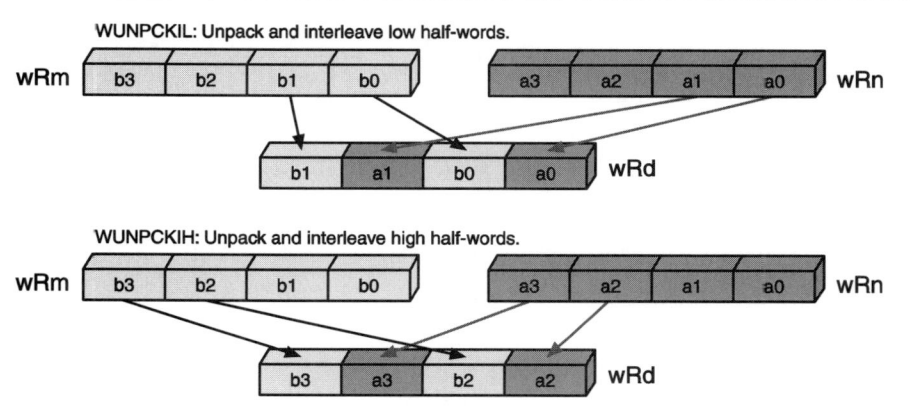

Figure 3.8   WUNPCKI Interleaving Data

Transposing a matrix

Matrix transposition is a useful operation for reformatting matrices to make them suitable for SIMD processing. The unpack operation with interleave can be used to implement a transposition in an efficient manner, as shown in Figure 3.9. Here the original matrix is loaded into registers wR0-wR3. The first step is to interleave both the high and low parts of the two source operands using half-word data types. Doing so yields four partial results in wR4-wR7. These partial result pairs are interleaved again, this time using a word data type to get the final transposed matrix in registers wR8-wR11.

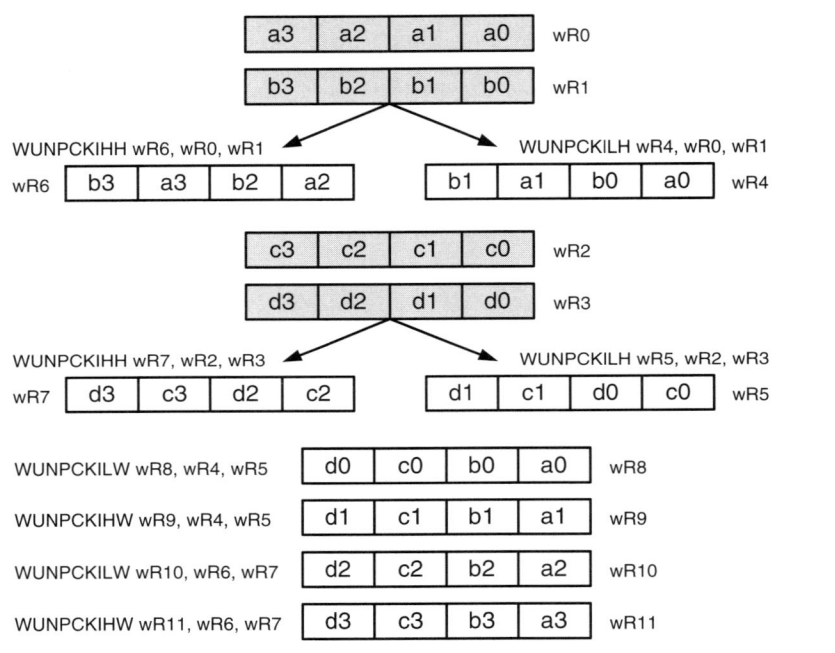

Figure 3.9   Transpose Using Unpack

Arbitrary Rearrangement

Sometimes an arbitrary shuffle of elements is required to get the data into the right order for processing. If so, you can use the WSHUFH instruction for half-word data. The instruction performs an arbitrary mapping of the source half-words to the destination half-words. Any half-word in the source can be mapped to any half-word in the destination, and a source half-word can also map to multiple-destination half-words. An 8-bit immediate value is specified with the instruction, so that two bits are used to encode the selection for each destination half-word. Use bits 0 and 1 to determine which half-word to select for the destination half-word 0. Repeat this action for the rest of the bits in the immediate value and for any half-words in the destination. Figure 3.10 shows how the WSHUFH operation works. In the example, an immediate value of 0x9C has been selected, so bits 0 and 1 equal the value 0b00, which selects b0 for destination field 0. The immediate value for destination field 1 is 0b11, which selects field 3 from the source. This action is repeated for the remaining fields. An example of the usage of WSHUFH is:

```
WSHUFH wR4, wR13, #0x9C
```

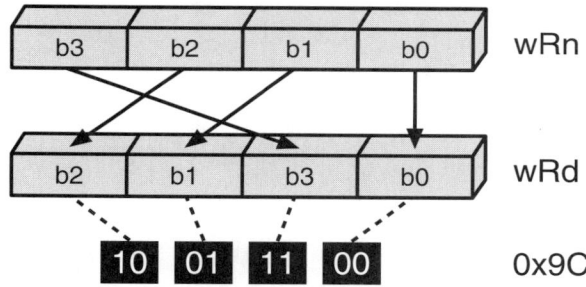

Figure 3.10   WSHUFH Arbitrary Half-Word Shuffle

With the data loaded into the registers and in the right format, the next step in SIMD processing is to perform operations on the data.

The Basic Operations

Intel Wireless MMX technology provides the basic operations that one expects of any instruction set: addition, subtraction, logical operations, and shift. This section describes the key features of these basic operations.

Saturating Arithmetic

Normal arithmetic allows the operation to wrap around if it exceeds the maximum value that can be represented. For example, adding two 16-bit values might result in a 17-bit answer—an unsigned addition of 0xFFFE+2=0x10000. If only the lower 16 bits are kept, the result would be 0x0000. This result is clearly wrong. To reduce the error when overflow occurs, saturation arithmetic clamps the value to the maximum or minimum that can be represented in the data type being processed. In the same example, the addition result would be 0xFFFF instead of 0x0000 with unsigned saturation. Here the result error is now only 1.

Saturation is particularly useful for audio processing where it is preferable to accept some small amount of error if the audio sample goes out of range, rather than getting an audible click if the data wrapped around from 0xFFFF to 0x0000. Figure 3.11 shows how clipping can be used to limit the range of a signal.

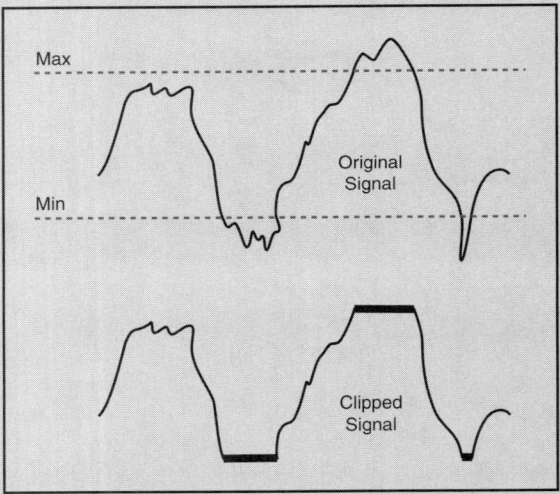

Figure 3.11 Clipping a Signal to Maximum and Minimum Values

Addition and Subtraction

The WADD instruction, as the name suggests, provides the addition functionality for Intel Wireless MMX technology. The instruction adds the data elements of the source operands and places the result in the destination register. The WSUB instruction subtracts the contents of the secondary source register, wRm, from the contents of the primary source register, wRn.

If the result of either operation is larger than the maximum value that can be represented in the destination register field, the result wraps around by default. For example, if a WADDH instruction is specified, as shown in Figure 3.12, and the result is larger than 0xFFFF, the result wraps, and only the lower 16 bits are written to the destination.

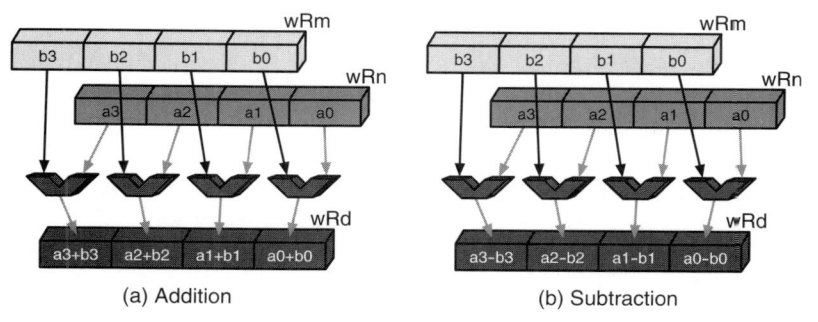

(a) Addition   (b) Subtraction

Figure 3.12   WADD/WSUB Addition and Subtraction

If the size of the result after the addition or subtraction would overflow, these instructions optionally allow the result to be clipped to the largest value that can be represented in the destination data type. This clipping is also known as *saturation*.

The destination values can be saturated using either signed or unsigned limits, as specified in the instruction mnemonic. Saturation is specified using the optional qualifiers of US, unsigned saturation, or SS, signed saturation.

If unsigned saturation is specified, as it is in Figure 3.12, the clipping limits are 0x0000 and 0xFFFF, the minimum and maximum unsigned values for half-words. For signed saturation, the clipping limits are 0x8000 and 0x7FFF, the minimum and maximum signed values for the destination half-word data type, as in the following example:

```
WADDH:        0x8000 + 0xFFFF = 0x7FFF
WADDHUS:      0x8000 + 0xFFFF = 0xFFFF
              (Clipped to maximum unsigned value)
WADDHSS:      0x8000 + 0xFFFF = 0x8000
              (Clipped to maximum negative signed value)

WSUBH:        0x8000 - 0x0001 = 0x7FFF
WSUBHSS:      0x8000 - 0x0001 = 0x8000
              (Clipped to minimum signed value)
WSUBHUS:      0x8000 - 0xFFFF = 0x0000
              (Clipped to minimum unsigned value)
```

Example usages of the WADD and WSUB instructions are:

```
WADDH wR3, wR6, wR9
WSUBH wR6, wR2, wR9
```

Here the WADD adds the corresponding half-words in the wR6 and wR9 source registers and writes the result to wR3. The WSUB subtracts elements of wR9 from the elements of wR2 and the result written in wR6. No saturation is specified.

Logical Operations

Intel Wireless MMX technology also supplies a full complement of logical operations. All of these logical operations perform bitwise operations on the two 64-bit source operands and write the result to the destination register. Since the operation is bitwise on 64-bit data, *only the double-word data type is supported*. All of the logical operations follow the same general flow as shown in Figure 3.13.

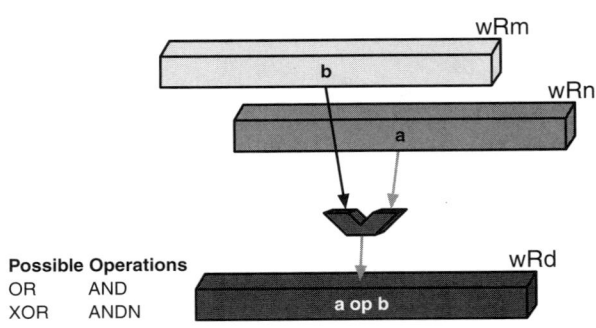

Figure 3.13   WAND, WOR, and WXOR Logical Operations

The supported 64-bit, bitwise logical operations are:

■ WAND—bitwise logical AND

■ WANDN—bitwise logical AND with one operand negated

■ WOR—bitwise logical OR

■ WXOR—bitwise XOR

Two pseudo-instructions are provided for programmer convenience. WMOV moves one register to another and WZERO simply sets the destination register to the value zero, as the name suggests. Examples of all these logical operations are:

```
WAND   wR2,   wR4,   wR9
WANDN  wR7,   wR8,   wR3
WOR    wR9,   wR13,  wR1
WXOR   wR12,  wR11,  wR5
WMOV   wR6,   wR15
WZERO  wR15
```

Shift

The Intel Wireless MMX instruction set specifies four basic classes of shift operation: shift left (WSLL), shift right arithmetic (WSRA), shift right logical (WSRL), and rotate right (ROR). All of these shift operations can operate on either half-word, word, or double-word operands. The register to be shifted is specified by the wRn register identifier. The shift amount can either be specified by the contents of another packed register file (wRm) or, if the G qualifier is specified, the count operand is obtained from an auxiliary register (wCGRx).

The WSLL instruction shifts the source operand to the left by the number of bits specified in the count operand. During the shift operation, the empty low-order bits are cleared, or set to zero. If the value specified by the second operand, also called the or count operand, is greater than the size of the data type that is being shifted, the destination is set to all zeros. The WSRA instruction shifts the source operand to the right by the number of bits specified by the count operand; the empty high-order bits of each element are filled with the initial value of the sign bit of the data element. This time, if the shift amount is greater than the data type, the result is filled with the initial value of the sign bit. The WSRL performs a similar operation to the WSRA, but with one difference: the empty high-order bits for WSRL are filled with zero instead of the sign bit. Finally, the WROR instruction rotates the value in each data element right by the amount specified. In this case, the destination register contains the result of rotation, so the register contains no empty bits because the source bits are rotated instead of shifted out. That is, the least significant bits are rotated back into the element via the high-order bits.

A sample use of each of the four instruction classes follows:

```
WSLLW wR0, wR3,  wR4    ; Shift logical left
WSRAH wR4, wR2,  wCGR0  ; Shift arithmetic right
WSRLD wR4, wR2,  wR8    ; Shift logical right
WRORH wR7, wR15, wCGR3  ; Rotate right
```

Comparing Data Elements

Data comparison is an important part of algorithm development; it can help to determine whether a particular boundary condition has been reached by the data. Has the operand exceeded some predetermined value? Which operation produced the biggest or smallest result? Intel Wireless MMX technology provides three ways to evaluate packed data elements. Two of them use specific instructions; the other uses the SIMD arithmetic flags. In conjunction with the standard Intel XScale core, the SIMD arithmetic flags can be used as a conditional execution mechanism to compare data and then take action based on the result. Use of SIMD flags is discussed later in this chapter.

The instruction support for data comparison comes in two forms. The first form of comparison examines the values using a specific logical test and creates a mask of all ones or all zeros depending on the outcome. This mask can be used in conjunction with the logical operations to select particular fields in the source operands. The logical tests that are directly supported for this class of instruction are equality, WCMPEQ, and greater than, WCMPGT.

For WCMPEQ, if the data elements are equal, the corresponding data element in the destination register is set to all ones; otherwise, the corresponding element is set to all zeros. Similarly for WCMPGT, if the data element in the primary operand is greater than the data element in the secondary operand, the corresponding field in the destination register is set to all ones; otherwise, it is set to all zeros. WCMPGT can perform either a signed or unsigned comparison, depending on whether the S qualifier, signed WCMPGTS, or U qualifier, unsigned WCMPGTU, is specified. The following examples show both uses of these instructions:

```
WCMPEQB      wR3, wR5, wR7
WCMPGTUB     wR8, wR3, wR14    ; signed byte
WCMPGTSH     wR4, wR9, wR2     ; unsigned half-word
```

Masks from other logical tests can be created by using the WCMP instructions in combination with the logical operations to get the comparisons less than, less than or equal to, and greater than.

The second method of comparison is to analyze the magnitude of data elements and select either the maximum, WMAX, or minimum value, WMIN, of the corresponding elements in the two source operands.

The WMAX instruction compares the data elements in the two source operands, selects the maximum value from each field, and writes the value to the corresponding field in the destination register. Using the S qualifier, the WMAX instruction selects the maximum signed data elements or, using the U qualifier, the WMAX instruction selects the maximum unsigned data elements. WMIN performs a similar function, but in this case, the minimum value rather than the maximum value is selected. Examples of both WMAX and WMIN are:

```
WMAXBU  wR0, wR7, wR9    ; unsigned byte maximum
WMINWS  wR4, wR6, wR13   ; signed word minimum
```

Here the WMAX instruction selects the maximum unsigned byte value for each element of the two source registers, wR7 and wR9, and writes the result to the destination register, wR0. The WMIN instruction selects the minimum signed word value for each element of the two source registers, wR6 and wR13, and writes the result to the destination register, wR4.

Signal Processing

Multiplication is a cornerstone of many digital signal processing algorithms. Finite impulse response filters (FIR), infinite impulse response filters (IIR), discrete cosine transforms (DCT), and fast Fourier transform (FFT) are but a few of the popular algorithms. This section introduces some of the key multiplication building blocks that you can use to implement these algorithms. Chapter 13 takes signal processing algorithms even further with a case study of DSP kernels implemented using the co-processor multiplication instructions that support Intel Wireless MMX technology.

The coprocessor multiplier instructions are aimed at the fixed point processing of 16-bit data that is common in multimedia applications, such as the manipulation of 16-bit pixels in color conversion and alpha plane processing. These common applications also include the manipulation of audio samples used in compression and in an audio voice codec such as GSM-AMR. One instruction, TMIA, does provide support for a 32×32 multiply operation, but the primary data type for the multipliers is half-word.

The multiply class of instructions contains two distinct types:

■ *Accumulating*. The multiplication result is added to a previously calculated value.

■ *Non-accumulating*. The multiplication result is not added to an existing value.

The accumulating capability is new to Intel Wireless MMX technology since the limitation of having only two register operands in the original MMX technology prevented accumulation.

Finite Impulse Response (FIR) Filter

The FIR can be viewed as a delay line where a single output D', is a linear combination on n data samples D_{t-n+1} through D_t, as shown in Figure 3.14. The mathematical form can be written as:

$$Z_n = \sum_{i=0}^{i=N-1} C_i * X_{n-i}$$

where N is the length of the filter, X_{n-i} and C_i are the input samples and filter coefficients respectively, and Zn is the current output sample.

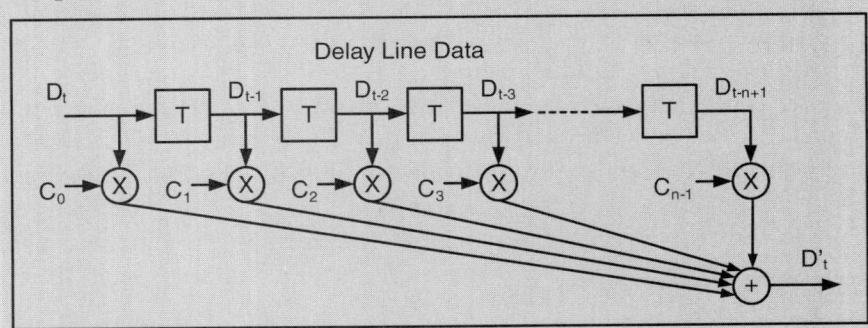

Figure 3.14   Delay Line Representation of a FIR Filter

Multiply Accumulate Instructions

Intel Wireless MMX technology provides two classes of multiply with accumulation. The first instruction class takes its source operands from the core register file, TMIA. The second instruction class, WMAC, takes source operands from the coprocessor's packed data registers. Both types of multiply accumulate write the result to a packed data register. The T prefix of the TMIA instruction indicates that it is transferring data from the Intel XScale microarchitecture to the coprocessor registers, and, in this case, performing a data processing operation during the transfer.

Multiplying 32-Bit Operands

The TMIA instruction provides the only 32×32 multiply capability in Intel Wireless MMX technology. The instruction takes two 32-bit operands from the core register file, performs a 32×32 multiply on the operands, then adds the result to the original value contained in the destination register wRd. This three-part action provides the same functionality as the original core MIA instruction and uses the same binary encoding—the core acc0 register maps directly onto wR0. The Intel XScale microarchitecture provides a 40-bit accumulator; however, the Intel Wireless MMX TMIA instruction provides a full 64-bit precision in the accumulator to prevent overflow of the result. This instruction is useful for processing high precision audio data, such as 24-bit data for MP3 decode.

Figure 3.15 shows the 32×32 TMIA operation with the multiplication results being accumulated with the previous value of the destination wRd. A sample usage is:

```
TMIA wR4, R2, R3
```

Here the source operands are taken from the core source registers R2 and R3, and the product is added to the previous value of the destination register wR4.

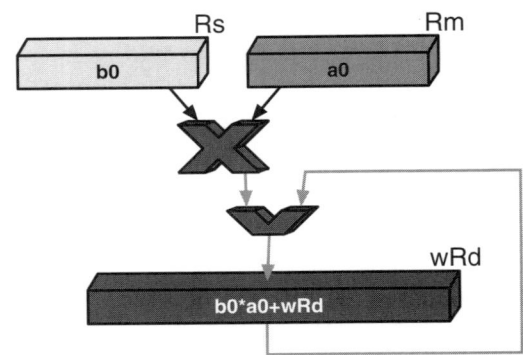

Figure 3.15 TMIA 32×32 Multiply Accumulate

Transfer 16×16 Multiply Accumulate

The TMIA instruction also has variants that perform various flavors of 16×16 multiplies. The TMIAPH instruction performs a dual 16×16 multiply accumulate operation where the source operands are taken from a core register. Both multiplication results are added together with the previous value of the destination, as shown in Figure 3.16(a).

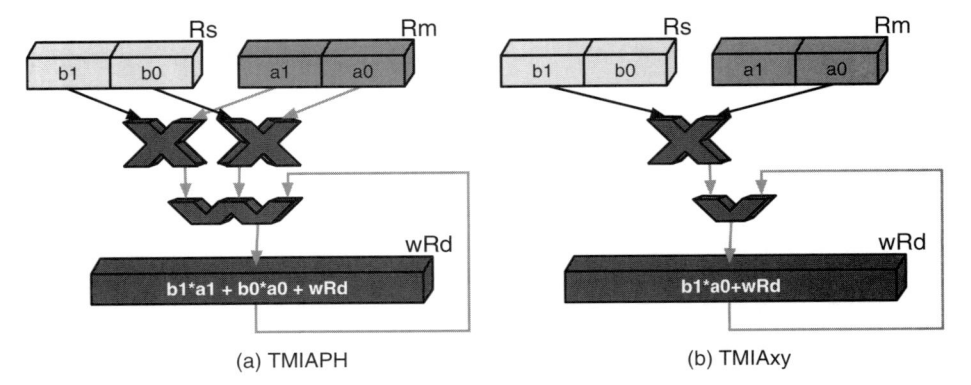

Figure 3.16 TMIAPH/TMIAxy 16×16 Multiply Accumulate

The TMIAxy instruction provides a single 16×16 multiply accumulate capability for which you can specify the source operands to be the top or bottom 16 bits of the two 32-bit core source registers. Two single-letter suffixes are added to the instruction to indicate the parts of the two source operands that should be multiplied. The letter T selects the top half of a source register, and the letter B selects the bottom half of each source register. Figure 3.16(b) shows the TMIABT instruction where the bottom of Rm (a0) is selected and the top of Rs (b1) is selected for multiplication. The possible combinations of the T and B qualifiers are:

```
TMIATT gives the result (a1*b1) + wRd
TMIATB gives the result (a1*b0) + wRd
TMIABB gives the result (a0*b0) + wRd
TMIABT gives the result (a0*b1) + wRd
```

Both the TMIAPH and TMIAxy instructions provide equivalent functionality to the corresponding core MIAPH and MIAxy instructions, but with a 64-bit accumulator. An example of both the TMIAPH and TMIAxy instructions is:

```
TMIAPH wR4, R3, R4
TMIATB wR6, R2, R4
```

For the TMIATB, the top 16 bits of R2 and the bottom 16 bits of the core R4 register and the product are added to the existing value in the destination register wR6.

WMAC

The multiply accumulate operation is a basic staple of many DSP algorithms. Intel Wireless MMX technology provides explicit instruction set support for this operation in the form of the WMAC instruction. The WMAC instruction performs four 16×16 multiplications and adds all of the products to the existing value of the 64-bit result register. The operands can be specified to be either signed or unsigned by selecting either the S, signed, or U, unsigned, qualifier. Figure 3.17 shows the WMACS operation. The instruction also allows optional clearing of the destination prior to the final addition by using the Z, zero qualifier.

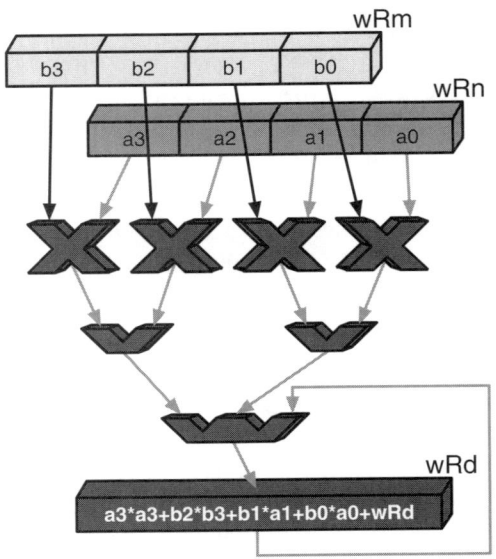

Figure 3.17   WMAC Four-way 16×16 Multiply

This instruction is well suited to filter applications where it can calculate four filter tap multiply-accumulate operations at a time. An example of the WMAC usage is shown below:

```
WMACS wR3, wR5, wR7
```

This instruction multiplies the signed half-word elements of wR5 and wR7, adds the result products together, and accumulates them with the previous value in the result register wR3.

FIR Filter Implementation

The WMAC instruction is ideally suited for a block FIR operation where many data elements are processed. The critical inner loop of the algorithm for one output could be represented with the simple code sequence shown in Figure 3.18.

```
Loop:
    WLDR wR1 [R1], #4      // get 4 data elements
    WLDR wR2 [R2], #4      // get 4 coefficients
    SUBS r0, r0, #1        // loop repeat count decrement
    WMAC wR0, wR1, wR2     // process four mac operations
    BNE  Loop              // repeat for all coefficients
```

Figure 3.18   Simple FIR Implementation

The example code sequence shows the advantage of the WMAC instruction in such filter operations. However, simple code sequences could contain performance hazards such as data dependencies that may need further optimization. Chapter 13 describes an efficient implementation of the FIR filter using Intel Wireless MMX instructions.

Multiply Instructions

The remaining two multiply instructions do not provide an accumulation capability. WMUL provides a four-way 16×16 multiply. WMADD also provides a four-way 16×16 multiply, but adds together the upper two products and the lower two products.

WMUL

A multiplication of two 16-bit quantities can generate a result of up to 32 bits. The WMUL instruction multiplies together the four corresponding 16-bit half-words in each of the source operands and provides four half-word results packed into the destination register. To enable the result of each 16×16 product to fit into the destination register, the WMUL instruction provides the capability to select the most significant (M qualifier), or least significant (L qualifier), 16 bits of the intermediate product. The operands for WMUL operation can be signed or unsigned data depending of whether the U, unsigned, or S, signed, qualifier is selected.

Figure 3.19(a) shows the MULSM form of the instruction where only the most significant 16 bits of the intermediate product are written to the destination field of the result. The S qualifier indicates that data is signed.

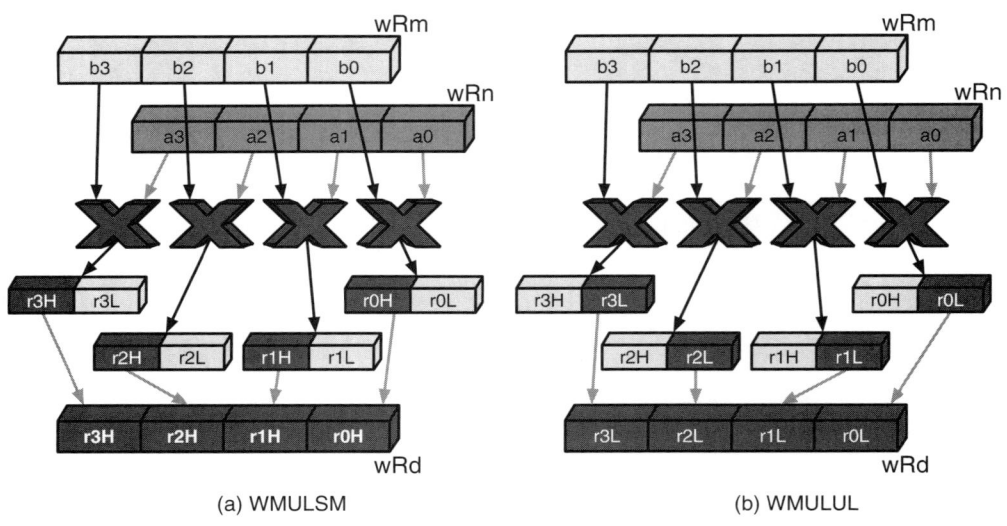

Figure 3.19   WMULSM/WMULUL Four-way 16×16 Multiply Selecting Half the Product

The WMULUM instruction performs a similar operation to WMULSM but with unsigned data. This operation is particularly useful when one of the inputs represents a fractional value, such as the cosine of an angle or an alpha-channel numerator with an implicit denominator of 255.

The WMULUL instruction shown in Figure 3.19(b) also multiplies together the four corresponding 16-bit half-words in each of the source operands, but this time only the least significant 16 bits of the intermediate product are written to the destination field of the result. Notice that the type of the incoming arguments—signed or unsigned—does not affect the final result, because only the lower 16 bits are selected from the intermediate product.

An example usage of the WMUL instruction is:

```
WMULSM wR4, wR7, wR9
WMULUL wR5, wR8, wR10
```

WMADD

The WMADD instruction also multiplies the four 16-bit operands from each source operand. To accommodate the results in the destination register this time, the two high-order products are added together and placed in the upper word of the result and the two lower-order products are added together and placed in the lower word of the result. Figure 3.20 illustrates this instruction. The incoming operands can be either signed or unsigned data, and the data type is specified with either the S, signed, or U, unsigned, qualifier. Hence, WMADDS performs signed multiplication and WMADDU performs unsigned multiplication. An example usage of WMADD is:

```
WMADDS wR7, wR5, wR15
```

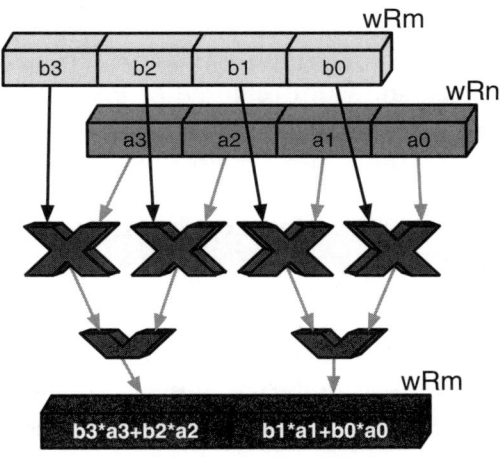

Figure 3.20   WMADD Multiplying and Summing High and Low Products

The WMADD instruction can be combined with the saturating addition operation to also achieve a multiply accumulate operation. The difference between this and the WMAC instruction is that the WMADD/WADD combination can support two parallel accumulators; one in the upper word, one in the lower word. The operands and results in the upper and lower half can therefore be treated as independent data streams.

The WMADD instruction does not have saturating arithmetic. Wraparound can occur only in one situation. If all operands of each register half are 0x8000, the result only wraps around to 0x80000000, which is negative, not positive. In most cases, the coefficients to be used are prepared ahead of time, so this limitation is easy to avoid.

Video Instructions

Intel Wireless MMX technology contains two special instructions that are explicitly targeted at accelerating video encoder and decoder applications. The sum of absolute differences instruction, WSAD, is aimed at accelerating video encoder operations, and the average instruction, WAVG2, is targeted to accelerate video decoding operations.

Sum of Absolute Difference

The sum of absolute difference (SAD) is a fundamental operation used in video encode during motion estimation. In video encode, it is desirable to reduce the bandwidth required to encode a video stream. Instead of encoding and sending every pixel in a video frame, you want to employ techniques to reduce the amount of data. With respect to this particular instruction, one technique used is motion estimation. Here each new frame is analyzed to determine whether it contains any blocks from the previous image. If a match is found, a motion vector is sent instead of sending the block itself. This motion vector tells the video decoder to use a block from the previous frame and move it to the specified location in the new frame. To provide the motion vectors, the video encoder must search the new frame to see whether a block from the old frame is present. The sum of absolute differences is often used as the fundamental measure of how similar a source and destination block are to each other. Typically, the SAD operation is performed on all the pixels in a block and a measure of "goodness" is determined. The SAD operation is repeated on a number of candidate blocks in the new image to find the best match—the one with the lowest SAD value. Motion estimation and the use of the WSAD instruction are described in more detail in Chapter 15.

The WSAD calculates the absolute difference between corresponding fields of the source operands, sums all the differences together, and then adds this to the previous value contained in the destination register. The final result that is placed in the destination register can be used to give a measure of how different the two source operands are. The more similar they are, the smaller the accumulated difference is. Using the accumulating behavior of the instruction allows the comparison to be extended to multiple words. Figure 3.21 shows the operation of the WSADB instruction, which performs the operation on eight 8-bit data items. Similarly, WSADH performs the operation on four 16-bit values. The instruction also optionally allows the destination register to be cleared before the operation. Here's an example of the WSAD instruction in which the absolute differences between the byte elements in wR6 and wR7 are calculated and all are added to the existing contents of the destination register wR4:

```
WSADB wR4,wR6,wR7
```

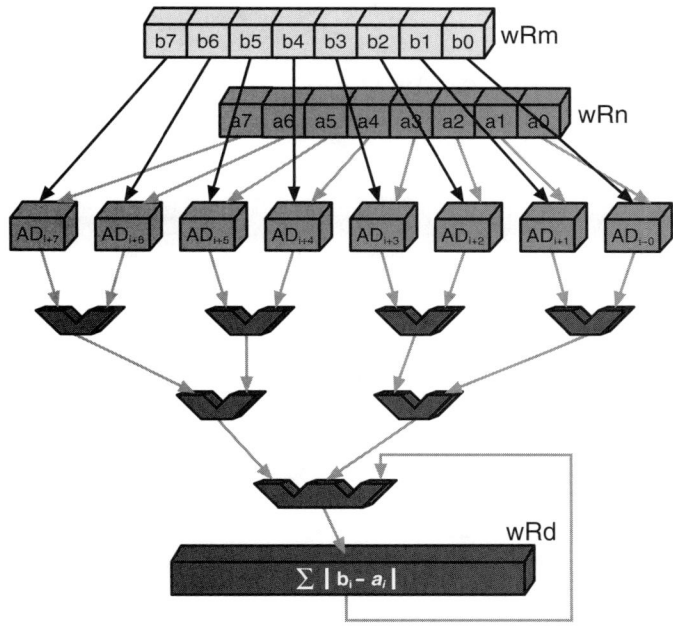

Figure 3.21   WSAD Accumulating Sum of Absolute Difference

Pixel Average

A key component of video decoding is motion compensation. One key operation of this task is to determine the average of two adjacent pixels. The WAVG2 instruction provides support for this operation by performing an averaging operation between corresponding fields in the source operands and writing the result into the destination register. The average-taking operation is performed by adding the two source fields together, dividing the result by two, and then writing the result to the destination register. Extra precision is maintained during the intermediate calculation.

The WAVG2H instruction is shown in Figure 3.22. The WAVG2 also provides an optional capability to add 1 to the intermediate result before the divide by 2, which can prove useful for supporting different rounding modes that are specified in various video decoding standards. An example usage is:

```
WAVG2HR wR4, wR6, wR8
```

Here, the half-word elements of the source operands wR6 and wR8 are averaged with rounding specified.

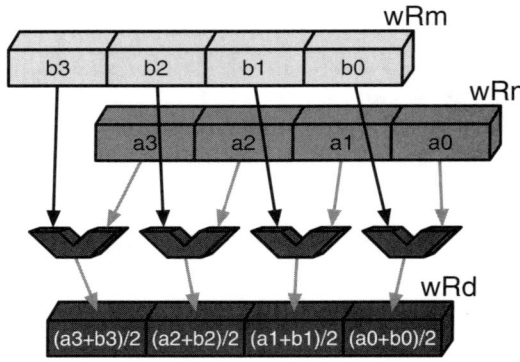

Figure 3.22   WAVG2 Four Concurrent Two-Element Average Operations

Use of these special instructions in video compression algorithms is described in more detail in Chapter 15.

Miscellaneous Instructions

The final two instructions fall into the miscellaneous category. The first instruction, WACC, performs a horizontal add of the elements of the source register. This action is useful if the results of a number of previous parallel operations must be added together. As shown in Figure 3.23, all the elements in the source register are added together and the result is placed in the destination register. In this example, WACCB is used to add all eight bytes of the source register together.

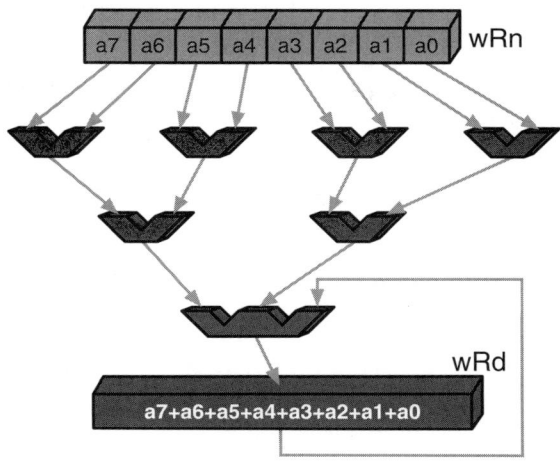

Figure 3.23   WACC Adding All the Fields in a Register Together

The second instruction, TMOVMSK, extracts the top bit, usually a sign bit, of each field and sends it to a core register. The TMOVMSK instruction extracts the top bit of every data element and places them consecutively in the lower order bits of the destination register, with the rest of the core destination register being set to all zeros. Figure 3.24 shows the TMOVMSKH operation, where the top bits of each of the four fields are extracted and transferred to the lower four bits of the destination register.

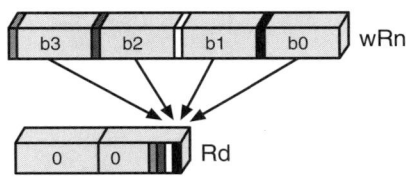

Figure 3.24   TMOVMSK Extracting Sign Bits

Example usages for both WACC and TMOVMSK are:

```
WACCB     wR3,  wR6
TMOVMSKH R3,   wR4
```

Conditional Execution

The current programmers status register, CPSR, contains four arithmetic flags that indicate the state of the results of the last operation that set the flags. The four flags are as follows:

- N – the result is negative
- Z – the result is zero
- C – the result had a carry out
- V – the result overflowed

The ARM architecture specifies a mechanism for using these flags to determine whether a particular instruction should be executed. This mechanism is commonly known as *conditional* or *predicated* execution. Each instruction can be suffixed by an optional mnemonic, which indicates the condition that must be true for the instruction to execute. Table 3.2 shows all the possible condition mnemonics specified by the ARM architecture.

Table 3.2 Condition Code Mnemonics

Condition	Meaning	Flag State Required
EQ	Equal	Z Set
NE	Not equal	Z Clear
CS	Carry set	C Set
CO	Carry clear	C Clear
MI	Minus/negative	N Set
PL	Plus/positive	N Clear
VS	Overflow	V Set
VC	No overflow	V Clear
HI	Unsigned higher	C Set & Z Clear
LS	Unsigned lower or same	C Clear | Z Set
GE	Signed greater than or equal	N == Z
LT	Signed less than	N != V
GT	Signed greater than	Z==0, N==V
LE	Signed less than or equal	Z==1, N!=V
AL	Always (unconditional)	N/A

> The conditions are tested by evaluating the current state of the arithmetic flags in the CPSR. The third column in Table 3.2 shows the test that is performed to indicate whether the condition is satisfied. An example of conditional execution is:
>
> ```
> WADDBEQ  wR0, wR1, wR2
> ```
>
> This byte addition is executed if the EQ condition is satisfied; that is, the Z flag is set in the CPSR. If the condition test failed, then the instruction does not change any processor state and it becomes a NOP.

Controlling Program Flow

You can control program flow in a number of ways when using Intel XScale microarchitecture with Intel Wireless MMX technology. In compliance with the ARM coprocessor framework, the main core is responsible for all flow control decisions. These decisions can be made by an implicit operation such as load to register R15 or by explicit branch operations. Individual instructions can also be predicated to execute only if the arithmetic flags of the Intel XScale core are in a particular state. You can apply the same conditional execution predicates to Intel Wireless MMX instructions, but the arithmetic flags that are used as a basis for the test are those contained within the CPSR core register, not within the SIMD coprocessor unit.

SIMD Arithmetic Flags

To seamlessly integrate SIMD-style programming into the core conditional execution mechanism, Intel Wireless MMX technology provides a set of arithmetic flags, one for each packed data element processed. For example, if byte operands are processed, eight sets of arithmetic flags are produced. When half-word elements are processed, four sets of flags result, and if word operands are processed, only two sets of flags are produced. The flags are stored in the SIMD arithmetic flag register, wCASF. Figure 3.25 shows what the wCASF register looks like after an instruction of each particular data type is executed. The regions shaded gray are set to zero. The register contents reflect the state of the flags, depending on the last instruction that changed the flags and the data type of that instruction.

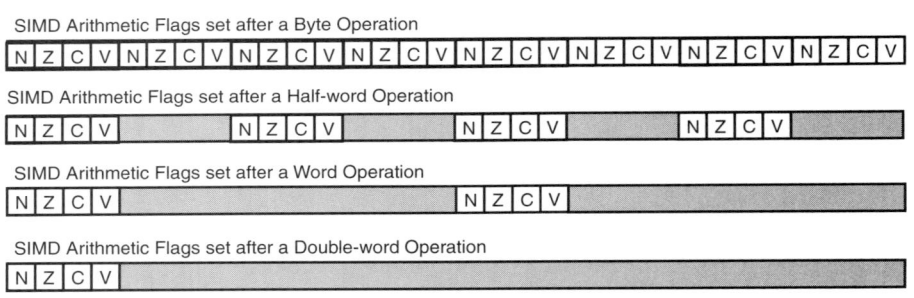

Figure 3.25   SIMD Arithmetic Flags

A unique feature of the programming model for Intel Wireless MMX technology is its ability to logically combine the SIMD arithmetic flags and use these in conjunction with the ARM conditional execution mechanism to provide new execution predicates. This technique is known as *group conditional execution*.

Group Conditional Execution

The arithmetic flags can be transferred to the CPSR core register by performing a logical operation to combine the flags in the SIMD PSR, wCASF, and then transferring these to the CPSR register. Figure 3.26 shows the flags set after a half-word instruction has been combined with a logical or operation and transferred to the CSPR. The TORC instruction provides this functionality for Intel Wireless MMX technology; it may operate on byte, half-word, word, or double type data-generated flags.

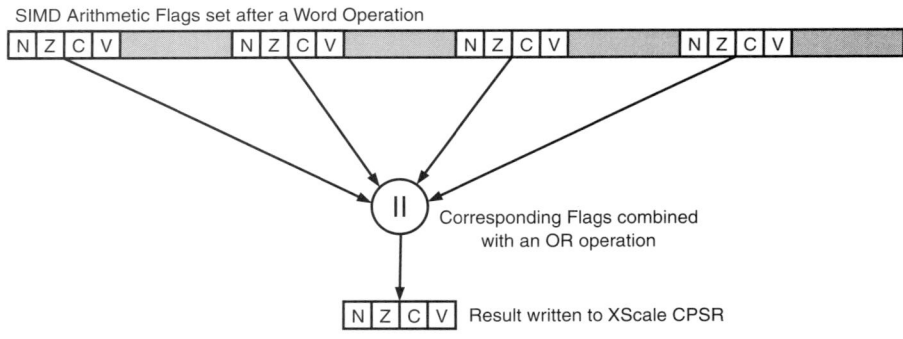

Figure 3.26   Combining SIMD Flags with a Logical or Operation

Once the flags are transferred to the CPSR, subsequent conditional instructions can use them—both Intel XScale microarchitecture and Intel Wireless MMX conditional instructions. However, the flags now contain extra meaning because they were derived from the SIMD PSR. For flags that were transferred using an or operation, the corresponding flag in the CPSR is set *if any* of the same flags in the SIMD PSR were set. This characteristic gives rise to powerful new predicates, which are best demonstrated by the following code example:

```
WADDB   wR0, wR6, wR7
TORCB   wR15
BEQ     Loop
```

Here the WADDB instruction first sets the byte SIMD PSR flags. Then, the TORCB combines the flags with an or operation and transfers them to the CPSR. Finally, the branch is executed conditionally on the state of these flags. The branch is executed if the Z flag is set, which effectively means the branch is executed if any packed data element in wR0 is a zero and had set the SIMD flags accordingly. Other flags could be used to realize group conditional predicates such as *take the branch if any SIMD element is negative* (BMI) or *take the branch if any SIMD element has overflowed* (BVS).

The SIMD flags can also be combined using a logical and operation. This time, the sample code uses the TANDC instruction to perform a similar function to TORC, except that the logical function is an and instead of an or. If the flags are combined with the and operation (TANDC) instead of an or operation, the branch (BEQ) is taken *if all* elements in wR0 were zero.

The *if any* and *if all* group conditional qualifiers are useful for search algorithms and determining boundary conditions of execution. An example would be the following sequence of actions: loop again unless any packed data element has overflowed, branch if any field matches (Z Set) after a comparison operation.

In addition to logical combination of the SIMD flags, elements and individual set of flags may be transferred by the use of the TEXTRC instruction. This instruction specifies the data type of interest and indicates the position of the required flags using an immediate value.

The following example uses all three instructions:

```
TORCH    R15
TANDCW   R15
TEXTRCH  R15, #2
```

For TEXTRCH the set of half-word flags at position 2 in the word is selected and transferred to the CPSR. Note that the least significant set of flags is identified by an offset #0.

Remembering Saturation

During a computation, it is often useful to know whether any intermediate calculation saturated during the overall operation. Many DSP algorithms use this capability to optimize performance. Instead of checking input operands and intermediate values for overflow, the algorithms typically run through the complex calculation and then just check a saturation indicator at the end. If saturation did occur, the input operands are typically scaled to prevent saturation and the operation is repeated, this time without saturating.

Only three Intel Wireless MMX instructions—WADD, WSUB, and WPACK—can force the results to saturate to the maximum or minimum value rather than causing wrap-around. To indicate that saturation has occurred, a saturation history register is provided. In this register, eight flags indicate which of the possible packed data elements has been saturated. The register is called the SIMD saturation flag register, wCSSF.

The saturation flags indicate that saturation occurred at a particular byte, half-word, or word position in the 64-bit double word. The saturation flags are sticky, in that they remain set until explicitly cleared by writing to the register. For a byte saturation operation, all eight flags are set according to the saturation status. For a half-word operation, only every other flag is set, four in total, one for each packed half-word element. Similarly, for word operations, only two flags are set to indicate that saturation occurred in one of the two words. For both the word and half-word operations, the saturation flags that are not used for that data type remain at their previous value, as shown in Figure 3.27.

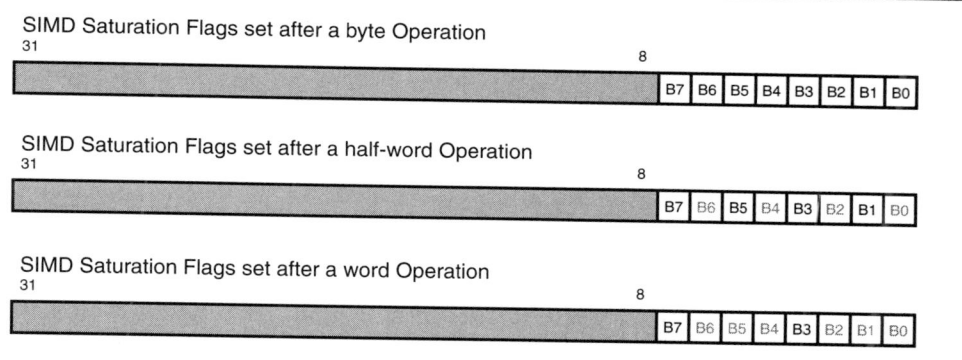

Figure 3.27 wCSSF SIMD Saturation Register

![Key Points]

Key Points

This chapter introduced the basic components of Intel Wireless MMX technology. In particular, the following key points should be remembered:

■ The Intel XScale core with Intel Wireless MMX technology is a load-store architecture where SIMD data processing operations operate only on registers.

■ A typical algorithm is processed by loading data into the register, rearranging for SIMD processing, performing the operation, then repacking before ultimately storing in memory.

■ Intel Wireless MMX technology provides a large register file with sixteen 64-bit registers.

■ Intel Wireless MMX technology provides a rich set of instructions for manipulating and operating on packed data types, including support for video and DSP functions commonly found in multimedia applications.

■ Intel Wireless MMX instructions can be conditionally executed, depending on the state of the current program status register (CPSR).

Chapter 4

Understanding the Hardware

It is quite a three-pipe problem.

—Sir Arthur Conan Doyle

To write highly optimized applications using Intel® Wireless MMX™ technology, it is very useful to understand how the underlying hardware executes instructions and how hardware architecture can constrain the performance of an application. This chapter provides an overview of the hardware architecture and how instructions map onto these structures.

You must gather five types of information to understand the co-processor operation of Intel Wireless MMX technology.

- What basic functional building blocks are available?

- How are these building blocks connected together in a pipeline structure to achieve the instruction functionality required?

- How are multiple pipeline structures organized?

- How does an instruction use the pipeline organization to achieve the desired result?

- When is the result available for other operations to use?

When you understand the inter-instruction dependencies that the hardware creates, you can reorder instruction sequences to avoid redundant processor stalls.

Coprocessor Framework

The ARM[†] architecture supports extension of the baseline processor functionality by using a predefined framework for adding up to 16 coprocessors. Intel Wireless MMX technology is incorporated into a coprocessor on the Intel XScale® microarchitecture that uses this standard ARM coprocessor framework. The coprocessor framework includes definitions of instruction encoding space that can be used to extend the instruction set and basic classifications of instruction types. The ARM coprocessor model supports three classes of coprocessor instruction:

■ *Load and Store*–transfers data to or from the coprocessor to main memory.

■ *Register transfer*–transfers the contents of registers between the coprocessor and the main core.

■ *Coprocessor Data Processing (CDP)*–operates on data from the coprocessor registers and retains the result in a coprocessor register.

All Intel Wireless MMX instructions belong to one of these classes of instruction. The load and store instructions WLDR and WSTR clearly belong to the coprocessor load and store class of instruction. All other instructions starting with the W prefix are data processing operations that belong to the CDP class of instructions. The remaining instructions with a T prefix belong to the register transfer class of instruction. The register transfer class includes instructions that allow an operation to be performed as data to be transferred from one register file to the other. For example, TMIA transfers contents from the core register file, performs a 32×32 multiply, and writes the result into a coprocessor register.

For the application developer, Intel Wireless MMX technology appears as a seamless extension to the instruction set and programming model of the Intel XScale microarchitecture. For convenience, the mnemonics of Intel Wireless MMX instructions are provided to ease programming, but it is also possible to refer to instructions using the standard ARM nomenclature. However, using this method is not recommended because the code is not easy to understand and maintain. Figure 4.1 demonstrates the difference in code legibility.

Mnemonics for Intel® Wireless MMX™ Technology

```
WADDB    wR0, wR1, wR2
WSUBB    wR4, wR5, wR0
```

Nomenclature for Standard ARM CDP

```
CDP    p1, CR0, 0, CR1, CR2, 4
CDP    p1, CR4, 0, CR5, CR0, 5
```

Figure 4.1   Comparison of Instruction Mnemonics

The ARM CDP format is only useful if a particular assembler does not support Intel Wireless MMX instructions; it is not a productive way to write the code because it is more difficult to understand and maintain.

Dealing with Memory

The ARM architecture specifies that the main core is responsible for fetching instructions and data from memory and delivering them to the coprocessor. For applications using Intel Wireless MMX technology, instructions are fetched and dispatched by the Intel XScale core; Intel Wireless MMX instructions are routed to the coprocessor for execution. The Intel XScale core is also responsible for all communications with the data memories. The address calculations for memory transactions are calculated from values stored in the core register file, and the data is either sent to or retrieved from the coprocessor registers. The coprocessor to Intel XScale core arrangement is shown in Figure 4.2

Intel Wireless MMX technology takes advantage of the existing memory subsystem of the Intel XScale microarchitecture without the need for extra dedicated memories and the power consumption associated with them. Power efficiency is further improved by using advanced power management, where the coprocessor unit is only activated, when required, on an instruction-by-instruction basis.

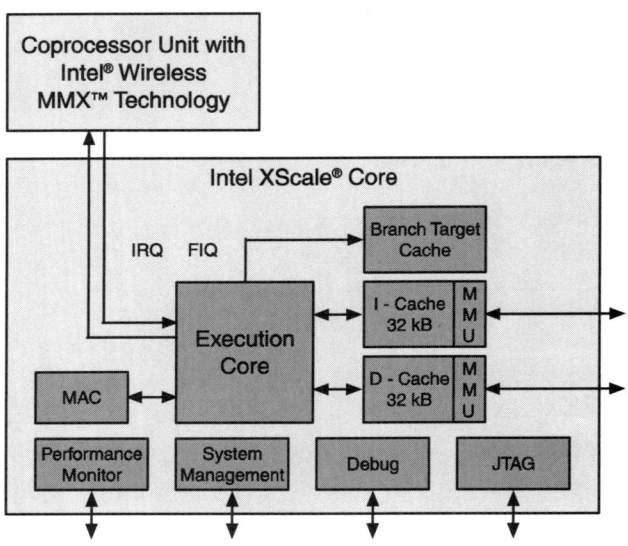

Figure 4.2   Relationship to the Core

The Intel XScale® Microarchitecture

The Intel XScale microarchitecture is a high-speed, power-efficient Intel implementation of the ARM† V5TE Architecture. The microarchitecture surrounds the core with instruction and data memory management units; instruction, data, caches, and branch-target buffer; and power management, performance monitoring, debug, and JTAG units. The key features of the core are as follows:

■ Seven-stage to eight-stage superpipelined RISC technology achieves high speed and ultra low power.

■ Dynamic voltage management means voltage and frequency on-the-fly scaling to allow applications to use the right blend of performance and power. Intel Wireless MMX technology also supports data voltage management.

■ Power management provides power savings via idle, sense, sleep, deep-sleep, and standby modes.

■ 128-entry branch target buffer keeps the pipeline filled with statistically correct branch choices.

- 32-kilobyte instruction cache keeps local copies of important instructions to enable high performance and low power.

- 32-kilobyte data cache keeps local copy of important data to enable high performance and low power.

- 2-kilobyte mini-data cache avoids thrashing of the 32-kilobyte data cache for frequently changing data streams.

- 32-entry instruction-memory management enables logical-to-physical address translation, access permissions, and instruction cache attributes.

- 32-entry data memory management unit enables logical-to-physical address translation, access permissions, data cache attributes.

- Four-entry fill and pending buffers promote core efficiency by allowing hit-under-miss operation with data caches.

- Performance monitoring unit furnishes two 32-bit event counters and one 32-bit cycle counter for analysis of hit rates.

- Debug unit uses hardware breakpoints and 256-entry trace history.

- Eight-entry write buffer allows the core to continue execution while data is written to memory.

More information about the Intel XScale microarchitecture can be found in the *Intel XScale® Core Developer's Manual* (Intel 2004), listed in "References."

Hardware Building Blocks

Five hardware functional units are provided to execute Intel Wireless MMX instructions. These are connected so that data may be routed in and out of each functional unit during instruction execution. A register file provides the temporary storage area for all operands and results. A typical operation proceeds by initially retrieving the operand data from the register file, routing this to the functional unit required to provide the instruction operation, and then sending the result back to the register file until it is needed again. Figure 4.3 shows how the units are connected together.

The five key functional units that form the basis of the coprocessor, shown in Figure 4.3, are as follows:

■ The shift and permute unit (SPU) is responsible for performing shift and permute operations. These operations include alignment WALIGN, logical shift WSLL and WSRL, arithmetic shift WSRA, rotation WROR, packing WPACK and WUNPCK, and shuffling WSHUF.

■ The execute unit (EXU) is responsible for performing arithmetic and logic operations; it also provides a saturation capability. Operands may be received from the SPU when saturation is required and from the CIU when the transfer instructions are issued. The execution unit is the workhorse general execution unit for addition and subtraction WADD/WSUB and all the logical operations WAND, WANDN, WOR, and WXOR.

■ The multiply and accumulate unit (MAU) is responsible for performing all multiply and accumulate operations. Operands are also received from the EXU when executing the sum of absolute difference instruction. The MAU unit is a three-stage pipeline with internal accumulator forwarding. This unit supports multiply instructions TMIA, TMIAPH, TMIAxy, WMAC, WMUL, and WMADD. The multiplier accumulation hardware is also used to implement the sum of absolute difference with WSAD and WACC instructions.

■ The coprocessor interface unit (CIU) transfers data between the coprocessor unit registers and the Intel XScale core. In addition to supporting coprocessor data transfer, it is also responsible for storing and loading data to and from the memory. This unit deals with all the T-prefixed instructions as well as coordinating data transfers for the WLDR load and WSTR store instructions.

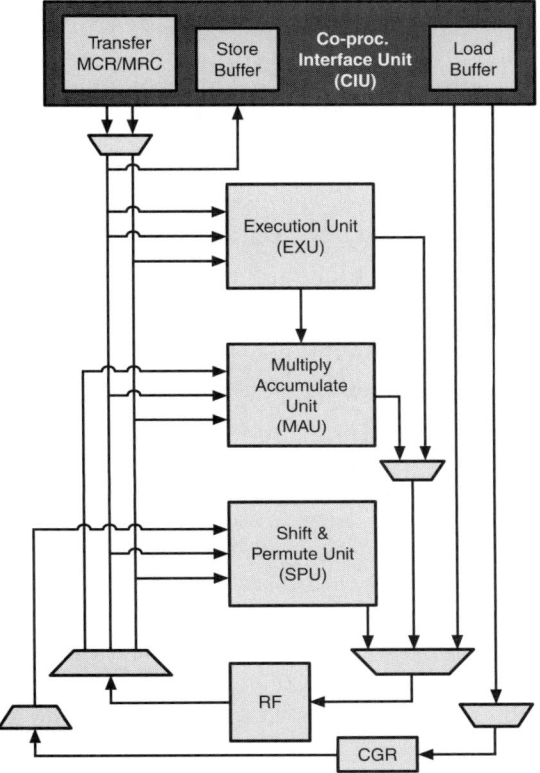

Figure 4.3   Microarchitecture

■ The register file unit (RFU) is organized as sixteen 64-bit registers, located in the coprocessor 0 space (CP0). The large register file allows the Intel Wireless MMX instructions to support an increased number of intermediate values in complex calculations. For example, multiple output samples of a filter may be calculated in parallel. The increased storage allows the programmer to take advantage of the spatial and temporal data locality as found in many multimedia applications. This reduces the required load and store bandwidth and improves processing efficiency. Alignment support instructions also increase the effectiveness of this data reuse. You will learn more about algorithm techniques that utilize the large register file in Chapter 5. The register file also contains control and status registers that are mapped into coprocessor 1 space (CP1). Four 32-bit general-purpose control registers can be used for alignment and shift control. Because the shift and alignment offset is usually invariant across the inner loops of many multimedia algorithms, the registers are designed to hold constant values. This design feature saves the use of a packed data register. The four status registers are:

- wCASF, which contains the SIMD arithmetic flags
- wCSSF, which contains the SIMD saturation flags
- wCID, which contains the coprocessor identification and revision number
- wCON, which is a general purpose control status register

Both the packed data registers and the control registers are shown in Figure 4.4.

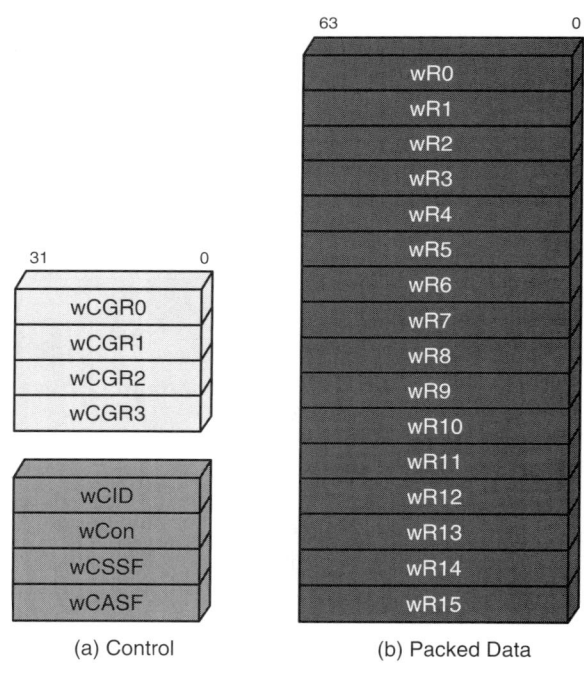

(a) Control   (b) Packed Data

Figure 4.4   Register File Organization

Pipeline Structure Overview

The basic building blocks are connected in a manner that provides the required instruction functionality. To achieve higher performance, multiple instructions are in progress at any given time. In these sections you will learn how pipelines are used to improve performance and how this impacts instruction-to-instruction dependencies and overall performance.

Pipelining

To support high-frequency operation, modern microprocessors employ a technique known as *pipelining*. As shown in Figure 4.5, this technique involves breaking a task down into smaller chunks that can be processed over a number of clock cycles, rather than all at once in a single clock.

In the non-pipelined case shown in Figure 4.5(a), the operand is taken from the input storage element, the task takes a time duration (T_{task}) to perform, and the result is stored in the output element.

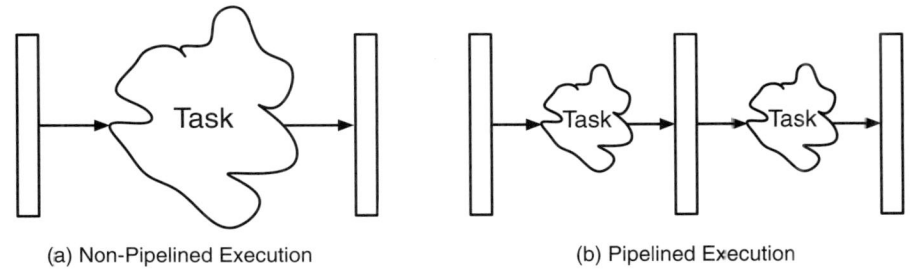

(a) Non-Pipelined Execution   (b) Pipelined Execution

Figure 4.5   Pipelining a Task for High-frequency Operation

In the pipelined case shown in Figure 4.5(b), the task is divided into two halves; each half of the task is performed in separate stages. The time taken for each stage to compute its answer is now T_{task} divided by two. The reduction in the delay for each individual stage allows the clock frequency of the design to be increased; in this example, the increased clock rate allows twice the frequency.

The elapsed time for the task to complete does not change for the pipelined case—two stages, each taking T_{task} divided by two. However, the benefit results from a two-stage simultaneous effort. As soon as the first stage has completed its task and stored its result, it may start processing the next data element while stage 2 is finishing the task on the first data element. The ability to process two data elements at the same time allows the pipeline to produce a result every $T_{task}/2$.

Pipelining a design has many advantages for increasing performance, but you also need to consider potential consequences. Pipeline performance is usually measured in two ways:

■ Latency—how long does the task take to get from start to finish?

■ Bandwidth—how many results per second can be generated?

In the previous example, the pipeline shown in Figure 4.5(a) would have a latency of 1 clock and a bandwidth of 1 result per time (T_{task}). The pipeline example shown in Figure 4.5(b) has a latency of 2 clock cycles but a bandwidth of 1 result per time ($T_{task}/2$). So in the same time period, (b) would produce twice as many results as (a).

Unfortunately, life is not this simple. In real-world examples, there are data dependencies between data elements. For example, consider the following two instructions:

```
A = B + C (1)

D = A + F (2)
```

The dependency in this example is that the value of A must be calculated before the calculation of D can commence. If the addition operation is mapped onto the two-stage pipeline shown in Figure 4.5(b) and it requires both stages to complete, the calculation of A has to complete before D can start processing. The cycle-by-cycle progress in the pipeline storage elements is shown in Figure 4.6. During the first cycle, instruction (1) arrives at the input. In the second cycle, half of the A calculation is complete and instruction (2) arrives at the input. In the third cycle, the calculation is completed but the calculation of D cannot start because it is waiting for the value of A. Finally, in the fourth cycle, the calculation of D can commence, and in the fifth cycle, the calculation of D is complete.

In this case, D must wait for 1 full clock cycle until the value of A has been completely calculated. The cycle that D must wait for is commonly referred to as a *pipeline stall*.

To help understand the different forms of stalls and how a particular instruction sequence flows through the pipeline, it is convenient to classify characteristics of each instruction using standard terminology.

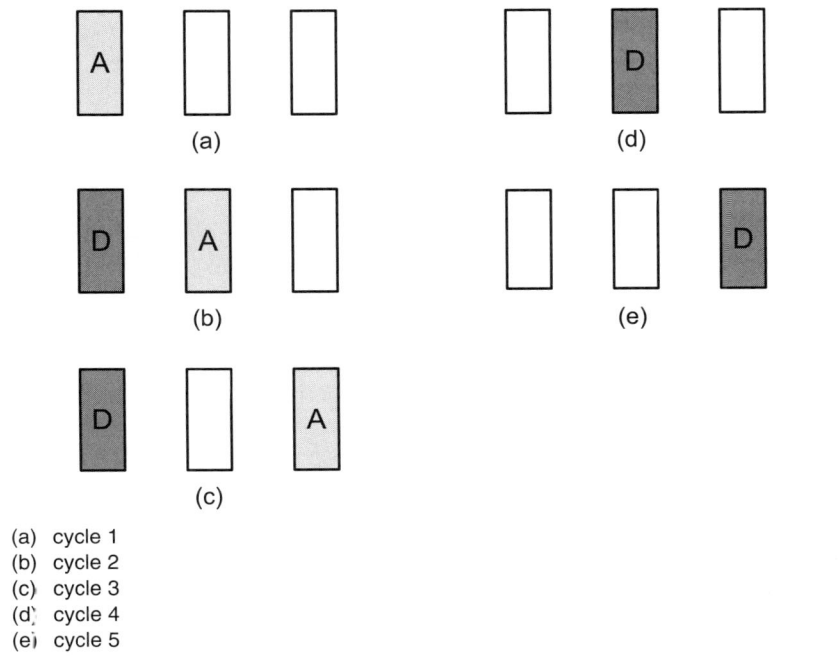

(a) cycle 1
(b) cycle 2
(c) cycle 3
(d) cycle 4
(e) cycle 5

Figure 4.6   Pipeline Progress of Two Dependent Instructions

Terminology

Some common terminology is used to describe the characteristics of instruction behavior in a given pipeline. The following terms are used in this book:

■ *Result latency* is the number of cycles it takes an instruction to calculate a result and make that result available to a following instruction. A result latency of 1 clock cycle indicates that the result is immediately available to the next following instruction without stalls. In the example shown in Figure 4 6, instruction (a) has a result latency of 2 cycles. If the result is used immediately in the following instruction, any result latency above 1 cycle translates directly into stall cycles for the following instruction. Using the same example in Figure 4.6, the number of stalls for instruction (d) can be calculated from:

```
Stalls = Result latency -1 =  2 - 1 = 1
```

Similarly, an instruction with a result latency of 4 would cause an instruction immediately behind it to stall 3 cycles if that following instruction requires as input the result currently being calculated.

A stall caused by result data not being available in time is usually called a *data hazard*. That is, if an instruction has a result latency greater than 1 and the following instruction tries to use the result immediately, a stall occurs.

◼ *Issue Latency* describes the number of clock cycles an instruction spends in a particular pipeline stage—usually the first stage. In some cases, an instruction might take two clock ticks to perform a more complex task because it uses the same hardware twice. For example, a 32-bit add operation may be calculated by using a 16-bit adder twice. In this case, the following instructions cannot enter the pipeline stage when it is still busy. An instruction that occupies a pipeline stage for a single cycle has an issue latency of one clock cycle. An instruction that occupies a stage for two cycles has an issue latency of two clock cycles, and so on. A following instruction wishing to enter the pipeline stage stalls if the issue latency of the previous instruction is greater than 1. The number of cycles stalled is calculated by:

```
Stall Cycles = Issue latency - 1
```

An issue latency of 1 has no stalls.

A stall caused by an instruction occupying a stage for more than one cycle is often called a *resource hazard*. That is, the resource is busy and cannot be used immediately by a following instruction.

Pipeline Structure

To achieve the same clock speed as the Intel XScale core, the coprocessor unit employs the same pipeline structure as the core. This structure is shown in Figure 4.7. Here, in the first two stages of the pipeline (F1,F2), the instructions are fetched from the instruction cache. In the next stage (ID), the instruction is decoded and the operation is determined. At this point, if an Intel Wireless MMX instruction is identified, it is transferred to the coprocessor during the ID stage. After decode, the operands are read from the register file in the RF stage. Once the operands are available, the main execution of the operation happens in X1 and X2, with the final result writeback in XWB. The coprocessor pipeline operates in lockstep with the main core pipeline, providing a single thread of control; no complex synchronizations are required between the two units.

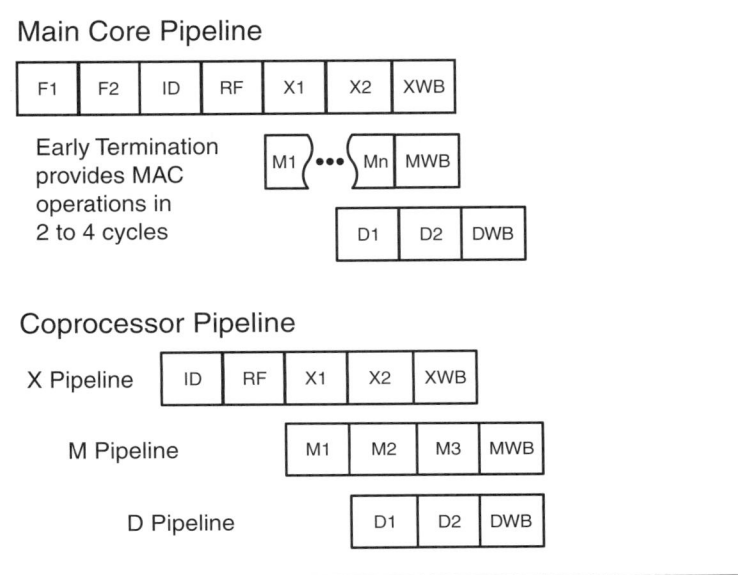

Figure 4.7   Pipeline Structure

In addition to the main execution pipeline, the coprocessor unit contains two other side pipelines: one for memory operations D1, D2, and DWB routed via the Intel XScale core and another side pipeline for multiply operations M1, M2, M3, and MWB. A fourth implicit pipeline for the coprocessor unit is the pipeline to the Intel XScale core, which is used for register transfer operations.

Pipeline Organization

Multiple parallel pipelines provide a choice as to where to dispatch the next instruction. After reading the packed data operands, an Intel Wireless MMX instruction can be sent to one of the four possible pipeline structures identified in the previous section, as shown in Figure 4.8. The combined Intel XScale microarchitecture with Intel Wireless MMX technology can only issue one instruction per clock cycle. An instruction can be issued to any resource in the main core pipeline or coprocessor pipeline that is not busy.

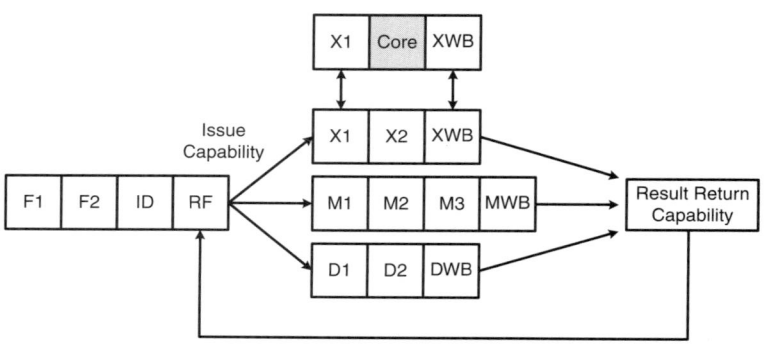

Figure 4.8   Pipeline Issue and Return Capability

When the operation in a pipeline structure is complete, the result is returned to the register file. Three independent routes lead back to the register file; returning results may arrive back in the register file in a different order than that in which the instructions were dispatched. The common terminology used to describe this rearrangement is that results can be "retired out of order." For example, multiply operations generally take longer to complete than execution pipeline instructions such as addition. Therefore, the result from a WADD dispatched immediately after a WMAC operation will return to the register file before the WMAC result is completed.

Special hardware interlocks in the coprocessor ensure that if dependencies or conflicts exist, the results return in the correct order. For example, if two consecutive instructions write to the same register but the first is in the multiply pipeline and the second is in the execution pipeline, then the original order is preserved for writing the result to the register file to ensure that the correct result remains; that is, the multiply result is written first and then the execution operation overwrites the value.

Fortunately, write-after-write dependencies are uncommon—it is rarely useful to write a register and then immediately overwrite without reading the contents first.

The out-of-order result capability is particularly useful for working around load dependencies. A load instruction may take many cycles to fetch data if a cache miss is encountered, especially if the access has to go off chip to SDRAM. In this case, nondependent instructions can continue to execute and write their results back while the load is still outstanding. Since the memory interface can support up to four outstanding loads without stalling the processor, data may be fetched well ahead of when it may be needed to mitigate the effects of external memory latency. Fetching the data early may reduce the number of cycles the processor is stalled waiting for data. This is an especially important consideration in a deeply embedded system-on-a-chip application, where the external memory may be shared with other functions such as an LCD controller or camera interface. Memory optimization is discussed in more detail in Chapter 9.

Putting It All Together

So far you have seen the basic building blocks, how they connect in a pipeline, and how the pipelines are organized. The final step is to understand how instructions map to these resources and how this affects inter-instruction dependencies and stalls.

Understanding How Instructions Execute

Figure 4.9 shows a concise method of describing which pipeline stages a particular instruction operates in and when the result is available. Figure 4.9(a) shows the mapping for execution pipeline instructions; the meaning of the table is as follows. Each instruction occupies a row of the table and each column represents a pipeline stage that is used for this instruction execution. The action in each pipeline stage can be either execute (X) with no result available or the result is available (R). For each instruction, the left-most column containing an R indicates the earliest point at which the result is available.

For example, the WOR instruction in this table shows an X in the ID and RF columns, indicating that the instruction executes in the instruction decode (ID) and register file (RF) stages, and no result is yet available. The R in the X1 column indicates that the result of WOR is available at the end of the X1 stage.

Dependency checks are performed in the X1 stage. If the required operand is not available and cannot be immediately forwarded, the processor stalls in the X1 stage and waits for the operand to become available. If the result is available in X1—indicated by the first R in the X1 column—then the next instruction is guaranteed never to stall while waiting for this data. The WOR instruction always produces its result in X1, so it never causes a data dependency stall for a subsequent instruction using the result.

Trace of ALU Operations:

Instructions	ID	RF	X1	X2	XWB
WADD	X	X	X/R	R	R
WSUB	X	X	X/R	R	R
WCMPEQ	X	X	X	R	R
WCMPGT	X	X	X	R	R
WAND	X	X	R	R	R
WANDN	X	X	R	R	R
WOR	X	X	R	R	R
WXOR	X	X	R	R	R
WAVG2	X	X	R	R	R
WMAX	X	X	X	R	R
WMIN	X	X	X	R	R
WSLL	X	X	R	R	R
WSRA	X	X	R	R	R
WSRL	X	X	R	R	R
WROR	X	X	R	R	R
WPACK	X	X	X	R	R
WUNPCKEH	X	X	R	R	R
WUNPCKEL	X	X	R	R	R
WUNPCKIH	X	X	R	R	R
WUNPCKIL	X	X	R	R	R
WALIGNI	X	X	R	R	R
WALIGNR	X	X	R	R	R
WSHUF	X	X	R	R	R

Trace of CIU Operations:

Instructions	ID	RF	X1	X2	XWB
TANDC	X	X	X		
TORC	X	X	X		
TEXTRC	X	X	X		
TMOVSK	X	X	X		
TINSTR	X	X	X	X	X
TBCST	X	X	X	X	X
TMRRC	X	X	X	X	R
TMRC	X	X	X	R	
TMCR	X	X	X/R		
TMCRR	X	X	X	X/R	

An instruction in MAC can forward to another instruction within MAC (in M2)

Forwarding to other functional unit takes place in M3

X = Execute

R = Ready for forwarding

R'= Forwarding within the functional unit

X'= Spends additional cycle

(a) Execute Pipeline   (b) Transfer Operations

Figure 4.9   Mapping Instructions to Execution Pipeline Stages

In contrast, the WPACK instruction executes in the ID, RF, and X1 stages, with the result not being available until the X2 stage. Therefore, if the following instruction is waiting for this result, it will stall for one cycle.

A rule of thumb: any instruction with the leftmost R in the X1 column can never cause a data dependency stall to subsequent instructions. If the first R is in the X2 column—as with the WPACK instruction—then a one-cycle stall is possible if the instruction result is used immediately by the next instruction. Similarly, if the first R is in the XWB column—as with TMRC—then using the result of this instruction immediately will cause a two-cycle stall.

If you understand when the result is available, you can arrange instruction sequences to avoid trying to use a result value before it is known to be available. For example, in the following code sequence, the WADD instruction stalls for one cycle waiting for the result of the WPACK instruction to become available.

```
WPACKWUS      wR4, wR0, wR1
WADD          wR6, wR4, wR2
WMOV          wR8, wR10
```

It takes four cycles to execute three instructions. This same code can be written in a different order while maintaining the same functionality.

```
WPACKWUS      wR4, wR0, wR1
WMOV          wR8, wR10
WADD          wR6, wR4, wR2   <- No stalls
```

Now, it takes three cycles to execute three instructions. This time the stall is avoided and the task completed in three cycles rather than the original four cycles. The reordering of instruction sequences is commonly known as *instruction scheduling* and is an essential part of optimizing an application. You will learn more about this in Chapter 10.

Some columns in Figure 4.9 have both an X and an R in the column (X/R). This indicates that sometimes the result is available and sometimes the instruction is just executing and no result is available. For example, in the WADD instruction row, X/R is in the X1 column. This configuration indicates that the result is available in X1 when no saturation is specified for the add operation, and the result is not available until X2 if saturation is required. In this case, a WADD without saturation never causes a data dependency stall for a subsequent instruction; whereas, a WADD with saturation can cause a one-cycle stall if the result is required immediately afterward.

Figure 4.10 shows the more complex arrangement of the multiply instructions. This figure introduces some new symbols. An R' indicates that the result is available but can only be used by subsequent instructions in the multiply pipeline. If a non-multiply instruction requires a result, it is available in the M3 pipeline stage with only an R symbol. For example, the WACC instruction executes in the ID and RF stages and then the M1 stage. In the M2 stage (R'), the result is available for internal M pipeline use; in the M3 pipeline stage (R), the result is available for use outside the multiply pipeline.

The rule of thumb here is that if an R' is in the M2 column—which all instructions have—then you incur no data dependency penalty for using the result within the multiply pipeline. When the first R is in the M3 pipeline, the other non-multiply instructions experience at least a two-cycle stall waiting for the result.

Trace of MAU instructions:

Instructions	ID	RF	X1	X2	XWB	M1	M2	M3	MWB
WSAD	X	X	X			X	X/R'	X/R	R
WACC	X	X				X	X/R'	X/R	R
WMUL	X	X				X/X'	X/R'	X/R	R
WMADD	X	X				X/X'	X/R'	X/R	R
WMAC	X	X				X/X'	X/R'	X/R	R
TMIA	X	X	X			X/X'	X/R'	X/R	R
TMIAPH	X	X	X			X	X/R'	X/R	R
TMIAxy	X	X	X			X	X/R'	X/R	R

An instruction in MAC can forward to another instruction within MAC (in M2)	X = Execute
	R= Ready for forwarding
Forwarding to other functional unit takes place in M3	R'= Forwarding within the functional unit
	X'= Spends additional cycle

Figure 4.10   Mapping Instructions to the M Pipeline

For example, a WACC followed by a WMAC using the same accumulator does not stall as shown below:

```
WACCB wR0, wR1
WMAC  wR0, wR2, wR3   <- wR0 available in Mpipe, no stall
```

However, a two-cycle stall would result if the second instruction is not in the list, as shown in Figure 4.10. One example might be a WADD instruction that uses the main execution pipeline, as follows.

```
WACCB wR0, wR1
WADDB wR4, wR0, wR3   <- 2 stall cycles
```

Fortunately, the common case is accumulator forwarding within the multiply pipeline. Use outside of the M pipeline is usually a load or store operation, and the result availability stall can usually be hidden by code rescheduling.

The other new symbol in Figure 4.10 is X'. This symbol indicates that a particular instruction takes multiple cycles in that pipeline stage. The net result is that a following instruction cannot use the pipeline stage and must stall. For example, the WMAC instruction uses the M1 stage twice, so it is not possible to use the first pipeline stage for one cycle after the WMAC enters. In the following example, the second WMAC stalls for one cycle because the M1 stage is not available. This situation is known as a *resource hazard*.

```
WMAC wR0, wR1, wR2
WMAC wR0, wR3, wR4   <- Stalls for 1 cycle
```

Most practical signal processing algorithms load data from memory to process, using multiply operations such as WMAC. The data load operations can usually be interleaved with the MAC instructions to prevent occurrence of the resource hazard, as shown in this example:

```
WMAC wR0, wR1, wR2
WLDR wR6, R8
WMAC wR0, wR3, wR4   <- No stalls
WLDR wR7, R9
```

Some instructions—WSAD, TMIA, TMIAPH, and TMIAXY—operate in both the execution pipeline and the multiply pipeline. This type of operation is shown in Figure 4.10 by an X in the X1 column and an X in the M1 column, indicating that the instructions operate in just the X1 stage of the execution pipeline before transferring to the multiple pipeline. Extra care has to be taken when looking at resource stalls in this case because a following instruction cannot use the M1 stage until these instructions have executed in X1 and finished in M1. If the next instruction tries to use the multiply pipeline, it will stall for one cycle until the resource is available.

Figure 4.11 shows the instruction pipeline mapping for load and store instructions. In the case of store operations, no result is available in a pipestage because the value is being stored in external memory.

Trace of load and store instructions:

Instructions	ID	RF	X1	D1	D2	DWB
WLDR	X	X	X	X	X	X
WSTR	X	X	X			

Figure 4.11   Execution of Memory Operations in the Pipeline

By using your understanding of Figures 4.9, 4.10, and 4.11 to reschedule your instruction sequences, you can avoid data dependencies and resource conflicts. You can also use profiling tools such as the Intel VTune™ Performance Analyzer to help identify data and resource dependencies. These tools are discussed in detail in Chapter 7.

Issue and Result Latency

In this chapter, you have seen how the instruction characteristics can create stalls in processor execution because of the particular pipeline structures and organization of Intel XScale microarchitecture with Intel Wireless MMX technology. To formally describe these hazards, it is useful to relate the data in Figures 4.9, 4.10, and 4.11 back to the issue latency and result latency terminology discussed earlier.

The issue latency of each instruction is easy to extract from these tables. By default, the issue latency is one cycle, unless the instruction is a multiply pipeline instruction with an X' in the M1 column or is a multiply pipeline instruction with an X in both the X1 and M1 columns. In both of the latter two cases, the multiply pipeline issue latency becomes two cycles.

Result latency can be determined by counting how many columns to the left of X1 before an R is encountered, and then adding one. For example:

- WAND is 0 (R is in the X1 Column) + 1 = result latency 1

- WMAX is 1 (R is in the X2 Column) + 1 = result latency 2

- WSAD to non-multiply pipeline is 3 (X1,M1,M2) + 1 = result latency 4

For internal forwarding of the result in the multiply pipeline, the result latency is always one cycle.

Using these rules of thumb, you can easily determine whether a particular sequence of Intel Wireless MMX instructions will have data or resource dependencies.

Key Points

The key points you should take away from this chapter are:

- Intel XScale and Intel Wireless MMX technologies employ pipelining techniques to improve performance.

- Dependencies between instructions in a pipeline can cause the processor to stall while the dependency is resolved.

- Instructions operating in pipelines can be characterized by result and issue latencies.

- By understanding when a result is available, code sequences can be rearranged to avoid processor stalls and improve performance.

Part II
Enabling Applications with Intel® Wireless MMX™ Technology

Chapter 5

The Art of Optimization

It's clever, but is it ART?

—Rudyard Kipling

In an ideal microprocessor, one that can issue one machine instruction per clock cycle, the best performance that can be achieved is that, for every cycle, one useful instruction is completed. The processor's choice of instructions then leads to an efficient implementation of the task at hand. The two goals of optimization are: (1) to reduce the total number of cycles required to achieve a particular task by reducing the number of cycles wherein no useful work is done and (2) to make the most effective use of the cycles consumed.

In real-world microprocessors, many factors conspire to cause deviation from ideal performance. The art of optimization lies in figuring out how to work around a particular factor or how to mitigate its effect on performance.

Optimization Strategy

The overall strategy for optimization is straightforward and can be summarized by the following recipe:

1. Identify the hotspots.

2. Identify the cause of the performance bottleneck and assess the suitability of using SIMD techniques.

3. Select a suitable SIMD optimization and method of applying it.

4. Repeat steps 1–3 until the performance goal is reached.

This chapter introduces you to the concepts and the terminology associated with performance optimization, laying the foundation for the optimization techniques described in detail in the rest of Part 2.

Identifying the Hotspots

Identifying those places where the application spends most of its time is the first step in looking for performance bottlenecks. Many tools are available for profiling an application to determine which subfunctions are used the most. For Intel® Personal Internet Client Architecture (Intel® PCA) based devices, Intel VTune™ Performance Analyzer is the usual choice for application profiling; this tool is available for multiple operating systems. While you run the application on the target system, under the operating system, performance data is captured so that it can be analyzed to find the parts of the application that are consuming the most time. For detailed information about the mechanics of using the VTune analyzer, see Chapter 6.

The subfunctions that consume the most run-time of the application are selected first as optimization candidates. Typically, a function shows up in this group for one of two reasons:

■ The function is a computationally intense calculation.

■ The function contains some simpler computation, but it is repeated many times.

A profiling tool can determine the reason a particular subfunction is a hotspot. The repeated operation type is more easily optimized because the function itself is usually simpler.

Once a candidate function is selected, the suitability for SIMD acceleration is evaluated by using the *multiple*, *independent,* and *many* criteria described in Chapter 2.

If the function is suitable for SIMD acceleration, the next step is to ensure that the optimal solution using Intel Wireless MMX™ technology is selected.

■ Pipelined Microprocessors

All modern microprocessors employ pipelining techniques in one form or another. In Chapter 4, you saw that the Intel XScale® microarchitecture uses a seven-stage pipeline and it also has a side pipeline for the multiply and memory operations.

Chapter 4 also showed how Intel Wireless MMX technology uses a similar pipeline structure. Both the main core and the coprocessor use a technique called *data forwarding* to send recently calculated data directly to the next instruction as soon as it is available, rather than waiting until the value has been written back to the destination register. This hardware helps minimize the number of data hazards, but does not completely eliminate them.

■ Understanding the Impact of Stalls

Every cycle in which the processor is stalled is a cycle in which no useful work is being done. The object of optimization is to reduce or eliminate the number of wasted cycles in a given application. Stalls are the result of either of two conditions:

- ■ Instructions cannot be processed because they are not available or the resource to process them is not available.

- ■ Data is not yet available.

The Supply of Instructions

To keep the microprocessor busy, a ready supply of instructions to execute is required. Modern microprocessors are designed to keep frequently used instructions in fast memory close to the core. This memory usually contains a cache of recently accessed instructions. Slower and larger backing memory is supplied to store the less frequently used instructions. If the instruction is not in the fast cache memory, it must reside in the slower memory, quite often off-chip. The arrangement of the different types of storage is often called the *memory hierarchy*. The small faster caches are known as *level 1* memory.

If the required instruction is not found in the level 1 cache, the instruction has to be retrieved from the next level in memory. If this memory is off-chip, retrieving the data can take many clock cycles. For example, retrieval times in excess of 50 clocks are not uncommon.

During this time, the core has no instructions to process, so it stalls. The impact of cache-miss stalls can quite quickly have a dramatic effect on performance.

Effect of Missing the Cache

To demonstrate the effect of cache misses, consider the case of an ideal 400-megahertz core that can execute one instruction every cycle. If the instructions are always located within the cache, the number of clocks required per instruction (CPI) remains at one. The equation to calculate the time taken to execute 100 instructions is:

```
#Clocks for 100 Instructions (C100) =
          (#Instructions did not stall)*1 +
          (number of stalls)*(time for each stall)
```

This calculation can be generalized to a short form, as follows:

```
C100 = Icache hit rate*1 + Icache miss rate*stall time
```

Thus, if all instructions are found in the instruction cache every time—that is, a 100 percent hit rate—the time for 100 instructions is:

```
C100 = 100*1 + 0*50=100
CPI  = 100 Instructions/100 Clocks = 1
```

If in this example the next level memory, level 2, is external memory requiring 50 clocks cycles to access and two instruction cache misses occur every 100 instructions, the calculation of CPI becomes:

```
C100 = 98*1  + 2 * 50 = 198
CPI  = 198/100 =  1.98
```

This result shows that the time taken to complete the same 100 instructions has nearly doubled or, to put it another way, the performance has been halved. The hit rate of the instruction cache and the miss penalty thus play a very important role in performance. Figure 5.1 shows a graph of the effect of instruction cache hit rate on the performance of a system. Here the graph shows a processor with a 400-megahertz clock where the miss penalty is 50 clock cycles. The X-axis shows the impact of the instruction cache hit rate. The Y-axis shows the rate at which instructions are consumed, taking stalls into account. The instruction rate can be calculated from the equation:

```
Instruction rate = Clock Frequency/CPI
```

The graph in Figure 5.1 shows that the effective instruction rate, or observed performance, drops off dramatically as the hit rate decreases. With a 100 percent hit rate, instructions are consumed at one per cycle or at a rate of 400 megahertz in this case.

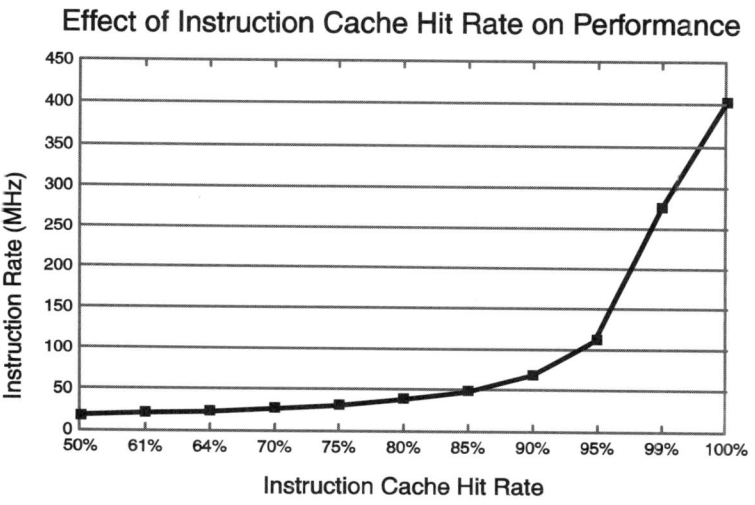

Effect of Instruction Cache Hit Rate on Performance

Figure 5.1   Effect of Instruction Cache Misses on Performance

With a hit rate of 90 percent, the effective instruction rate has dropped to approximately 70 megahertz or just 17.5 percent of the ideal performance.

The objective of optimization is to get as close to ideal as possible. Once again, the factors affecting the performance equation are:

```
C1C0 = Icache hit rate*1 + Icache Miss Rate*stall time
```

Clearly you can improve the performance in two ways:

■ Reduce the instruction cache miss rate.

■ Reduce the stall time.

Instruction Locality

Reducing the instruction cache miss rate relies upon getting good code reuse. Fortunately, many multimedia algorithms tend to have computationally intense inner loop calculations that are repeated many times on the multimedia data stream, as shown in Figure 5.2.

```
snippet() {

  unsigned char a1[64];
  unsigned char a2[64];
  unsigned char a3[64], a4[64];

  for (i=0; i<64; i++) {
    a3[i] = a1[i] + a2[i];
    a4[i] = a1[i] - a2[i];
  }
}
```

Figure 5.2   Instruction Locality

The first pass through the loop causes the loop body instructions to be loaded into the cache, and the remaining 63 loop iterations are likely to find the instructions required already in the level 1 cache.

Reducing the Stall Time

Reducing the stall time is usually a hardware implementation decision. Typically, such reductions are achieved by carefully designing the path to the next level of memory and ensuring the next level of memory is as economically fast as possible.

Resource Conflicts

Not being able to execute an instruction because the hardware resource is busy is known as a *resource conflict*. This event can lead to a processor stall and wasted cycles.

Some Intel Wireless MMX instructions occupy a particular pipeline stage for more than one cycle, which can lead to stalls if the following instruction needs to use the same resource. For example, the Intel Wireless MMX multiply accumulate instruction, WMAC, uses the first stage of the multiplier pipeline twice. The code sequence below shows two WMAC instructions back to back.

```
WMAC wR0, wR1, wR2
WMAC wR0, wR3, wR4
```

The second WMAC incurs a one-cycle stall because it cannot start until the first WMAC has finished its two cycles in the first stage of the multiplier pipeline. Usually, it is quite easy to schedule other instructions between resource-constrained instructions. In this case, a typical operation would be to load data—using WLDR—for the WMAC in a sequence such as:

```
WLDR
WMAC
WLDR
WMAC
```

This sequence would not stall because the WMAC instructions no longer have a resource hazard. Instruction resource hazards are discussed in more detail in Chapter 10.

Finding the Data

Not having the data needed to start a calculation is the other reason that cycles can be wasted in a microprocessor. Typically, the data is not available because it is:

- In memory.

- Being calculated by a previous instruction.

- In transit from the memory or previous instruction.

- Available in the registers.

These causes are ordered according to the impact on performance. Fetching data from memory has the greatest potential impact; using readily available data in the registers has the fewest wasted cycles.

Accessing Data Memory

Data memory is organized using a hierarchical scheme similar to the instruction memory. Again, fast level 1 cache is provided for frequently accessed data values. A similar performance equation can be constructed for the impact of data cache misses, and a similar graph of performance impact would result.

```
C100 = Dcache hit rate*1 + Dcache Miss Rate*stall time
```

The total performance impact of a cached subsystem is a function of both instruction and data cache hit rates.

To reduce the impact of data cache misses, data structures can be organized so that frequently accessed data is grouped together in the same area of memory. Data can also be preloaded into the fast caches by special instructions. Chapter 9 describes how other techniques such as loop unrolling and load pipelining can be employed to reduce stall times due to memory data availability. All these techniques should be considered when writing optimal code.

Internal Data Hazards

Internal data hazards occur when the data being calculated by a previous instruction is not yet available. If the processor cannot get the data to the right place by use of elaborate data forwarding schemes, it must stall until the data is available. The magnitude of the stalls for internal data hazards is much smaller than for external memory, but even a single cycle stall can impact performance. For example, if the inner loop is only four instructions and one stall is present, the task would take five clocks instead of four. To put it another way, the data hazard reduces performance by 25 percent.

Data hazards can usually be avoided by scheduling instructions carefully and finding other instructions to complete while waiting for data to become available. The result latency gives an indication of the result availability of each instruction and when each instruction can be safely used without incurring a stall. Understanding these relationships and how to schedule instructions to minimize internal data hazard stalls is described in detail in Chapter 10.

Identifying Algorithm Techniques

Some key architecture features of Intel Wireless MMX technology can be effectively utilized to improve code efficiency. A common issue in the optimizing of any code sequence is that a finite number of registers are available to store frequently used variables. Register file "pressure" occurs when the limited number of registers in a processor is not sufficient to conveniently implement an algorithm. In response, developers often reorganize the algorithm to execute using multiple code sequences or take a performance hit by saving intermediate values back to memory.

Intel Wireless MMX technology, with its 16 64-bit SIMD registers, and Intel Xscale microarchitecture, with its 15 32-bit registers, reduce the pressure on register storage and allow more variables to be stored in registers to create a corresponding improvement in performance. With a larger register file, a number of optimization techniques can be applied, trading off cycle consumption for memory bandwidth and code size. Some of the best techniques include:

- Software pipelining
- Multi-sample calculations
- Data and coefficient preloading
- Algorithm fusion

All of these techniques are illustrated in later chapters with real multimedia algorithm mapping examples in the areas of video compression, color image processing, and digital filtering.

Software Pipelining

Software pipelining, or loop unrolling, is the best-known optimization technique. It involves reducing the number of iterations for a loop by increasing the number of calculations done in each iteration. The advantage with Intel Wireless MMX technology is in reduced cycle consumption; however, additional performance enhancements may also be achieved. Load-to-use stalls may be more easily eliminated with scheduling, and multi-cycle instructions may be interleaved with other instructions. The disadvantages of applying the technique include an increase in code size for critical loops and restrictions on the minimum and multiple number of operands that are processed. Software pipelining is an important technique that forms one of the pillars of algorithm mapping with Intel Wireless MMX technology.

Multi-Sample Calculations

The multi-sample technique is one of the more popular optimization methods with Intel Wireless MMX technology. This technique—a form of software pipelining—may be applied to algorithms that can be described through nested loops. These types of algorithms appear quite often in multimedia applications.

The multi-sample approach involves loop unrolling at two levels. The first level maps to the parallel execution resources, and the second level calculates as many outputs as possible through maximum use of loaded data. In addition to cycle count improvements, an advantage is realized through reduced memory bandwidth. Amortization of the overhead cost is achieved for other aspects of the calculation, including both data formatting and loop management operations. The disadvantages of applying this technique include an increase in code size for critical loops and restrictions on the minimum and multiples of operands. Examples are discussed in following chapters that cover digital filtering, image filtering, and video motion estimation algorithms.

Register File Loading

The large register file enables an important optimization technique. When combined with the multi-sample approach, near-ideal throughput is possible for many important algorithms. Filter coefficients can be effectively cached for multiple applications in audio and voice processing. In video motion estimation, a source block can be preloaded and then compared to multiple candidate reference blocks. The organization of the register file is an important step in mapping an algorithm to Intel Wireless MMX technology.

Algorithm Fusion

In multimedia applications, sequences of algorithms are used. The output from one algorithm often becomes the input to the next. If two algorithms can be combined, a single more efficient routine can be developed in many cases. Identifying algorithms that can be merged can be a complicated task. However, the potential reduction in both cycle consumption and memory bandwidth reduction is appealing. When applied effectively, load amortization can be achieved with dramatic results.

Using the Right Approach

With the performance issue identified and the cause of the degradation understood, the next step is to choose the method of attacking the problem. Intel Wireless MMX technology provides a number of options to address the problem with varying degrees of difficulty and return. The four key approaches to optimizing the application are:

■ *Intel Integrated Performance Primitives (Intel IPP)*: This library of useful routines is pre-optimized for Intel Wireless MMX technology. A rich set of signal-processing and image-processing constructs is provided. If the hotspot identified is a library function, the routine can be swapped out for the Intel IPP routine.

This substitution of library routines is potentially the easiest approach to enabling an application with Intel Wireless MMX technology, and the recommended approach if the right functions are available in the library. The Intel IPP libraries are described in more detail in Chapter 7.

- *Vectorizing complier*: The vectorizing compiler can identify code segments in C code that exhibit data parallelism and automatically take advantage of the SIMD processing capability of Intel Wireless MMX technology. This optimization is described in more detail in Chapter 8.

- *C intrinsics*: This library of C-callable functions contains one-to-one representations of each variety of Intel Wireless MMX instruction. The programmer explicitly selects the instructions to use, and the compiler takes care of register allocation and detailed instruction scheduling. The C intrinsics are also described in more detail in Chapter 8.

- *Assembly code*: The use of assembly code gives the developer ultimate control over which instructions and registers to use, and which sequences to follow. Although this method is the most complex, it can indeed result in the most optimized code. It is worth noting that the Intel IPP libraries themselves use assembly coding in some of their inner loops.

The choice of optimization implementation is a trade-off between development time versus control of the code sequences and ultimate performance. The other factor that you must consider is how difficult maintenance of the code base becomes. Figure 5.3 shows the relative complexity of the various approaches, with the quicker, easy-to-maintain Intel IPP libraries on the left and the more time-consuming, difficult-to-maintain detailed assembly code on the right.

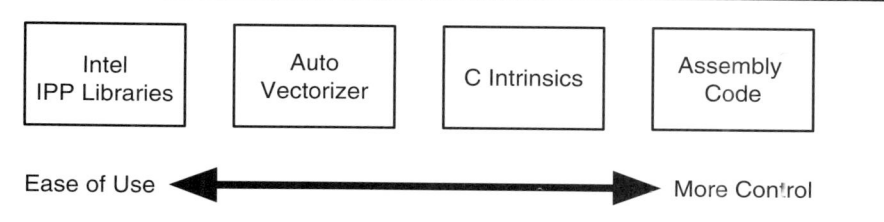

Figure 5.3   Selecting the Method to Write the Multimedia Code

In general, the choice of optimization approach should be evaluated from left to right to determine how much effort is required to accelerate a particular hotspot. The approach that yields the required performance with the minimum of effort should be selected.

Getting Started

This chapter has identified the fundamentals required to start optimizing an application with Intel Wireless MMX technology. The rest of Part 2 looks at each element of optimization in more detail to give you all the information you need to get started. Part 3 applies these techniques to some real-life multimedia problems.

Key Points

The key points from this chapter are:

- Memory performance has a big impact on overall performance.

- Restricted supply of instructions and unavailability of data are the two main causes of performance degradation.

- From the four approaches to optimizing a hotspot, select the approach that takes the minimum effort to reach the performance goals.

Chapter 6

Finding the Bottleneck

It is a capital mistake to theorize before you have all the evidence.

—Sir Arthur Conan Doyle

Determining which part of an application to optimize with Intel® Wireless MMX™ instructions can be the single most important decision for successful deployment of Intel Wireless MMX technology. Chapter 2 introduced the *multiple*, *independent*, and *many* characteristics required to successfully deploy SIMD techniques. These characteristics identify the type of code that can be optimized with Intel Wireless MMX technology but do not indicate which code gives the maximum return on optimization investment. To get the most improvement, you should find the portions of the application that consume the most time and start optimizing these portions in order of their time consumption. To do this, you profile the application while it is running and find out where it spends most of its time.

Figure 6.1 shows a sample profile for an MPEG-4 video decoder application. It is obvious from this figure that the motion compensation routines occupy the biggest proportion of the execution time—40 percent of the application.

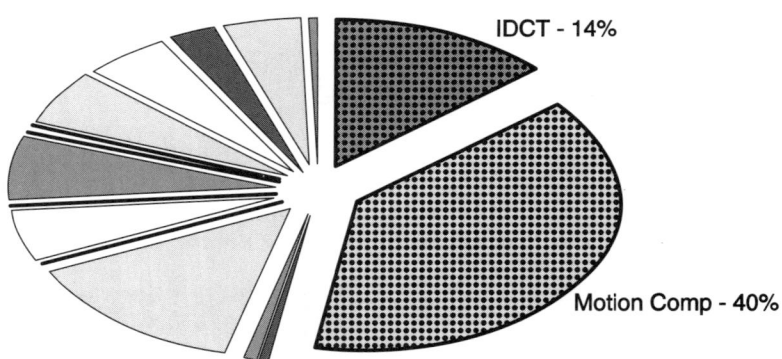

Figure 6.1   Example MPEG-4 Decoder Profile

If the performance of the motion compensation routine is doubled using SIMD techniques, the routine executes in half the time, and the overall impact is 20 percent—40 percent divided by 2—on the application. In contrast, the IDCT function in Figure 6.1 only occupies 14 percent; so, even if this function is optimized to the same extent as motion compensation, the overall impact at the application level is only seven percent—14 percent divided by 2.

The message is clear: start with the function that has the biggest impact on overall application performance—in this case, motion compensation—then work down the list of candidate functions for optimization in decreasing complexity. For each optimization candidate, evaluate the suitability for SIMD processing using the multiple, independent, and many criteria; perform the optimization; and then move on to the subroutine with the next biggest impact—in this case, IDCT. This sequence is repeated until the point of diminishing returns is reached, which means that the remaining candidate routines do not have much impact on overall performance.

You must weigh the amount of time spent optimizing routines against your goal of getting the best performance. By choosing to optimize the most critical routines first, you get the biggest return on effort expended.

Intel® VTune™ Performance Analyzer

Ideally, when you run a program, you know everything that is happening as it runs. You could do this hypothetically by watching a system and continuously noting everything that occurs. Unfortunately, such an approach would intrude on the performance of the very system you want to examine. At a minimum, this approach would create unacceptable delays, and most likely, it would distort system performance so much that the information would be useless.

The Intel VTune™ Performance Analyzer is a tool that profiles a system to determine where the system is spending its time. The VTune analyzer solves the problem of distorting the system under test by interrupting normal system execution only occasionally to take a sample. This kind of interruption is so slight that it is almost always non-intrusive. Such a method is sometimes called *statistical sampling*.

The VTune analyzer implements sampling in a way that requires no source code modification and no instrumentation of the compiled code. This approach allows system-wide sampling regardless of what application or part of the system code may be of interest and can even examine code running in an operating system such as a device driver.

Users of tools such as `prof` and `gprog` know that time-based sampling of just one application leaves a great deal unknown about system performance, especially since the key bottleneck in a system may not even occur in the application you are examining. By taking a system-wide perspective, sampling with the VTune analyzer avoids the pitfalls associated with more limited solutions that only give you part of the picture.

To recap, sampling with the VTune analyzer has these advantages:

- It requires no code modifications.

- It requires no instrumentation.

- Low overhead means minimal intrusion.

- Sampling is system-wide.

- You can even sample drivers in the operating system.

What Are We Looking For?

The VTune Performance Analyzer is used to identify the part of the program where *something* happens more often than it happens elsewhere. These areas of the program are often known as *hotspots*. If that something is time, then a hotspot is a place where your program spends more time than other parts of your code.

The VTune analyzer adds interest by allowing the hotspot to be some event other than time. Examples include cache-misses and pipeline stalls. Although you might not expect your program to do any of these things, the ability to highlight unexpected or undesirable activities is a big part of what locating hotspots is all about.

In addition to sampling an application or *module of interest*, the VTune analyzer tracks and records processor time spent on modules running as part of your operating system. In fact, while sampling, the VTune analyzer monitors all the software executing on your system—including your application and the operating system. As mentioned earlier, since the VTune analyzer conducts sampling non-intrusively and does not modify any binary files, it has next to no impact on your application's performance.

After the sampling program of the VTune analyzer examines all the code associated with the collected samples, the program summarizes the hotspots or bottlenecks in the Hotspot View shown in Figure 6.2. Whereas hotspots are locations of significant activity, *bottlenecks* are areas of significant performance constraint. Finding software hotspots is one way the analyzer can help you identify bottlenecks.

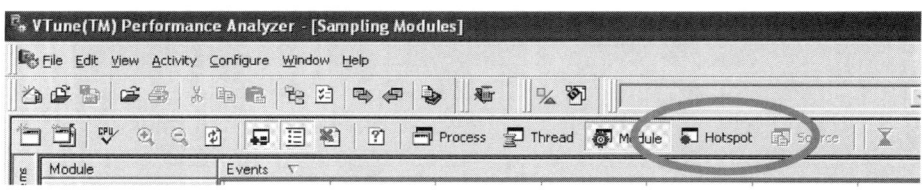

Figure 6.2   Hotspot View Icon on the Toolbar of the VTune™ Performance Analyzer

Once you find a hotspot, the VTune Performance Analyzer makes it easy to move from Hotspot View to the source or assembly code. This is called *drill down* in the analyzer documentation. Once you view the source causing the hotspots, you can determine how to modify your code to remove the bottlenecks and improve the performance of your application.

Before You Begin Sampling

Before you begin sampling, be aware that the VTune Performance Analyzer requires *line number information* and *symbol information,* also referred to as *debug information,* in order to display the function names in sampling, call graph, and static module analysis views. It also uses this information to display the source view.

Depending on how you configure settings, your compiler generates line number and symbol information either in a separate file or as part of the binary file.

The VTune analyzer recognizes many types of line information and symbol files and tries to obtain this information as follows:

- It searches for symbol information in the binary it launches, such as an .exe, .obj, .ocx, .dll, or .VxD file.

- If it doesn't find the symbol information, the VTune analyzer prompts you to specify a file that contains the symbols, such as a file in .pdb, .dbg, or .sym format.

- If you can't supply a symbol file, the VTune analyzer resorts to showing you virtual addresses in hexadecimal and assembly code instead of your source code. This use of assembly code makes it much harder to decipher what is happening, so it is not the recommended way to use the VTune analyzer.

Don't worry about overhead concerns in your target code. Generating line number and symbol information properly during compilation does not modify any existing optimizations in your application, and the generated code remains unchanged.

Sampling

Sampling comes in two flavors: *time-based* and *event-based.* Both types collect samples of active instruction addresses.

- Time-based sampling (TBS) collects the samples at regular time-based intervals—1 millisecond by default.

- Event-based sampling (EBS) collects the samples after a certain number of processor events.

In either case, the sampling results from the VTune analyzer show you where your program is doing *something*. When the *something* happens more in one place than another, you have located a hotspot. In the case of time-based sampling, the *something* being counted is *time spent*. You can think of time-based sampling as simply a special form of event-based sampling, where the event just happens to be the tick of a clock. However, two reasons for making the distinction are:

■ Many programmers are familiar with time-based sampling because of tools like `prof` and `gprof`.

■ Time-based sampling is most often implemented without using an event register in the processor—since time-based interrupts are available separately on many processors. Thus, you may be able to use time-based sampling with processors that are not specifically supported by your copy of the VTune Performance Analyzer.

Sample Interval

The *sample after* interval is a programmable value indicating how many events or clock ticks have to occur before the performance analyzer takes another sample. Each item being monitored has its own sample interval.

For time-based sampling, the sampling interval represents the amount of time the VTune analyzer waits before collecting each sample. The sampling interval is the frequency of data collection.

For event-based sampling, the sampling interval is used to calculate the target number of samples and the sample-after value. To calculate the average number of samples collected per second per event, use the formula:

```
Duration(sec) * 1000ms/1sec * 1/(Sampling interval(ms)/sample)
```

For example, if Duration = 10 seconds and Sampling interval = 1 millisecond, the number of samples collected per second is calculated as follows:

```
10(sec) * 1000ms/1(sec) * 1 sample/1ms = 10000 samples
```

The number of samples collected per second is multiplied by duration in seconds to get the target number of samples to be collected for an event in an activity run.

When the sample-after value is too small, the sampling interrupts occur too frequently. In this case, the processor spends a lot of time in the analyzer's sampling interrupt handler instead of doing what it is supposed to do. Once you get to extremely small sample-after values, you could run into different problems even if you can keep the analyzer running. The recommendation and the target of event calibration is 1,000 samples per second per processor.

For example, running at a clock speed of 1 gigahertz, a sample-after value of 2,000 for clock ticks means that the result would be 500,000 samples per second, a number that is considered too large and would mean only 2,000 CPU clocks between samples. If the analyzer sampling interrupt consumes 1,000 clocks, for example, the CPU is spending 50 percent of its time responding to analyzer interrupts and not responding to OS interrupts, disk I/O, and so forth.

In fact, the analyzer calculates the default sample-after value for clock ticks to produce 1,000 samples per second. You should not change that value unless you have some compelling reason to do so

The Plan of Attack

Before you start any optimization work, you must establish a metric to measure performance so that you know when you have done enough optimization and can stop. This metric can be an application level quantity such as frame rate in a video decoder application or graphical game, or the metric can be more abstract like elapsed time or processor utilization during the applications. Using the same video decoder example, performance could be measured as frames processed per second, elapsed time to complete N frames of a movie, the percent of time the processor is used to perform the required task, or the average time in clocks that each instruction takes to complete.

The main consideration of using the metric is that it can quantify changes in performance and that it is an easy and convenient thing to measure. Measuring performance should not take longer than optimizing the code!

With the termination condition defined, Figure 6.3 shows the steps to follow to profile and optimize the application.

The first step in optimization is to perform a time profile using the time-sampling approach of the VTune analyzer. This step identifies the hotspots of the application for a more focused investigation. Event analysis using the VTune analyzer can help establish the likely cause of each candidate hotspot. Using the event counter information in conjunction with the MIM SIMD suitability test discussed in Chapter 2, it is possible to determine whether the candidate routine should be optimized with Intel Wireless MMX technology or by using standard optimization techniques, both of which are described in later chapters.

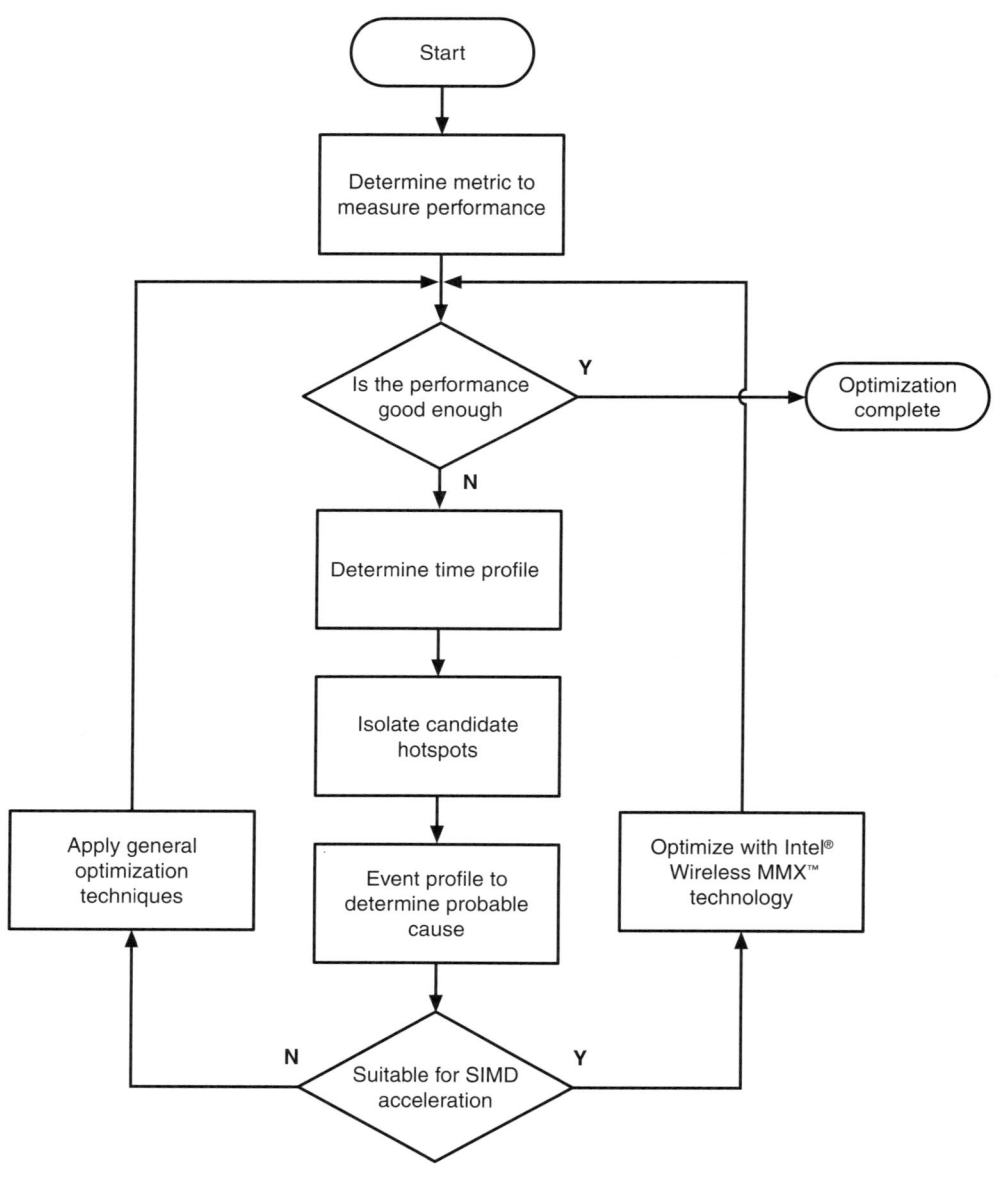

Figure 6.3   The Plan of Attack

Determining the Time Profile

The time profile is created by using the processor interrupt mechanism to temporarily suspend an application to determine the value of the program counter, and hence the function, in the application that is currently executing. Each time the application is suspended, a copy of the program counters is logged. Each interruption of the process is a sample of what the application is currently doing. By capturing enough samples, it is possible to build a profile of application activity over time.

The period of time between the successive interrupts, called *sample interval*, is usually controlled by a system timer set to approximately 1 millisecond. The cost of performing the sample is small compared to the executing application, so this procedure has very little impact on the application under investigation. Reducing the sample interval could improve sample accuracy, but improved accuracy comes at the cost of interfering with the execution of the application as more time is spent in sampling and less in running the actual application.

The VTune analyzer collects all the program samples in a buffer until the buffer is full, after which the application program is suspended so that the sample data can be uploaded to the host application of the VTune analyzer for analysis. The buffer usually is specified to be large enough to collect samples for many elapsed seconds of program execution. The large buffer also minimizes the impact to the application under analysis.

The host application of the VTune analyzer uses the collected time-based program counter samples in conjunction with the application line number and symbol information to build a histogram of where in the application, on average, the time is being spent.

Figure 6.4 shows a sample time profile produced by the VTune analyzer. The basic time-based view is known as the Hotspot View. In this example, it is clear that the bottom function consumes most of the time and would therefore be the first candidate for further investigation.

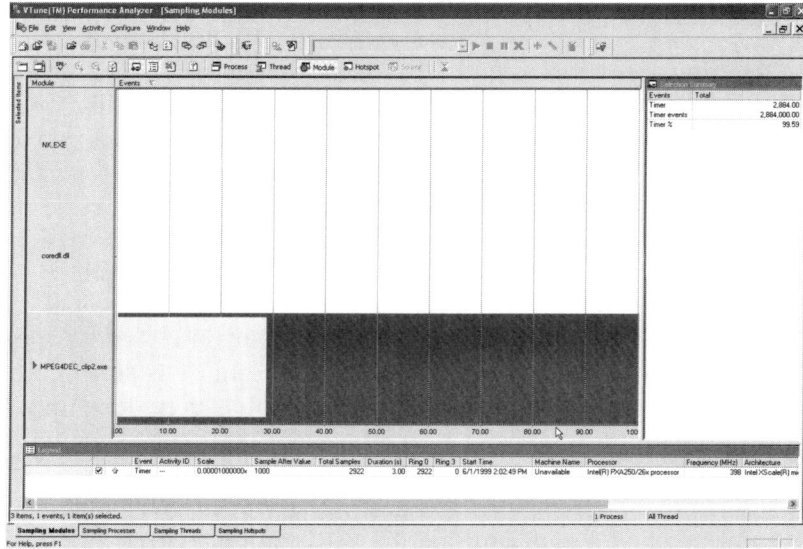

Figure 6.4   Time Profile of a Simple Application

The VTune analyzer allows the time-based samples to be displayed in four formats:

■ Process-based

■ Module-based

■ Thread-based—a breakdown of which threads are most active

■ Virtual Address—a breakdown of which address regions are most active

Figure 6.5 shows an example of a process-based profile, and Figure 6.6 shows the same application viewed as a virtual address profile. It is clear from Figure 6.5 which process is dominant and should be investigated further. In Figure 6.6, it is not clear what is happening because you lack the symbol information to help you. This example reinforces the statement that using the VTune analyzer without debug information in the application under test, although feasible, is much harder and should be avoided.

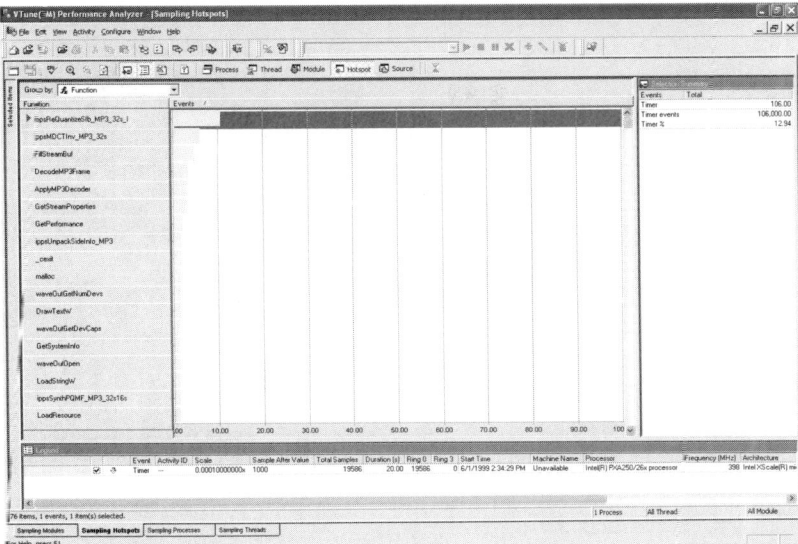

Figure 6.5   Process-Based Analysis

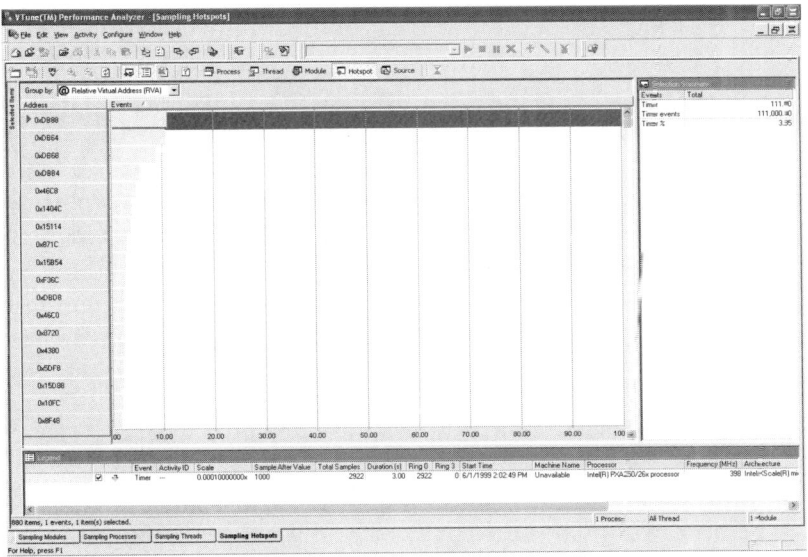

Figure 6.6   Relative Virtual Address-Based Analysis

Using Events to Analyze Hotspots

The Intel XScale microarchitecture provides a performance monitoring unit (PMU) for counting important events that happen in the system. These event counters used in conjunction with the VTune analyzer can help you understand why a particular function is taking so long to execute. Figure 6.7 shows an overview of the PMU and how it collects and counts events from around the Intel XScale core and coprocessor functional units.

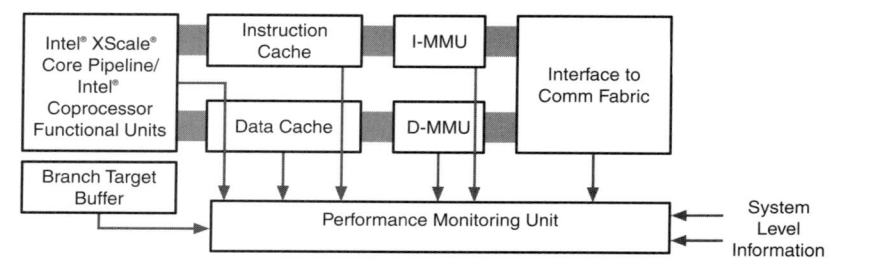

Figure 6.7   Performance Monitoring Unit (PMU)

The PMU can count four different event types concurrently out of all the possible events. The events of interest are selected by the user. The counters in the PMU are set up by the VTune analyzer before application launch and run continuously in the background while the application is running. If a counter overflows, the application is briefly suspended, a sample is taken, and the corresponding counter is reset to the sample interval. Each counter is 32 bits wide, so the time between counter overflows is relatively long.

The next step is to understand what events you can count and then what to do with the information you have to optimize the application.

What Are the Important Events?

Fifteen events can help you with event-based analysis. Table 6.1 provides an overview of the events with the event number and the intended use of the information for optimization. The event number is used by each of the four event counters to determine what sort of event will be counted.

Table 6.1   Event Counters

Event #	Event Definition	Usage for Optimization
0x0	Instruction cache miss	Instruction traffic and CPI estimation and cache locality
0x1	Instruction cache cannot deliver instruction	
0x2	Data dependency stall	Amount of time waiting for core data
0x3	Instruction TLB miss	Page locality
0x4	Data TLB miss	
0x5	Branch instructions executed	CPI determination
0x6	Branch mis-predicted	CPI determination
0x7	Instruction executed	CPI determination
0x8	Stall cycles due to D-cache buffer full	Data traffic, data access congestion, congestion rate, and congestion lengths
0x9	Count of stall events due to D-cache buffer full	
0xA	Data cache access	Data access rate
0xB	Data cache-miss	Data traffic and CPI estimation
0xC	Data cache write-back	Data traffic
0xD	Software changed the PC	Number of function calls
0x17	Intel Wireless MMX data dependency stall	Amount of time waiting for coprocessor data

All core PMU events, from 0x0 to 0xD, include all events generated by Intel Wireless MMX technology except for event 0x2—data dependency stall—which is Intel XScale core only. The following sections provide a brief overview of each counter.

Event 0x0: Instruction Cache Miss

This event count is incremented when the required instruction is not in the L1 instruction cache or not in the buffers. A hit in the fetch buffer is considered a hit.

Event 0x1: Instruction Cannot Be Delivered

This event count is incremented when the instruction cache cannot deliver an instruction, which could be due to an instruction cache miss.

Event 0x2: Intel XScale Core Data Dependency

This event count increments whenever the result of a previous instruction in the Intel XScale pipeline creates a dependency. It does not include the stalls specific to Intel Wireless MMX, which are counted separately in event count 0x17 discussed later.

Event 0x3: Instruction TLB Miss

Translation look-aside buffers (TLBs) are used to accelerate page table lookups used in virtual memory systems. The event counts misses to the instruction TLB (ITLB) due to instruction fetches.

Event 0x4: Data TLB Miss

This event counts misses to the data TLB caused by load, store, and swap instructions.

Event 0x5: Branches Executed

This event counts explicit branch operations executed. In particular, B and BL—taken/not-taken and predicted/mis-predicted—are counted in Arm and Thumb modes.

Event 0x6: Branch Mis-predicted

This event counts every B and BL mis-prediction. It does not include mis-predictions for branch operations, which are not counted in event 0x5— BX, BLX, MOV, LDR, and LDM.

Event 0x7: Instructions Executed

This event counts the number of instructions retired. Multiple cycle instructions are counted as one.

Event 0x8: Data Cache Buffer Stall Cycles

This event counts the *duration of* the stall because the data cache buffers are full. This event occurs every cycle in which the condition is present. The event only counts buffer full conditions.

Event 0x9: Data Cache Buffer Stall Count

This event counts the *number of* stalls because the data cache buffers are full. This event occurs once for each contiguous sequence of this type of stall. Only counts buffer full conditions.

Event 0xA: Data Cache Accesses

This event counts accesses to the data cache including load, store, and preload operations (PLD).

Event 0xB: Data Cache Misses

This event counts the number of time the request data was not in the data cache. If an access misses the data array but a previous access to the same cache line has already generated a fetch for the cache line, it is still considered a miss. A hit in the fill buffer still counts as a miss.

Event 0xC: Data Cache Write Back

This event counts the number of data cache write-back operations. This event occurs once for each half line, or four words, written back from the cache.

Event 0xD: Software Changed the Program Counter

This event occurs any time the program counter (PC) is changed by software. All of the following instructions cause the PC to change and are counted:

```
B
BL
BLX
MOV[S] PC, Rm
LDM Rn, {Rx, PC}
LDR PC, [Rm]
```

Event 0x17: Intel Wireless MMX Data Dependency

This count includes all dependency stalls caused by the coprocessor. It includes the data hazards and resource hazards discussed in Chapter 5.

Event View

Figure 6.8 shows an example display from the Intel VTune Performance Analyzer for an event-based analysis. In this case, the data cache access and data cache miss events are analyzed as well as the time profile. In this example, you have 1,776 data cache miss events, each with a sample interval of 1,570, which gives a total data cache miss event count of 1,776 * 1,570 = 2,788,320.

The data cache miss event total (DCache miss events) is shown in the box in the upper-right of Figure 6.8.

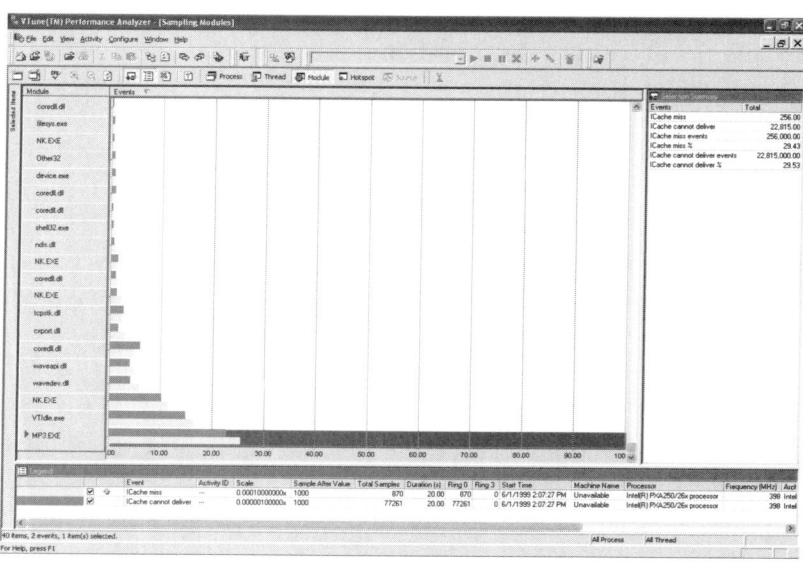

Figure 6.8　Event Display from Intel® VTune™ Performance Analyzer

While analyzing events, you must ensure that you are in fact measuring the application you intended. The VTune analyzer can examine all activity in the system, including the OS and other applications, so you should ensure that you locate the particular function you are interested in. For example, GenSample in Figure 6.8 would be the function of interest to analyze further. Alternatively, make sure that the application under analysis is the dominant application in the system—that is, close all other applications and reduce system activity.

Deriving Performance Metrics

PMU events can be used to determine the state of the system and the characteristics of the application running in the system. Some key general metrics are used to characterize a system:

- Clocks per instruction
- Data cache miss rate
- Instruction cache miss rate
- Number of data stalls

These metrics can be calculated from the event counter data, and they can be used as a method of determining optimization progress and direction. It is also possible to determine many other metrics by combining the different event counts shown in Table 6.1. These calculations are beyond the scope of this book, but you might find them useful for developing new metrics depending on the application.

Clocks per Instruction

Clocks per instruction (CPI) represents the number of clock ticks it takes, on average, to execute each instruction. This metric indicates overall efficiency of the processor. Sometimes, instructions per clock (IPC) is quoted as a metric; IPC is simply the reciprocal of CPI. To calculate CPI using the event counters, the total number of clock cycles is measured using the timer. The number of instructions executed is monitored by using event counter 0x7. CPI is calculated as follows:

```
CPI = (Timer Counter)/(Event 0x7 Counter)
```

Conversely, IPC is calculated as follows:

```
IPC = (Event 0x7 Counter)/(Timer Counter)
```

The target of optimization is to get the CPI as low as possible.

Data Cache Miss Rate

Data cache miss rate gives a measure of how effective the caches are at keeping data in the fast local memories of the core. Data cache miss rate is usually quoted as a percentage of all data accesses that are not found in the cache. The data cache miss rate is calculated by counting the number of data accesses, event 0xA, and counting the number of data cache misses, event 0xB. The miss rate is:

```
D Cache Miss rate % = [(event 0xB)/(event 0xA)] * 100
```

Similarly, the hit rate is:

```
D Cache Hit rate % = [1 - (event 0xB)/(event 0xA)] * 100
```

Chapter 5 describes how cache hit rate has a big impact on performance. The target of optimization is to reduce the data cache miss rate as close to zero as possible. A high data cache miss rate is an indication that there may be a memory bottleneck. Using the memory optimization techniques such as preload and load pipelining described in Chapter 9 can often reduce the miss rate and improve performance.

Instruction Cache Miss Rate

Instruction cache miss rate is calculated in a similar way to the data cache miss rate. Instruction cache miss rate is a ratio of the instruction cache misses (event 0x0) and the number of instructions executed (event 0x7):

```
I Cache Miss rate % = [(event 0x0)/(event 0x7)] * 100
```

Similarly, the hit rate is calculated as:

```
I Cache Hit rate % =  [1 - (event 0x0)/(event 0x7)] * 100
```

Data Stall

The time spent stalled waiting for data is a critical measure of wasted cycles. To calculate this metric, the data dependency stall for the Intel XScale core (event 0x2) is added to the Intel Wireless MMX data dependency stall (event 0x17):

```
Data Stall Cycles = (event 0x2) + (event 0x17)
```

The data stall time includes both the time stall due to internal dependencies, such as the resource hazards described in Chapter 5, and external dependencies such as memory accesses. In most systems, the stalls due to external memories are the dominant factor, so it is also useful to measure the average stall time per data cache miss by the approximation:

```
Stall per D Miss = (Data Stall Cycles)/(# D Cache Misses)

                 = (Data Stall Cycles)/(event 0xB)
```

The target of optimization in this case is to reduce the data stall time per data cache miss. Again, the memory optimization techniques such as preload and load pipelining described in Chapter 9 can help improve this. A high data cache miss rate in conjunction with a high data stall count is a strong indication of an external memory bottleneck.

After improving the memory component of the data stall by using data memory optimization techniques, it is useful to use the static code analysis tool of the VTune analyzer to help schedule the instructions to avoid any internal data or resource hazards.

Static Analysis

The static analysis tool of the VTune analyzer operates on basic blocks of code in-between branch statements. It can analyze a contiguous sequence of instructions with one entry and one exit bounded by a branch or branch target. The VTune analyzer can determine whether a particular sequence of instructions has any resource or data hazards by using the issue and result latency information described in Chapter 4.

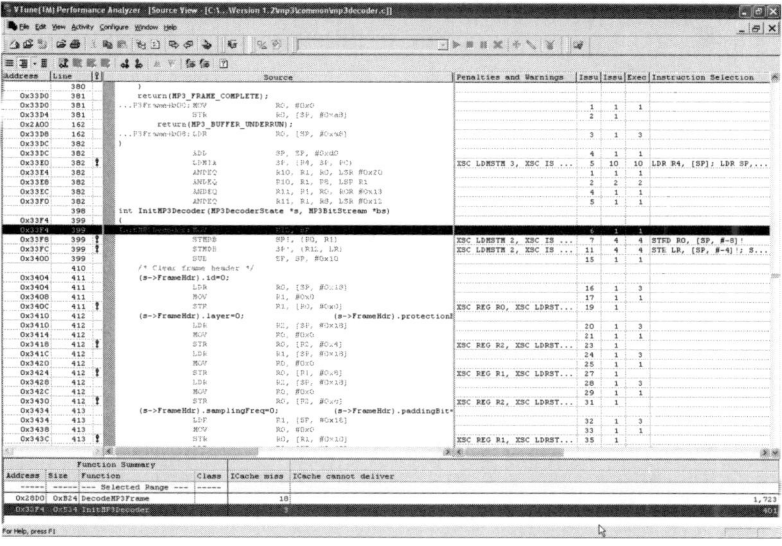

Figure 6.9   Static Analysis—Looking for Internal Stalls

In addition to identifying performance hazards, the VTune static analyzer also provides a brief explanation of the cause of each stall so that you can attempt to reschedule the instructions to remove the wasted cycles. Figure 6.9 shows an example of the VTune static analyzer tool in action.

More About VTune Performance Analyzer

More information about the VTune Performance Analyzer can be found on the Web site for the VTune analyzer. Additional information on the VTune analyzer specific to Intel Wireless MMX technology is available on the Web site for Intel PCA. The URLs for both of these Web sites are listed in "References."

Using the VTune™ Performance Analyzer (Reinders, 2004) is a comprehensive book from Intel Press about the VTune analyzer.

Key Points

The following key points have been covered in this chapter:

■ To find bottlenecks, profile the application and find out which functions consume the most execution time. These functions are the prime targets for acceleration.

■ VTune Performance Analyzer provides a user-friendly mechanism for determining hotspots in an application.

■ The Intel XScale microarchitecture provides hardware to assist counting important system events to help optimization.

■ VTune Performance Analyzer can profile an application by analyzing how much time is spent in each part of the application or by analyzing the characteristics of each part using event counters.

■ VTune Performance Analyzer provides static analysis of Intel Wireless MMX instruction sequences to detect internal data dependencies and resource hazards. This analysis can be used to reschedule code sequences to improve performance.

Chapter 7

Intel® Integrated Performance Primitives

A library is a thought in cold storage.

—Lord Samuel

Constructing software out of existing optimized building blocks is the fastest and easiest way to accelerate the execution speed of an application with Intel® Wireless MMX™ technology. Intel provides a library of useful functions called the Intel Integrated Performance Primitives, or Intel IPP for short. The library includes about 2,500 elements, ranging from basic building blocks such as filters to more advanced examples such as audio and video codecs.

The recommended practice for enabling an application with Intel Wireless MMX technology is to use the Intel IPP library wherever possible, because doing so saves time and resources while still achieving the benefits of acceleration with Intel Wireless MMX technology. In this chapter, you will learn about the features and advantages of using the Intel IPP library.

What Are the Intel Integrated Performance Primitives (Intel IPP)?

Intel IPP provides a set of library functions for accelerating code development. This library covers a range of functionality that includes a broad class of computational tasks and almost every media type. Almost any time-consuming function, particularly those that operate on arrays of data

121

at a time, is a reasonable candidate for Intel IPP. The functionality provide by Intel IPP can be divided into six key areas:

- Digital signal processing
- Speech codecs
- Audio codecs
- Image processing
- Video and image coding
- Graphics

Integrating all this functionality in one library has an obvious advantage; moving from domain to domain within one library takes less development time than adopting a new set of conventions for each of several separate libraries. To gain the most benefit, you should understand the major Intel IPP domains and the typical functions that you find in each domain.

Digital Signal Processing Functions

Intel IPP supports a broad range of digital signal processing functions that are commonly found in many multimedia algorithms. These routines are the nuts and bolts used to build more complex algorithms. Figure 7.1 shows some of the common functions that are used.

Transforms	FFT, IFFT, DCT, IDCT, MDCT, IMDCT
Filters	FIR, IIR, IIR Biquad FIR LMS Adaptive
Windowing	Kaiser, Bartlett Hamming, Hann
Signal Generation	Sinusoidal, Square, Triangular Uniform Random, Gaussian Random
Vector Statistics	Min, Max, Mean, Std_Dev AutoCorr, CrossCorr, Norms
Vector Manipulation	Add, Sub, Mul, Abs, Sqr, Sqrt, Ln Log10, Exp, Dotprod, Set, Zero, Copy

Figure 7.1   Intel® IPP DSP Building Blocks

Speech Codecs

Speech compression is commonly used on handheld and wireless platforms to reduce the amount of network bandwidth used to transmit a voice conversation. Intel IPP includes optimized speech codec examples for the ITU G.723.1 and GSM-AMR (3GPP 3G TS26.090, v3.1.0) standard encoders and decoders.

Audio Codecs

Audio data is usually coded to reduce its size. Raw digital audio is too large for the storage and bandwidth available in handheld devices. For example, compact disc audio has 16 bits per sample in stereo at 44,100 samples per second, which is over 10 megabytes of data per minute. In portable audio, the trend is to put more audio on smaller devices, so compression is essential—particularly when compressed audio is reasonably about one tenth the size of uncompressed audio. In networked and wireless audio, you must make efficient use of the available bandwidth, so your application must target a reduced amount of bandwidth per stream. Thus, both trends lead to the same conclusion: audio compression is crucial.

Intel IPP supports audio coding in general, but has a particular focus on two popular open codec formats: MP3 and AAC. MP3 is the most advanced audio format derived from MPEG-1 and AAC is the Advanced Audio Codec from MPEG-2. MPEG-4 AAC is supported to the extent that it is an expansion of MPEG-2.

Other formats that are not directly supported today can still use the horizontal Intel IPP functions where applicable to accelerate code development.

Image Processing

The Intel IPP imaging function set covers the types of operations that are found in such imaging tools and applications as image and video editing, image and video compression, human-computer interface, and image analysis. The main functions are those that filter images and those that transform them geometrically.

Intel IPP includes an extensive set of functions that perform vector and matrix arithmetic to support calculations for three-dimensional geometry of the sort required by computer graphics and physical modeling. These operations are particularly geared toward operation on small vectors and small square matrices, orders 3–6.

Image and Video Compression

Intel IPP support of image and video compression takes several forms. Intel IPP provides portions of codecs and includes samples that are partial codecs for several compression algorithms. In particular, Intel IPP includes the following:

- General functions, such as transforms and arithmetic operations, applicable across one or more compression algorithms.

- Specific functions, such as Huffman coding for JPEG, that you can think of as *codec slices*. At present, such functions exist for MPEG-1, MPEG-2, MPEG-4, DV, H.263, and H.264.

- Sample encoders and decoders of several major video and imaging standards, including JPEG, JPEG-2000, MPEG-2, and MPEG-4.

Graphics

The graphics routines of Intel IPP are collectively referred to as the Intel Graphics Performance Primitives, or Intel GPP for short. The Intel GPP functions accelerate the commonly used operations in 2D and 3D graphics, providing the essential building blocks to construct a graphics engine. The routines include data type conversion, arithmetic calculations, matrix operations, trigonometric functions and rasterization support.

Horizontal and Vertical Functions

The terms horizontal and vertical indicate whether the designated Intel IPP elements are basic building block elements or more complete algorithms. Figure 7.2 breaks these two categories down by showing example functions. The term *horizontal* refers to Intel IPP elements that are a low-level building block and the term *vertical* refers to an application-specific API.

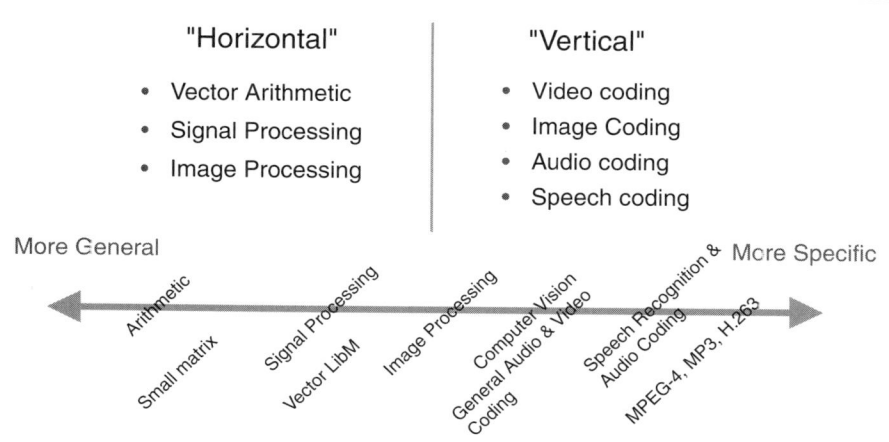

Figure 7.2   Types of Intel® IPP Functions

For a horizontal Intel IPP element, the emphasis is on primitives that can be used in many domains. The horizontal Intel IPP functions were designed to be small, low-level, low-overhead functions. One advantage of this approach is that little branching occurs within each function. The small functions in Intel IPP tend to support one data type and one flavor of the function. As a result, these functions incur no overhead in switching between versions supporting multiple data types.

Another advantage of these smaller functions is their smaller memory and disk footprint. Usually, an application only needs one or two versions of a function, and the fine-grained approach allows that application to link in exactly the needed functions.

Using the low-level horizontal API has one difficulty: it might not be as powerful or full-featured as a high-level API. In particular, some common components, such as video compression, are difficult to implement even when a primitive layer is provided. For this reason, the library also provides the vertical Intel IPP functions, which are example implementations of image, video, audio, and speech compression and decompression. These sample codecs are provided in source code, so that you can enhance and expand them to suit your needs. The vertical Intel IPP functions are in turn made out of the lower level horizontal Intel IPP functions. Figure 7.3 illustrates how the sample vertical functions are constructed out of the primitive horizontal functions.

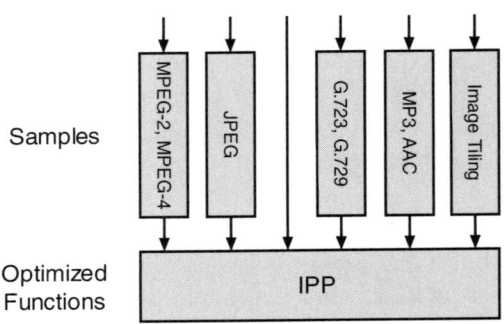

Figure 7.3   Primitives and samples

Where Does Intel IPP Fit with the OS?

The Intel IPP source code is a mixture of C code with Intel Wireless MMX technology and assembly code for the Intel XScale® microarchitecture for critical functions. The source code is completely operating system (OS) independent, with one Intel IPP source generating multiple OS target binaries. The primitives do not use any OS services such as memory allocation, the use of semaphores, or message passing. However, the binary format from one OS to the next does change to support the different linker format and tool chains available in each operating system. The Intel IPP libraries are available only as precompiled libraries for each operating system. The currently supported operating systems and tool chains are:

- Windows† CE—Pocket PC and Smartphone
    - Microsoft eMbedded Visual C++ 4.0
    - Microsoft Windows CE Platform Builder
- Symbian OS†
    - gcc derived tool chain
- Palm OS
    - ARM† ADS
- Linux (ELF-32)
    - arm-linux-gcc tool chain
    - xscale-elf gcc tool chain

While the Intel IPP library contains no OS-specific routines, nothing prevents an OS itself from using Intel IPP to accelerate a particular service or driver. Figure 7.4 shows how an Intel IPP function is used to accelerate an audio driver in the OS. It also shows that Intel IPP functions themselves can be integrated into third-party libraries as well as directly into application code.

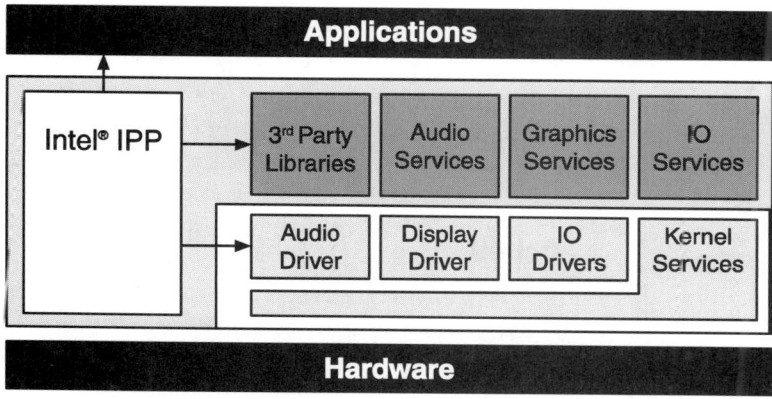

Figure 7.4   Where Intel® IPP Fits in the System Software

Why Use Intel IPP?

The key reason for using the Intel IPP library is that you can optimize your applications quickly to take advantage of Intel Wireless MMX technology without worrying about the details of assembly level programming. The library supports a rich set of building blocks commonly used in many multimedia applications, and it provides a high-level abstraction away from both hardware architecture issues and detailed algorithm internals.

Development Time

The Intel Integrated Performance Primitives may provide the fastest route to optimizing an application with Intel Wireless MMX technology. The hard work of optimizing the computational hotspots has already been taken care of and the developer needs only to select the required function from the existing library. Not having to write assembly code reduces development time and reduces the burden of ongoing code maintenance. An added benefit is the reduction of development time needed for porting applications to new hardware platforms because the application is simply recompiled with the latest platform-optimized Intel IPP library files. The API interfaces remain the same from one processor generation to the next. Therefore, Intel IPP may offer the shortest time to market to enable applications with Intel Wireless MMX technology.

Code Quality

The Intel IPP libraries are developed by a group of algorithm experts at Intel who work closely with the microprocessor architects to make sure that the libraries extract maximum performance from a particular platform. The library is crafted to minimize code and memory footprint, while taking full advantage of underlying architectural features such as Intel Wireless MMX technology. The performance improvements achieved by Intel IPP allow increased performance at the application level and lead to more efficient use of the battery in handheld applications.

Code Portability

One of the key advantages to using the Intel Integrated Performance Primitives is that the optimization for Intel Wireless MMX technology is already provided. In addition, as the underlying hardware architecture of the Intel PCA product line evolves and new features become available, you can incorporate them through a corresponding new release of the Intel IPP library. By design, the API remains the same across successive generations so that application developers need only to recompile their application with the latest Intel IPP library to take advantage of the new hardware features. Figure 7.5 shows how the API for the motion compensation routine remains the same across successive product generations, from native applications for Intel XScale microarchitecture, to applications supporting Intel Wireless MMX technology, and on into future new generations of Intel Wireless MMX technology.

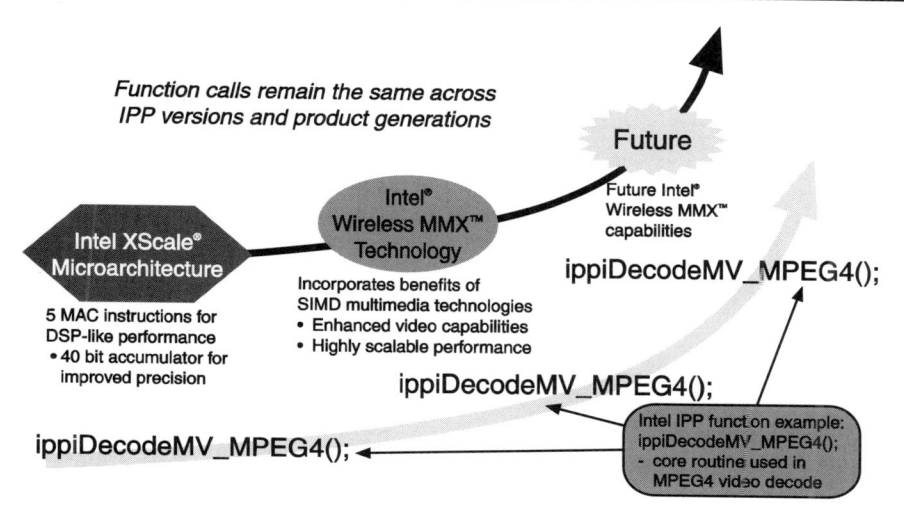

Figure 7.5   Intel® IPP Portability across Intel® PCA Products

Figure 7.5 shows that in addition to supporting the same API across multiple generations of Intel PCA applications processors. Intel IPP also supports the migration of applications between different processor architectures. A similar Intel IPP API exists for Intel architecture processors, for Itanium® microprocessors, and for the handheld version of Intel PCA processors. For example, if your code is written to run on Intel architecture and it only uses Intel IPP library functions as a means for optimization, you can migrate the application easily to the handheld Intel PCA platform by recompiling with the Intel IPP library for Intel PCA instead of the library for Intel architecture.

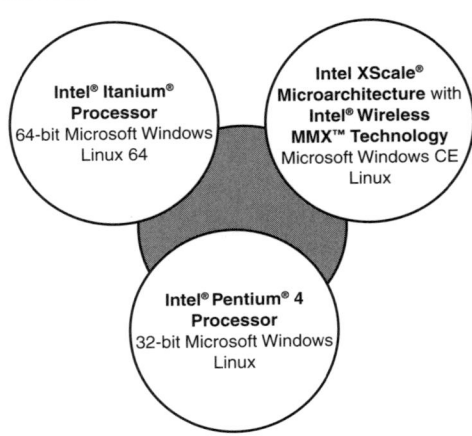

Figure 7.6   Intel® IPP Portability across Intel Processor Architectures

When Not to Use Intel IPP

Intel IPP may not be suitable for use when the binary file format is neither available nor suitable for your particular system configuration. The supported operating systems for Intel IPP are always evolving, so it is worth checking the Intel IPP page on the Intel developer Web site, cited in "References," for the latest information and availability.

Another reason not to use the Intel IPP library is that the exact function required is not in the library. When you have a proprietary algorithm that is not a standard—for example, if you have a novel search algorithm for motion estimation in MPEG-4 video encoding—you may choose not to use the existing routines in the library. Even if you are writing assembly code for Intel Wireless MMX technology, it still makes sense to use Intel IPP code where it is applicable to reduce the development time.

Understanding Intel IPP Names

As a large API, Intel Integrated Performance Primitives contains thousands of functions. To make so many functions intelligible to the developer, the set of naming and interface conventions is extensive. Ideally, the experienced user should be able to determine the name and arguments of a complicated Intel IPP function without consulting the manual. At the very least, you should find the Intel IPP behavior predictable be cause the names are uniform and consistent across all functions in the API.

Intel IPP function names describe their operation using the following components:

- Intel IPP return status

- Domain

- Operation type

- Function-specific descriptor

- Data type

- General description of function

- Arguments, or parameter list

Here is the API convention based on the naming components:

```
IppStatus
ipp<domain><operation>_
   <functionSpecificDescriptor>_
   <datatype>_<generalDescriptor>
 ( <paramList> );
```

The Three Prefixes

Intel IPP supports operations on three fundamental data types, each of which has a corresponding function prefix:

- Array (prefix `ipps`)

   The prefix `ipps` denotes a one-dimensional array of data, which includes, as a corner case, functions that operate on a single scalar. Examples are:

   - Vectorized scalar arithmetic operations, such as adding two arrays element-wise into a third array

   - Vectorized `math.h` type functions, such as taking the sine of each number in an array

   - Digital signal processing (DSP) operations

   - Audio processing and encoding

   - Speech recognition

   - Cryptographic operations

   - String operations

■ Image (prefix `ippi`)

An image is a two-dimensional array of pixels. Images are expected to have multiple channels representing, usually, separate color planes. Examples are:

— Image processing: arithmetic, filtering, manipulation, etc.

— 2D signal processing, for applications such as radar imagery and medical imagery

— Computer vision

— Video coding

— Raster-based graphics

■ Matrix/Vector (prefix `ippm`)

Vectors and matrices are one-dimensional and two-dimensional arrays that are treated as linear equations or data vectors, and subjected to linear algebra operations. Examples are:

— Matrix-vector multiplication

— Basic graphics geometry operations, such as coordinate transformations

— Matrix inversion

— Equation solving

The determination of the domain to which a function belongs is based primarily on the input arrays that are taken by that function, with related functions taken into account. If a function operates on scalars but is specifically an algorithm in support of imaging operations, it might be an `ippi` operation and follow the `ippi` conventions. For example, the function `ippsUnpackSideInfo_MP3` takes a bit stream as input rather than a signal, but it is an `ipps` function because it belongs to a tight group of audio coding functions.

Fundamental Data Types

C and other languages emphasize architecture independence for fundamental types at the expense of some needed specificity. For example, the `int` type has been specified in general terms as the core type of the executing architecture. While the convention for these languages is for `int` to be a 32-bit type even on 64-bit architectures, its long term future is still uncertain. In fact, at the inception of Intel IPP, the future size of a `long` on 64-bit architectures was uncertain.

For most Intel IPP functions, the exact size in bits is the key characteristic of input and output data. For this reason, the prudent course was to emphasize the size of the data, and the fundamental types of arrays in Intel IPP are specified to be of a certain bit length.

The abbreviations for types are of the form:

`IppNN<u|s|f>[c]`

`NN` represents the number of bits in the type, such as 8 or 32. The characters `u` and `s` indicate signed and unsigned integers, respectively, while `f` indicates a floating-point number, and `c` indicates that the number is interleaved complex. Table 7.1 is a complete list of types used.

Table 7.1   Fundamental Types in Intel® IPP

Code	IPP Type	Usual C Definition
8u	Ipp8u	unsigned char
8s	Ipp8s	char
16u	Ipp16u	unsigned short
16s	Ipp16s	short
32u	Ipp32u	unsigned int
32s	Ipp32s	int
32f	Ipp32f	float
64f	Ipp64f	double
1u	Ipp8u	unsigned char* bitstream, int offset
16sc	Ipp16sc	struct { Ipp16s re; Ipp16s im; } Ipp16sc;
32sc	Ipp32sc	struct { Ipp32s re; Ipp32s im; } Ipp32sc;
32fc	Ipp32fc	struct { Ipp32f re; Ipp32f im; } Ipp32fc;
64fc	Ipp64fc	struct { Ipp64f re; Ipp64f im; } Ipp64fc;

The "Code" column in Table 7.1 indicates the characters found in the function name for functions that take arrays of that type. Multiple versions of the same function that take different data types are distinguished in this way.

Signals and Arrays

The function names for signal/array, or `ipps` functions, follow this format:

`ippsBasename[_modifiers]_types[_descriptors]`

Where:

Basename is one or more words, acronyms, and abbreviations that identify the algorithm/operation.

_modifiers are abbreviations that choose among flavors of the Basename that recur across more than one entry point.

_modifiers are function-specific, and new modifiers can be created to make function groups.

_types are shorthand codes for the input and output data types.

_descriptors are characters that indicate particulars of the operation.

Base Name

The `ippsBasename` identifier takes the general form VerbAdjective or NounAdjective. Each word, acronym, or abbreviation is capitalized.

Examples:

■ `Add`

■ `RandUniform` generates a uniform random number

■ `VectorJaehne` generates a Jaehne vector

■ `WinBartlett` applies the Bartlett windowing function

In some cases, the words remain the commonly accepted order for clarity. Examples might be the following: `CrossCorr`, `StdDev`, `DotProd`

Abbreviations

Letters of acronyms are capitalized. Function names are generally abbreviated by truncating the name rather than removing vowels. Examples are:

■ `Norm` for normalize

■ `Sub` for subtract

- `Mul` for multiply
- `Conv` for convolve

Some exceptions exist, such as `cplx` for complex, `indx` for index, and a few standard abbreviations such as `sqr` and `sqrt`.

Fixed-point Operations

When a function has a "Q" notation in the base name, it indicates fixed-point operation. The type of fixed-point used is expressed as "Qn", where n is the number of bits of precision. This code is found after the text of the base name. For example, the `ippsToneQ15_16s` function would generate tone data that has one bit of sign and 15 bits of precision to the right of the binary point.

Specific Function Groups

Some function groups have conventions that are consistently applied within the group, but won't generally be found elsewhere.

Conversions. The base names for functions that perform conversions are written as "XxxToYyy". Examples are `ippsCplxToReal` and `ippsCart-ToPolar`.

Arithmetic operations. The character C, for arithmetic operations, indicates that one of the inputs is a constant. Examples are:

- `ippsAddC` to add a constant to each element of an array
- `ippsDivC` to divide each element of an array by a constant

The base name postfix `One` indicates that the arithmetic operation is a scalar rather than array operation.

Transforms. For transforms such as the discrete cosine (DCT) or the discrete Fourier transform (DFT), the abbreviations `Fwd` and `Inv` indicate forward and inverse transforms.

Filters. The postfix `One` indicates that the filter takes one element of input and produces one element of output. For example, the function `ippsFIROne_32f` filters one additional 32f sample.

A data type postfix, such as `32f` or `64f`, indicates that the filter taps are a different data type than the input and output arrays. An example is: `ippsFIR64f_16s_Sfs` filters a 16s array with a 64f filter.

Modifiers

Modifiers are used to define multiple flavors or multiple stages of a single operation. For example, functions that can occur in many different codecs with some variation in interpretation have the codec abbreviation in the name. Functions that are closely grouped but have slightly different formulae are usually distinguished by a modifier. Here are some illustrative examples:

- Variations on the threshold function include `ippsThreshold_LT`, `ippsThreshold_GT`, and `ippsThreshold_LTInv`.

- Three types of `Norm` are defined: "level 1" (`Norm_L1`), "level 2" (`Norm_L2`), and "infinite" (`Norm_Inf`).

- `ReQuantize_MP3` is the MP3-specific version of the inverse quantization function.

- `FFT` takes five types of inputs and outputs: `R`, `C`, `CCS`, `Pack`, and `Perm`. The layout taken by each FFT function can be identified using the modifier, as in `ippsFFT_CCSToR` and `ippsFFT_RToPack`.

Types

Of the full list of types, only a few are supported as broadly as possible. The following are supported for most functions and are therefore considered the primary types for the signal and array functions: `Ipp16s`, `Ipp32f`, and `Ipp64f`. Examples are:

    ippsMul_64f, ippsMul_32f, ippsMul_16s

    ippsAdd_64f_I, ippsAdd32f_I, ippsAdd_16s_I

In some cases, different types are used for input and output. When multiple types are used, both or all types are listed in this spot with the inputs specified first, followed by the outputs. Examples are:

- All of the following take one type of input(s) and produce one type of output(s): `ippsConvert_8s16s`, `ippsALawTo-Lin_8u32f`, `ippsAdd_8u16u`, `ippsExp_32f64f`

- This dot product function takes `Ipp16s` and `Ipp16sc` inputs and produces an `Ipp32sc` output: `ippsDotProd_16s16sc32sc`

For cases in which a function supports or initializes an operation on arrays, that function has the type or types of the arrays that is taken by the
supported function. If the function supports multiple types of operation,
the type usually is omitted or it is replaced by an appropriate modifier.

For example, these two functions initialize table structures for transform functions of certain data types but do not take arrays of those types
themselves:

```
ippsFFTInitAlloc_C_16s
```

```
ippsWTInvInitAlloc_32f16u
```

Intel GPP Naming Conventions

The format of the Intel GPP functions, although following the general
trend of Intel IPP does follows a slightly different format as shown in
Figure 7.7.

```
gpp<graphics/data entity><action>_, <fraction_part>
_<datatype> (parameter list)
```

Where:

> `<graphics/data entity>` describes the graphics function be-
> ing specified, such as `Vec3D` for 3-D vector
>
> `<action>` abbreviates the functional behavior, such as `Add`
>
> `<fraction_part>` specifies the number of bits that repesent the
> fractional part of fixed point representations
>
> `<data_type>` specifies the bit depth and signed or unsigned data

Figure 7.7   Intel® GPP Naming Conventions

An example of this format is:
```
gppMUL_16_32s(l32 src1, l32 src2, l32 *dst)
```

The function is a Intel GPP multiply operation with 16 bits of fractional
data that uses 32-bit signed integers as operands.

Intel IPP in Action

In this section, you'll see two specific examples of Intel IPP routines. The complete list of Intel IPP routines available can be found at the Intel IPP page on the Intel Developer Web site, listed in "References."

FIR Example

The finite impulse response filter (FIR) is a common component of many digital signal processing algorithms. This algorithm was briefly introduced in Chapter 3 along with an example implementation using Intel Wireless MMX technology. In this section, you'll see how a similar function is available in the Intel IPP library. Finally, FIR will come up again in Chapter 13 where more advanced techniques for optimizing the FIR algorithm using Intel Wireless MMX technology are examined.

Figure 7.8 shows the classic mathematical description of a FIR filter and the corresponding Intel IPP API. Using the naming conventions discussed previously, you can see that the first "s" in ipp**s**_FIRDirect_16s indicates that this function operates on one-dimensional data. The operation is the FIRDirect function, which operates on 16-bit signed data (_16s).

The Intel IPP library supplies generic forms of the functions where the number of data elements processed is configurable—in this case, the number of coefficients. This flexibility does incur a small performance overhead, but if the specific size and type of operation is not available, you can use assembly code to squeeze the last bit of performance out of the function instead. Doing so is an obvious trade-off of effort for performance.

(a)
$$y(n) = \sum_{k=0}^{K} b_k x(n - k)$$

where

$y(n)$	output sequence
$x(n)$	input sequence
b_k	taps

(b)

```
Ipps_FIRDirect_16s( Ipp16s *pSrc,
                    Ipp16s *pDst,
                    int     sampLen
                    Ipp16s *pTapsQ15
                    int     tapsLen,
                    Ipp16s *pDelayLine,
                    int     pDelayLineIndex )
```

where

pSrc	input vector pointer
pDst	output vector pointer
sampLen	input vector length
pTapsQ15	filter taps, Q0.15
tapsLen	tap vector length
pDelayLine	filter memory
pDelayLineIndex	internal state variable

(a) Function description
(b) IPP FIR API

Figure 7.8   FIR Intel® IPP Example

MPEG Video Encode

Figure 7.9 shows a block diagram overview of the functional elements of the Intel IPP MPEG-4 video encoder. The details of video compression algorithms are discussed in more detail in Chapter 15, but this figure demonstrates how a complex Intel IPP codec is broken down and constructed out of horizontal primitive functions. Note that the subfunctions all start with `ippi`, which according to the naming conventions means that they all operate on two-dimensional data, such as an 8×8 or 16×16 pixel block.

(a)

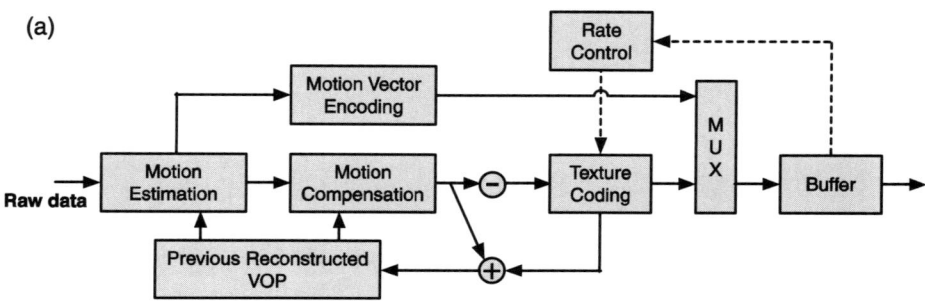

(b)

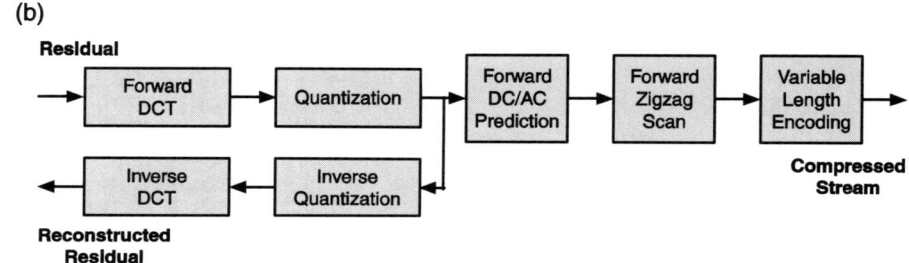

(a) Encoding process
(b) Texture encoding

Variable length encoding
```
ippiEncodeVLCZigzag_IntraDCVLC_MPEG4_16s1u
ippiEncodeVLCZigzag_IntraACVLC_MPEG4_16s1u
ippiEncodeVLCZigzag_Inter_MPEG4_16s1u
```

Block based texture encoding
```
ippiTransRecBlockCoef_Intra_MPEG4
ippiTransRecBlockCoef_Inter_MPEG4
```

Motion Compensation & Reconstruction
```
ippiMCBlock_RoundOff_8u
ippiMCBlock_RoundOn_8u
ippiReconBlock_RoundOff_8u
ippiReconBlock_RoundOn_8u
```

Motion Estimation
```
ippiMotionEst_16X16_SEA
ippiMotionEst_16X16_MVFAST
```

Rate Control
```
ippiUpdateRCModel_MPEG4
ippiUpdateQP_MPEG4
```

Figure 7.9 Intel® IPP MPEG Video Encoder and Intel IPP Sub-functions

What Do You Need to Get Started with Intel IPP?

All the collateral required to get started with Intel IPP is available on the Intel developer Web site listed in "References," where you can find the libraries in binary format for Windows CE and Linux. This Web site also includes supporting documentation, application notes, training materials and sample programs. Evaluation copies of Intel IPP libraries for Windows and Linux, along with collateral documents, are also available on the CD-ROM that accompanies this book. Another book from Intel Press, *Intel® Integrated Performance Primitives*, by Stewart Taylor, covers Intel IPP in greater depth (Taylor 2004).

Key Points

The key points to take away from this chapter are:

■ Intel IPP is the recommended way to accelerate your application with Intel Wireless MMX technology, if possible.

■ Intel IPP provides a fast route to release software with Intel Wireless MMX technology optimized for current and future Intel processors.

■ Intel IPP reduces the need for hand-coded assembly language and can help reduce development costs.

■ Intel IPP can provide increased battery life for handhelds via shorter execution times.

■ Intel IPP can increase available CPU headroom for running multiple applications.

Chapter 8

Embedded Software Development Tool Chain

Give us the tools and we will finish the job.

— Winston Churchill

Embedded software development requires very advanced and highly optimized development tools to make effective use of system resources—memory and processing capability—and still operate within the performance and power constraints. Programmable processors are used in embedded systems due to their flexibility and ability to perform software upgrades. As a result, high-level language compilers are a requirement for these processors, and the performance needs of these systems require these compilers to be highly optimized. In particular, this requirement concerns computation-intensive multimedia applications such as compression, filtering, imaging, and so on. Due to the complexity of the optimization problem, insight into the tools as well as the target architecture and application can make the developer even more effective. Earlier chapters provided insight into the architecture. This chapter introduces the tool chain provided by Intel and discusses some techniques that can take advantage of it.

Embedded System Software Design Flow

The increasing complexity of embedded handheld applications requires a well-defined development methodology. Although development methodology can vary from organization to organization, Figure 8.1 shows a typical design method for embedded software for mobile devices.

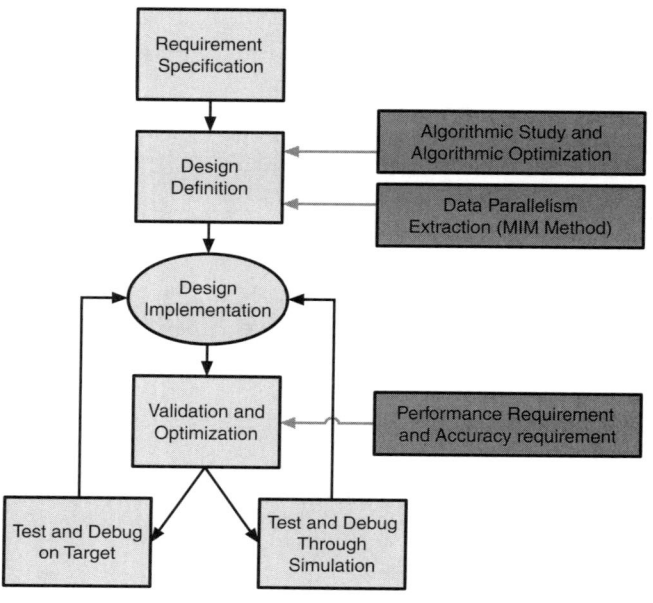

Figure 8.1   Typical Embedded Systems Software Design Flow

The diagram in Figure 8.1 outlines the following steps:

■ *Requirement Specification*—Capture system and application requirements. Typically, these requirements are captured in a document.

■ *Design Definition*—Define high-level design of software applications. Some aspects of the design definition will be independent of the target architecture. However, different aspects of the target architecture or platform can influence the design decisions, such as whether a hardware accelerator exists in the platform, or whether the processor does or does not support single instruction multiple data (SIMD). You can identify modules that map to Intel® Wireless MMX™ technology based on the criteria provided in Chapter 2.

■ *Implementation*—Implement the design. During the implementation phase, you can use different methods of implementation. In this phase, developers can use the high-level language of their choice. For enhanced processors that incorporate Intel Wireless MMX Technology, you may choose alternate methods of implementation other than a high-level language. Based on the acceleration desired, you can choose a target algorithm and method of implementation. During this phase, you can use many of the optimization techniques for Intel Wireless MMX technology that are described in Chapters 9, 10, and 12 through 15.

■ *Test and Debug on Simulation*—Validate the implementation functionally. The simulation can be functional- and/or cycle-accurate. This step is performed before the silicon or platform is ready. This step can proceed concurrently with the platform hardware development.

■ *Test and Debug on Target System*—Verify functionality and timing. Verification is performed either on the target system or on the reference platform that most closely resembles the target platform. During this phase, you can use the techniques described in Chapter 6, such as profiling, to expand the scope of optimization.

In embedded systems, the later stages are often more time consuming due to the fact that the software developer needs to adhere to many system-level constraints such as power, performance, and memory size The first few stages—requirements definition and specification definition—are done by other means and are not overly complex, since the size and complexity of the embedded applications are still significantly smaller than their desktop counterparts. In some cases, the later stages of embedded software development—performance and functional validation and optimization—consume four times the amount of effort as design and development. Thus, it is important for a given platform to have detailed capability to support the later stages. Intel XScale® microarchitecture and Intel Wireless MMX technology are supported by an integrated design environment with an enriched set of tools.

Integrated Design Environment

Intel offers a set of integrated tools for developers. In this framework, shown in Figure 8.2, a series of tools is integrated such that output of one tool can be consumed by another seamlessly. In addition, all the tools are accessible through a common user interface so that you can use different features of the tool chain without having to familiarize yourself with a new look and feel with every tool. The framework is also flexible; it allows you to easily incorporate new plug-ins for post-processing, which makes it easy to support varying development needs of different designers.

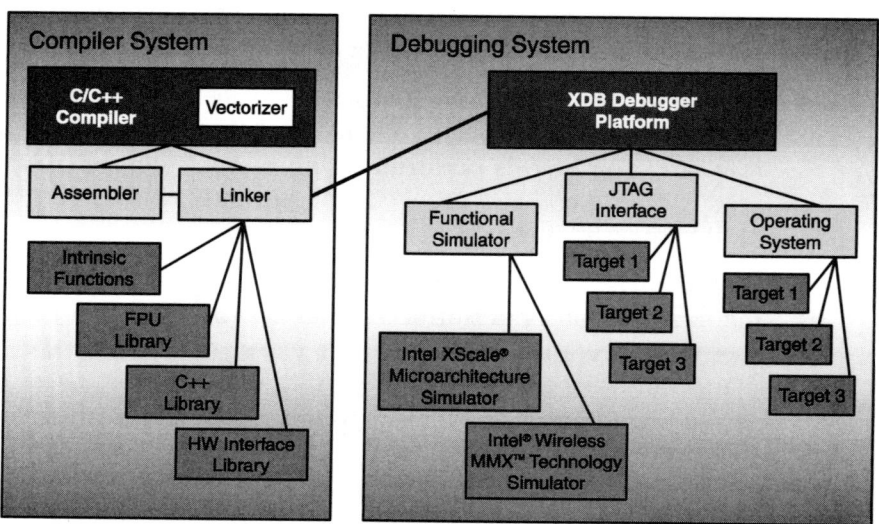

Figure 8.2   Components of the Integrated Design Environment (IDE) for Intel XScale® and Intel® Wireless MMX™ Technology

The integrated design environment (IDE) in the Intel C/C++ tool suite provides all the facilities needed for creating, editing, compiling, building, and debugging applications for processors with Intel XScale technology. The C/C++ compiler in the tool suite is highly optimized for this family of processors, containing powerful optimization algorithms that provide a high level of efficiency. The compiler provides control over the use of optimizations through compiler switches and directives that enable a knowledgeable engineer to achieve efficiency that comes close to hand-coded assembly language. The assembler and linker provide a high degree of flexibility by being compatible with other leading development tools and allowing mixing and matching of object files with the Intel tools. The XDB debugger shown in Figure 8.2 contains an easy-to-use GUI, models every aspect of the family of processors with Intel XScale technology, and works with a variety of interfaces—JTAG, ROM monitor, simulator, and a host of operating systems. The debugger also supports powerful scripting languages, enabling commercial-strength software development using these tools. In addition to standard libraries, the tool suite comes with a rich set of specialized libraries called Intel Integrated Performance Primitives (Intel IPP) that are highly optimized for processors with Intel XScale technology.

IDE-Based Design Flow

The tools' capability can be mapped to the embedded system software design flow described earlier. From a more pragmatic point of view, one could create a design flow based on the tools especially for design, implementation, and debugging.

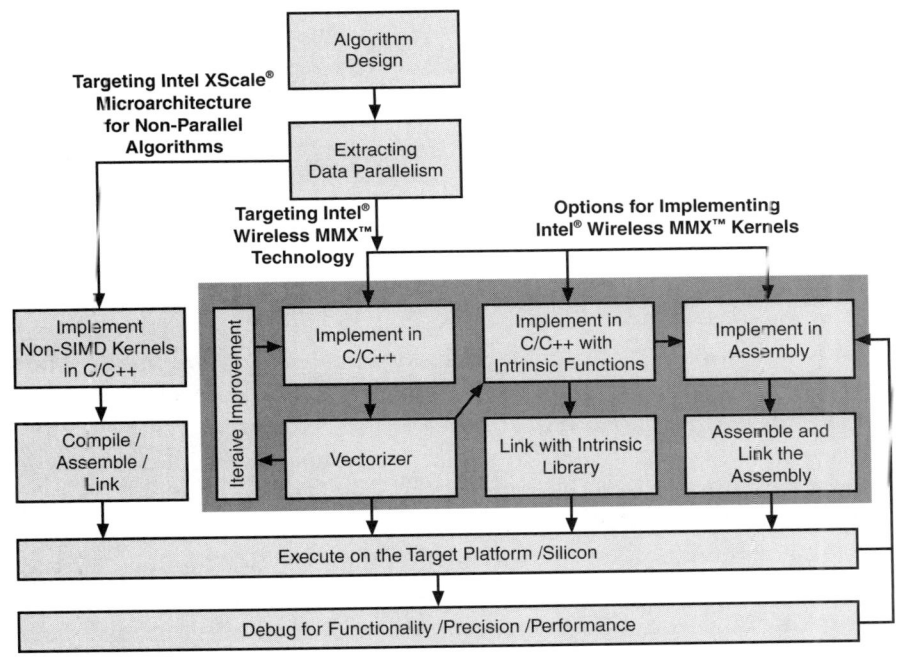

Figure 8.3   IDE Supported Design Flow for Intel® Wireless MMX™ Technology

The tool suite hides the complexity of developing efficient software using Intel XScale microarchitecture and Intel Wireless MMX technology quite effectively. The tool suite does so by hiding the complex details of efficient use of Intel Wireless MMX instructions in the compiler and allowing debug of the related code through a familiar, easy-to-use interface that displays registers and controls system issues. For power users who need the flexibility of accessing all the resources and facilities offered by the platform, the tools provide a variety of features, such as intrinsics, inline assembly, performance counter access, and hardware debug features. The software development methodology for the family of processors with Intel Wireless MMX technology is shown in Figure 8.3. You can create a software development flow based on the tool chain.

Applications can be accelerated with Intel Wireless MMX technology by using the following design approach based on the tools provided by the IDE. In this flow, an application is decomposed into data-parallel components and non-data-parallel components. Using techniques described in Chapter 2, you can determine which components should be targeted to Intel Wireless MMX technology. Non-parallelizable components can be compiled and optimized using compilers and assemblers that support Intel XScale technology, as shown in the left part of the diagram in Figure 8.3. For those application components that you intend to optimize using Intel Wireless MMX technology, you can follow a set of methods based on three distinct approaches:

■ Vectorizer

■ Intrinsic function

■ Hand-coded assembly

You can also use these three techniques in combination. These approaches differ in terms of development flexibility, level of control, code generation, and performance efficiency. Whether you use the approach based on the vectorizer, intrinsic functions, hand-coded assembly, or some combination of the three, you essentially go through the same iterative process of development, debugging, and code tuning. The hand-coding approach might be the most commonly used technique for SIMD or data-parallel machines. Several other chapters describe techniques appropriate to this method of development. This chapter focuses vectorization and intrinsic functions, with possible hybrid approaches.

The following sections show how to use the various tools for software development on processors supporting Intel XScale technology, specifically focusing on those aspects relating to Intel Wireless MMX technology.

■ Intel C++ Compiler

Compiler technology for embedded systems has increased the productivity of embedded software development efforts tremendously. Software written in a high-level language can be compiled targeting a new architecture. Modern compilers are capable of performing many microarchitecture-specific optimizations. To provide good performance, the Intel C++ Compiler is highly optimized to support Intel Xscale and Intel Wireless MMX technologies. The Intel C++ Compiler can perform loop optimizations, interprocedural optimizations, instruction scheduling, register allocation, and profile-guided optimizations. The compiler can generate code for traditional ARM† mode or for thumb mode with the use of the appropriate compiler driver, using the following syntax:

```
ccxsc  [options] file1 [file2 file3 ..]
[/link linker_options]

ccxscthb [options] file1 [file2 file3 ..]
[/link linker_options]
```

where *fileN* is a C/C++ source (.c .cc .cpp .cxx .i), assembly, object, library, or other linkable file, and `ccxsc.exe/ccxscthb.exe` is simply a driver that invokes the compiler [`mcpcom.exe`], the assembler [`asxsc.exe`], and the linker [`ldxsc.exe`].

C/C++ source specifies the behavior of the code in a sequential manner. It inherently hinders the developer from expressing certain algorithmic characteristics—concurrency in particular. For example, in C/C++ two lines of code expressing addition operations are treated as sequential operations; although, if they are not interdependent, they can be concurrent. While targeting a high-level language to SIMD or similar sub-word parallel machines, these concurrencies need to be extracted by the compiler. A compiler optimized for concurrency extractions is often called a *parallelizer* or *vectorizer*. An important component of the Intel compiler is the vectorizer that generates the Intel Wireless MMX instructions to exploit the parallelism present in the application.

Consider the following example. The 32-bit addition operations in a loop shown by the C code are independent across iterations; two such operations can be performed in a single Intel Wireless MMX instruction. The code generated by the Intel vectorizer shown in Figure 8.4 demonstrates that concurrency of operations can be extracted successfully.

The following extract from a program was exposed by the vectorizer and changed from a loop to sequential code using Intel® Wireless MMX™ instructions:

```
short a[128],b[128],c[128];
for (i=0; i<128; i++) {
    a[i]=b[i]+c[i];
}
```

After vectorizing the code:

```
.L1.2:
        wldrd   wR0, [r1, #0] @loading c
        sub     r4, r3, #416
        add     r14, r4, r2
        wldrd   wR1, [r14, #0] @loading b
        waddw   wR0, wR0, wR1
        add     r5, r3, #416
        add     r14, r5, r2     @ r14 now points to a
        wstrd   wR0, [r14, #0] @ storing a
        wldrd   wR0, [r1, #8]
        add     r14, r4, r0
        wldrd   wR1, [r14, #0]
        waddw   wR0, wR0, wR1
        add     r14, r5, r0
        wstrd   wR0, [r14, #0]
        add     r2, r2, #16     @updating offset
        add     r1, r1, #16     @updating offset
        add     r0, r0, #16     @updating offset
        add     r12, r12, #4    @updating offset
        cmp     r12, #128
        bcc     .L1.2
```

Figure 8.4   Concurrency of 32-Bit Vector Operations Extracted from Sequential High-level Language Using Vectorizer

Consider another example, shown in Figure 8.5, where the data types used for the additions are of 8-bit precision. You can see in the generated code that WADDB has been used instead of the WADDW instruction used in the previous example.

The following extract from a program was exposed by the vectorizer and changed from a loop to sequential code using Intel® Wireless MMX™ instructions

```
unsigned char a1[8] = {1,1,1,1,1,1,1,1};
unsigned char a2[8] = {1,1,1,1,1,1,1,1};
unsigned char a3[8];
foo() {
for (i=0; i<8; i++)
    a3[i] = a1[i] + a2[i];
}
```

After vectorizing:

```
foo:
        ldr     r0, .Llp.0
        ldr     r1, .Llp.0+4
        ldr     r2, .Llp.0+8
        wldrd   wR0, [r0, #0]
        mov     r0, #0
        wldrd   wR1, [r1, #0]
        waddb   wR0, wR0, wR1 @Byte operation for char
        wstrd   wR0, [r2, #0]
        bx      r14
```

Figure 8.5 Concurrency of 8-Bit Vector Operations Extracted from Sequential High-Level Language Using Vectorizer

From a programmer's perspective, you can think of the vectorizer as having two fundamental tasks: extracting concurrency and mapping concurrent operations onto the most effective instruction. Due to the complexity of these operations, the vectorizer might not offer the most optimal solution. From the programmer's perspective, the best result could be achieved by writing programs that are vectorizer-friendly. Later in the chapter, a few such techniques are described. Also, the code-generation process using the vectorizer can be an iterative process in which you adopt a trial-and-error scheme.

The vectorizer can be invoked by a command-line option during compilation. The option /QTPxsc3 enables code generation using Intel Wireless MMX instructions and, by default, enables the vectorizer. Additional features such as loop unrolling can be enabled by using the command-line option /Qunroll0.

For code segments that cannot be vectorized, the programmer can use intrinsic functions, detailed later, and inline assembly to make use of Intel Wireless MMX technology while working in a high-level language.

Macroassembler

The Intel-supplied macroassembler supports both ARM assembler and GNU assembler syntax with all the assembler directives for various versions of processors with Intel XScale technology. The assembler supports various file output formats.

The assembler generates Microsoft COFF/CV4 output when used for Windows† CE targets, where *COFF* is the executable and *CV4* is the executable with debug information. For other operating systems, the assembler generates ELF/DWARF2 output, where *ELF* is the executable and *DWARF2* is the executable with debug information.

The assembler has full support for Intel Wireless MMX instructions and can be accessed as a part of the tool-chain IDE or by command-line commands. The syntax is as follows:

```
asxsc [<options>] sourcefile
```

The following shows differences between different syntax formats:

GNU syntax example:

```
.section add_example, "ax"
.export Add
Add:
      ADD r0, r0, r1
      BX lr
      .end
```

ARM syntax example:

```
AREA add_example, CODE, READONLY
GLOBAL Add
Add
      ADD r0, r0, r1
      BX lr
      END
```

The assembler also has an enriched set of preprocessing capabilities such as conditional code declaration. For a complete list of assembly instruction syntax and the set of supported directives, refer to the assembler guide, *Intel Assembler for Intel XScale® Microarchitecture, rev 1.17*, in the tool suite supporting Intel XScale technology (Intel 2003).

■ Intel Linker

The Intel linker processes relocatable input files created by the assembler and creates a single executable file. ELF/DWARF is the object format of these files. The Intel linker works in *final link mode*, where the logical section fragments are bound to physical segments at absolute addresses. All relocation is completed, and a single absolute symbol table is output. The Intel linker supplies the following features:

- ELF/DWARF object format support
- Public-external resolution
- Relocation processing
- Assignment of addresses
- Construction and destruction of static C++ objects
- Command-line options to control the link process
- Creation of debug information
- Creation of a listing file
- A rich linker definition file specification language to control the link process in terms of location of sections

The linker is invoked in the following manner:

```
ldxsc [options] [input-files]
```

The link process can be controlled through the build files that enable you to locate sections and segments, to change the link order, to specify alignment information for sections, and so on. An example of a build file is shown in Figure 8.6.

```
LABEL SEGMENT SYMBOLS
LABEL SECTION SYMBOLS
LAYOUT
      SEGMENT CODE BASE  0x0
          LOAD SECTION Init OF main
               SECTION _RO_
      SEGMENT CTORS BASE ALIGN 1
          LOAD SECTION .ctors
      SEGMENT DATA BASE ALIGN 4
          LOAD SECTION _RW_
      SEGMENT BSS BASE ALIGN 4
          LOAD SECTION _BSS_
INPUT
```

```
LABEL  GLOBAL  _seg_CODE_beg_    Image$$RO$$Base
LABEL  GLOBAL  _seg_CODE_end_    Image$$RO$$Limit
LABEL  GLOBAL  _seg_DATA_beg_    Image$$RW$$Base
LABEL  GLOBAL  _seg_DATA_end_    Image$$RW$$Limit
LABEL  GLOBAL  _seg_BSS_beg_     Image$$ZI$$Base
LABEL  GLOBAL  _seg_BSS_end_     Image$$ZI$$Limit
```

Figure 8.6   Example Demonstrating a Build File

For details on the syntax of the build file, refer to the linker description manual, *Intel Linker, rev 2.0, Set 2003*, that is supplied with the tool suite supporting Intel XScale technology.

Intel Library Manager

The Intel library manager organizes object files, or modules, into library files. The format of object files is the ELF relocatable object format. ELF relocatable files can be generated by compilers, assemblers, or other utilities. You can create, examine, or change library files using the library manager. The library manager allows you to:

■ Create new libraries.

■ Update existing libraries by adding or deleting modules.

■ Extract modules from the library.

■ Display information on the library, such as names of modules and names of public symbols.

■ Move modules to a specific location within the library.

■ Restore libraries.

The library is invoked with the following command:

```
libxsc [options] object-files
```

The tools supporting Intel XScale technology contain the *C standard library*, provided for ANSI C support and consisting of two main parts. The first part is the *C library,* which is target independent and contains ANSI C functions, C run-time functions, and additional library functions. The second part is target dependent, consisting of the *system library* and the start-up module.

The *C++ library* is provided for C++ support. It contains run-time support functions, functions used for exception handling, input and output services, and templates. The C++ library *does not replace* the C standard library. When a C++ application is linked, both the C standard library and the C++ library are required.

Intel Debugger

The suite of tools for the Intel XScale microarchitecture includes a debugger that can work with the simulator and the hardware development board in a seamless manner. The Intel Debugger can work at the assembly level or at the high-level language source code level. It has significant support for debugging the optimized code generated by the Intel compiler. The Intel Debugger contains several modules, referred to as *plug-ins*, that make it OS-aware. Currently, plug-ins for Symbian[†] OS, Palm[†] OS, and Windows CE are provided with the tool chain. In addition, the debugger seamlessly supports several features of the Intel XScale microarchitecture. These features include:

- On-chip execution trace support

- Angel[†] Software interrupt call support

- Flash memory writer plug-in support

- Performance counter support

- Memory-mapped registers

The debugger works with the hardware development board using a ROM monitor or the JTAG interface. The debugger also supports several Intel XScale cores or other cores on a single JTAG scan chain in a seamless manner, providing facilities for complex break points and synchronization. The debug tool can be used in three different configurations, as illustrated in Figure 8.7.

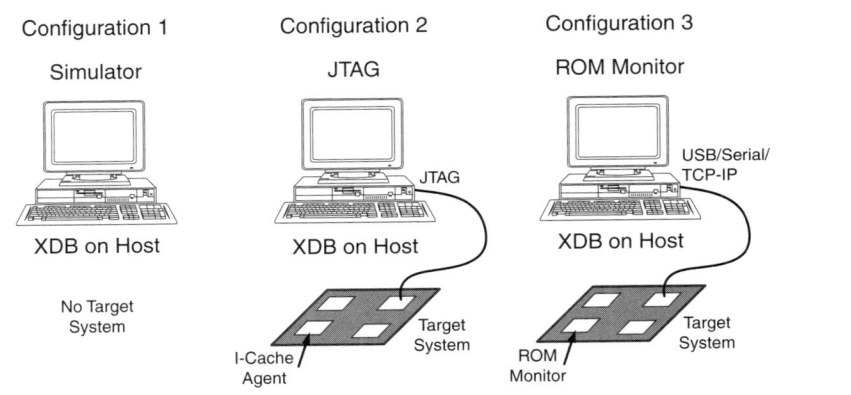

Figure 8.7   Three Different Configurations for XDB Debugger

XDB Simulator—The Intel XScale Microarchitecture XDB Simulator for Intel Wireless MMX Technology is a fully functional simulator. It models the Intel XScale microarchitecture, Intel Wireless MMX technology, and other system-level peripherals such as DMA and LCD. This multi-model coverage allows software debugging at a system level in contrast to the other development tools, which only model the core. With the capability of setting breakpoints and viewing co-processor registers, one can track the execution of Intel Wireless MMX instructions. Simulation is effective since you can test your code without the target platform. You can use this feature to perform functional validation of the kernels and the whole application in general.

XDB JTAG Debugger—The XDB JTAG Debugger fully supports and utilizes the on-chip debug capabilities of Intel XScale microarchitecture, including the low-level JTAG debug mode. This debugger provides access to all the on-chip processor structures, including the co-processor and device registers, allowing the use of hardware breakpoints and disassembly from the on-chip trace supporting Intel XScale microarchitecture. This feature can be used for on-chip functional validation of the application and performance validation. A performance-monitoring counter along with the VTune analyzer can be used to evaluate the time taken by the application as a whole and also the time taken by each kernel. The effect of all the optimization techniques described in other chapters can actually be measured in this configuration.

XDB ROM Monitor—JTAG debug assumes very little maturity of the target board and might not be well suited when a user is trying to debug an application in a complicated environment, such as running on an OS or concurrently with other applications. Once the XDB debugger is configured with a ROM monitor, it can debug the system in the presence of an OS. ROM monitor is a debug agent that runs on the target system and is aware of the operating system. This configuration can be used to debug applications that use Intel Wireless MMX instructions in complex scenarios such as videoconferencing.

Intrinsic Functions

The intrinsic functions model the data types and operations that are efficiently supported in hardware, but are difficult to express concisely in C or C++. Intrinsic functions eliminate the need to use inline assembly language or run-time library calls to efficiently use the underlying hardware features. Moreover, the semantics of intrinsics are known to the compiler, and it can optimize these functions like any other C/C++ arithmetic or logical operators.

You can use intrinsic functions by including the file `mnintrin.h`. This library file defines a data type `__m64`, which is the fundamental 64-bit data type in Intel Wireless MMX technology. The data type `__m64` can contain packed byte, word, or double-word data, which can be signed or unsigned. Several operations, which are classified into the broad categories listed in Table 8.1, are defined for this data type.

Table 8.1   Summary of Different Intrinsic Functions

Categories	Description	Example Names	Instruction Mapping
Packed Arithmetic Intrinsics	Arithmetic operations	_mm_adds_pu32	WADDWUS
Shift Intrinsics	Shift operations	_mm_sll_pi32	WSLLW
Logical Intrinsics	Logical operations	_mm_and_si64	WAND
Pack/UnPack Intrinsics	Extraction and creation of packed data	_mm_packs_pi16	WPACKHSS
Utility Intrinsics	Setting register constants	_mm_set1_pi8	TBCSTB
General Support Intrinsics	Extracting from 64-bit numbers	_mm_extract_pi32	TEXTRMSW

The compiler maps the intrinsic functions into Intel Wireless MMX instructions and, in many cases, applies optimizations based on the algebraic properties of these intrinsic operations. Figure 8.8 shows the use of intrinsic functions in C. The assembly code generated by the compiler containing Intel Wireless MMX instructions is shown in Figure 8.9.

```
__m64 a, b, c;
int dd;
a = _mm_set_pi32( 0xffffffff, 0xffffffff);
b = _mm_set_pi32( 0x80000000, 0x80000000);
c = _mm_add_pi32(a,b);
dd = _mm_extract_pi32(c, 0);
```

Figure 8.8   Example of Intrinsic Code

The compiler maps the C code in Figure 8.8 into the code shown in Figure 8.9, which uses Intel Wireless MMX instructions.

```
ldr       r1, .L2.16
ldr       r2, .L2.16+4
add       r3, r13, #0
wldrd     wR0, [r1, #0]
mov       r14, #0
wldrd     wR1, [r2, #0]
waddw     wR0, wR0, wR1
textrmsw r4, wR0, #0
ands      r1, r3, #3
add       r2, r3, #36
mvn       r3, #35
bne       .L2.14
```

Figure 8.9   Generated Assembly Code from the Intrinsic Functions

The use of intrinsic functions is typically a replacement for the vectorizer in the current generation of processors supporting Intel XScale technology. The intrinsics operate on packed data types, so in order to use them, you have to vectorize the program yourself and then use the intrinsics to issue the vector operations. Although this operation eliminates the need for the compiler to perform vectorization, the program must be in written in C, which in turn means portability and ease of maintenance. You can depend on the compiler to allocate variables to registers and to schedule the Intel Wireless MMX instructions in an efficient manner. Using the intrinsics is recommended only when you find that you have no way in which to convey the information needed to the compiler so that it can vectorize the code. Using intrinsics, you do not have to worry about register allocation and scheduling. While allocating registers, the compiler uses the maximum number of registers to increase the data reuse-and-gain load amortization. For example, a 16-tap FIR filter, implemented as shown in Figure 8.10, yields code as optimized as hand-coded assembly. Hand-coded assembly is demonstrated in Chapter 13. You can use an iterative approach to check that the compiled intrinsic codes are scheduled optimally.

```
_m64 input[64], output[64], _m64 coeff[16], temp;

for (i=0; i< 40 ; i=i+4) {
    for (j=0 ; j< 16; j=j+4) {
        _mm_macz_pi16 (output[i], input[i], coeff[j]);
        _mm_align_ (temp, input [i], input[i +1])
        _mm_macz_pi16 (output[i+1], temp, coeff[j]);
        _mm_align_ (temp, input [i+1], input[i+2])
        _mm_macz_pi16 (output[i+2], temp, coeff[j]);
        _mm_align_ (temp, input [i+2], input[i+3])
        _mm_macz_pi16 (output[i+3], temp, coeff[j]);
    }
}
```

Figure 8.10   A FIR Filter Implemented Using Intrinsic Functions

■ Vectorization Programming Guidelines

Vectorizing compilers exploit single instruction multiple data (SIMD) processing automatically. Users can help the compiler by writing their code to accommodate SIMD processing—that is, the code is vectorizer-friendly. Using the vectorizer to generate Intel Wireless MMX instructions can be an iterative approach. The vectorizer outputs detailed information on the vectorizability of a given high-level language code. Based on the reports from the vectorizer, you can adapt your code to vectorize more effectively. This section introduces differing techniques you might use to vectorize a kernel better; it also shows you how best to interpret the messages from the vectorizer.

Making Kernels of the Loop Vectorizer-Friendly

The programmer has a better understanding of the application being developed than the automated tools. The programmer can offer a set of hints and adopt a set of programming techniques to help the vectorizer work effectively. To ensure successful vectorization, you can follow this set of tips.

Loops with Single Basic Blocks

Make sure that the body of the loop does not have conditional statements, GOTO statements, break statements, or continue statements. Also, make sure that the loop is has a single entry and single exit. The loop shown as Example 1 in Figure 8.11 cannot be vectorized since it is not a single exit loop.

```
// Example 1
for (i=0;i<1024;i++) {
   if (foo())
      break;
   else
      a[i]=b[i]+c[i];
}

// Example 2
for (i=0;i<1000;i++) {
   foo();
   a[i]=b[i]+c[i];
}
```

Figure 8.11   Example of a Case Wherein the Inner Loop is Not a Basic Block

Similarly, loops that contain function calls cannot be vectorized since function calls cannot be reordered without potentially changing the semantics of the program. Example 2 in Figure 8.11 shows a loop that contains a function call that cannot be vectorized.

Avoid Inline Assembly Statements Inside Loops

With inline assembly instructions—using the asm statement—you can ensure that a specific instruction is placed in the generated code. However, inline assembly is not recommended while using the vectorizer. The effect of assembly code inside asm statements is not known to the compiler, so it does not apply any optimizations across asm statements. This situation prevents vectorization in loops containing asm statements.

Avoid Volatile Variables in Loops that Need to Be Vectorized

Access to a volatile variable inside a loop prevents the loop from being vectorized because a volatile variable prevents reordering of instructions, which is a fundamental requirement for vectorization.

Avoid Complicated Array Expressions Inside Loops

The compiler might not vectorize complex expressions efficiently. Consider the example shown in Implementation A of Figure 8.12. In the first example, the index to the array is computed on the fly based on the running variable of the outer loop. The vectorizer could have difficulty generating robust code for such on-the-fly index computation. This complex expression can be modified to the form of the code shown in Implementation B of Figure 8.12, where only on-the-fly index computation is based on the running variable of the current loop. Then, the compiler can vectorize the latter implementation.

```
// Implementation A

void cse(double a[][N], double b[][N],double c[][N]){
  for(int i=0; i<N; i++) {
    for(int k=0; k<N; k++) {
      for(int j=0; j<N; j++) {
        c[i][j] = c[i][j] + a[i][k] * b[k+1][j+1];
      }
    }
  }
}


// Implementation B

void cse2(double a[][N], double b[][N],double  c[][N]){
  for(int i=0; i<N; i++) {
    for(int k=0; k<N; k++) {
      int kxx=k+1;   //Index computation done separately
      for(int j=0; j<N; j++) {
        c[i][j] = c[i][j] + a[i][k] * b[kxx][j+1];
      }
    }
  }
}
```

Figure 8.12   Simplifying Complicated Array Expression Inside the Loop

Use Arrays Instead of Pointers

Although programmers might like to use pointers in their code, especially for accessing arrays and vectors, the compiler can extract more information out of the program if arrays are used. For instance, when variables are declared as arrays, the compiler can ensure that the variables are aligned in memory when processing Intel Wireless MMX instructions. Moreover, arrays have certain properties—known lengths—that enable the compiler to handle them more efficiently than pointers. In Figure 8.13, Implementation B is more favorable for vectorizing than Implementation A because it uses arrays instead of pointers inside the for-loop.

```
// Implementation A

short a[512], b[512], c[512];
short *x=a, *y=b, *z=c;
foo() {
    for(int i=0; i<512; i+=2) {
        x[i] = y[i] + z[i];
    }
}

// Implementation B

short a[512], b[512], c[512];
foo() {
    for(int i=0; i<512; i+=2) {
        a[i] = b[i] + c[i];
    }
}
```

Figure 8.13   Programming Technique That Avoids Pointer Usage

Avoid Using Global Pointers

Local variables are limited in scope to the function in which they are defined, so the compiler can have complete information about them and can apply aggressive optimizations. But for global variables, a compiler typically cannot have complete information, such as where global variables will be used, so the compiler does not optimize them effectively.

Also, details of global declarations can be outside the scope of local function optimization in the compiler. The vectorizer cannot generate Intel Wireless MMX instructions in many instances with global pointers; whereas, with local pointers, it can do so. This situation is illustrated in Figure 8.14. In the example, local pointers are used to point to the arrays to ensure that the compiler can associate the alignment property of the array to the local pointers.

```
// Implementation A

short int a[100],b[100],c[100];
short *a1=a,*b1=b,*c1=c;
foo() {
    int i;
    for (i=0; i<100; i++)
        a1[i] = b1[i] + c1[i];
}

// Implementation B

short int a[100],b[100],c[100];
foo() {
    int i;
    short *a1=a,*b1=b,*c1=c;
    for (i=0; i<100; i++)
        a1[i] = b1[i] + c1[i];
}
```

Figure 8.14   Coding Technique That Avoids Using Global Pointers

Use Local Variables to Avoid Aliasing Issues

Consider the example shown in Figure 8.15, Implementation A. The compiler needs to make sure that x[23] does not alias with a[i] to vectorize this loop. Therefore, the compiler generates two versions of the loop: one vectorized and guarded by the check for aliasing between arrays x and a, and another that is a non-vectorized version.

To eliminate the need for these multiple versions, the programmer need only change the code slightly, as shown in Implementation B, conveying the information that x and a do not alias with each other.

```
// Implementation A

int a[100];

foo(int *x) {
int i;

    for (i=0; i<100; i++)
        a[i] = a[i] + x[23];
}

// Implementation B

int a[100];

foo(int *x) {
int i;
int temp=x[23];

    for (i=0; i<100; i++)
        a[i] = a[i] + temp;
}
```

Figure 8.15   Removing Dependency Between Vectors

Vectorizer-Friendly Addressing

The vectorizer examines memory access patterns in the code so it can map similar operations on consecutive memory spaces into one or a sequence of Intel Wireless MMX instructions. A set of programming techniques exist that helps make memory addressing "friendly" for the vectorizer.

Use Unit Stride Instead of Non-Unit Stride

SIMD architectures, such as those using Intel Wireless MMX technology, offer the highest efficiency if operations are homogeneous in a vector. If a non-unit stride is used, as in Implementation A in Figure 8.16, adjacent elements in the vectors possibly are not operated on uniformly. Cases similar to the example might not be efficient in Intel Wireless MMX technology due to the additional shuffling required to organize the data. The vectorizer does not vectorize the loops that are non-unit stride. Implementation B in Figure 8.16 is, however, vectorizable.

```
// Implementation A

for(int i=0; i<512; i+=2) {
   a[i] = b[i] + c[i];
}

// Implementation B

for(int i=0; i<512; i++) {
   a[i] = b[i] + c[i];
}
```

Figure 8.16 Example Showing Unity Stride versus Non-Unity Stride

Traverse the Arrays in Natural Order—Row Major for C/C++

The following 4×4 matrix is used in the example in Figure 8.17, where each of the elements is a 16-bit quantity.

```
a1 a2 a3 a4
b1 b2 b3 b4
c1 c2 c3 c4
d1 d2 d3 d4
```

C/C++ uses *row major order*. In row major order, the last subscript changes most rapidly. Therefore, in C/C++, the memory layout would look like this:

```
a1 a2 a3 a4 b1 b2 b3 b4 c1 c2 c3 c4 d1 d2 d3 d4
```

For C/C++, you would want to access these values using a loop similar to the one in Figure 8.17.

```
for(int i=0; i<4; i++) {
   for(int j=0; j<4; j++) {
      matrix[i][j] += 5;
   }
}
```

Figure 8.17 Row Order Addressing of Arrays

A stride 1 access to an array accesses contiguous memory. So, stride 1 access would get a1, then a2, then a3, then a4. A stride 2 (j+=2) access would get a1, then a3, then b1, and so on. Intel Wireless MMX instructions can load four contiguous values at a time into a register supporting Intel Wireless MMX technology with a single load instruction.

Consequently, when the loop is vectorized, the vectorizer moves a1, a2, a3, and a4 into a register where it can operate on all four of them simultaneously—in this case, by adding five to the value. The vectorizer sees that it is accessing four contiguous pieces of memory and that it can perform a legal SIMD operation on them—in this case, a packed add, so it can vectorize the loop.

If the loops are interchanged, with the j being incremented in the outer loop and i being incremented in the inner loop, you would get a1, b1, c1, d1 for your first four values. Because these elements are not contiguous in memory, they can't all be moved into a register at the same time, even though the operation is the same. Consequently, the loop remains unvectorized.

Loop Iteration Count Must Be a Compile-Time or a Run-Time Constant

For a vectorizer to vectorize a loop, the iteration count of the loop must be known at compile time or at run time. An example of a loop whose iteration count is not known is shown in Figure 8.18.

```
while (!found) {
    found = (a[i] == val);
    i+=1;
}
```

Figure 8.18   Example of Indeterministic Loop Count

Vectorizer-Friendly Loop Organization

During extraction of concurrency, the vectorizer examines multiple iterations of a loop. A set of simple steps can make concurrency extraction easy.

Avoid Unrolling the Loop by Hand

The compiler can decide upon the loop unroll factor by employing very effective heuristics that generate highly efficient code. Manually unrolling loops usually prevents these loop-unrolling heuristics from working in an efficient manner. An example of an unrolled loop that the compiler cannot vectorize is shown in Implementation A in Figure 8.19.

```
// Implementation A

for (i=0; i<1000; i+=2) {
   a[i] = b[i] + c[i];
   a[i-1] = b[i+1] + c[i+1];
}

// Implementation B

for (i=0; i<1000; i++) {
   a[i] = b[i] + c[i];
}
```

Implementation A is inefficient for vectorization.
Implementation B is efficient for vectorization.

Figure 8.19   Demonstration of Hand-Loop Unrolling

A semantically equivalent loop that the compiler can vectorize is shown as Implementation B of Figure 8.19.

Keep Loops Simple through Loop Splitting

Try to keep the loops simple so that the compiler can better understand all the interactions between various statements inside the loop. An example of loop splitting is shown in Figure 8.20.

```
// Implementation A

for (i=0; i<100; i++) {
   a[i] = b[i] + c[i];
   x[i] = y[i] + z[i];
}

// Implementation B

for (i=0; i<100; i++)
   a[i] = b[i] + c[i];

for (i=0; i<100; i++)
   x[i] = y[i] + z[i];
```

Implementation A shows two loops together.
Implementation B shows two loops split for efficiency of vectorization.

Figure 8.20   Loop Splitting

Inherent in the nature of this loop split is the lack of dependence between the write to array a and the write to array x. The compiler must deduce this information through its analysis in the first case to enable vectorization.

For the sake of simplicity, only inner loops are vectorized. When programming, try to keep all the vectorizable expressions in inner loops so that the vectorizer can generate efficient code for them.

Express Loop Counters as Variables

Due to the limitations of alias analysis algorithms used in the compiler, vectorization of loops operating on pointers is disabled if the addresses of loop control variables are expressed as pointers. In Figure 8.21, the loop is not vectorized since the address of the upper bound of the loop variable is taken as input.

```
int a[100], b[100], c[100];

foo(int *n) {
    int i;
    int *a1=a, *b1=b, *c1=c;

    for (i=0; i<n; i++) {
        a1[i] = b1[i] + c1[i];
    }
    foo(&n);
}
```

Figure 8.21   Work-around Demonstrating How to Vectorize in the Presence of Pointers

By modifying the function call which takes the value of variable n instead of its address, the loop can be vectorized.

Data Type Considerations

The order of parallelism depends on the basic data types used in a loop. Vectorization efficiency depends on the data types used for algorithm development. In this section, a set of guidelines are provided for the data-type usage.

Avoid Using Mixed Data Types in Expressions Inside Loops

It is preferable to have similar data types participating in the expressions computed inside loops. This similarity eliminates the need for the compiler to marshal the arguments into the coprocessor registers to be processed by the Intel Wireless MMX instructions. It makes the generated code efficient. Figures 8.19 through 8.22 illustrate how using similar data types helps boost efficiency. In Figure 8.19, mixed data types—int and short—are used. The program also specifies mixed operation between short and int. For Intel Wireless MMX technology, operations are homogeneous in nature typically; that is, both the operands are considered as the same data type. Due to the complexity involved in handling mixed data mode, the vectorizer often chooses to operate with the lowest common data size between different data types, which in this case, is a byte. In Figure 8.20, the code generated operates the loads and data manipulation by primarily using byte-based operations, which are not the most optimal. However, this inefficiency can be avoided by using similar data sizes.

```
int a[100],b[100];
short c[100];

foo()
{
   int i;
   for (i=0; i<100; i++) {
      a[i] = b[i] + c[i];
   }
}
```

Figure 8.22   Code Example Using Mixed Data Types

```
@The generated code
.L1.2:
        ldrb    r0, [r14, #1] @byte addressing is used
        ldrb    r1, [r14, #2]
        ldrb    r2, [r14, #3]
        ldrb    r8, [r14, #4]
        tbcstb  wR1, r6
        orr     r0, r0, r1, lsl #8
        orr     r0, r0, r2, lsl #16
        ldrb    r9, [r14, #6] @byte addressing is used
        ldrb    r10, [r14, #7]
```

```
orr       r0, r0, r8, lsl #24
tmcrr     wR0, r0, r5
wunpckilh wR0, wR0, wR0    @additional manipulation
ldrb      r8, [r14, #5]
wsraw     wR1, wR0, wR1
add       r2, r4, #224
add       r0, r2, r12
wldrd     wR0, [r0, #0]
waddw     wR0, wR0, wR1
add       r1, r4, #640
add       r0, r1, r12
wstrd     wR0, [r0, #0]
ldrb      r0, [r14, #8]!
tbcstb    wR1, r6
orr       r8, r8, r9, lsl #8
orr       r8, r8, r10, lsl #16
orr       r0, r8, r0, lsl #24
tmcrr     wR0, r0, r5
wunpckilh wR0, wR0, wR0
wsraw     wR1, wR0, wR1 @byte addressing is used
add       r0, r2, r3
wldrd     wR0, [r0, #0]
waddw     wR0, wR0, wR1
add       r0, r1, r3
wstrd     wR0, [r0, #0]
add       r12, r12, #16
add       r3, r3, #16
add       r7, r7, #4
cmp       r7, #100
bcc       .L1.2
```

Figure 8.23   Inefficient Code Generation Due to Mixed Data Types

If array c were an integer, the generated code would be a lot more efficient, as shown in Figures 8.24 and 8.25.

```
int a[100],b[100], c[100];

foo()
{
   int i;
   for (i=0; i<100; i++) {
     a[i] = b[i] + c[i];
   }
}
```

Figure 8.24   Code Example Which Removed Mixed Data Types

The code in Figure 8.24 generates the assembly code shown in Figure 8.25.

```
.L1.2:
        wldrd   wR0, [r1, #0]
        @double word loads instead of byte loads
        sub     r4, r3, #416
        add     r14, r4, r2
        wldrd   wR1, [r14, #0]
        waddw   wR0, wR0, wR1
        add     r5, r3, #416
        add     r14, r5, r2
        wstrd   wR0, [r14, #0]
        wldrd   wR0, [r1, #8]
        add     r14, r4, r0
        wldrd   wR1, [r14, #0]
        waddw   wR0, wR0, wR1
        add     r14, r5, r0
        wstrd   wR0, [r14, #0]
        add     r2, r2, #16
        add     r1, r1, #16
        add     r0, r0, #16
        add     r12, r12, #4
        cmp     r12, #100
        bcc     .L1.2
```

Figure 8.25 Efficient Assembly Code Generated from the Code Using Homogeneous Data Types

Use Integer as a Loop Control Variable

It is preferable to use a signed integer as the loop control variable in for loops. The loop in Figure 8.26 is vectorized when the loop control variable is an integer instead of a short.

```
// Implementation A

int a[100],b[100],c[100];

foo(short n)
{
   short i;
   for (i=0; i<n; i++)
      a[i] = b[i] + c[i];
}
```

```
// Implementation B

int a[100],b[100],c[100];

foo(short n)
{
    int i;
    for (i=0; i<n; i++)
        a[i] = b[i] + c[i];
}
```

Implementation A: the loop control variable is not an integer
Implementation B: the loop control variable is an integer.

Figure 8.26   Code Demonstrating Preferred Loop Control Variable

Compiler Directives to Help Vectorization

The programmer can help vectorization by using compiler directives and pragmas. These constructs are hints or guides for the compiler to optimize in a particular fashion. Better results can be expected since these hints narrow the optimization search on behalf of the compiler.

Pragma Vector always

The pragma vector always overrides the heuristic decision about profitability and vectorizes non-unit strides or even unaligned accesses by packing the unaligned data items into vector registers. The code shown in Figure 8.27 generates the vectorizer code shown in Figure 8.28.

```
void vec_add(short *a, short *b, short *c) {
    int i;
#pragma vector always

    for (i=0; i<n; i++)
        a[i] = b[i] + c[i];
}
```

Figure 8.27   Example Code Demonstrating Usage of #pragma Vector

```
.L1.4:
        ldr     r12, .Llp.0
        add     r1, r1, #4
        cmp     r1, r3
        add     r14, r12, r2
        wldrd   wR1, [r14, #0]
        sub     r14, r12, #256
        add     r14, r14, r2
        wldrd   wR0, [r14, #0]
        waddhus wR0, wR1, wR0
        add     r12, r12, #256
        add     r12, r12, r2
        wstrd   wR0, [r12, #0]
        add     r2, r2, #8
        bcc     .L1.4
```

Figure 8.28   Result of the Vectorizer from the Example C Code

Pragma ivdep

To vectorize a loop that contains—or might contain—dependencies, add #pragma ivdep to ignore vector dependencies, as shown in Figure 8.29.

```
void foo(int k) {
#pragma ivdep

    for(int i=0; i<1000; i++) {
        a[i] = a[i+k] + c[i];
    }
}
```

Figure 8.29   Using ivdep Pragma to Ignore Dependencies

When vectorizing the loop in this example, the compiler assumes a dependence across iterations involving the array a, due to the use of the variable k passed into the function. If you know that k will not interfere with data access, adding a #pragma ivdep tells the vectorizer it's okay to ignore vector dependencies and attempt to vectorize. In essence, it says that you know what your dependencies are and that you are sure they won't be a problem.

Keyword `Restrict`

To vectorize a loop that contains—or may contain—pointer references that may cause dependencies, use the `restrict` keyword if needed, as shown in Figure 8.30.

```
void foo(short *restrict a, short *restrict b,
         short *restrict c) {
int i;

    for(i=0; i<512; i++) {
       a[j] = b[i] + c[i];
    }
}
```

Figure 8.30 Example Demonstrating `restrict` Keyword

Note that the use of the `restrict` keyword requires the use of the `/Qrestrict` switch. When vectorizing this loop without the `restrict` keyword, the compiler assumes dependence across iterations involving each array reference and statement in the loop. The compiler makes this assumption because, when pointers are used in the loop to access the data, the compiler cannot know whether the pointers are referencing the same memory, commonly known as *aliasing*, and must err on the safe side. The `restrict` keyword indicates that the data to which the pointers point is restricted and it may only be accessed by the given pointer variable. In other words, no pointer aliasing is occurring.

Pragma `Align`

For certain code, the programmer could know that certain pointers are aligned on a proper boundary for vectorization to be enabled. This information can be communicated to the compiler by using the pragma `align` as shown in the example in Figure 8.31.

```
void vec_add(short *a, short *b, short *c) {
    int i;
    __assume_aligned(a, 8);
    __assume_aligned(b, 8);
    __assume_aligned(c, 8);

    for (i=0; i<n; i++)
       a[i] = b[i] + c[i];
}
```

Figure 8.31 Example Code Demonstrating `Align` Pragma

The compiler vectorizes this loop with a check for aliasing guarding the vectorized loop.

Pragma novector

For certain algorithms, the programmer might know beforehand that vectorization cannot be helpful. The novector pragma can be used to indicate not to vectorize the loop following the pragma even if it is qualified to be vectorized, as shown in Figure 8.32.

```
void vec_add(short *a, short *b, short *c) {
int i;
#pragma novector

    for (i=0; i<n; i++)
        a[i] = b[i] + c[i];
}
```

Figure 8.32   Example Code Demonstrating novector pragma

In general, you should use pragmas in your code to provide explicit hints to guide the vectorizer in following these schemes. Future versions of the compiler could contain even more enhanced pragmas. Be sure to get the latest list of such pragmas from the tools-related manuals, cited in "References."

Vectorizer Messages

Following the programming tips in the previous sections, you can program code that is suitable for vectorization. Should you happen to miss any of these programming tips, the vectorizer can provide further hints. The Intel Compiler can produce detailed messages to indicate the behavior of the vectorizer on your programs. These messages can help you to understand the behavior of the vectorizer and enable you to rewrite the code so that the vectorizer can work better. The option /Qvec_report [0,1,2,3] generates detailed vectorizer output.

The parameter [0,1,2,3] indicates the level of output detail. In its most verbose mode—level 3—the Intel Compiler tells you what the vectorizer is "thinking" as it generates your code. At level 1, the vectorizer generates LOOP WAS VECTORIZED for each vectorized loop; at level 2, it identifies which loops were not vectorized. You can use these hints and the programming tips mentioned earlier to modify the code and attain successful vectorization.

Figure 8.33 shows an example of standard vectorizer output.

```
// Input Code
for (i=0; i<1000; i++) {
    foo();
    a[i] = b[i] + c[i];
}

// Vectorizer Message
C:\TEMP\Text1.cpp(16) : (col. 1) remark: LOOP WAS
VECTORIZED.
```

Figure 8.33   Typical Success Message from Vectorizer

Figure 8.34 is an example of vectorizer output using the level 3 switch. In this example, the code cannot be vectorized. The message from the vectorizer also specifies the reason that the loop could not be vectorized.

```
// Input Code
char *p;
p = "aeiou";
while (*p++) {
    cout << *p;
}

// Vectorizer Message
C:\TEMP\Text1.cpp(20) : (col. 1) remark: loop was not
vectorized: nonstandard loop is not a vectorization
candidate.
```

Figure 8.34   Typical Error Message from the Vectorizer

Have a look at two more examples that are not as straightforward. In the example in Figure 8.35, the vectorizer did not work due to the use of mixed data types. Based on the programming tips in the earlier section, you can modify the code by splitting the loop and thus achieve vectorization.

```
// Input Code Example
short x[100], y[100];
int z[100];
for(int j=0; j<100; j++)
{
   x[j] = y[j] + 3;
   z[j] = z[j+1];
}

// Vectorizer message
C:\TEMP\Text1.cpp(29) : (col. 5) remark: loop was not
vectorized: mixed data types.
```

Figure 8.35 Vectorizer Message Example Showing Mixed Data Types

Consider another example. In the example in Figure 8.36, the loop has two issues: vector dependence and the use of mixed data types.

```
// Input Code
short x[100], y[100];
int z[100];
for(int j=0; j<100; j++)
{
   x[j] = y[j] + 3;
   y[j+1] = z[j+1];
}

// Vectorizer message
C:\TEMP\Text1.cpp(26) : (col. 1) remark: loop was not
vectorized: existence of vector dependence.
```

Figure 8.36 Example Demonstrating Vectorizer Message Prioritization

Note that the vectorizer reports only one error. In situations where the compiler finds more than one reason for not vectorizing, the vectorizer indicates the higher priority error only.

In the last few sections, we described programming techniques for effective use of the vectorizer. For complete coverage of the vectorizer and its underlying technologies, see *The Software Vectorization Handbook: Applying Multimedia Extensions for Maximum Performance*, (Bik 2004).

Key Points

Intel XScale microarchitecture and Intel Wireless MMX technology are supported by a rich set of software development tools that hide the complexity of software development effectively. The Intel C++ Compiler supports multiple development methodologies based on autovectorization, intrinsics, and hand-coded assembly. This chapter presents a brief overview of various approaches to vectorization that can improve performance. The vectorizer phase in the compiler is responsible for generating the Intel Wireless MMX instructions for your program, but for the vectorizer to work effectively, you must write your program using conventions presented in this chapter.

- Identify kernels targetable to SIMD. Choose the method of code development as it fits your need.

- Use the vectorizer wherever you can for productivity.

- Follow the programming guidelines for the vectorizer and the vectorizer messages.

- If you encounter a case where the vectorizer does not yield, use intrinsic functions.

Chapter 9

Optimizing for
Memory Subsystems

Memory is the thing you forget with.

—Alexander Chase

With the growth of integration in system on chip (SOC) technology, memory subsystems of an embedded system have also grown in complexity. The memory subsystem of an embedded system is composed of memory that is internal and external, volatile and nonvolatile. Efficient use of the memory subsystem is the key to gaining performance on multimedia applications. The Intel XScale® microarchitecture offers features that help programmers to use memory subsystems efficiently. Optimizing applications for memory subsystems can substantially accelerate performance and reduce power consumption. This chapter explains the following key techniques for optimizing an application to make effective use of memory:

- ■ Configuring the memory subsystem correctly

- ■ Determining the type of memory to use for distinct purposes

- ■ Writing code to make best use of the architectural features

Characteristics of Memory Subsystems

Chapter 5 demonstrated the importance of the memory subsystem's performance for an embedded system on a chip. The characteristics of the memory subsystem that impact performance are:

- *Memory latency*—The amount of time it takes to get data from the memory to the processor, as measured by the number of core clock cycles or actual time in nanoseconds.

- *Memory throughput*—The maximum amount of data that can be loaded from the memory or written to the memory in a given time. In some systems, read throughput from the memory and store throughput to the memory might not be the same. Memory throughput is measured in megabytes per second.

These characteristics are affected by type of memory (static, dynamic RAM, flash), load-store capability in the processor, level of integration—that is, whether memory is integrated onto the same silicon die as the processor or is located on a separate die—communication fabric architecture, frequency setting, and so on. The memory characteristics latency and throughput are interdependent to some extent. Therefore, a slow memory yields higher latency and lower throughput. However, latency and bandwidth can be decoupled so that a system can obtain very high throughput despite larger latency.

Memory Subsystems in Intel Application Processors

Intel® Personal Internet Client Architecture (Intel® PCA) products utilize the Intel XScale microarchitecture and incorporate Intel Wireless MMX™ technology. The products integrate memories and multimedia components such as an LCD controller, camera interface, and a set of other peripherals such as UART, USB, and the like. The memory subsystem of an Intel PCA processor with Intel Wireless MMX technology contains caches for instruction and data, with one or two levels of caching capability, integrated internal SRAM for on-chip storage, and external memory for off-chip storage. Current systems using Intel Wireless MMX technology incorporate 32 kilobytes of instruction cache, 32 kilobytes of data cache, and 256 kilobytes of integrated internal SRAM. The caches have the least latency and fastest throughput; the external memories are the slowest. Intel Wireless MMX technology can also be incorporated in a system that has a different memory architecture than is described here. Figure 9.1 shows a typical memory architecture for Intel Wireless MMX technology.

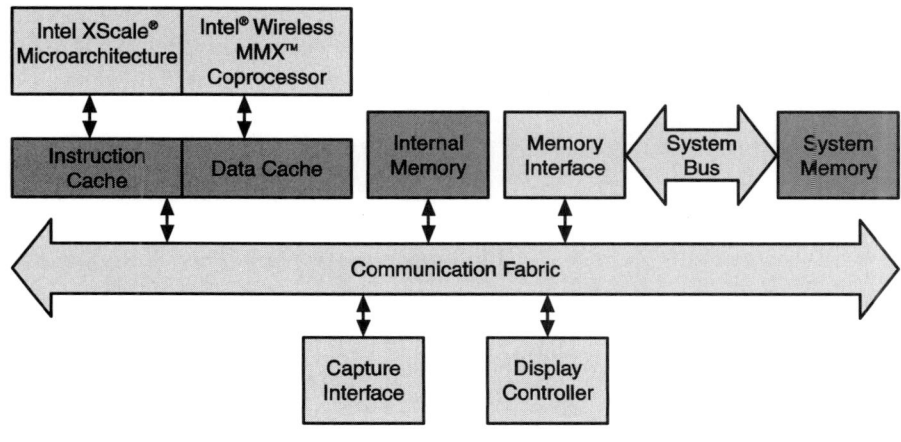

Figure 9.1   Typical Memory Architecture for Intel® Wireless MMX™ Technology in a System on a Chip

Memory Subsystems-based Optimization

Highly integrated systems on a chip impose stringent packaging constraints. To decrease pin count and keep the package size small, a single memory interface must be shared among the processor core and other peripherals. For any application, sharing the memory interface among different agents constrains the usable bandwidth and increases perceivable latency.

Software developers can use a number of key features of the Intel XScale microarchitecture to optimize software for memory subsystems:

■ *Page table attributes*—The system's memory space is divided into small units called *pages*. The operating system maintains attributes for each page. You can use these attributes to describe the way that the core and caches handle any data from that memory page. Setting these attributes correctly is the key to getting the desired system behavior.

■ *Multiple outstanding loads*—During a miss, relevant data is loaded to the core register and also to the data caches. Data load operations generate memory read transactions. The Intel XScale microarchitecture allows nonblocking loads. As a result, the Intel XScale microarchitecture has the capability to issue multiple memory read requests and to maintain those requests as outstanding or pending at any given time. The Intel XScale microarchitecture can sustain four such cache-line loads.

■ *Hit under miss*—If a data cache miss occurs, subsequent access to the caches is allowed while the missed data is being fetched from the memory. Called *hit under miss,* this access allows the processor to continue processing until the data for the miss is needed. Your code can access caches and continue computation even if a load is outstanding.

■ *Data preloading*—Every data miss can stall the core, potentially leading to inefficient usage of the system. Preloading is a hint to the memory subsystem to read in a particular cache line and store that data in the data cache. Preloading data ahead of its use allows you to reduce stalls due memory access latency during a miss.

■ *Write coalescing*—The Intel XScale microarchitecture allows *write buffer coalescing,* which combines as many as four words when the stores go to the same line of the cache line. The Intel XScale microarchitecture can buffer eight such cache-line data combinations.

So, how do you make the best use of these key features while writing code? Read on.

Configuring Memory with the Correct Properties

Virtual memory is used to manage the development complexity of large software systems and allow portability of applications. In a virtual memory system, the addresses used and generated by an application are translated to physical addresses. The virtual addresses are divided into a set of pages, and those pages are organized with sizes of 1 kilobyte or 4 kilobytes. Large page sizes are called *sections*, which are 4 megabytes in size. Each page has a property that defines cache behavior and how a memory access to that particular page is handled while loading from or storing to the memory. The loading and storing property refers to the way that a cache line is allocated in the cache and updated in the memory.

Properties of the pages are a part of the page translation entry, which has three attribute bits: the cacheability bit (C), the bufferable bit (B) and extension bit (X). The cacheability bit indicates whether or not the data that is being loaded from the memory can be placed in the cache. The bufferable bit indicates that multiple loads or stores to this page of the memory can be issued consecutively without waiting on the previous one to finish. The extension bit offers further levels of granularity in terms of controlling read and write policies. Table 9.1 summarizes the implications of these attribute bits.

Table 9.1   Page Table Policies Based on the Attribute Bit Setting

X bit	C bit	B bit	Cacheable	Bufferable	Write Policy	Line Allocation Policy	Notes
0	0	0	N	N	-	-	Stall until complete
	0	1	N	Y	-	-	
	1	0	Y	Y	Write-through	Read Allocate	
	1	1	Y	Y	Write-back	Read Allocate	
1	0	0	—	—	—	—	Not to be used
	0	1	N	Y	—	—	Writes do not coalesce into buffers
	1	0	(Mini-data cache)	—	—	—	
	1	1	Y	Y	Write-back	Read/Write Allocate	

As an application or system developer, you need to use these attributes to configure the pages appropriately.

Optimizing Instruction Accesses

Instructions for an application are read from the memory during the execution. When the processor encounters an instruction cache miss, the processor examines only one of the attribute bits, namely the C bit. If the C bit is clear, the instruction cache treats a code fetch from that memory as non-cacheable and does not fill a cache with that entry. If the C bit is set, fetches from the associated memory region are cached. Typically, a processor executes instructions in a sequence. Media applications usually are composed of a set of algorithmic loops. Thus, loading an instruction cache line despite a cache miss offers an application the ability to reuse the loaded data. For this reason, you should always keep the instruction pages cacheable for maximum performance.

Optimizing Data Accesses

Multimedia applications operate on a set of data buffers for input, output, and intermediate results. These applications read data from a file system, from an input device such as a microphone or camera, or from the wireless receiver. After processing the input data, these applications produce output to the speaker, display, or the wireless transmitter. From the application's perspective, not all the data buffers are used in the same manner, so assigning different page-table characteristics to different buffer types could make performance better. When selecting the page attributes for data objects, consider the following questions:

- How could you optimize the read operations or get data into the caches optimally?
- How could you optimize the write operation or get data to the memories?

Getting Data from the Memory Efficiently

Allocation policy for a memory region determines when a cacheline is loaded from the memory to the cache. Page allocation policy can be set to be read-allocated or read/write-allocate in systems based on Intel XScale microarchitecture. For pages with read-allocate policy, cache lines are loaded from the memory when the processor encounters a read-miss. On the other hand, for pages in read/write-allocate mode, cache lines are loaded when a write or read access misses. Once a cache line is loaded using write-allocation policy, subsequent accesses see cache hits.

However, the downside is that potentially every write can cause a memory load, which could deteriorate the performance for memory intensive algorithms. Some intermediate buffers for algorithms where a write followed by a read is likely to take place can benefit from the write-allocate setting. One such example is intermediate buffer in-place computation for DSP algorithms. Apart from such special cases, the data sections should be kept as read-allocate only.

Saving Data to the Memory Efficiently

To allow for faster access by the processor, caches contain a copy of the data from the main memory. Sooner or later, any data written to the caches needs to update its copy in the main memory. The write policy determines the manner in which the main memory—whether it is internal SRAM or external SDRAM—is updated from the caches. You can configure memory regions with two different write policies:

■ *Write-back mode* only updates main memory with the cache-line content when a cache line is evicted. Write-back mode avoids some memory transactions by allowing data to collect in the data cache before being written to memory when the cache line is evicted. When cache lines are evicted, the writes coalesce and are written to memory efficiently.

■ *Write-through mode* updates the main memory whenever data is written to the cache line. Memory regions configured in write-through mode usually generate more data traffic on the bus and consume more power due to increased bus activity. If a system with Intel Wireless MMX technology has multiple masters, such as an Intel XScale core and an external communication processor, the application might have to maintain coherency on the shared data across multiple masters. In such a situation, all shared memory regions should use a write-through policy.

Thus, write-back is the recommended policy when considering performance and power.

Interacting with the Peripheral Devices

Input, output, and control registers of peripheral devices in a handheld system on chip are memory-mapped, meaning the processor can access them like memories. Software using any of these devices must track the state of the device. By keeping the device registers in a cacheable space, the application would see cache hits for subsequent reads from the device register and would read stale data from the cache. For these devices, the relevant device registers and memory spaces should be mapped as non-cacheable memory, setting the bits as X=0, C=0, and B=0. However, if a device has an input or output buffer, one would like to keep the bufferable bit set. The B=1 setting can offer two potential advantages:

■ Multiple loads from the buffer are issued as a series of outstanding loads, effectively increasing the throughput for the load buffer.

■ Similarly, multiple writes to a non-cacheable region with B=1 can coalesce into one write, improving the store efficiency or throughput for that region. However, this technique cannot be applied to any device where consecutive writes to the same address could be overwritten in the write buffer before reaching the target device, as in FIFOs, or to devices where read/write order needs to be strictly maintained.

Streamlining Updates of Display Buffers

A typical handheld product uses an LCD display to output information in a graphical fashion. The LCD controller displays content of a memory space onto the screen following a specified color format. This memory location is called the *frame buffer* or display buffer. Different applications write data in the frame buffer. A typical multimedia application updates the frame buffer 30 or more times per second, even up to 60 times per second for gaming applications. A VGA-sized display (640×480 pixels) could require 20–30 megabytes for data updates by the core every second.

For most products, the LCD frame buffer should be allocated in a non-cacheable region so that the updates from the application immediately update the display. The pages in the frame-buffer region should be set to non-cached but bufferable mode, with the bits set as X=0, C=0, and B=1. Bufferability improves write performance by allowing consecutive writes to coalesce in the write buffer. To achieve more efficient bus transactions in this way, you should set the LCD frame buffer as non-cached but bufferable.

Ensuring Correct Data Objects Placement

Compared to external RAM memories, on-chip integrated memory has lower latency, higher throughput, and better frequency scaling. You must ensure that this high performance memory is used most effectively. With the virtual-to-physical translation table, data objects from any application can be mapped to the internal memory. This translation can be controlled statically by the system engineer or dynamically by the operating system. This section provides a set of approaches for using the internal memory effectively.

An application's data footprint is defined by the data space that it uses. By analyzing the usage characteristics of the data footprint, you can decide which data objects should be put in the internal memory. Any data object that requires higher throughput and lower latency can be placed in the internal memory. All data objects not placed in the internal memory are placed in the external memory.

Optimal Placing of Video Display Buffer

The LCD can be a significant bandwidth consumer in the system, depending on the LCD display size and refresh rate. You may choose to place the LCD frame buffer in the internal memory. The LCD can be configured with multiple display planes, such as a base plane with video and graphics overlays. With multiple overlays, all the frame buffers might not fit into the internal memory. The rule of thumb for such cases is to keep the most commonly accessed memory spaces in the internal memory. For instance, during a video capture the processor core accesses the video overlay more frequently than the base plane, since the base plane does not change too often. Thus, keeping the overlays in the internal memory improves performance.

Using Internal SRAM for Storing Streaming Data Objects

Video conferencing is one of the many multimedia applications that demonstrate data streaming behavior because data is consumed and produced in a regular fashion. These streaming applications maintain a nice system-wide data flow. Streaming data objects are the intermediate data buffers between different agents. Figure 9.2 demonstrates the intermediate buffers to be managed at a high level in the case of video conferencing.

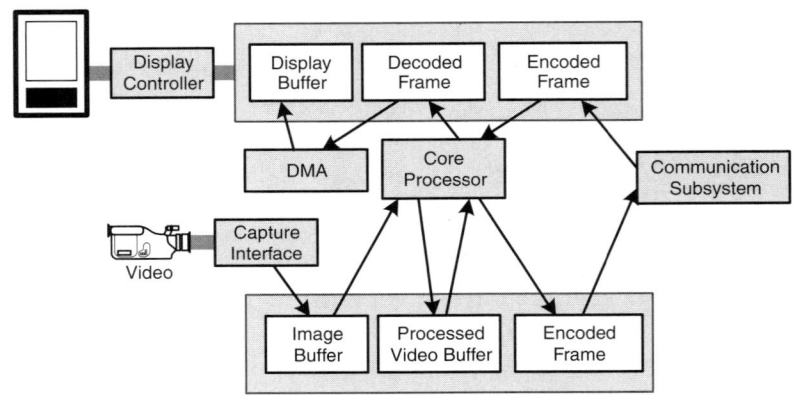

Figure 9.2 Shared Buffers between Different Hardware and Software Components

Notice how different processing components share the streaming data objects. The critical streaming data objects for this case are the image buffer and the video encode and decode buffers. Shared buffers that are accessed most commonly should be placed in the internal memory. The developer can also use the DMA in the system to transfer data from different sources effectively to the internal memory periodically, so the core is operating as much as possible out of the internal memory. This method does require a fair amount of data and flow analysis, an activity that we'll leave as an exercise for the reader.

How to Use the Internal Memory for Speeding Up the OS

Operating systems and general applications can benefit from internal SRAM in two ways:

■ *Critical code and library storage*—Much of the code related to the operating system is used in a periodic fashion, in the form of device drivers and OS daemon processes. Not meeting the real-time constraints of these functions impacts the performance of a system. For some peripheral devices, interrupt service latency is the key to avoiding buffer overflow or underrun. Storing the code for these routines in the internal memory reduces the instruction-cache miss penalties for the periodic routines. Similarly, internal memory can be used for storing instructions or libraries for relevant applications—for example, libraries for Java Virtual Machine

(JVM). Another example is telephony software, where a packet must be processed within a hard deadline or in a deterministic manner every time. Caches often introduce some timing non-determinism, since what will hit and what will miss in the cache often is not apparent. Putting critical code in the internal memory is an option to provide deterministic execution.

■ *Critical data storage*—For many applications such as graphics and gaming, the working set often could be larger than the data cache. Due to the random access nature of the application, effective preload could be difficult to perform. Thus, you might use some part of the internal RAM for storing these critical data structures. Similarly, data segments critical to the operating system, such as context or state of an application, can be saved in the internal memory.

Reducing the Impact of Data Cache Misses

As described in Chapter 5, memory latency during a cache miss can directly impact the cycles per instruction (CPI) or the performance of an application. Therefore application code should be optimized to reduce its dependence on the memory latency, if not to become insensitive to it. Two Intel XScale microarchitecture features can be used for this purpose: the "hit under miss" and the prefetching capability. The actual time for a read transaction to go through the processor and memory subsystem until it reads the first cache line does not change. However, much of this time can be made up in one of two ways:

■ Loading data early

■ Preloading data into the cache

Loading Data Early

Typically, data in an application is loaded to a register, then it is operated on. Consider the following example:

```
waddhus   wR6,  wR7,wR6
waddhus   wR8,  wR7,wR6
wldrw     wR0,  [r1]
waddhus   wR2,  wR0,  wR2
waddhus   wR4,  wR5,  wR6
```

In this code segment, data loaded from the memory by the load operation is immediately used by the add operation. If the load operation does not hit the cache, the add operation stalls until the memory transaction invoked by the WLDRW has completed. The difference in the program counter between the load instruction and use instruction is called the load-to-use-distance and represented as D. In this case, $D=1$ cycle. The processor stalls if $D<L$, where L is the effective memory latency. Effective memory latency is simply 3 if a cache is hit during the load. Otherwise, the effective memory latency can be tens of cycles. Scheduling the load instruction further ahead of the use instruction reduces the stall. If D can be made higher than L, data stalls can be avoided altogether.

Moving the load instruction ahead into the program flow is referred to as *load hoisting*. Modern compilers often perform load hoisting, assuming the load is hitting the cache—that is, $D=3$ cycles for WLDRW and $D=4$ cycles for WLDRD. This approach benefits from the hit-under-miss feature of the Intel XScale microarchitecture because hoisting a load beyond another load does not stop the loads from accessing the cache. For instance, by hoisting the WLDRW in the previous example, one could have a code sequence as follows:

```
wldrw      wR0, [r1]
wldrw      wR5, [r2]
waddhus    wR6, wR7, wR6
waddhus    wR8, wR7, wR6
waddhus    wR2, wR0, wR2
waddhus    wR4, wR5, wR6
```

In the modified code sequence, the first WLDRW can look up data from the cache while the second WLDRW is loading data into the wR5. The drawback to this approach is that it consumes a register from the register file space. However, the SIMD coprocessor has 16 registers, which makes it easy to employ this method.

Preloading Data into the Cache

Another method of hiding latency is prefetching the data into the cache. The Intel XScale microarchitecture has a prefetch instruction (PLD). The purpose of the PLD instruction is to preload data into the data cache without actually occupying any of the processor's registers with the loaded data. Data prefetching allows hiding of memory transfer latency while the processor continues to execute instructions. The prefetch is important to high-level languages and assembly code because appropriate use of the prefetch instruction can improve throughput performance of Intel XScale microarchitecture-based processors enormously.

The Intel XScale microarchitecture prefetch is ignored when its use causes a fault or a table-walk. In such cases, the processor takes no action on the prefetch instruction, the fault or table-walk, and it continues processing the next instruction. This response is particularly advantageous in the case where a linked list or recursive data structure is terminated by a NULL pointer. Prefetching the NULL pointer does not fault or halt the program flow.

The Intel XScale microarchitecture PLD instruction encoding translates to a "never execute" opcode in the ARM† V4 ISA. This translation creates compatibility between code using PLD on application processors with Intel XScale microarchitecture and equivalent code on older devices. Code running on both architectures can include the PLD instruction, thus gaining performance on the Intel XScale microarchitecture, while maintaining compatibility for ARM V4, for example, systems with Intel® StrongARM† technology.

Although preload (PLD) is an assembly instruction, it also has been abstracted into C-callable form, `prefetch()`, by numerous tools and operating systems. Programmers who are familiar with data usage characteristics of different data structures can incorporate the `prefetch()` form into the code to take better advantage of this feature.

However, similar to load hoisting, preloads or prefetching must be scheduled ahead of time. The following are typical preloading concerns:

- Maintaining prefetch distance
- Managing prefetching in a loop
- Calculating prefetch address

Prefetch Distances in the Intel XScale® Microarchitecture

The preload distance is optimal if the preload distance is equal to the memory latency. Depending on whether the target is in the internal memory or in the external memory, you might need to vary the prefetch distance.

Consider the following code sample:

```
    add  r1, r1, #1
@ Sequence of instructions that use r2.
@ These instructions leave r3 unchanged.
    ldr  r2, [r3]
    add  r3, r3, #4
    mov  r4, r3
    sub  r2, r2, #1
```

The `sub` instruction in the last line would cause a stall if the data to be loaded missed the cache. These stalls can be avoided by using a PLD instruction well ahead, as shown in the first line of the following code.

```
    pld  [r3]
    add  r1, r1, #1
@ These instructions leave r3 unchanged.
    ldr  r2, [r3]
    add  r3, r3, #4
    mov  r4, r3
    sub  r2, r2, #1
```

In the previous two examples, the load-to-use distance was 3 ($D=3$). Upon a miss in the first example, the `sub` instruction would stall for $L-3$ cycles, whereas in the latter example the number of stalls would be $L-5$ cycles, or less if the preload had been scheduled even earlier. Here L represents memory latency. Similar to load hoisting, a preload with a larger distance makes the result better. The value of the distance should be the same as the value of the memory latency. Typically, data resides in external memory, so in most cases, you need only optimize for external memory latency, since external memory latency is higher than internal memory latency. Another benefit of pre-fetching over load hoisting is that it avoids register pressure, or running low on the number of available registers.

Preloading in a Loop

Generally, multimedia applications contain a number of tight loops performing data intensive operations on one or two dimensional array structures. The regularity of the data structure makes it easy to perform prefetch operations, since the preload addresses of the data are easy to compute. When adding prefetch to these loops, you can measure the prefetch distance as the number of loop iterations. Prefetching can be performed ahead by one, two, or more iterations.

    Determining Prefetch Distance in a Loop. While scheduling `prefetch()` in a loop, the optimal distance of prefetching is the prefetch distance (PD), where PD can be shown as :

```
PD >= Memory_Latency/Number of cycles per iteration
```

While processing an image, the application can apply preloads to data from the next block or the next row. For example, if a loop takes 20 cycles to complete, assuming no data misses, and if the memory latency is 40, then scheduling a `prefetch()` hint two iterations ahead would hide the memory latency.

Balancing Prefetch Rate in a Loop. Apart from the preload distance, you should also consider the data consumption per loop. To maintain ideal throughput without stalls from memory, each iteration should prefetch the same amount of data it consumes. For example, if a loop consumes two cache lines of data, the code should preload two cache lines using two PLDs to attain effective latency hiding. However, the challenge often comes with the cases where the prefetching rate is lower than a cache line. In those cases, a new cache line is not needed for more than one
iteration. Consider the following example:

```
for(i=0; i<NMAX; i++) {
   prefetch(data[i+2]);
   sum += data[i];
}
```

Iterations `i-1` and `i` could attempt to prefetch the same cache line of data, which is inefficient. You can avoid the problem by unrolling the loop, as follows.

```
for(i=0; i<NMAX-8; i=i+8) {
   prefetch(data[i+8]);
   sum += data[i];
   sum += data[i+1];
   sum += data[i+2];
   sum += data[i+3];
   sum += data[i+4];
   sum += data[i+5];
   sum += data[i+6];
   sum += data[i+7];
}
```

Another thing to watch out for is excessive data loads in the last iteration of the data preload. Since those data loads lie outside of the usable range, the last few iterations might be performed outside the critical loop. The above code example can be modified the following way:

```
for(i=0; i<NMAX-8-1; i=i+8) {
   prefetch(data[i+8]);
   sum += data[i];
```

```
      sum += data[i+1];
      sum += data[i+2];
      sum += data[i+3];
      sum += data[i+4];
      sum += data[i+5];
      sum += data[i+6];
      sum += data[i+7];
   }
   sum += data[NMAX-9];
   sum += data[NMAX-9+1];
   sum += data[NMAX-9+2];
   sum += data[NMAX-9+3];
   sum += data[NMAX-9+4];
   sum += data[NMAX-9+5];
   sum += data[NMAX-9+6];
   sum += data[NMAX-9+7];
```

Optimizing Data Location and Sizing for Prefetch. Aligning data on a cache-line boundary is always beneficial. Cache-line alignment is conducive to prefetching data. Consider the following data structure example:

```
struct {
   unsigned int ia;
   unsigned int ib;
   unsigned int ic;
   unsigned int id;
} tdata[IMAX];

for (i=0, i<IMAX; i++) {
   prefetch(tdata[i+1]);
   tdata[i].ia = tdata[i].ib + tdata[i].ic +
                 tdata[i].id;
   ....
   tdata[i].id = 0;
}
```

Note that the size of array tdata is 16 bytes. If tdata[i] is not aligned to any of first four words of a cache line, the prefetch using the address of tdata[i+1].ia will not include element id and a separate prefetch would have to be placed on &tdata[i+1].id. Thus, data structures should be aligned such that preloading gets the maximum benefit.

If the structure is not sized to a multiple of the cache line size, the prefetch address must be advanced appropriately and doing so requires extra prefetch instructions, as shown in the following example:

```
struct {
   unsigned int ia;
   unsigned int ib;
   unsigned int ic;
   unsigned int id;
   unsigned int ie;
} tdata[IMAX];

ADDRESS predata = tdata;

for (i=0, i<IMAX; i++) {
   prefetch(predata+=16);
   tdata[i].ia = tdata[i].ib + tdata[i].ic +
                 tdata[i].id + tdata[i].ie;
   ....
   tdata[i].ie = 0;
}
```

In this case, the prefetch address is advanced by the size of half a cache line and every other prefetch instruction is turned into a no-op. Thus, try to use data structures which fits within one or integer multiple of a cacheline and align the data structure on a cacheline boundary to get the most out of your preloading scheme.

Calculation of Prefetch Address. Calculating the address to prefetch is overhead that you should keep to a minimum. You should structure the code so that from one interaction to the next the prefetch address can be computed by using load-offset. For a vector operation, the address computation becomes an addition with an offset. Thus, when the application is prefetching 2D data structures, preloading along the line of the row is relatively easy.

Prefetching in a Linked List

Not all looping constructs are as straightforward as prefetching a 2D structure. However, you can still apply prefetching techniques like the linked list traversal in the following example.

```
while(p) {
   do_something(p->data);
   p = p->next;
}
```

The pointer variable p becomes a pseudo induction variable and the data pointed to by p->next can be prefetched to reduce data transfer latency for the next iteration of the loop. Linked lists should be converted to arrays as often as possible.

```
while(p) {
    prefetch(p->next);
    do_something(p->data);
    p = p->next;
}
```

Knowing the Limitations

Adding prefetch to a loop is not always advantageous. The following loop characteristics limit the use and value of prefetch:

- *Throughput bound versus latency bound*—If a loop is bounded by the memory throughput, the loop cannot benefit from increasing the prefetch distance. Typically, with an optimal prefetching scheme, the application can hide memory latency completely, and the loop processing performance becomes bounded by the throughput.

- *Low number of iterations*—Loops with a low number of iterations might not offer much prefetching opportunity, since the prefetch distance is constrained by the maximum number of iterations.

- *Bandwidth consumption and cache pollution*—Prefetches consume load buffer from the regular loads. Thus, overusing the prefetches does not produce any benefit. For example, more than four PLDs in a row cause a stall until the first preload is done. Moreover, each prefetch loads a different cache line, potentially evicting one cache line and leading to cache pollution.

Increasing Memory Throughput

To summarize, memory latency can be hidden using the techniques of preloading. The previously mentioned approaches help to decouple the memory latency from the application's performance. If dependency on memory latency can be hidden completely, performance of the application depends on the memory throughput. You can use the Intel XScale microarchitecture's load store buffering features to ensure that an application gets the most throughput from the memory subsystem, as explained in the sidebar "Load Buffer Behavior in the Intel XScale® Microarchitecture: Read Buffer." Load pipelining provides a way to handle multiple loads in a nonblocking fashion and store buffering makes the stores efficient.

Load Buffer Behavior in the Intel XScale® Microarchitecture: Read Buffer

The Intel XScale microarchitecture has four fill buffers and four pending buffers that allow four outstanding loads to the cache from external memory. Four outstanding loads increase the memory throughput and bus efficiency. Page-table attributes affect the load behavior. For a section with attribute bits set to C=0 and B=0, only one load is outstanding from the memory. Thus, the load performance for a memory page with settings of C=0 and B=1 is significantly better than a memory page with C=0 and B=0. Figure 9.3 illustrates the difference between a single outstanding load and multiple outstanding loads.

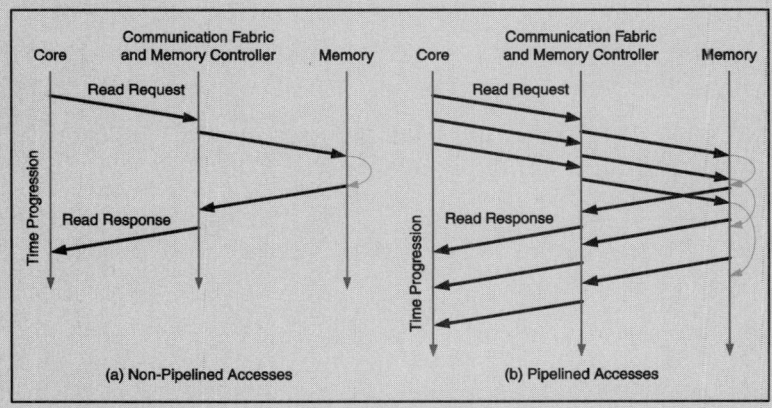

Figure 9.3　Amortizing Overhead Using Load Pipelining

Utilizing the Nonblocking Multiple Loads

Effective use of the outstanding loads can ensure higher efficiency of the memory load throughput. Multiple loads benefit by the concurrency between different components in the system. For instance, while one load is being serviced by the external memory, the communication fabric can be processing a subsequent load and the core can be processing yet another load. This simultaneous activity is also called *load pipelining*.

Data-demanding applications often contain a series of load instructions, such as `ldr` and `wldr`. Typically, these load instructions are followed by instructions that use the loaded data. Such load-to-use dependencies do not take advantage of the multiple load feature and the instructions only issue one outstanding load at a time. You can use a technique called *register rotation* to allow multiple outstanding loads. The following code sample allows one outstanding load at a time due to the data dependency between the load and add instructions. Throughput falls drastically in cases where a cache miss occurs.

```
Loop:
wldrw    wR1, [r0], #32
@ r0 be a pointer to some initialized memory
waddwus wR2, wR2, wR1
wldrw    wR1, [r0], #32
waddwus wR2, wR2, wR1
wldrw    wR1, [r0], #32
waddwus wR2, wR2, wR1
  .
  .
  .
bne Loop
```

However, the following example uses multiple registers as the target for loads and allows multiple outstanding loads.

```
wldrw wR1, [r0], #32
@ r0 be a pointer to some initialized memory
wldrw wR2, [r0], #32
wldrw wR3, [r0], #32
wldrw wR4, [r0], #32

Loop :
waddwus wR5, wR5, wR1
wldrw    wR1, [r0], #32
waddwus wR5, wR5, wR3
wldrw    wR2, [r0], #32
waddwus wR5, wR5, r3
wldrw    wR3, [r0], #32
waddwus wR5, wR5, r4
wldrw    wR4, [r0], #32
  .
  .
  .
bne Loop
```

The modified code increases the throughput by allowing multiple loads to be outstanding at a time. Typically, the register rotation algorithm implementation consumes more registers. With Intel Wireless MMX technology you have 16 additional registers, and they all can be used for load pipelining. When using load pipelining, keep in mind that the Intel XScale microarchitecture allows four single-word or two double-word loads to be outstanding.

Store Buffer Behavior in the Intel XScale® Microarchitecture: Write Buffer

Through the use of write coalescing, the Intel XScale microarchitecture has enhanced write performance or write throughput. Coalescing is performed by combining a new store operation with an existing store operation that is already resident in the write buffer. The new store is placed in the same write buffer entry as an existing store when the address of a new store falls in the 4-word aligned address of the existing entry.

The core can coalesce any of the four entries in the write buffer. The Intel XScale microarchitecture has a global coalesce-disable bit located in the Control Register (CP15, register 1). Figure 9.4 shows how coalescing transforms multiple memory transactions into a single one.

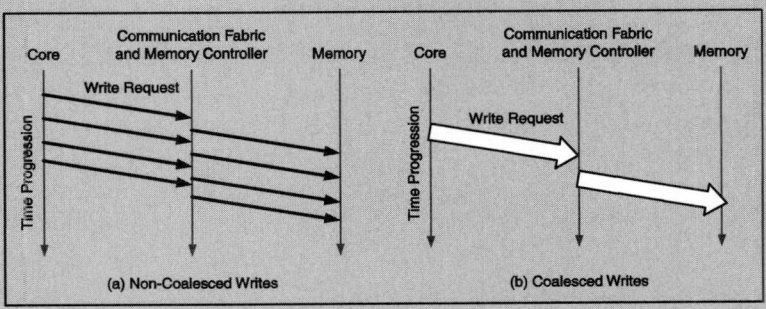

Figure 9.4 Write Buffer Behavior

Utilizing Write Combining

Increasing store throughput is important in applications that generate large amounts of data, as do video processing applications. Video decoding or gaming applications update the display buffer 30 to 60 frames a second, giving rise to large data store requirements. In processors incorporating Intel Wireless MMX technology, write coalescing—which is set by the page table attributes—combines multiple stores going to the same half of the cache line into a single memory transaction. This approach increases the bus efficiency and throughput. The coalescing operation is transparent to software. However, software can cause more frequent coalescing by placing stores that are going to the same cache line next to each other and configuring the target page attributes as bufferable. For example, the following code does not take advantage of coalescing:

```
waddwus wr1, wr1, wr2
wstrw   wr1,[r0],#4
        @ A separate bus transaction
waddwus wr1, wr1, wr3
wstrw   wr1,[r0],#4
        @ A separate bus transaction
waddwus wr1, wr1, wr4
wstrw   wr1,[r0],#4
        @ A separate bus transaction
waddwus wr1, wr1, wr5
wstrw   wr1,[r0],#4
        @ A separate bus transaction
```

However, the code can be modified to allow coalescing to occur, as follows:

```
waddwus wr1, wr1,wr2
waddwus wr6, wr1,wr3
waddwus wr7, wr6,wr4
waddwus wr8, wr7,wr5
wstrw   wr1,[r0],#4
wstrw   wr6,[r0],#4
wstrw   wr7,[r0],#4
wstrw   wr8,[r0],#4
@ 4 writes coalesce into 1 bus transaction.
```

Programming Techniques for Memory and Cache Efficiency

You can adopt a set of additional programming techniques to improve cache and memory efficiency. This section offers some generic techniques that focus on increasing cache efficiency.

Choosing Data Types and Alignment

Many applications inherently use data sizes that are smaller than a word. Packing a set of them into a single word is beneficial for memory accesses and memory bandwidth. Packed data formats can be processed using Intel Wireless MMX technology without unpacking. Due to architectural constraints, any data load to the coprocessor registers should be aligned on an eight-byte boundary. When declaring a variable in the application code, desired alignment for the variable can be indicated to the compiler.

To maximize cache line use and minimize cache pollution, you should align data structures on 32-byte boundaries or on a cache-line boundary and size the structures to a multiple of the cache-line size. Aligning data structures on cache address boundaries simplifies the addition of prefetch instructions to optimize performance.

Increasing Cache Locality

Caches contain recently accessed data. Efficiency of the caches depends on the access pattern in the application or algorithm, which is referred to as the *locality of accesses*. This access pattern has two aspects:

- *Spatial locality* refers to how close the addresses of successive data accesses are to each other.

- *Temporal locality* refers to how soon data from the same cache line is accessed since its previous access.

Organizing any algorithm to increase the spatial or temporal locality can improve cache utilization.

Increasing Spatial locality

The Intel XScale microarchitecture data cache has 32 sets of 1,024 bytes. Choosing a data structure size so that it fits within one of the sets increases spatial locality. The cost of a cache-line load can be amortized by using all the data from the cache line. Thus, restructuring algorithms to localize the accesses of the subsequent data can increase cache efficiency. Array merging is a classic example of this technique, as shown in this example:

```
int a[NMAX];
int b[NMAX];
int ix;

for (i=0; i<NMAX]; i++) {
```

```
        ix = b[i];
        if (a[i] != 0)
            ix = a[i];
        do_other calculations;
}
```

In this code, data is read from both arrays a and b, but a and b are not spatially close. They are at least NMAX*4 bytes apart. Array merging can place a and b spatially close, as shown in the following example:

```
struct {
    int a;
    int b;
} c_arrays;

int ix;

for (i=0; i<NMAX; i++) {
    ix = c[i].b;
    if (c[i].a != 0)
            ix = c[i].a;
    do_other_calculations;
}
```

As an example of rearranging often written to sections in a structure, consider the code sample:

```
struct employee {
    struct employee *prev;
    struct employee *next;
    float   Year2DatePay;
    float   Year2DateTax;
    int     ssno;
    int     empid;
    float   Year2Date401KDed;
    float   Year2DateOtherDed;
};
```

In the data structure shown above, the Year2DatePay, Year2DateTax, Year2Date401KDed, and Year2DateOtherDed fields are likely to change with each paycheck. However, the remaining fields rarely change. If the fields are laid out as shown in the previous example, assuming that the structure is aligned on a 32-byte boundary, modifications to the Year2Date... fields are likely to use two write buffers when the data is written out to memory. However, you can restrict the number of write buffers that are commonly used to one by rearranging the fields in the data structure as shown in the following example:

```
struct employee {
    struct employee *prev;
    struct employee *next;
    int     ssno;
    int     empid;
    float   Year2DatePay;
    float   Year2DateTax;
    float   Year2Date401KDed;
    float   Year2DateOtherDed;
};
```

Thus, organize the data elements in a structure such that you can take advantage of the write buffering and spatial locality.

Increasing Temporal Locality

Temporal locality is a measure of how soon a data element is reused once it is loaded into the cache. You can apply C coding techniques to increase temporal locality of data access. While operating on a large data vector or array in a loop, data can be divided into smaller chunks so that data loaded into the cache in the first iteration can be reused during subsequent iterations. This technique is known as *cache blocking*.

As an example of cache blocking, consider the following code:

```
for(i=0; i<10000; i++)
    for(j=0; j<10000; j++)
        for(k=0; k<10000; k++)
            C[j][k] += A[i][k] * B[j][i];
```

The variable `A[i][k]` is completely reused. However, accessing `C[j][k]` in the j and k loops can displace `A[i][j]` from the cache. Using cache blocking, the code becomes:

```
for(i=0; i<10000; i++)
    for(j1=0; j<100; j++)
        for(k1=0; k<100; k++)
            for(j2=0; j<100; j++)
                for(k2=0; k<100; k++) {
                    j = j1 * 100 + j2;
                    k = k1 * 100 + k2;
                    C[j][k] += A[i][k] * B[j][i];
                }
```

The cache-blocking technique can be applied to many video and multimedia applications. Tile-based graphics algorithms are similar in concept. An additional advantage of cache blocking is that it encourages scheduling of preloads since the preload address calculation would be simpler.

Intelligent Addressing for Reducing Cache Eviction

To minimize cache thrashing and increase cache utilization, data is best accessed in a spatially contiguous address range. However, arrays of data might have been laid out so that indexed elements are not physically next to each other. Consider the following C code, which places array elements in row major order.

```
for(j=0; j<NMAX; j++)
    for(i=0; i<NMAX; i++) {
        prefetch(A[i+1][j]);
        sum += A[i][j];
    }
```

In this example, A[i][j] and A[i+1][j] are not in the memory sequentially. This situation causes inefficiency in bus traffic when prefetching loop data, since only a part of the cacheline may be used. In addition, data misses can occur while processing large blocks of data. While processing A[i][j+1], the cacheline loaded in iteration A[i][j] may be evicted by the cachelines for A[i+X][j]. In some cases where the loop's mathematics are unaffected, you can resolve the problem by induction variable interchange. As a result, the preceding example becomes:

```
for(i=0; i<NMAX; i++)
    for(j=0; j<NMAX>>3; j=j+8) {
        prefetch(A[i][j+8]);
        sum += A[i][j];
        sum += A[i][j+1];
        sum += A[i][j+2];
        sum += A[i][j+3];
        sum += A[i][j+4];
        sum += A[i][j+5];
        sum += A[i][j+6];
        sum += A[i][j+7];
    }
```

Notice that a bit of loop unrolling has been used in the example to further optimize the prefetches.

Increasing Data Reuse

Many signal-processing and media-processing applications operate on data in stages, where each stage can be a tight kernel loop. If an application is composed of a series of such loops, you can apply *loop fusion*, a process of combining multiple loops that reuse the same data into a single loop. The advantage of loop fusion is that the reused data is immediately accessible from the data cache. Consider the following example:

```
for(i=0; i<NMAX; i++) {
    prefetch(A[i+1], c[i+1], c[i+1]);
    A[i] = b[i] + c[i];
}
for(i=0; i<NMAX; i++) {
    prefetch(D[i+1], c[i+1], A[i+1]);
    D[i] = A[i] + c[i];
}
```

The second loop reuses the data elements A[i] and c[i]. Fusing the loops together produces:

```
for(i=0; i<NMAX; i++) {
    prefetch(D[i+1], A[i+1], c[i+1], b[i+1]);
    ai = b[i] + c[i];
    A[i] = ai;
    D[i] = ai + c[i];
}
```

In some instances, loop fusion actually can cause performance degradation. In general, loop fusion should be used only when the data to be operated on in each loop is the same and when all of the contents within the fused loop can fit entirely in the instruction cache. Another generalized form of loop fusion is algorithm fusion, which can be used for many applications such as accelerating graphics applications, where a set of pixel-level operations can be performed all in the same loop although logically they are different algorithmic operations.

Key Points

This chapter demonstrated how an application can be optimized for the memory subsystem of Intel XScale core, especially with different memory characteristics in mind. You can use various features of the Intel XScale microarchitecture to attain efficient memory utilization. The key points to remember:

- Set up the attributes correctly for your memory subsystem.

- Keep your frame buffer in a non-cacheable but bufferable space to get write efficiency.

- Carefully partition your use case to decide how to map internal SRAM.

- Use preloading to hide memory latency. Adapt preloading for the data structure: a block, linked list, and the like.

- Use an appropriate preload distance in a loop and maintain a balanced preload rate.

- Use multiple outstanding loads to get the maximum read throughput.

- Use array merging or loop fusion to increase the spatial locality of the caches.

- Use cache blocking and intelligent data addressing to increase temporal locality of the caches.

Chapter 10

Optimizing for
Pipelines

More computing sins are committed in the name of efficiency (without necessarily achieving it) than any other reason.

— William A. Wulf

Optimization of a code segment can contribute greatly to its performance. An optimized application makes best use of all the available microarchitectural features. In a pipelined processor, the key to optimization is to keep all the stages of the pipelines and functional units occupied with meaningful tasks. The instruction set and the pipeline architecture of the Intel XScale® microarchitecture and Intel® Wireless MMX™ technology are described in Chapter 4. This chapter explains the implications of the pipelined structure in terms of performance and offers best-known ways to utilize all the available resources. The chapter focuses on low-level instruction sequences to demonstrate different optimization techniques. Most techniques described herein are generic to all processors, but some are specific to the Intel XScale microarchitecture and Intel Wireless MMX technology.

Microarchitectural Optimization Philosophy

The optimization process is a hierarchical one that needs to be addressed at different levels during the application development cycle. During algorithm selection, high-level code development, and kernel development, an optimization effort is necessary. The focus here is simply on the optimizations useful for developing assembly routines or kernel-level coding.

Two sets of instructions are used. Intel XScale microarchitecture implements ARM[†] V5TE-compliant instructions, and Intel Wireless MMX technology implements an instruction set specifically designed to accelerate multimedia applications. The implementation uses two concurrent pipelines to handle the respective instruction set architecture (ISA). You have two aspects of the optimization to consider with regard to the pipeline and ISA:

■ Choosing the right instruction

■ Choosing the right sequence of instructions

Choosing the Right Instruction

The combined instruction sets of the Intel XScale microarchitecture and Intel Wireless MMX technology have a large variety of instructions from which the programmer can choose those most appropriate for a given application. For example, 32-bit addition can be performed on the register file of Intel XScale core using an add instruction. An addition of this kind can also be performed on the coprocessor register file using a WADDW instruction. Choosing the correct instruction for the operation and partitioning the desired kernel between both the register files are the first challenges in optimizing for the pipeline. Intel Wireless MMX instructions are relatively orthogonal; that is, each instruction supports the same operations on different data types—byte, half-word, and word. Based on the algorithmic need of the kernel, selecting the correct data types offers you the most efficient use of the resources. For example, if the required accuracy for an algorithm is only 16-bit data, you can use a 16-bit data type and process four data samples concurrently using Intel Wireless MMX technology. However, when using 32-bit data, you meet the accuracy requirement, but you can enjoy only two-way concurrency.

Choosing the Right Sequence

Intel XScale microarchitecture with Intel Wireless MMX technology has two processing pipelines. Chapter 4 presented details of the pipeline organization and explained the concept of resource and data hazards. Resource and data-dependency hazards introduce inefficiencies into the system, since, for the duration of the stalls, the concurrency between the pipe stages is not utilized, thus hurting performance and power. You can employ different techniques for instruction scheduling to reduce such stalls. *Instruction scheduling* refers to the rearrangement of a sequence of instructions for the purpose of helping to minimize pipeline stalls.

When you are writing code in a high-level language, you cannot specifically control the selection of the right instruction or the selection of the right sequence of instructions. The compiler tool chain can handle some of these concerns. However, for performance-critical applications, critical and heavily used routines might need to be written or optimized by hand in assembly language or using intrinsic functions. The majority of this optimization effort is spent in stall reduction.

Stall-Directed Instruction Scheduling

The initial step in basic pipeline optimization is to understand the pipeline and delay characteristics of each instruction. Two parameters, defined in Chapter 4, characterize an instruction:

- *Resource, or issue, latency*—When a functional unit is processing an instruction, it can be busy for one or more cycles. Resource or issue latency for an instruction is the number of cycles that the functional unit will be busy before the next instruction using the same functional unit can be scheduled.

- *Result latency*—Result latency for an instruction is the number of cycles that the functional unit takes to produce the result. If two instructions are back to back and the later instruction uses the data produced by the earlier instruction, then the later instruction stalls for the period of result latency.

In Chapter 4, Figures 4.9 and 4.10 describe execution of trace for each instruction in terms of how they flow in the pipeline. Based on those figures, the resource and result latency for the instructions can be extracted. The only way to solve the stall and hazard problem is to avoid it. Stall avoidance is achieved by reordering instructions while maintaining the same functionality.

Looking for Stalls

Attempting to reschedule a complete application one kernel at a time can be very cumbersome, especially when you are working with code written in assembly language. Once a piece of code has been developed with functional correctness, the developer can optimize it piece by piece. Using existing knowledge of the application or a VTune™ analyzer profile, you can identify which critical piece of code has the greatest impact on the application. After applying the profiling and critical component analysis techniques explained in Chapter 6, you must measure the number of stalls in that piece of code to determine whether you should reschedule. To decouple the contribution of the memory subsystem stalls from the pipeline stalls, assume that all the data for the kernel is in the data cache. This operation can be done by making multiple function calls to the same kernel with the same data set during the test. Once you have measured stalls per instruction and determined that an optimization to reduce stalls is necessary, you need to evaluate rescheduling opportunities.

Begin by considering a window of instructions for reordering, then gradually slide the window down as you reorder the instructions, as shown in Figure 10.1. This method is typically known as the *sliding window* approach. You need to choose the peeping window size such that it fits a small loop or *Bbasic block* of code, which in our context is defined by a sequence of code that does not have any branches. For particular application classes, such basic blocks could be too small; for those cases, larger window sizes should be considered.

Avoiding Stalls

Using a sliding window approach, you can find opportunities for stall reduction. Depending on the complexity of the code, the window size can be limited to a single loop or a small kernel. Once a stall is detected within the observation window, one of the following techniques can be applied: moving instructions up or down, loop unrolling, loop-fusion, register renaming, footprint adjustment, and so on. After optimizing code in the current window, it slides into next set of instructions. Two windows should moderately overlap.

If a resource hazard between two instructions exists, you can do one of two things. Either the first instruction of the hazard can be *moved up* or the later instructions can be *moved down*, thus creating enough distance between the two instructions. You can apply the same technique to stalls due to data dependency. This approach is referred to as *simple translation,* since the instructions are simply moved up or down.

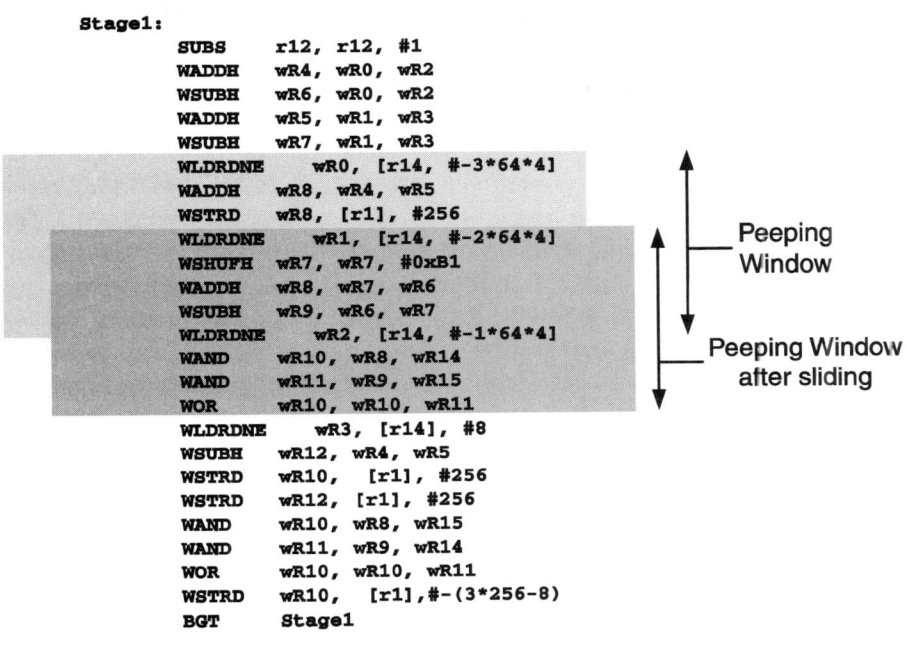

Figure 10.1   Sliding Window of Optimization

In a tight kernel loop, reordering might be limited to a single iteration of processing due to the lack of a sufficient number of instructions. *Unrolling the loop* allows more instructions within a basic block. In addition, two consecutive loops can be combined to obtain the same effect. Later in this chapter, you will find case studies in which this technique has been used quite extensively.

Register renaming is another approach to remove undue dependencies. By renaming registers, certain parts of a computation can be decoupled and performed independently; the result can be combined later. Care should be taken not to perform excessive register renaming, so that registers used in one window do not overwrite the register in the next window of optimization.

Reducing the register *footprint,* or using the least number of registers, is a good programming technique. Reducing register footprint can save the overhead of *hot save.* The term hot save refers to storing data to the stack and reading it back as a result of using a high number of registers. However, when the rescheduling opportunity is limited, increasing the register footprint can help. Especially during loop unrolling and loop fusion, using more registers could be necessary to compute data values concurrently for different iterations. Intel Wireless MMX technology has a large register file that can be effectively used in these cases. Keeping track of the registers and usage for each window under investigation is a good practice. Keeping track ensures that no register is overwritten unnecessarily, and that the optimization effort has not introduced any functional bugs.

Another commonly used technique to avoid stalls is to extract the concurrency between the pipelines—more specifically, to reduce resource hazards. This technique is known as *pipeline interleaving.* The technique allows the programmer to interleave instructions between both the pipes, providing greater opportunities for avoiding stalls. The next level of concurrency extraction is at the functional unit level, or intracore level. For example, when an Intel Wireless MMX multiply instruction is operating, another instruction can be processed concurrently in the ALU pipe. Similarly, reordering with concurrency in mind also helps avoid stalls due to resource hazards.

Decomposition of an Application

An application can be decomposed into a set of connected basic blocks, where the basic blocks are data processing tasks and the control operations that determine the flow between the basic blocks, as shown in Figure 10.2.

Thus, for the sake of simplicity, this discussion focuses on two categories:

- Optimization for control-oriented operations
- Optimization for data-processing operations

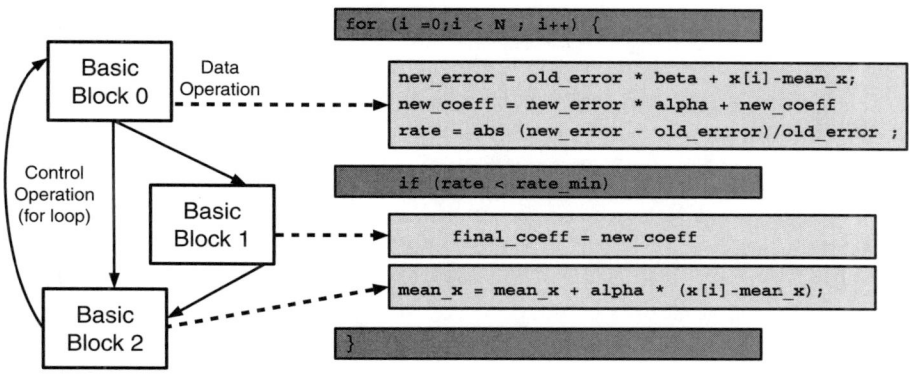

Figure 10.2   Decomposition of a Code Segment into Data Blocks and Control Constructs

Optimization for Data-Processing Operations

Data-processing operations are at the heart of any multimedia application. In Chapters 3, 4, and 5, details of the instructions and their potential applicability are discussed. The impact of the pipeline delay characteristics on the coding style is the focus of this section.

Fast Multiply Operations

The core has two sets of multiplication units, one in the Intel XScale microarchitecture and the other in the Intel Wireless MMX instructions. These two sets of multipliers support different levels of precision of data-processing capability. The Intel XScale microarchitecture supports half-word and word multiplication with results of word and double-word width. Selecting the correct precision for the algorithm under implementation helps reduce the execution time; for example, SMULxy has a latency of one cycle whereas SMULL has a latency of two cycles.

Multiply instructions can cause pipeline stalls due to resource conflicts or result latencies. The following code segment incurs a stall of zero to three cycles depending on the values in registers r1, r2, r4, and r5 due to resource conflicts:

```
mul    r0, r1, r2
mul    r3, r4, r5 @0-3 stalls
```

The second multiply operation would stall by three cycles if r1 and r2 did not have any trivial value and the S bit was set. Just as issue latency depends on the values of the operands, the result latency can vary between one and three cycles. In the following example, the mov instruction incurs the result penalty:

```
mul    r0, r1, r2
mov    r4, r0   @stall until previous mult
```

However, if an arithmetic operation follows the multiplication operation, it does not stall as long as no register dependency exists. Multiply instructions should be separated out from each other by the worst-case latency, especially if you have no *a priori* knowledge of the data value.

ARM[†] instructions can set conditional flags so that following instructions can execute conditionally based on the flags. A multiply instruction that sets the condition codes blocks the multiply and arithmetic pipeline. Blocking stalls any subsequent instructions. For instance, in the following example, the add instruction waits three to four cycles for the muls instruction to finish.

```
muls   r0, r1, r2 @mult that updates flags
add    r3, r3, #1 @stalls until the mul finish
sub    r4, r4, #1
sub    r5, r5, #1
```

Thus, it is not efficient to use the multiplication operation to update the flags. The modified code is as follows:

```
mul    r0, r1, r2
add    r3, r3, #1
sub    r4, r4, #1
sub    r5, r5, #1
cmp    r0, #0
```

The issue latency of the WMUL and WMADD instructions is one cycle; the result and resource latency are two cycles. The second WMUL instruction in the following example stalls for one cycle due to the two-cycle issue latency.

```
WMULUM wR0, wR1, wR2
WMULSL wR3, wR4, wR5 @one cycle stall
```

Hence, two WMUL instructions should be separated by one instruction. The WADD instruction in the following example stalls for one cycle due to the two-cycle result latency.

```
wmulm wR0, wR1, wR2
waddhus wR1, wR0, wR2 @two cycle stall
```

Thus, any instruction waiting on the result should be separated by two other instructions. However, if the latter instruction is another SIMD-multiplication instruction, then the stall is one cycle despite data dependency.

Fast Multiply and Accumulation

For DSP and multimedia applications, multiply and accumulate (MAC) is the most commonly used operation. In addition to multipliers, Intel Wireless MMX technology offers accumulation capabilities. In the SIMD coprocessor, any of the registers can be used as an accumulator.

Performing MAC Operations on Registers in Intel XScale Core

A MAC operation can be done using TMIA 32-bit and TMIAPH 16-bit instructions. TMIA and TMIAPH instructions allow the use of two registers in the Intel XScale core as two operands and produce the result of multiplication and accumulation to any of the coprocessor registers.

The issue latency of the TMIA instruction is one cycle; the result and resource latency are two cycles. The second TMIA instruction in the following example stalls for one cycle due to the two-cycle resource latency.

```
tmia wR0, r2, r3
tmia wR1, r4, r5 @stall 1 cycle
```

The WADD instruction in the following example stalls for one cycle due to the two-cycle result latency.

```
tmia    wR0, r2, r3
waddhus wR1, wR0, wR2
```

Refer to Figures 4.9 and 4.10 for more information on instruction latencies for various multiply instructions. The multiply instructions should be scheduled taking their respective instruction latencies into consideration.

Performing MAC Operations on Registers in Intel Wireless MMX Technology

Intel Wireless MMX technology supports 16-bit SIMD multiply and accumulate operations, where the sources and the destination use SIMD coprocessor registers. Similar to the TMIA instruction, any of the coprocessor registers can be used as an accumulator for this case. The issue latency of the WMAC instruction is one cycle, and the result and resource latency is two cycles. The second WMAC instruction in the following example will stall for one cycle due to the two-cycle resource latency.

```
wmacs wR0, wR2, wR3
wmacs wR1, wR4, wR5 @stall 1 cycle
```

The WADD instruction in the following example stalls for one cycle due to the two-cycle result latency. However, the second WMACS does not stall for two cycles due to the internal forwarding supported by the multiplier and accumulate unit (MAU) of the coprocessor.

```
wmacs  wR0, wR4, wR5
wmacs  wR0, wR2, wR3   @stall 1 cycle
waddhss wR1, wR0, wR2 @stall 2 cycles
```

It is often possible to interleave instructions and effectively overlap their execution with multicycle instructions that use the multiply pipeline. The two-cycle WMAC instruction may be easily interleaved with operations that do not use the same resources:

```
wmacs  wR14, wR2, wR3
wldrd  wR3, [r4] , #8
wmacs  wR15, wR1, wR0
waligni wR5, wR6, wR7, #4
wmacs  wR15, wR5, wR0
wldrd  wR0, [r3], #8
```

In the preceding example, the WLDRD and WALIGNI instructions do not incur a stall, since they are utilizing the memory and execution pipelines respectively and have no data dependencies. For interleaving WMACS with other instructions, instructions of the Intel XScale core can be used.

```
wmacs wR14, wR1, wR2
add   R1, R2, R3
wmacs wR14, wR1, wR2
mul   R4, R5, R6
```

Scheduling in the Addition and Logical Pipeline

Most data-processing instructions for Intel XScale microarchitecture technology and Intel Wireless MMX technology—including logical and addition instructions—have a result latency of one cycle. Therefore, the current instruction can use the result from the previous data processing instruction without any penalty. For example, a series of additions can be performed without any stalls, such as:

```
waddh wR4, wR2, wR1
waddh wR5, wr4, wR1
waddh wR6, wR2, wR1
```

The preceding code segment does not incur any stall. The only exception to the above is the saturation arithmetic operation. During saturation, the result is generated one cycle later. Thus, subsequent instructions using the result stall by a cycle, as in this instance:

```
waddhss wR4, wR2, wR1
waddhss wR5, wR4, wR1 @single cycle stall
waddhss wR6, wR2, wR1
```

In this example, the second saturating SIMD instruction stalls for one cycle due to the read-after-write dependency on register wR4; however, the third saturating SIMD instruction does not stall since the two have no data dependency between each other. This code segment can be easily modified via *translation* such that there is no stall. To make this modification, case swapping the locations of the second and the third WADDH is sufficient to remove the stall. The pipeline for the Intel XScale microarchitecture also has no stalls on its logical and simple arithmetic operations. For many applications, this feature offers high performance.

Shifting an operand by an immediate value during an arithmetic operation is a feature of core processor instructions. This feature can save an extra instruction for explicit shifting. You need to be mindful of the subtle constraints posed by this feature; if the current instruction uses the result of the previous data processing instruction for a shift by immediate, the result latency is two cycles. As a result, the following code segment incurs a one-cycle stall for the MOV instruction:

```
sub   r6, r7, r8
add   r1, r2, r3
mov   r4, r1, LSL #2
```

The following code removes the one-cycle stall:

```
add    r1, r2, r3
sub    r6, r7, r8
mov    r4, r1, LSL #2
```

Similarly, you can use a register to specify the shift or rotate amount for an operand. This instruction option can be very effective if the shift amount is not known beforehand; however, a longer latency is involved. All data-processing instructions incur a two-cycle issue penalty and a two-cycle result penalty when the shifter operand is shifted or rotated based on a register. For instance, in the following code sequence, the sub incurs a two-cycle stall since the add instruction uses a register as a shift operand.

```
mov    r3, #10
mul    r4, r2, r3
add    r5, r6, r2, LSL r3
sub    r7, r8, r4 @ Stalls for two cycles
```

Getting Data from Cache to Register and Back Efficiently

Cache memory allows taking advantage of the data locality of the program. Even if a data segment is in the cache, data has to be loaded to the registers for data processing operations. For critical data processing kernels, data cache optimization and register moving should be optimized.

Knowing the Load-to-Use Penalty

An increased number of pipeline stages and increased complexity in design gives rise to non-unity load latency. Any load operation of word, byte, and half-word size has a result latency of three cycles if the load is the cache. Thus, a load followed by a use should be avoided. For cases when the load gets a cache miss, the latency can be high. Approaches to reduce miss-and-hide latency are discussed in Chapter 9. An example of the load-to-use stall follows:

```
wldrw    wR0, [r3],#4
waddw    wR8, wR0, wR8 @stalls for 2 cycles
wldrw    wR0, [r3],#4
waddw    wR8, wR0, wR8 @stalls for 2 cycles
wldrw    wR0, [r3],#4
waddw    wR8, wR0, wR8 @stalls for 2 cycles
```

Here, the stall of six cycles can be easily reduced by scheduling other instructions in the shadow of the load. A modification of the preceding code follows:

```
wldrw  wR0,  [r3],#4
wldrw  wR1,  [r3],#4
wldrw  wR2,  [r3],#4
waddw  wR8,  wR0,  wR8  @ no stall
waddw  wR8,  wR1,  wR8  @ no stall
waddw  wR8,  wR2,  wR8  @ no stall
```

Note that the modified code segment uses multiple registers to target its load. This modification is known as *register rotation*. This technique hides cache access latency and utilizes the multiple-load buffering capability offered by Intel XScale microarchitecture. This particular technique is applicable to all other load operations—those of different sizes and also those in the co-processor space.

Double-Word Loading and Storing

The Intel XScale microarchitecture supports double-word loads and stores from a pair of 32-bit registers on an even boundary. Intel Wireless MMX technology supports load and store operations on 64-bit registers.

When the LDRD instruction is used to load a pair of core registers, it has a result latency of three or four cycles depending on the destination register being accessed, assuming the data being loaded is in the data cache. When WLDRD is used to load a 64-bit coprocessor register, the latency is four cycles.

```
@ load double using Intel XScale core
ldrd   r0, [r3]
orr    r8, r1, #0xf @stalls for 4 cycles
mul    r7, r0, r7

@ Another example
ldrd   r0, [r3]
orr    r8, r0, #0xf @stalls for 3 cycles
mul    r7, r1, r7

@ Load using Intel Wireless MMX technology
wldrd  wR0, [r3]
waddw  wR1, WR0, wR2 @stalls for 4 cycles
```

Any memory instruction followed by a load double instruction has a resource hazard of one cycle, as shown in the next example:

```
@ str instruction below will stall for 1 cycle
ldrd  r0, [r3]
str   r4, [r5] // 1 cycle

@ For Intel Wireless MMX technology
wldrd wR3,[r4],#8
wldrd wR5,[r4],#8       @ STALL 1 cycle
wldrd wR4,[r4],#8       @ STALL 1 cycle
waddb wR0,wR1,wR2
waddb wR0,wR0,wR6
waddb wR0,wR0,wR7
```

The coprocessor supporting Intel Wireless MMX technology can buffer incoming load operations up to two double-word loads at a time, or four word loads, byte loads, or half-word loads.

The overhead on issuing load transactions can be minimized by instruction scheduling and load pipelining. In most cases, interleaving other operations to avoid the penalty with back-to-back LDRD instructions is straightforward. In the following code sequence, three WLDRD instructions are issued back-to-back, incurring a stall on the second and third instruction.

```
wldrd wR3,[r4],#8
wldrd wR5,[r4],#8   @ STALL
wldrd wR4,[r4],#8   @ STALL
waddb wR0,wR1,wR2
waddb wR0,wR0,wR6
waddb wR0,wR0,wR7
```

The same code sequence is reorganized to avoid a back-to-back issue of WLDRD instructions.

```
wldrd wR3,[r4],#8
waddb wR0,wR1,wR2
wldrd wR4,[r4],#8
waddb wR0,wR0,wR6
wldrd wR5,[r4],#8
waddb wR0,wR0,wR7
```

Always try to separate three multiple WLDRD instructions so that only two are outstanding at any one time and the loads are always interleaved with other instructions.

```
wldrd  wR0,[r2],#8
wzero  wR15
wldrd  wR1,[r4],#8
subs   r3,r3,#8
wldrd  wR3,[r4],#8
```

Always try to interleave additional operations between the load instruction and the instruction that will first use the cached data.

```
wldrd  wR0,[r2],#8
wzero  wR15
wldrd  wR1,[r4],#8
subs   r3,r3,#8
wldrd  wR3,[r4],#8
wmacs  wR15,wR1,wR0
subs   r4,r4,#1
```

Similarly, WSRTD and STRD store data from coprocessor registers and from core register pairs. Like WLDRD and LDRD, store instructions also offer a stall for any memory operation followed by double-word store instructions.

Scheduling Load and Store Multiple (LDM/STM)

Load and store multiples are two instructions—LDM and STM—that can be used to load a set of core registers. These instructions are often used for saving and retrieving the state of the processor. LDM and STM instructions have an issue latency of 2 to 20 cycles, depending on the number of registers being loaded or stored. The issue latency is typically two cycles plus an additional cycle for each of the registers loaded or stored, assuming a data cache hit. The instruction following an LDM stalls whether or not this instruction depends on the results of the load. While these instructions are useful to ease code development, they have two drawbacks: they have a two-cycle delay of issue latency and they are not used for loading and storing registers that support Intel Wireless MMX technology.

Optimizing Align and Shift

The auxiliary registers are designed to hold constants that are invariant across the lifetime of an inner loop calculation. For this reason, values loaded into the auxiliary registers are not forwarded to data operations. The intended use of the registers is that the shift or alignment offset is loaded into a wCGRn register before the main loop is entered, and then the shift to alignment offset is used repeatedly inside the loop without change. If the value in a wCGRx register is changed and an instruction immediately afterward tries to use the loaded value, then the coprocessor stalls until the loaded value has reached the control register file. For most kernels, the alignment values and shift amount values do not change during the execution of the kernel. For example, consider an algorithm that accesses a large data array where each element has 16-bit accuracy and has been stored in a packed fashion in the memory. Using Intel Wireless MMX technology, four elements of this data array can be processed concurrently. If the data structure is aligned at a 64-bit boundary, Intel Wireless MMX technology can access the data by a simple WLDRD instruction. For instance:

```
wldrd wR0, [r1],#8
.. use wR0 now ..
```

However, if the data is not aligned to a 64-bit boundary, it will be necessary to perform alignment. For the unaligned case, the data segment can be from a 64-bit boundary by an amount of one to seven bytes. The last three bits of the pointer's address can determine the exact offset. Be aware that the misalignment for successive double words does not change throughout the array. You can keep the misalignment constant stored in a control register and perform alignment on successive accesses.

```
bic  r1, r2, #7  @ r1 gets aligned address
xor  r0, r2, r1  @ r0 now contains misalignment

tmcr wCGR0, r0  @ WCGR0 now gets misalignment
wldrd wR0, [r1],#8
wldrd wR1, [r1],#8
..
..
waligni wR2, wR0, wR1, #0
.. use wR2 now..
```

Similarly, control registers can be used to determine a shift amount. Some algorithms require a certain level of accuracy—range and precision—during the computation. Following any multiplication or accumulation, you need to use a right shift of the resultant value. This correction can be maintained easily by using a control register-based shift operation.

Optimization for Control-Oriented Operations

A typical application has a set of control-oriented operations, such as compare, branching, and looping. Certain applications, such as a data sort operation, are control heavy. Even in a more data-intensive application such as video processing, control operations can consume a significant part of the application's execution time. The optimizing control-oriented operation has three key components: branch overhead reduction, conditional execution, and addressing techniques.

Reduce Branch Cost

In a deeply pipelined device, branches can be expensive since, during a branch, many stages of a pipeline can potentially be flushed, thus causing stalls of five cycles. Intel XScale microarchitecture has branch prediction logic and branch target buffers to ensure that branch penalties are as small as possible. From the application developer's point of view, avoiding unnecessary branches and ensuring that the branches are predictable helps improve performance. The following set of examples demonstrates how to eliminate potential branches, eliminate unnecessary loop overhead, and make control flow efficient.

The branch prediction and branch target buffers can reduce branch-related penalties a great deal. The operating system and platform level software must ensure that the branch target buffer (BTB) is enabled. The BTB has only 32 entries. The size of the branch target buffer limits the number of correctly predictable branches. Because the total number of branches executed in a program is relatively large compared to the size of the branch target buffer, it is often beneficial to minimize the number of branches in a program. Consider the following C code segment:

```
int foo(int a) {
   if (a > 10)
      return 0;
   else
      return 1;
}
```

The code generated for the `if...else` portion of this code segment using branches is:

```
    cmp    r0,#10
    ble    L1
    mov    r0,#0
    b      L2
L1:
    mov    r0,#1
L2:
```

This code takes three cycles to execute the `else` statement and four cycles for the `if` statement assuming best-case conditions and no branch misprediction penalties. In the case of the Intel XScale microarchitecture, a branch misprediction incurs a penalty of four cycles. If the branch is mispredicted 50 percent of the time and if both the `if` statement and the `else` statement are equally likely to be taken, on an average the code above takes 5.5 cycles to execute.

Using the Intel XScale microarchitecture to execute instructions conditionally, the code generated for the preceding `if...else` statement is:

```
cmp    r0,#10
movgt  r0,#0
movle  r0,#1
```

The preceding code segment would not incur any branch misprediction penalties and would take three cycles to execute assuming best-case conditions. Using conditional instructions helps to speed up execution significantly.

Use Conditional Instruction

Many embedded applications, such as parsing of a packet or looking for a peak in a spectrum, are loop intensive. Branch density—the number of instructions per branch—can be high, which could mean that the number of instructions in a loop or number of instructions between two branches is low. Each loop has management overhead—counting the loop pointer and comparing for the exit condition—associated with it.

Intel XScale microarchitecture provides the ability to execute instructions conditionally based on a set of conditional flags. Refer to Chapter 3 for more information. This conditional execution feature, combined with the ability of the instructions to modify the condition codes, makes a wide array of optimizations possible.

Optimizing Condition Checks

Core instructions can selectively modify the state of the condition codes. When generating code for if...else and loop conditions, it is often beneficial to make use of this feature to set condition codes, thereby eliminating the need for a subsequent compare instruction. Consider the following C statement.

```
if ((a + b) !=0)
    c = c + 1;
```

Code generated for the if condition without using an add instruction to set condition codes is:

```
add     r2, r0, r1
cmp     r2, #0
addne   r3, r3, #1
```

However, code can be optimized making use of an add instruction to set condition codes:

```
adds    r2, r0, r1
addne   r3, r3, #1
```

Condition checking for coprocessor registers can also be performed. SIMD flags in the wCASF register are updated during execution of Intel Wireless MMX instructions. Then, using one of the three flag extraction operations—TANDC, TORC, or TEXTRC—flags for the Intel XScale core can be updated. This method allows checking of all or one of the SIMD fields for conditional execution. Called group conditional execution, this method is shown in the following example:

```
wsubhus wR1, wR2, wR3
@ Saturating subtraction minimum of wR1
@ is zero
torch R15
@ Updating core flags with ORed
@ coprocessor flag values
addeq r2, r2, #1
@ now executes conditional coprocessor flag
```

All preceding techniques of effectively using conditional execution can also be applied to the group conditional execution. For cases such as peak detection or finding a match in a vector, you can use group conditional techniques.

The instructions that increment or decrement the loop counter can also be used to modify the condition codes. Modifying the codes eliminates the need for a subsequent compare instruction. A conditional branch instruction can then be used to exit or continue with the next loop iteration.

Consider the following C code segment:

```
for (i = 10; i != 0; i--) {
   perform inner_kernel;
}
```

The optimized code generated for the preceding code segment would look like:

```
L6:
@equivalent to inner_kernel
   subs r3, r3, #1
   bne  .L6
```

Using the above argument, it is also beneficial to rewrite loops whenever possible to make the loop exit conditions check against the value 0. For example, the code generated for the following code segment needs a compare instruction to check for the loop exit condition.

```
for (i = 0; i < 10; i++) {
   perform inner_kernel;
}
```

If the loop is rewritten as follows, the code generated avoids using a compare instruction to check for the loop exit condition.

```
for (i = 9; i >= 0; i--) {
   perform inner_kernel;
}
```

However, the use of conditional instructions should be considered carefully to ensure it improves performance. To decide when to use conditional instructions over branches, consider this hypothetical code segment:

```
if (cond)
   if_stmt
else
   else_stmt
```

Using the following data:

- N_{1B} = number of cycles to execute the if_stmt, assuming the use of branch instructions
- N_{2B} = number of cycles to execute the else_stmt, assuming the use of branch instructions
- P_1 = percentage of times the if_stmt is likely to be executed
- P_2 = percentage of times likely to incur a branch misprediction penalty
- N_{1C} = number of cycles to execute the if...else portion using conditional instructions, assuming the if condition to be true
- N_{2C} = number of cycles to execute the if...else portion using conditional instructions, assuming the if condition to be false

Use conditional instructions when:

$$N_{1C}P_1 + N_{2C}(1 - P_1) \leq N_{1B}P_1 + N_{2B}(1 - P_1) + 4P_2$$

The following example illustrates a situation in which it is better to use branches instead of conditional instructions.

```
    cmp    r0, #0
    bne    L1
    add    r0, r0, #1
    add    r1, r1, #1
    add    r2, r2, #1
    add    r3, r3, #1
    add    r4, r4, #1
    b      L2
L1:
    sub    r0, r0, #1
    sub    r1, r1, #1
    sub    r2, r2, #1
    sub    r3, r3, #1
    sub    r4, r4, #1
L2:
```

The CMP instruction takes one cycle to execute, the if statement takes seven cycles to execute, and the else statement takes six cycles to execute. If the code were changed to eliminate the branch instructions by using conditional instructions, the if...else statement would take 10 cycles to complete.

Assuming an equal probability of both paths being taken and that branch mispredictions occur 50 percent of the time, the cost of using conditional instructions is 11 cycles and the cost of branches is 9.5 cycles.

Optimizing Complex Expressions Using Conditional Execution

Using conditional instructions helps improve the code generated for complex expressions such as the C shortcut evaluation feature. The use of conditional instructions in this fashion helps improve performance by minimizing the number of branches, thereby minimizing the penalties caused by branch mispredictions.

```
int foo(int a, int b) {
    if (a != 0 && b != 0)
        return 0;
    else
        return 1;
}
```

The optimized code for the if condition is:

```
cmp    r0,#0
cmpne  r1,#0
```

This approach also reduces the utilization of branch prediction resources. With Intel Wireless MMX technology, the flag registers can be set based on data values in the coprocessor registers or SIMD flag registers.

Use Addressing Modes Efficiently

Intel XScale microarchitecture and Intel Wireless MMX technology provide a variety of addressing modes that make indexing an array of objects highly efficient. The following code samples illustrate how various kinds of array operations can be optimized to make use of these addressing modes:

```
@ Set the contents of the word pointed to
@ by r0 to the value contained in r1 and
@ make r0 point to the next word

    wstrw wR1,[r0], #4

@ Increment the contents of r0 to make it
@ point to the next word and set the
@ contents of the word pointed to the
@ value contained in r1

    wstrw   wR1, [r0, #4]!

@ Set the contents of the word pointed to
@ by r0 to the value contained in r1 and
@ make r0 point to the previous word

    wstrw   wR1,[r0], #-4

@ Decrement the contents of r0 to make it
@ point to the previous word and set the
@ contents of the word pointed to the value
@ contained in r1

    wstrw   wR1,[r0, #-4]!
```

Various addressing modes save you from explicitly spending an instruction on updating the pointer.

Miscellaneous Approaches

Apart from the techniques mentioned earlier, you might consider these tricks geared towards interesting use of the instructions. Consider the following two cases.

Optimizing the Use of Immediate Values

For programming purposes, constant values might need to be used. Constant values are created to be used as masks or known coefficients in different calculations. The MOV or MVN instruction should be used when loading an immediate, or constant, value into a register. However, immediate move is restricted to a 12-bit number. One could load the constant from memory. Loading 32-bit or 64-bit constant values requires loading from the memory. The compiler typically places all the constants in a literal pool close to the instructions. Literal pools are not likely to be in the data cache, which makes loading constants expensive—a main memory access. Also, LDR instruction has the potential to pollute the data cache. It is possible to generate a whole set of constant values using a combination of MOV, MVN, ORR, BIC, and ADD instructions. Use a combination of the above instructions to set a register to a constant value. An example of this is shown in these code samples.

```
@ Set the value of r0 to 127
    mov    r0, #127
@ Set the value of r0 to 0xfffffefb.
    mvn    r0, #260
@ Set the value of r0 to 257
    mov    r0, #1
    orr    r0, r0, #256
@ Set the value of r0 to 0x51f
    mov    r0, #0x1f
    orr    r0, r0, #0x500
@ Set the value of r0 to 0xf100ffff
    mvn    r0, #0xff, LSL 16
    bic    r0, r0, #0xe, LSL 8
@ Set the value of r0 to 0x12341234
    mov    r0, #0x8d, LSL 2
    orr    r0, r0, #0x1, LSL 12
    add    r0, r0, r0, LSL #16
@ shifter delay of 1 cycle
```

It is possible to load any 32-bit value into a register using a sequence of four instructions. With Intel Wireless MMX technology, two such 32-bit values can be generated in core registers, and then transferred to co-processor registers using TCMR, TMCRR, and TBCST instructions.

Bit Field Manipulation

Different encryption algorithms such as Data Encryption Standard (DES), Triple DES (T-DES), and hashing functions (SHA) perform many bit-manipulation operations. The shift and logical operations of the Intel XScale microarchitecture provide a useful way of manipulating bit fields. Bit field operations can be optimized using regular instructions:

```
@ Set the bit number specified by
@ r1 in register r0

mov    r2, #1
orr    r0, r0, r2, asl r1

@ Clear the bit number specified by
@ r1 in register r0

mov    r2, #1
bic    r0, r0, r2, asl r1

@ Extract the bit value of the bit
@ number specified by r1 of the
@ value in r0 storing the value in r0

mov    r1, r0, asr r1
and    r0, r1, #1

@ Extract the higher order 8 bits of the
@ value in r0 storing
@ the result in r1

mov    r1, r0, lsr #24
```

This approach helps other applications such as video stream parsing. Intel Wireless MMX technology supports 64-bit-wide bit-wise manipulation—for instance, shift, and, or—which can be effectively used for different bit-wise algorithms.

Key Points

This chapter offers a set of optimization techniques based on the pipeline constraint of Intel Wireless MMX technology and Intel XScale microarchitecture. These methods are intended for assembly language development and can also be applied during development using intrinsic functions and in-line assembly. High-level language programming styles based on these techniques have also been presented. These programming styles demonstrate how best to use different instructions and, more specifically, how the sequence of instructions should be scheduled to reduce stalls. However, the list of methods described here is not exhaustive. A few points to remember are:

■ Use the correct precision for the algorithm, and choose instructions accordingly.

■ Interleave instructions between the pipe to hide result and issue latency.

■ Schedule load and stores with the correct data-addressing mode.

■ Watch out for load-to-use penalty and shifter-processing latency.

■ Count down on loops to reduce loop control overhead.

■ Use conditional instructions to avoid branch costs.

Chapter 11

Porting Existing Code

> *When it is not necessary to change, it is not*
> *necessary to change.*
>
> —Lucius Cary

Today, a large base of software applications is installed on desktop and mobile PC platforms. Bringing existing software from these PC platforms to the Intel® Personal Internet Client Architecture (Intel® PCA) gives handheld users a rich library of multimedia applications that are familiar. Intel Wireless MMX™ technology is designed to make the job of porting multimedia applications from the desktop to platforms based on Intel PCA as simple as possible.

This chapter describes the particular features of Intel Wireless MMX technology that help you port original code and Streaming SIMD Extensions (SSE) from the desktop to platforms based on Intel PCA.

Application Porting

To port an application from one architecture to another involves many considerations, such as operating system specific API calls, compiler idiosyncrasies, and library primitives. With many operating systems and tools suites now available on both desktop and handheld platforms, the barrier to porting the code is substantially reduced. The significant architectural differences between the source and destination platforms are the perennial difficulty in porting applications. Today, use of the original MMX technology and SSE is the cornerstone of multimedia

233

applications on the desktop. Intel Wireless MMX technology is designed specifically to make the conversion of applications containing these SIMD extensions easier.

Porting Options

Choosing a code-porting method boils down to a function of available time and resources versus performance efficiency of the resulting code. The more time and resources that you invest, the better the results you can expect. Figure 11.1 shows the three main styles of code porting that you can follow, and the relationship between ease of porting and performance of code.

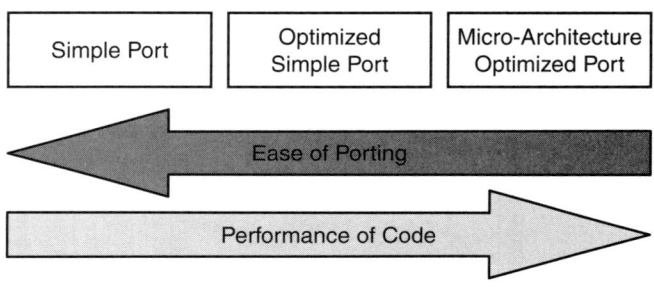

Figure 11.1   Core Porting Strategy Trade-offs

The basic characteristic of each porting strategy is:

■ *Simple port.* Take the algorithm original from the desktop and simply translate the mnemonics from original MMX to Intel Wireless MMX technology. The advantage with this approach is the speed with which the platform translation can be completed. This style of conversion is useful if time to market is an overriding consideration. However, the disadvantage is that the resulting code may not be optimal for the new platform.

■ *Rescheduled simple port.* This strategy takes the simple port one step further by using the techniques described earlier in this book to identify and eliminate performance hazards from the code. Identify hazards through use of performance analysis tools and eliminate the hazards through rescheduling the instruction sequence to avoid them. The advantage of this approach is that for only a small amount of optimization effort, the code performance can be dramatically improved.

- *Algorithm optimization.* The approach that yields the most optimum solution is to reoptimize the algorithm to take advantage of the microarchitecture-specific features of Intel Wireless MMX technology, such as the large register file. Techniques for getting the most out of the microarchitecture are discussed in Chapter 5. While algorithm optimization may yield the best results, it also may take the most time and resources to complete.

These three approaches allow you to trade off the amount of core porting effort invested against the level of performance achieved.

Intel® MMX™ and SSE Technology Mapping

Intel Wireless MMX technology follows the same SIMD programming paradigm as the original MMX technology. Here special instructions operate on packed data types in special architecture registers. Intel Wireless MMX technology uses the same programming style and provides a one-to-one instruction mapping from the original MMX core. To further ease the porting, the Intel Wireless MMX instruction mnemonics have also been chosen to reflect the functionality being reproduced from MMX technology.

Understanding the relationship between the two platforms has two phases. First, you have to understand where the similarities are. In the second phase, you have to understand how the two platforms differ and how these differences are accommodated in the porting process.

Instruction Syntax

On the desktop, MMX technology uses a prefix of "P" on all instruction mnemonics to indicate a packed data operation is being performed, whereas Intel Wireless MMX technology has two different prefixes. The prefix of "W" indicates the instruction operates on coprocessor data registers only, where as a "T" prefix is used to indicate that data is transferred between coprocessor registers and core registers. Table 11.1 shows how the mnemonics of MMX instruction can be translated to its wireless counterpart.

Table 11.1 Instruction Mnemonic Mapping from MMX™ Instructions

MMX™ Instruction	Intel® Wireless MMX™ Instruction	Description
PADD PSUB	WADD WSUB	Add or subtract eight bytes, four 16-bit half words, or two 32-bit words.
PCMPEQ PCMPGT	WCMPEQ WCMPGT	Compare eight bytes, four 16-bit half words, or two 32-bit elements in parallel. Result is mask of all ones if true or all zeros if false.
PMULLW PMULHW	WMULL WMULH	Multiply four signed 16-bit words in parallel. Low-order or high-order 16 bits of the 32 result are produced.
PMADD	WMADD	Multiply four 16-bit values and add two upper products and add lower two products.
PSRA PSLL PSRL	WSRA WSLL WSRL	Short arithmetic right, logical right and left of 4 half-words, 2 words or the full 64-bit double word in parallel.
PUNPCKL PUNPCKH	WUNPCKIL WUNPCKIH	Interleave and merge eight bytes, four 16-bit half words or two 32-bit words.
PACKSS PACKUS	WPACKSS WPACKUS	Pack double words to words or words to bytes, with signed on unsigned saturation.
PAND, PANDN, POR, PXOR	WAND, WANDN, WOR, WXOR	64-bit logical operations.
MOV	WMOV/WLDR	Move or load a register.

In addition to providing equivalent functionality for all MMX instructions, Intel Wireless MMX technology provides a one-to-one mapping for all of the Integer SSE instructions. The same convention for mapping the mnemonic names between the two platforms is observed for the integer SSE instructions, as shown in Table 11.2.

Table 11.2   Instruction Mnemonic Mapping from Integer SSE Instructions

SSE Instruction	Intel® Wireless MMX™ Instruction	Description
PMAX PMIN	WMAX WMIN	Vector maximum/minimum selection between 8-bit or 16-bit elements.
PMOVMSKB	TMOVMSK	Selects the most significant bit of each element in the source register.
PAVG	WAVG2	Two element average on unsigned vectors of 8- or 16-bit data.
PINSRW	TINSR	Insert an element at a specified position in a packed register.
PEXTRW	TEXTRM	Extract an element from a specified position in a packed register.
PROR	WROR	Rotate right 4 half-words, 2 words or the full 64-bit double word.
PSADB	WSAD	Performs sum of absolute difference on unsigned vectors of 8- or 16-bit data.
PSHUFW	WSHUF	Shuffles 16-bit data values specified by an 8-bit immediate value.

Note: Intel® Wireless MMX™ technology does not support the floating-point operations in hardware, so it does not provide the floating-point extensions of SSE.

Using these two tables allows application developers to quickly map instruction functionality between the platforms.

Understanding the Differences

With a good understanding of the similarities between the two platforms, it is now time to look at the differences and how this is handled during the application porting process.

Terminology

One of the key differences between the Intel architecture-based MMX technology and the ARM[†] architecture-based Intel Wireless MMX technology is the fundamental definition of the "word" data type. When the original Intel architecture was defined, the base data quantity, a word, was considered to be 16-bits of data. Today in Intel architecture, although the basic quantity of data is now typically 32 bits, a word still refers to 16 bits, so a 32-bit data item is referred to as a double word.

In contrast, many newer microprocessor architectures, such as the ARM architecture, consider their 32-bit basic data quantity to be a word. This mismatch in the definition of a word could lead to confusion for software developers who are porting code from MMX to Intel Wireless MMX technology. However, the mapping from one data type to the next is very straightforward, as shown below in Table 11.3.

Table 11.3   Translating the Definition of Data Type Sizes

Data Size	MMX™ Technology	Intel® Wireless MMX™ Technology
8 bits	Byte (B)	Byte (B)
16 bits	Word (W)	Half-Word (H)
32 bits	Double Word (D)	Word (W)
64 bits	Quad Word (Q)	Double Word (D)

The table shows the single letter suffix that is added to the corresponding instruction mnemonic to specify the data type being operated upon. Figure 11.2 shows an example of the use of the data type suffix.

MMX™ technology	**Intel® Wireless MMX™ technology**
PADDW	WADDH

Figure 11.2   Specifying an Add Operation on 16-bit Packed Data

The other difference in terminology is the way that instruction qualifiers are used to specify the saturation type. In MMX technology, the S qualifier indicates that signed saturation is required and the US qualifier signifies that unsigned saturation is required. In the ARM architecture, using an S qualifier on an instruction sets the arithmetic flags, so to avoid confusion in Intel Wireless MMX instructions, signed saturation is indicated by an SS qualifier. Unsigned saturation remains the same US qualifier. The use of the signed saturation qualifier is shown in Figure 11.3.

MMX™ technology	Intel® Wireless MMX™ technology
PADDSW	WADDHSS

Figure 11.3   Specifying an Add Operation on 16-bit Packed Data Using Signed Saturation

Data Storage

Intel Wireless MMX technology provides sixteen 64-bit registers for data operand storage, eight more than the number supported in MMX technology. While you can port MMX code that uses only eight registers straight across, you can simplify register allocation and reduce redundant load/store operations by using more of the extra registers available with Intel Wireless MMX technology. For example, an application can calculate more intermediate values and keep them in the register file, or it can reuse already loaded data for improved performance.

Instruction Operands

MMX and SSE instructions allow two register operands to be specified. One is a source register and the other is a source and destination register. The instruction allows each operand to be one of eight registers. The general format for MMX and SSE instructions follows:

```
OPERATION  SRCDEST1, SRC2
```

Here, the operation is performed on the two source operands and the result is written back to the primary source register, SRCDEST1, as in the following example:

```
PADDSW mm0, mm1
```

This instruction takes as its operands the contents of registers mm0 and mm1, adds the corresponding 16-bit elements of the registers together, and places the result back in register mm0, overwriting the original contents. The common terminology for one of the source operands being overwritten by the operation result is a *destructive* write operation.

Intel Wireless MMX technology allows three register operands to be specified for each instruction: two source operands and a separate destination operand. Each operand may be one of sixteen registers. The general format of the instruction is:

```
OPERATION DEST, SRC1, SRC2
```

In this case, DEST can be different from both the source operands so destructive write behavior can be avoided, as shown in this example:

```
WADDHSS  wR2, wR0, wR1
```

This instruction adds the 16-bit elements in the two source registers—wR0 and wR1—and places the result in a different destination register, wR2. If exactly the same destructive write behavior is required, the same register can be specified for SRC1 and DEST, for example,

```
WADDHSS wR0, wR0, WR1
```

This instruction now has identical behavior to:

```
PADDSW mm0, mm1
```

Eliminating MMX MOV Instructions

In MMX code, you commonly see the MOV instruction used to save a copy of the original source operand that is overwritten, so that value could be reused later in the calculation. For example, in the following instruction sequence, the original source value in mm0 is saved in mm2 so that when the PADDSW instruction overwrites mm0 with the sum, the original source operands are still available in mm2 and mm1.

```
MOVQ    mm2, mm0
PADDSW mm0, mm1
```

In Intel Wireless MMX technology, the extra MOV instruction can be eliminated by selecting different source and destination registers, as in the following example.

```
WADDHSS wR2, wR0, wR0
```

Here, the source values in registers wR0 and wR1 remain unchanged after the addition is completed and the result is placed in another register, wR2. By careful allocation of register resources, you could eliminate all such usage of MOV instructions from MMX code during application porting.

The task of register scheduling is also simplified by the larger register set available with Intel Wireless MMX technology.

Memory Operands

As in the underlying Intel architecture, MMX technology allows one of the operands of an instruction to be a value stored in memory. In contrast, Intel Wireless MMX technology follows the strict load/store architecture of the Intel Xscale® microarchitecture, so memory operands cannot be used in instructions.

Therefore, to port MMX code that contains memory references as operands, you must add an explicit load operation, as follows. Replace the two-operand PADDSW instruction with a sequence in which the WLDRD instruction contains address of memory operand and the WADDHSS instruction uses the reference.

```
PADDSW   mm0,  mm64

WLDRD    wR1,  [R1]      ;R1
WADDHSS  wR0,  WR0,  wR1
```

The large register file supporting Intel Wireless MMX technology provides extra space to store the loaded value prior to the calculation, and if the memory operand is reused, it can be accessed directly from the register file. Operand reuse is common in multimedia applications, so the caching of loaded values in the register file can lead to performance enhancements. The WLDRD instruction should be scheduled as early as possible, to avoid any load-to-use penalties.

Memory Alignment

In MMX technology, memory values can be loaded from an arbitrary memory address, so that double word data values can be loaded from any byte-aligned address. The hardware in MMX technology takes care of the load and store operations necessary to retrieve the desired double-word value, but for unaligned memory access, you incur a performance penalty. In the Intel XScale microarchitecture, double-word loads can only be accessed from addresses that are double-word aligned—that is, they are aligned on a 64-bit boundary. If your application requires an arbitrary un-aligned 64-bit value, the aligned values of the two adjacent double words are loaded and the WALIGN instruction is used to extract the required 64-bit value.

For example, Figure 11.4 shows the code sequence for dealing with unaligned addresses in Intel Wireless MMX technology. Here, the exact byte offset that the application requires is extracted from the base address in register R4 and sent to auxiliary register 0, wCGR0, in the coprocessor. The two aligned data items are loaded, and the register offset variant of WALIGN is used to select auxiliary register 0 as the byte offset to extract the double word from.

```
AND    R2, R4, #3
TMCR   wCGR0, R2
WLDRD  wR0, [R4,#4]
WLDRD  wR1, [R4,#4]
WALIGNR0 wR2, wR0,WR1
```

Figure 11.4   Intel® Wireless MMX™ Instruction Sequence for Unaligned Double Word Load Operations

Even on today's desktop systems, the use of unaligned data is discouraged because of the performance penalty, even if the load alignment is implemented in hardware.

The use of WALIGN and the corresponding load instructions provides a means for explicit management of the data to be loaded and offers optimization opportunities to reuse the loaded data for extracting other data alignments, as in the following example.

```
WALIGNI wR3,wR0, wR1, #5
```

If placed at the end of the code sequence in Figure 11.4, the instruction would extract the double word at a byte offset of 5 and places it in the result register wR3.

New Instruction Capability

Intel Wireless MMX technology provides a superset of the MMX and integer SSE functionality. Some of these extensions should be considered when you look for ways to simplify the porting process and to improve the efficiency of the resulting code.

More Data Types

Intel Wireless MMX technology provides support for both signed and unsigned byte data types in the comparison instructions: WMIN, WMAX, WCMPEQ, and WCMPGT. Byte-processing varieties of these instructions are not present in the original MMX and SSE instruction set. These instruction data types allow lower precision calculations to be used and more parallelism to be exposed. The Viterbi decoder is a good example of how the byte parallelism can be utilized.

Intel Wireless MMX technology also provides a saturation capability for word addition and subtraction operations, for example WADDWSS. The Intel Wireless MMX WPACK instruction also allows unsigned saturation on word types, whereas the corresponding MMX instruction allows only signed saturation. The WPACK instruction also allows the packing of double-word data into word data, another feature not present in MMX technology.

Use of these extra data-type-specific operations could result in alternatives that achieve more efficient algorithm implementations.

Accumulating Instructions

The sum of absolute difference instruction in Intel Wireless MMX technology, WSAD, provides an accumulating function that is not possible in the two-operand instruction of SSE technology. This instruction can eliminate extra addition operations required in SSE code to perform the accumulate operation. The WSAD instruction also allows the optional zeroing of the accumulation with the "Z" qualifier. Figure 11.5 shows how these can be used to reduce the code complexity of accumulating SAD operations such as those used motion estimation algorithms for encoding video.

	MMX™ technology	Intel® Wireless MMX™ technology
Input:	mm0, mm2: Data set 1	wR0, wR2: Data set 1
	mm1, mm3: Data set 2	wR1, wR3: Data set 2
Output:	mm0: SAD of sets 1&2	wR4: SAD of sets 1&2
PSADB	mm0, mm1	WSADBZ wR4, wR0,wR1
PSADB	mm2, mm3	WSADB wR4, wR2,wR3
PADDDW	mm0, mm2	

Figure 11.5   Using the Accumulating SAD Operation

The other accumulating function to consider when porting from applications with MMX instructions is the four-way 16x16 multiply accumulate instruction of Intel Wireless MMX technology, WMAC. Again, the two-operand restriction of MMX instructions does not allow the accumulating functionality. The multiply accumulate operation is a staple of many filter operations in digital signal processing, so using this instruction could present an optimization opportunity during the code porting.

Data Reformatting

Reformatting packed data is an important part of SIMD processing. MMX technology provides several instructions that pack and unpack data in the MMX technology registers. Intel Wireless MMX technology extends this set of functions with the ability to unpack half of a packed register and convert the elements to the next higher level of precision, such as unpacking bytes into half-words. This operation is particularly common in video decoders, where values of different precision are added together in the residual calculation. An example extending the precision of half word data to word data is shown in Figure 11.6.

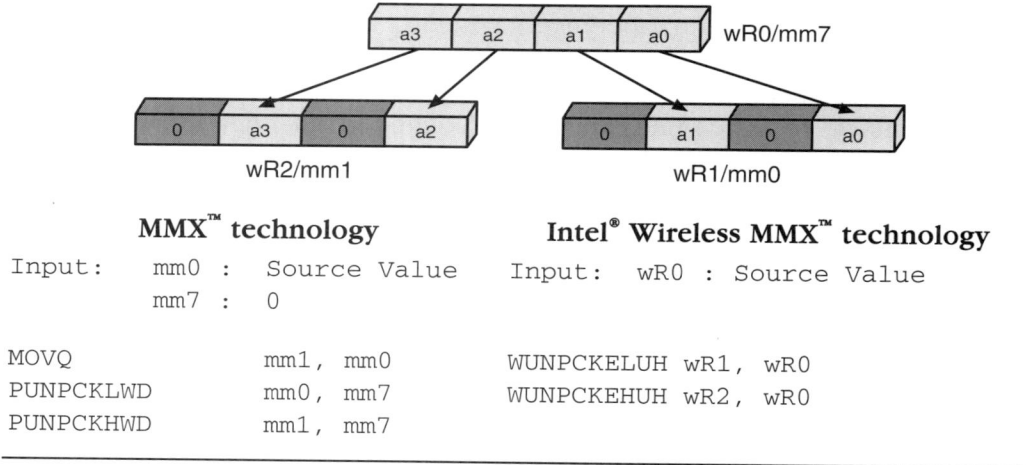

MMX™ technology		Intel® Wireless MMX™ technology	
Input:	mm0 : Source Value	Input:	wR0 : Source Value
	mm7 : 0		
MOVQ	mm1, mm0	WUNPCKELUH	wR1, wR0
PUNPCKLWD	mm0, mm7	WUNPCKEHUH	wR2, wR0
PUNPCKHWD	mm1, mm7		

Figure 11.6   Extending the Precision of Unsigned Data

As shown here, MMX technology requires an extra register to store the zero value that extends the unsigned value. With Intel Wireless MMX technology, the use of an extra register is eliminated.

For extending the precision of signed data types, the individual elements are sign extended, not zero-extended as with unsigned data. Intel Wireless MMX technology also provides additional support for extending the precision of signed data types, allowing the instruction count to be reduced for signed data precision extension, as shown in Figure 11.7.

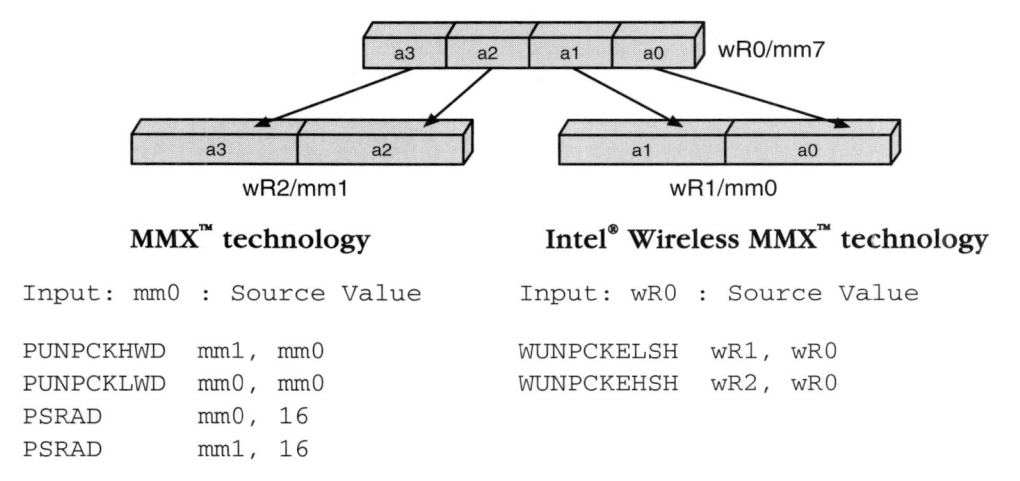

MMX™ technology   **Intel® Wireless MMX™ technology**

```
Input: mm0 : Source Value      Input: wR0 : Source Value

PUNPCKHWD   mm1, mm0           WUNPCKELSH   wR1, wR0
PUNPCKLWD   mm0, mm0           WUNPCKEHSH   wR2, wR0
PSRAD       mm0, 16
PSRAD       mm1, 16
```

Figure 11.7   Extending the Precision of Signed Data

Shift Operands

The basic shift operations of both MMX and Intel Wireless MMX technology are similar in that they allow shift left, shift right logical, shift left logical, and rotate right operations on data elements of 16-bit, 32-bit, and 64-bit widths. For both platforms, you can specify the shift amount in one of the packed data registers, mm0 or wR0 for example.

For MMX technology, the shift amount can be also specified as an immediate value. Immediate shift amounts are not possible in Intel Wireless MMX technology, so an equivalent code sequence must be used, as shown in Figure 11.8.

MMX™ technology	**Intel® Wireless MMX™ technology**
PSRLQ mm0, 16	MOV R1, #16
	TMCR wCGR0, R1
	WSRLD wR1, wR0, wCGR0

Figure 11.8   Translating Immediate Shift Operations

Notice that no special register forwarding is provided for auxiliary registers, wCGRn, so the TMCR instruction should be scheduled as early as possible to avoid a register dependency stall upon the value of the destination operand, wCGR0 in this case.

The use of an auxiliary register is also helpful if the required shift amount is a function of an address pointer that is held in the registers of the Intel XScale core. Figure 11.9 shows how this may be used.

```
AND   R1, R4, #16        ; Extract shift offset
TMCR  wCGR0, R1
.............
WLDR  wR0, [R4]
WSRLD wR1, wR0, wCGR0
```

Figure 11.9   Extracting the Shift Offset from an Address Pointer in Intel® Wireless MMX™ Technology

Miscellaneous

A number of small differences also need to be accounted for while porting code from MMX and SSE to Intel Wireless MMX technology.

The two-way average instruction in Intel Wireless MMX technology provides an option to perform biased and unbiased rounding during the average operation—that is, when one or zero is added to the intermediate sum before it is divided by two. This option is useful for supporting the different round schemes required by particular video standards. Code ported from MMX instructions that requires unbiased rounding has to perform this action by using discrete operations. To maintain accuracy,

MMX code would also have to increase the precision of the intermediate additions, which results in reduction of the data parallelism that can be used. Through use of the WAVG instruction that is available in Intel Wireless MMX technology without the "R" rounding qualifier specified, you can achieve all of these results in a single instruction while maintaining the accuracy of the final result.

Case Studies of Code Porting

The following sections provide case studies of converting exiting code sequences from MMX technology to sequences supporting Intel Wireless MMX technology.

Complex Multiply by a Constant

One example of a simple porting operation is complex multiplication by a constant. Complex multiplication is an operation that requires four multiplications and two additions, which is exactly how the PMADDWD instruction operates. To use this instruction, the data must be formatted into four 16-bit values. The real and imaginary components should be 16-bits each. Let the input data be Dr and Di, as follows:

```
Dr = real component of the data
Di = imaginary component of the data
```

The format of the constant complex coefficients in memory is four 16-bit values: Cr, -Ci, Ci, and Cr.

In this example, shown in Figure 11.10, the main effort in porting the code lies in mapping the mnemonic and register names correctly and ensuring that the specification of correct data type are mapped. In this case, D changes to W in the first instruction, and in the second instruction, W changes to H.

MMX™ technology	Intel® Wireless MMX™ technology
Input: mm0: Complex number [Dr,Di]	wR0: Complex number [Dr,Di]
mm1: Complex coeff. [Cr -Ci Ci Cr]	wR1: Complex coeff. [Cr -Ci Ci Cr]
PUNPCKLD mm0,mm0	WUNPCKILW wR2, wR0, wR0
PMADDW mm0,mm1	WMADDH wR3, wR2, wR1

Figure 11.10 Code Porting of Complex Multiplication by a Constant

Notice that the output is a packed word. If necessary, you could use a pack instruction to convert the result to a 16-bit value, thereby matching the format of the input.

Absolute Difference of Unsigned Numbers

The example in Figure 11.11 computes the absolute difference of two unsigned numbers. It assumes an unsigned packed-byte data type. Here, the subtract instruction is used with unsigned saturation. This instruction receives unsigned operands and subtracts them using unsigned saturation. This example also shows redundant MOV elimination.

MMX™ technology		Intel® Wireless MMX™ technology	
Input:	mm0 : Source Value 1	wR0 : Source Value 1	
	mm1 : Source Value 2	wR1 : Source Value 2	
MOVQ	mm2, mm0		
PSUBUSB	mm0, mm1	WSUBBUS	wR3, wR1, wR2
PSUBUSB	mm1, mm2	WSUBBUS	wR4, wR2, wR1
POR	mm0, mm1	WOR	wR5, wR3, wR4

Figure 11.11 Porting Unsigned Absolute Difference

This algorithm only works for unsigned operands; with signed operands, you must use the algorithm in the next section.

Absolute Difference of Signed Numbers

This example computes the absolute difference of two signed numbers. No MMX or Intel Wireless MMX subtraction instruction receives signed operands and subtracts them using unsigned saturation. The suggested technique here first sorts the corresponding elements of the input operands into packed-words of the maxima values and packed half-words of the minima values. Then, the minima values are subtracted from the maxima values to generate the required absolute difference. The key is a fast sorting technique, which uses the fact that B = XOR(A, XOR(A,B)) and A = XOR(A,0). Thus in a packed data type, having some elements that are XOR(A,B) and some that are 0, you could XOR the operand with A and receive in some places values of A and in some values of B. The example in Figure 11.12 assumes a packed half-word data type, each element being a signed value.

MMX™ technology		Intel® Wireless MMX™ technology	
Input: mm0 : Source Value 1		wR0 : Source Value 1	
mm1 : Source Value 2		wR1 : Source Value 2	
MOVQ	mm2, mm0	WCMPGTSH wR2, wR1, wR0	
PCMPGTW	mm0, mm1	WXOR	wR3, wR0, wR1
MOVQ	mm4, mm2	WAND	wR4, wR3, wR0
PXOR	mm2, mm1	WXOR	wR5, wR0, wR4
PAND	mm2, mm0	WXOR	wR6, wR1, wR4
MOVQ	mm3, mm2	WSUBH	wR2, wR5, wR6
PXOR	mm4, mm2		
PXOR	mm1, mm3		
PSUBW	mm1, mm4		

Figure 11.12 Absolute Difference of Signed Values

The absolute value of the most negative number—that is, 0x8000 for 16-bit data—cannot be represented in 16-bit signed format. This code produces the maximum positive value of 0x7FFF in this case.

Reducing Precision with an Interleaved Pack

Precision reduction is a common operation in many algorithms where an intermediate calculation is performed at higher precision and the final result packed back down into a lower precision to reduce the amount of storage required.

The example in Figure 11.13 shows a technique for reducing the precision of dual source operands and interleaving the values in the destination register. The example shows the classic way that this result is achieved using MMX technology, and how this same result can be achieved in fewer instructions using the SSE features of Intel Wireless MMX technology with the WSHUFH instruction.

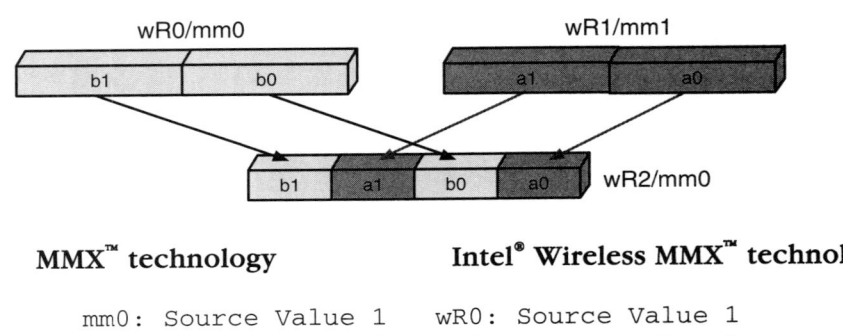

```
                  MMX™ technology           Intel® Wireless MMX™ technology

Input:      mm0: Source Value 1      wR0: Source Value 1
            mm1: Source Value 2      wR1: Source Value 2

PACKSSDW    mm0, mm1                 WPACKWSS  wR2, wR0, wR1
PACKSSDW    mm1, mm1                 WSHUFH    wR2, wR2, 0xD8
PUNPKLWD    mm0, mm1
```

Figure 11.13   Reducing Precision with an Interleaved Pack

If a noninterleaved pack is required, the standard pack instruction, WPACK, can achieve this in one cycle.

Alpha Saturation

Alpha saturation is used in 2D and 3D imaging to produce effects, such as fog, fade in/out, and blending of images. Typically, RGB values are used to represent the color component of a pixel. To represent the opacity of the color, a fourth component, alpha, can be added to RGB.

The objective of this code sequence is to ensure that none of the RGB elements exceed the value of corresponding alpha element. In the case shown here, the WMINUB instruction can be used to limit the RGB values to alpha, producing an image that is more or less saturated. The example in Figure 11.14 illustrates the conversion from SSE instructions to Intel Wireless MMX instructions.

MMX™ technology			Intel® Wireless MMX™ technology			
Input:	mm3/wR3	:	const_0xff00ff00ff00ff00			
	mm0/wR0	:	$\alpha_1 B_1 G_1 R_1 \alpha_0 B_0 G_0 R_0$			
	wR6	:	const_0x0008			
MOVQ	mm1,	mm0	WSHUFH	wR2 ,	wR0,	0xF5
PSHUFW	mm1,	mm1, 0xF5	WAND	wR1,	wR2,	wR3
PAND	mm1,	mm3	WSRLD	wR4,	wR1,	wR6
MOVQ	mm2,	mm1	WOR	wR5 ,	wR4,	wR1
PSRLQ	mm2,	8	WMINUB	wR0 ,	wR1,	wR5
POR	mm1,	mm2				
PMINUB	mm0,	mm1				

Figure 11.14 SSE Alpha Saturation Conversion to Intel® Wireless MMX™
Technology

Be aware of two main differences when converting this SSE instruction sequence:

■ The MOVQ instructions are eliminated.

■ The Intel Wireless MMX shift instructions do not provide for a shift by immediate, and they require a constant to be loaded from memory or from an ARM register. In this case, wR6 has been preloaded with the constant value 8.

Porting Code Using C-Intrinsics

The intrinsic functions provide an abstraction mechanism that keeps your design effort away from the detailed assembly code of each instruction, but still provides a way to specify which operation is required. The intrinsics are functions that can be called from a C program to perform an operation on the packed data types of MMX and Intel Wireless MMX technology, but the programmer does not have to worry about register allocation and instruction scheduling.

For both platforms, the intrinsic functions use the _m64 data type to describe the operands to the function; this description corresponds to the registers specified in the instruction. The _m64 data type can hold eight 8-bit values, four 16-bit values, two 32-bit values, or one 64-bit value.

Both platforms use the same naming convention for intrinsic functions, and they use a notational convention of:

`_mm_intrin_op_suffix`

where `intrin_op` indicates the base operation, such as `add`, and `_suffix` denotes the data type operated on by the functions.

An example of `_suffix` would be `pi32`, representing packed, signed, 32-bit integer. Since the data type is specified by the number of bits, there is no confusion of the different data type naming conventions—that is "H" versus "W".

To port from MMX C-code with intrinsics to Intel Wireless MMX technology is extremely easy; the names of the functions and data types are identical, so you need only recompile and be sure that the source file uses the correct include file for Intel Wireless MMX technology, `mmintrin.h`. The include file is found in the Intel compiler's include directory, and it defines the `_m64` data types and ANSI C prototypes of these intrinsics.

Figure 11.15 shows an example of some intrinsic mappings from MMX to Intel Wireless MMX technology.

Intrinsic	MMX™ technology	Intel® Wireless MMX™ technology
`_mm_add_pi8`	WADDB	PADDB
`_mm_add_pu16`	WADDHUS	PADDUSW
`_mm_unpackhi_pi8`	WUNPCKIHB	PUNPCHBW

Figure 11.15 Mapping Intrinsics from MMX™ to Intel® Wireless MMX™ Technology

The intrinsics also provide a mechanism to port functions such as shift by an immediate value easily. This function is available as a single MMX instruction, but requires multiple Intel Wireless MMX instructions. The form of the intrinsic remains the same, with the equivalent functionality synthesized below the function interface, as shown in Figure 11.16.

Intrinsic	MMX™ technology	Intel® Wireless MMX™ technology
_mm_srai_pi16	PSRAWI	Composite

Figure 11.16 Using Intrinsics to Map from a Single MMX™ Instruction to Multiple Intel® Wireless MMX™ Instructions

As shown in Figure 11.17, the superset functionality, which is present in Intel Wireless MMX technology but not in the original MMX technology, is also available in intrinsic form.

Intrinsic	MMX™ technology	Intel® Wireless MMX™ technology
_mm_cmpgt_pu8	None Available	WCMPGTUB

Figure 11.17 Intrinsics for New Functionality Using Intel® Wireless MMX™ Technology

Overall, C-code with intrinsics provides a very simple porting path from MMX to Intel Wireless MMX technology.

Key Points

The key points from this chapter are:

■ The three basic levels of porting are simple, simple optimized, and algorithm optimized. The amount of effort required to get more efficient results increases as you move from simple to algorithm optimized.

■ Intel Wireless MMX technology provides a one-for-one instruction mapping from MMX instructions and integer SSE.

■ Destructive write operations can be avoided with Intel Wireless MMX technology, so many redundant MOVQ instructions can be eliminated as a result of the port.

■ Memory operands must be loaded and stored explicitly when using Intel Wireless MMX instructions, and care must be taken with the alignment of the data.

■ C-intrinsics can be ported with minimal effort.

Part III
Intel® Wireless MMX™ Technology Case Studies

Chapter 12

Accelerating Graphics Applications

Starry, starry night, paint your palette blue and gray...

— Don McLean on Vincent Van Gogh

Demand for graphics and gaming applications has always outpaced the growth of processor capability. Graphics applications are becoming one of the "killer apps" for mobile and handheld devices. Enhanced graphics capability offers better user experience through an attractive user interface and an enjoyable gaming experience. Interactive games and graphics applications challenge the computational capabilities of the processor and memory subsystem. Optimizing for these applications requires an intimate understanding of the applications and the capabilities of the processing engine. This chapter, a brief overview of the graphics processing chain, demonstrates how Intel Wireless MMX technology can be used to accelerate the different components of the processing chain.

Graphics Pipeline

Graphics pipeline is a common term used to describe the graphics processing chain, which consists of the series of algorithmic stages that must be performed to create an image on the screen. The processing sequence is generally consistent across all implementations; however, it can be modified and optimized based on the content of the scene and hardware capabilities.

The graphics pipeline operates on a set of input data referred to as *primitives*. The primitives can be in the form of a triangle, strips of triangles, points, and lines. Primitives represented as vertices go in at one end of the graphics pipe and come out the other end as a set of pixels in the frame buffer. A display controller displays these pixels onto the LCD screen from the frame buffer. Figure 12.1 shows a generic flow in a graphics pipeline.

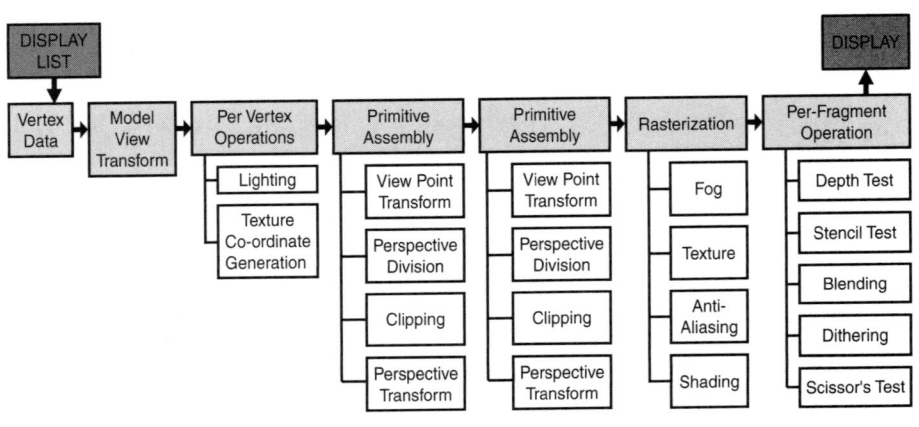

Figure 12.1 A Typical Graphics Pipeline Diagram

A real-world object, such as a car or a human, is represented as a collection of primitives in a graphics world. The primitives are a collection of vertices. The front end of the graphics pipeline consists of *geometry processing* stages, where the vertices of different primitives are operated on. These primitives are transformed into eye-space, or patterns as the eye would see them, then, the lighting and shading is performed on the vertex. This operation need not be done for those vertices that are not visible to the camera, or to the viewer's eye; thus, backface culling and clipping are performed on the primitives. Following these operations, the primitives are set up for the back end of the processing pipe, or for *rasterization*.

The back end of the graphics pipeline converts these primitives to the frame buffer or display buffer in a format acceptable by the LCD or the display screen. Based on the lighting and shading information, each of the primitives is filled with the correct color and written out to the frame buffer. Operations are performed to take into account the relative depth of each pixel—that is, making distant objects in the scene appear smaller. This characteristic is called *perspective correction*. A scene can contain multiple objects for which one object can occlude the view of other objects. Thus, when processing primitives, such occlusions must be detected. In this stage, a series of algorithms is applied to enhance the photorealism and to hide the imperfection of the image. These algorithms are filtering, blending, fogging, anti-aliasing, texturing, texture filtering, shading, and so on.

Indicators of Performance

Performance of the graphics pipeline is a nebulous topic. Performance can have two different aspects. One is the perceptual performance; the other is the mathematical performance metric. They need not correlate at all times. However, for gaming and interactive graphics, the application needs to adhere to a real-time deadline that also relies on the speed at which the interactions are being made. The performance of the graphics processing chain is a function of the content being displayed. Thus, comparing graphics performance between two platforms should ensure that all the preceding factors have been duly considered.

The most commonly used terms describing graphics pipeline performance are *fill rate* and *polygon rate*. Application performance is often measured in terms of *frame rate*. The optimization approaches discussed here focus on these metrics. Perceptual quality improvement is a more involved topic that is beyond the scope of this book.

Fill Rate

Fill rate represents the speed at which pixels are filled after converting the primitives. The fill rate depends on several factors: the algorithms that are used in the rasterization pipe, the size of the primitives, the filling method used, shading and texture complexity, the depth complexity, the output bit format, and the platform characteristics. However, by optimizing for performance, maximizing the fill rate across multiple test cases can be a very good approach for optimizing the pipe implementation. When setting a target for graphics pipeline implementation, one should consider the target frame rate of the application and display resolution. For example, in a system with a QVGA screen (320×240) with a content update rate of 15, the required fill rate should be 1.12 megapixels per second.

Polygon Rate

Often the primitives are triangles, and the polygon rate represents the number of triangles that can be processed per second. Polygon rate can be used instead of fill rate, since both indicate the level of complexity that is supported in the scene. The higher the number of triangles used to represent a scene, the more realistic the representation. Considering the screen size, content, and usage environment, the number of triangles for typical applications on handheld mobile devices may be considerably less.

Other performance representations include frame rate, vertex rate, and so on. While these different metrics measure different aspects of a graphics solution, an optimization approach tries to improve all aspects. In this chapter, some typical graphics workloads are analyzed and a set of methods and algorithms to use for optimizing Intel Wireless MMX technology are demonstrated.

Optimization Challenges

A graphics pipe is heterogeneous in nature. Different components of a graphics application demonstrate differing characteristics. They differ in terms of the data types they use—fixed versus float. The characteristics of the operations also differ in that they can be computationally bound or memory bound. This variation makes optimizing graphics more challenging. Thus, the general approach to optimization requires you to understand each of the algorithmic chains. This chapter provides a brief overview and a set of techniques.

Performance Profile

Profile-based optimization is described in Chapter 6, "Finding the Bottleneck." Graphics workloads can also be profiled to demonstrate their critical components and how these components can be accelerated in a system supporting Intel Wireless MMX technology. Let's consider a typical workload, as shown in Figure 12.2, one that follows the algorithmic flow of the graphics pipe shown in Figure 12.1. The workload uses approximately 10,000 triangles and a display resolution of QVGA (240×340). The statistics were gathered over a period of 1,000 frames using an Intel® PXA250 Applications Processor running at 400 megahertz. The results here are intended to show relative breakdown of different components of the graphics pipe.

Courtesy of Gopi K. Kolli, et. al., 3D Graphics Optimizations for Intel PCA Applications Processors with Intel XScale® Technology, Solutions Journal, Volume 3, Spring 2002.

Figure 12.2   Execution of a Typical Workload

It is important to understand the relative cycle consumption of different components in an application from the optimization point of view. Figure 12.3 shows the percentage breakdown of a workload in terms of number of cycles consumed. The key components of the workload are as follows:

■ *Application overhead*. This component represents the part of the workload that performs nongraphics operations such as file handling.

■ *Geometry processing*. This component of the workload performs model view transformation, per-vertex lighting, and texturing. It also assembles the primitives by clipping and perspective transformation. Most of these operations are done using floating-point or high-precision fixed-point operations.

Typical Breakdown of Graphics Workload

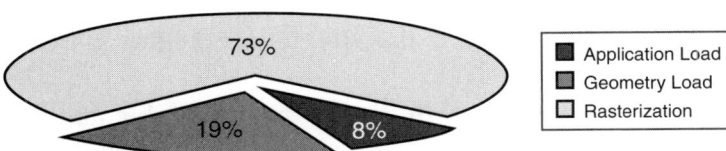

Figure 12.3   Approximate Decomposition of Key Contributors of a Graphics Workload

■ *Rasterization processing.* You can see from the profile that this stage contributes most to cycle consumption for a typical graphics application. At this stage, the transformed triangles are drawn on the screen one line at a time. While working on each line, a series of operations is performed on a per-pixel basis. Most of the operations are performed in fixed-point format. These pixel operations are uniform across different pixels and also across different color components of each pixel. Thus, Intel Wireless MMX technology can be used effectively to gain performance improvements on these algorithms. Rasterization can be further divided into a set of subcomponents, as follows:

– *Fogging.* The graphics primitives used for representing distant objects in the scene is fogged with a particular color to make it appear distant.

– *Texture mapping.* To reflect the material type—concrete, wood, and so on—in the scene, texture mapping is performed, where the color of the pixel or line is modulated with a particular pattern representing the material.

– *Anti-aliasing.* Due to the discrete nature of the display devices, some visual artifacts such as jagged edges for lines with a slope, can be introduced. Anti-aliasing is performed to reduce such visual artifacts. Anti-aliasing can also be used to improve the perceptual quality of fonts and lines when displaying smaller fonts in a smaller screen.

– *Shading.* Considering the lighting condition and relative orientation between the eye and the graphics object, most of the graphics primitives are not uniform in color throughout a realistic scene. Shading is performed to incorporate such variation in intensity while filling the faces of the graphics primitive. Given the two edges of a scan line that are covered by a triangle, this step fills in the line with a gradual intensity of color.

– *Alpha blending.* This algorithm blends an object with its background in a semitransparent manner. Common uses include creating a reflection of one object onto another or giving texture to clouds.

– *Depth test.* During the writing or rendering of each pixel, depth, or distance from the eye, is compared to ensure that the nearest pixel overwrites pixels that are farther away.

Figure 12.4 shows a typical flow of algorithms for a rasterization operation.

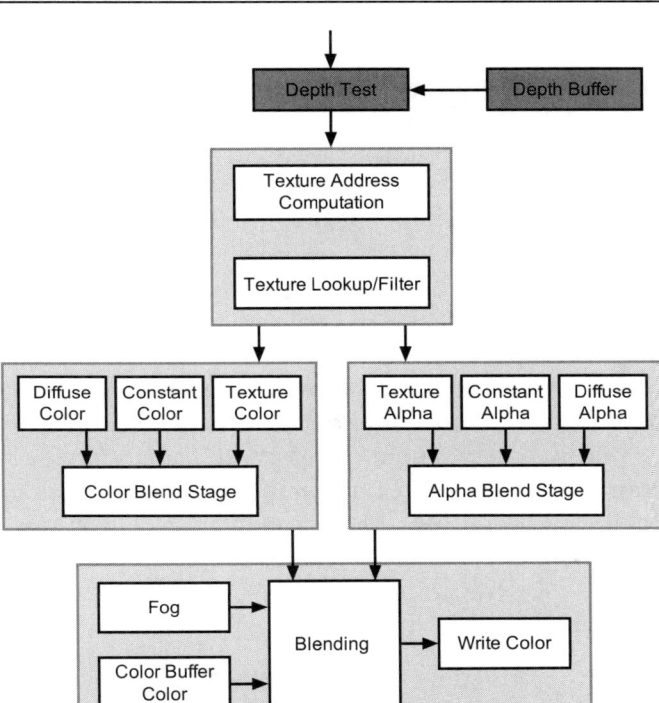

Figure 12.4   A Typical Algorithmic Chain for a Rasterizer

The following section focuses on acceleration of some of the key algorithms of the rasterization stage.

Performance Optimization Methods

Intel Wireless MMX technology combined with memory optimization techniques can be used to optimize graphics applications. Three aspects of optimizing graphics workload are:

- Algorithmic optimization
- Computational optimization
- Memory-based optimization

Algorithmic Optimization

One of the key methods of improving performance is to ensure that the algorithms chosen for the application are appropriate. For example, in many handheld multimedia devices, the display sizes are small and the user may be viewing the games or the graphics content while in motion or outdoors. By implication, you could assume that the user would not discern small flaws in the perceptual quality. Thus, choosing the correct level of detail may alone improve the interactivity of the games or graphics application. Algorithms can be used effectively to reduce overall computation by reducing unnecessary computations. For instance, performing a back-face culling saves the computation on lighting. In addition, performing a depth test first could save significant computational power in the rasterization operations. Similarly, the choice might force trade-offs between the number of triangles and the amount of texturing done per triangle. Using more textures could increase the perceived quality more than increasing the number of triangles. The graphics developer should consider these domain-specific optimizations while developing applications.

Computational Optimization

The front end of the graphics pipe—the geometry pipe—typically uses floating-point operations. Increased accuracy within the computation ensures that, as the graphics objects are transformed from model space to eye space, they appear accurate. For many gaming applications, floating-point computations are used to calculate the dynamics of motion, object collision, and so forth.

On the other hand, the rasterization is always performed in fixed-point format using 16-bit or 8-bit unsigned integers. Intel Wireless MMX technology offers single instruction multiple data (SIMD) support for 8-bit, 16-bit, 32-bit, and 64-bit data formats, both signed and unsigned. This section describes a set of example algorithms, primarily applicable for rasterization, which can be accelerated by using Intel Wireless MMX technology. Note that these examples are not conclusive. Many more algorithms can be designed and modified with SIMD implementation in mind. The fundamental techniques of optimization are similar to the techniques seen in earlier chapters. However, the discussion is intended to put the optimization approaches into context. The typical concerns for graphics applications are:

- Precision requirements
- Data-formation considerations
- Alignment considerations
- Level of pipelining
- Optimal use of resources

Precision Requirements

For floating-point-based geometry computation, emulation of floating-point arithmetic using fixed-point computation is a likely solution since most hardware does not inherently support floating-point data. Emulation of floating-point data may not be very efficient. However, in some cases, fixed-point data may be used instead. For performing geometric transformations, 16-bit fixed-point representation of signed integer values may be acceptable for many graphics applications and games. Such an algorithmic change can offer potentially significant performance acceleration.

For a rasterization pipe, a series of operations on the incoming data is performed. The precision of the input, output, intermediate results, rounding modes, and so on impact the overall perceptual quality on a graphics image. Choosing the correct precision and the correct set of instructions to attain these operations is important. Eight-bit precision for color—the RGB component—might not be sufficient for most operations. On the other hand, 32-bit precision for each color does not deliver significantly greater perceptual quality compared to 16-bit color component precision. Furthermore, using 16-bit precision as opposed to 32-bit precision allows larger parallelism. However, for some algorithms, higher precision—in fixed-point format—should be maintained. For example, for a Z-buffering algorithm, a precision error may lead to displaying some occluded primitives, leading to an unpleasant viewing experience. Thus, depth-buffer or Z-buffer management might be handled better in 32-bit format.

Data Formation Considerations

Data organization for graphics primitives contributes to how an algorithm is implemented. Each primitive is defined with a set of attributes. Note that a vertex has a set of attributes that are different than attributes for a scanline. A set of such primitives can be organized in different ways. The SIMD capability of Intel Wireless MMX technology allows operation on multiple data points at once. Algorithms can be designed such that entries from the same primitives are operated on concurrently. On the other hand, some algorithms may impose operation on attributes from different primitives concurrently. Two ways to organize data can be adopted: array of structures (AOS) and structure of arrays (SOA). Both are shown in the next code example. Traditionally, SOA is perceived to be SIMD-friendly, whereas AOS is thought of as software-development friendly. This perception lives on because AOS multiple structures might have to be loaded to extract and pack data elements for data-parallel operations. For SOA, this packing and unpacking might not be necessary. However, a set of examples later in this section shows that Intel Wireless MMX technology can be used effectively for both. Conversion between the formats, if necessary, can also be done efficiently using Intel Wireless MMX technology. Larger register files can be used for this purpose. Therefore, conversion between the formats can be done on the fly without an excessive number of loads. Another concern is the memory locality. For AOS with a larger structure, the cache preloading may not be efficient. One of the preloading techniques, pointer pre-fetch, as shown in Chapter 9, might not be effective. In addition, AOS with a larger structure could suffer from inefficient memory bandwidth use, since only a fraction of the data may be required for use. Thus, choosing between formats judiciously is recommended. You might also choose an intermediate hybrid approach where an array of structures is created with a structure of a small array, as shown here:

```
// Array of Structure (AOS)
struct { float x, y, z, r, g, b
} AoS_xyz_rgb[200];

// Structure of Array (SOA)
struct { float x[200], y[200], z[200];
        float r[200], g[200], b[200];
} SoA_xyz_rgb;

// Hybrid SOA
struct { float xx[4], yy[4], zz[4];
} Hybrid_xyz[50];
struct { float rr[4], gg[4], bb[4];
} Hybrid_rgb[50];
```

Hybrid structures may be used in both the front and back ends of the graphics-processing pipe. For instance, each object is presented as a set of triangles organized as AOS; whereas, each triangle may contain three vertices organized as SOA. As with the back end, the depth buffer can be represented as AOS, where each structure holds an array of depth buffer entries in one or two dimensions. Hybrid structures can be helpful for prefetching.

Alignment Considerations

Intel Wireless MMX technology offers two-way, four-way, and eight-way parallelism, whereas typical color formats are RGB—three elements. Thus, algorithm implementation should take alignment into consideration. While defining and placing data structures with multiple elements, the commonly used elements—RGBA or XYZW—should be aligned on a 64-bit address. This practice helps reduce the alignment overhead while processing using Intel Wireless MMX technology. For example, assume the following color format for an array of pixels:

```
typedef {
    U16 r; U16 g;
    U16 b; U16 a;
    //U16 represents unsigned shorts.
}SCAN_LINE_DATA;
SCAN_LINE_DATA input[32];
```

If the variable input is not aligned with a 64-bit addressing boundary, loading each of the pixels requires two loads (WLDRD) and an align (WALIGN) operation. Similar arguments can be extended toward aligning a data structure to the cache-line boundary for memory considerations, which is discussed in a later section.

Level of Pipelining

Typical algorithm definitions in graphics are mostly defined in a pixel-by-pixel manner. Regular software pipelining and enhanced pipelining such as multisample techniques should be applied to take optimal advantage of Intel Wireless MMX technology. Redesigning algorithms to take advantage of the pipelined execution is critical for performance acceleration. One approach can be to fuse a set of algorithmic stages together. Figure 12.5 shows how an algorithmic pipelining approach may need to work. In this figure, A, B, C, and D are per-pixel or per-primitive algorithmic stages. This type of pipelining allows better reuse of data by increasing the spatiotemporal locality of the data.

Another extension of computational pipelining is the tiling approach, where one tile-of-output image is created at a time; the computation for the particular tile is done concurrently as well. The advantage of tiling can be overshadowed by the additional effort of sorting and the cost of organizing graphics objects. Also, some graphics primitives could lie across more than one tile, which leads to decomposition of the object along the tile boundary. Thus, you have no clear winner in terms of the approaches. The right answer for the above trade-off is left up to each developer to measure for specific projects. However, fusing algorithmic stages and processing across multiple primitives in general offers efficiency, data reuse, and call-overhead amortization.

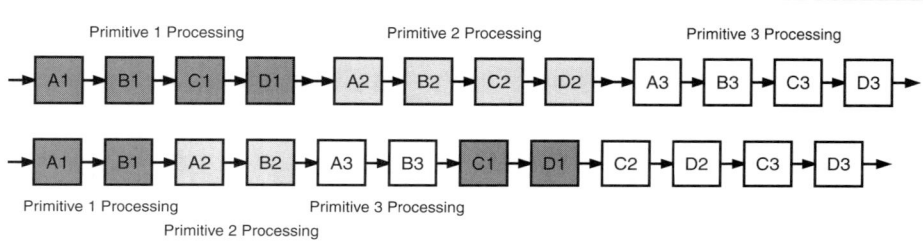

Figure 12.5   Pipelining Between Multiple Primitives

Optimal Use of Resources

As discussed in earlier chapters, ensuring that rescheduling hides all the pipeline stalls is mandatory to attain desired acceleration. It is also important to partition the data between the core register file and the coprocessor register file; typically, all the address computations can be kept in the former, whereas all the data elements can be processed in the latter.

Memory-Related Optimization

Graphics applications are, in general, hungry for memory and access bandwidth. For embedded systems, memory and access bandwidth are at a premium. Thus, optimizing for memory and access bandwidth utilization is extremely important.

Memory Footprint

The sum of data and instruction space that the application consumes defines the *memory footprint*. Keeping track of the memory footprint is important, since many service providers for personal communicators have restrictions on the maximum memory footage. The following elements can affect the size of the memory footprint:

■ *Depth buffer.* The depth buffer maintains the lowest depth of object that covers a particular pixel location. During rasterization, the depth of a pixel is compared against the depth buffer before rendering. Typically, the depth buffer is managed as an array of 32-bit integers. Using higher precision linearly increases the memory footprint. Considering the depth complexity of the application content, the designer can reduce the memory footprint by reducing the depth-buffer precision to 16 bits.

■ *Texture.* A scene may represent many different types of objects—trees, a river, walls, and so on. Each type of object has an associated texture map. Also, depending on the object size to be displayed, additional texture maps may be generated through MIP mapping. To limit the memory footprint, you might find it necessary to restrict the number of textures used and the size of the texture map. In addition, using synthetic textures—producing a texture as a combination of two other textures or computing the texture mathematically—reduces the memory footprint in exchange for more computation.

■ *Display back buffer.* This buffer space is where the content is updated at the desired content update rate and later moved over to the LCD frame buffer for display. These two buffers are kept in different physical locations to avoid unwanted image artifacts such as *image tearing.* Image tearing artifacts are introduced when an application updates the scene while it is being displayed on the screen. At the end of rendering, the LCD frame buffer is updated from the back buffer. For smaller screen sizes, this update can be done relatively smoothly. In some cases, more than one back buffer may be present, where the orientation of the graphics application is not same as the orientation of the display. One may be horizontal, and the other may be vertical. For the sake of the memory footprint, it is important to contain the number of buffers.

In summary, understanding the end application memory footprint requirement is the key to managing memory footprints. Apart from the specified methods above, there are many application-specific techniques that can be used. For instance, reusing characters or players in a gaming application can reduce its footprint.

Application Partitioning for Memory Subsystem

Embedded systems usually have a hierarchical memory subsystem. Each type of memory varies in its memory latency and memory throughput. Different data objects of the application can be placed in the memory in a way such that critical objects are in the memory space with lower latency. For example, texture maps can be stored in the internal memory for faster access. To maintain internal memory storage, the entire texture map need not be in the internal memory. Depending on use, different texture maps can be paged into the internal memory dynamically. In the paging scheme, only a part of the map is kept in the internal memory and updated. For many graphics applications, paging overhead can be justified since the performance boost due to paging can be large.

Memory Latency

The performance impact of memory latency during cache misses has been mentioned in earlier chapters. Also, a variety of methods for avoiding and hiding memory latency have been suggested in Chapter 9. Performing an aggressive and correct preloading scheme is very effective in hiding memory latency. While all suggested approaches hold true in the context of graphics applications, some more-specific methods can be offered for the graphics application domain. For example, rasterization is one of the biggest contributors to the graphics pipe because processing each pixel requires a certain set of data. Preloading can be done in various levels, shown in Figure 12.6.

Pixel level preloading. While processing one pixel (N^{th}), preload necessary data for a pixel down the line ($(N+P)^{th}$). This method is the simplest to adopt. For scan-line operation or operation on a block, the addressing mechanisms are deterministic, thus a certain level of look-ahead can be applied. Preloads are done by inserting `prefetch()` or `pld [Rx, #offset]` in the code, as discussed in Chapter 9. For pixel-level processing, the depth of the pixel is compared with the depth buffer value. Depth buffer values can be pre-fetched easily.

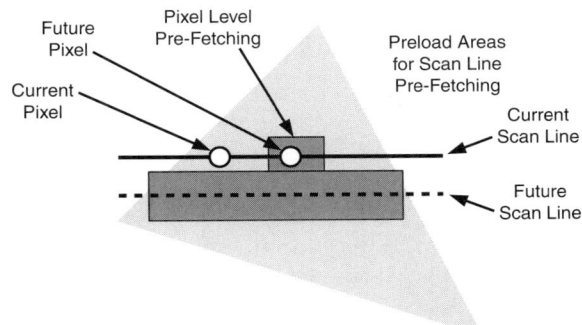

Figure 12.6   Pixel Level or Scan Line Level Pre-fetching

Scan-line level preloading. While processing one scan line (N^{th}), preload necessary data for a scan line down the line ($(N+P)^{th}$), even though no pixels are common between two adjacent scan lines. Texture map, alpha-plane, and Z-buffer values might be common between two adjacent scan lines. Thus, pre-fetching helps by hiding memory latency. To simplify the pre-fetch look-ahead computation, you might follow a general policy where the program preloads a tile or a strip of rows of data relevant for a set of scan lines. However, the biggest challenge is computation of the address to be pre-fetched. For smaller screen displays, sizes of the triangles are also smaller and the size of the texture maps is limited. Thus, a simpler tiled pre-fetching could work effectively. Note that tiled pre-fetching is the method of fetching a tile of data into the cache.

Primitive level preloading. While processing one primitive or triangle (N^{th}), preload necessary data for a primitive down the line ($(N+P)^{th}$). This approach could help with vertex processing. Each primitive contains a set of vertices and is organized as a linear list. While processing one primitive, the vertices for the next one can be preloaded following the linear list.

The preload distance (P) for all the above approaches should be determined correctly to benefit from the preloading.

P = memory_latency_in_cycle / (#cycles/loop + #cycles to issue preload)

Cache Usage

The memory subsystems in embedded systems have cache memories. Efficient programming of the graphics algorithms is necessary to achieve higher cache usage. Different cache utilization schemes have been introduced in earlier chapters. You can apply them to a graphics application by following a set of methods described in this section.

Choice of representation. An object is represented as a set of triangles that are often contiguous. For those cases, instead of representing these triangles as an array of triangles, they can be represented as an array of vertices. For an N triangle object, the amount of memory to represent the object with an array of triangles is: 3N * Memory_size(vertex). However, N triangles can also be represented as *N+2* number of vertices. Thus, representing the object as a vertex array would only consume memory space of the size: *(N+2)* * Memory_size(vertex). This approach is an example of choosing an appropriate representation. In this approach, memory footprint and in-turn cache utilization would increase, since each triangle uses the vertex information from the previous triangle.

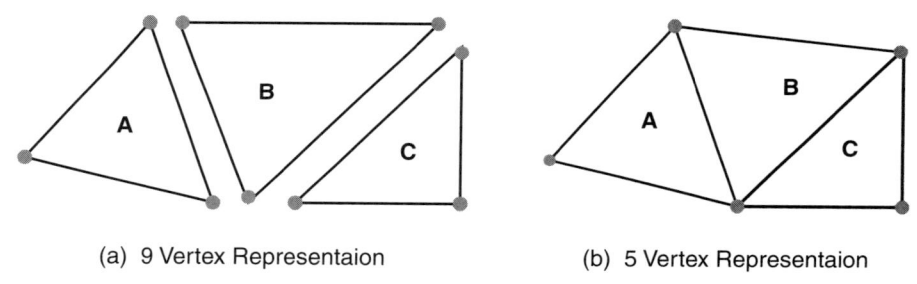

(a) 9 Vertex Representaion   (b) 5 Vertex Representaion

Figure 12.7   Representation of Primitives for Saving Memory

Choice of data structure. Data structures differ according to the stage in which they are used: vertex representation, scan-line representation, or output color representation. The data structure should be designed to be an integer multiple of the cache-line size, and the structure should be aligned on a cache-line boundary. This approach helps preload the data structure. For instance, if a data structure is of single cache-line size but is not aligned at the cache-line boundary, accessing the data structure can cause two cache misses. In addition, the typical pre-fetching approach might load only one part of the data structure into the cache. This concern applies to both the data organization methods shown previously: structure of array (SOA) and array of structure (AOS).

Having described different optimization concerns in mostly general terms, the following section demonstrates a few techniques of implementing graphics algorithms using Intel Wireless MMX technology. However, many of these examples are aimed at showing a few guidelines; the domain experts can achieve further optimizations.

Optimizing Graphics Application Kernels

The computational and memory optimization suggestions described previously need to be put to work on different components in a graphics chain. The best approach to demonstrate the optimizations is to apply them hands-on in a series of graphics algorithms. This section offers a series of algorithm examples with implementation suggestions where Intel Wireless MMX technology can best be utilized.

Shading

Color filling a triangle or primitive is called *shading*. Instead of flat shading—filling a triangle with one single color, realism can be attained by changing the intensity of the filled color pixel by pixel based on color intensity of the vertices.

Interpolation-based shading is used commonly for filling color in triangles. The approach of interpolation-based shading varies, with Gouraud shading and Phong shading the most commonly used approaches.

Gouraud Shading

Named after its inventor, Henri Gouraud, who developed this technique in 1971, this approach assigns to each triangle three projected vertices, *P1* to *P3*, and a reflected light intensity, *I1* to *I3*. For any given point inside the triangle, the intensity is evaluated by linear interpolation. Any point in the triangle can be defined using the following calculations:

$$P = \overline{P}_1 + \mu_1(\overline{P}_2 - \overline{P}_1) + \mu_2(\overline{P}_3 - \overline{P}_1)$$
$$I = I_1 + \mu_1(I_2 - I_1) + \mu_2(I_3 - I_1)$$

Since μ_1 and μ_2 are scalar parameters and the point being shaded is inside the triangle, $0 \le \mu_1 + \mu_2 \le 1$ and $0 \le \mu_1 \le 1$ and $0 \le \mu_2 \le 1$ are constraints on μ_1 and μ_2. Given a point inside the triangle, it would be possible to solve for μ_1 and μ_2 and then calculate I. Realistically, the program first interpolates between vertices and assigns intensity values along triangle edges.

Then it interpolates across the scan line based on the interpolated edge values. In the scan line approach, the intensity of points A and B is determined based on *(P2, P3)* and *(P2, P1)* respectively. Then the intensity for point *P* is determined by using the following equation, also illustrated in Figure 12.8:

$$Gradient = \frac{(B_s - A_s)}{(B_x - A_x)}$$

$$I = A_s + (P_x - B_x) \bullet Gradient$$

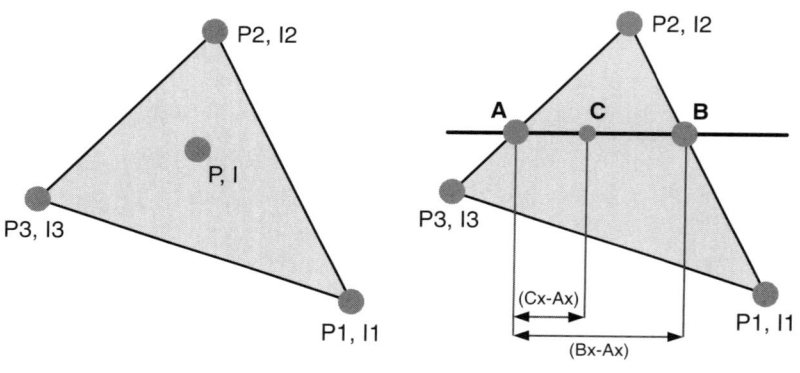

Figure 12.8 Illustrating Gouraud Shading

Using Intel Wireless MMX technology, the algorithm in Figure 12.8 can be effectively implemented two ways. The approaches differ in terms of how parallelism is extracted. The color component for each pixel can be computed in parallel; conversely, the same color component from multiple pixels can be computed in parallel. For a typical graphics pipe, 16-bit precision must be maintained for the intermediate operation, which means four-way parallelism can be achieved using Intel Wireless MMX technology. While operating on the same color component of multiple pixels, the program can achieve maximum efficiency if it works on multiples of four pixels. In addition, some rearranging of the incoming data might be necessary, since the pixels in the memory are likely to be stored in pixel-by-pixel fashion. On the other hand, if all the color components of each pixel are operated on concurrently, the RGB color components occupy only three out of four subfields. In the latter approach, three-way parallelism can be achieved by processing R, G, and B components in parallel. However, multiple pixels can be packed into a number of registers; that is, four pixels can be packed into three registers, allowing four-way parallelism. The differentiating factor between these two approaches is the overhead of data organization.

```
void GS_Scan_Line(int x0, int r0, int g0, int b0,
                  int x1, int r1, int g1, int b1,
                  int y)
// y is constant across the scan line
// output_r, output_b, output_c are the outputs
{
    int i;
    long gradient_r, gradient_g, gradient_b;
    int h_dist = x1-x0; //assuming x1 > x0
    gradient_r = (r1-r0)/h_dist;
    gradient_g = (g1-g0)/h_dist;
    gradient_b = (b1-b0)/h_dist;

    for (i=x0; i<=x1 ; i++) {
        output_r[i,y] = r0 + (i-x0)*gradient_r;
        output_g[i,y] = g0 + (i-x0)*gradient_g;
        output_b[i,y] = b0 + (i-x0)*gradient_b;
    }
}
```

Figure 12.9   C Code Implementation of Gouraud Shading Algorithm

The implementation in Figure 12.10 shows implementation of the algorithm shown in Figure 12.9. In the code, the loop of the RGB value of the vertex is assumed to be available in packed 16-bit per color format. One should note that in either implementation, multiple samples are processed at a time. The example provided here serves as a good example of the technique. The number of samples processed in each iteration has been chosen to take full advantage of the data parallelism.

```
@ r0 points to pixel_A
@ r0 = pntr to input buffer
@ r1 = pntr to delta_values buffer
@ r2 = pntr to output buffer

wldrd wR1, [r0] @16-bit precision for RGB
@r4 = 0x0000FFFF
@r5 = 0xFFFFFFFF
mov r4, #0
mov r5, #0xff
mov r4, r5, lsl #8
orr r4, r4, r5
mov r5, r4, lsl #16
orr r5, r5, r4
```

```
tmcrr wR2, r5, r4   @ wR2 [63:48]=0 wR2[47:0]=1
wand wR1, wR1, wR2 @ wR1 = 0   R   G   B
wldrd wR3, [r1]       @ wR3 = x dR dG dB
wand  wR3, wR3, wR2  @ wR3 = 0 dR dG dB
wzero wR15            @ wR15 = 0
waddh wR4, wR3, wR3 @ wR4 = 0 2dR 2dG 2dB
waddh wR5, wR4, wR3 @ wR5 = 0 3dR 3dG 3dB
waddh wR6, wR5, wR3 @ wR6 = 0 4dR 4dG 4dB
waligni wR14, wR15, wR4,#2   @ wR14 = 2dB 0 0 0
wor     wR3, wR3, wR14       @ wR3  = 2dB dR dG dB
waligni wR14, wR4, wR15,#2   @ wR14 = 0 0 2dR 2dG
waligni wR13, wR15, wR5,#4   @ wR13 = 3dG 3dB 0 0
wor     wr4, wR14, wR13      @ wR4  = 3dG 3dB 2dR 2dG

aligni wr14, wr5, wr15, #4   @ wR14 = 0 0 0 3dR
waligni wr13, wr15, wr6, #6  @ wR13 = 4dR 4dG 4dB 0
wor wr5, wR14, wR13          @ wR5  = 4dR 4dG 4dB 3dR
@Each iteration produces 4 pixels
Loop_set:
subs r3, r3, #4
wshufh wR7, wR1, 0x24        @ wR7  = B R G B
wshufh wR8, wR1, 0x49        @ wR8  = G B R G
wshufh wR9, wR1, 0x92        @ wR9  = R G B R
waddh  wR7, wR7, wR3 @ B+2dB R+dR G+dG B+dB
waddh  wR8, wR8, wR4 @ G+3dG B+3dB R+2dR G+2dG
waddh  wR9, wR9, wR5 @ R+4dR G+4dG B+4dB R+3dR
@Packing will be required to reduce color prec.
wstrd wR7, [r2],#8
wstrd wR8, [r2],#8
wstrd wR9, [r2],#8
waligni wR1, wR9, wR15,#2    @ 0 R+4dR G+4dG B+4dB
bne Loop_set
```

Figure 12.10 Implementation of Gouraud Shading using Intel® Wireless MMX™ Technology

In addition to demonstrating the acceleration capability of Intel Wireless MMX technology, this example shows how to address the overhead of alignment and data organization carefully. Using multisample techniques, data organization overhead easily can be amortized. The example assumed 16-bit precision RGB color format. However, some graphics engines could choose to use the RGB and Alpha (RGBA) color format. In this case, alignment overhead is reduced because the color information of each pixel is 64 bits wide. In the previous example, the AOS form was used, and neither AOS nor SOA conversion was needed due to the implementation design of the shading algorithm.

Z-Buffering

The Z-buffering algorithm is used in graphics applications to ensure that the perspective view works realistically, so that a solid object in the foreground blocks the view of the one behind it. Z-buffering works by testing pixel depth and comparing the current position, or z coordinate, with stored data in a buffer, called a Z-buffer, which holds information about the last position of each pixel. The pixel in the closer position to the viewer is displayed. Figure 12.11 shows a typical pseudocode for implementation.

```
Clear Z-Buffer to a certain value
For every primitive
    For every scan line of that primitive
        For every pixel
            If this is nearest pixel
                Write Pixel
                Write Z into zbuffer
            End If
        End For
    End For
End For
```

Figure 12.11 Pseudocode for Z-Buffer Algorithm

In a theoretical approach, Z-buffering would be a last step before writing data to the frame buffer. However, in a practical approach, Z-buffer testing is performed at the beginning of rasterization to avoid any rendering operations if the pixel does not pass the Z-buffer test. The code in Figure 12.12 is an effective representation of Z-buffer testing using Intel Wireless MMX technology. For the purposes of this implementation, assume that pixels passing the Z-buffer test are written to the memory. Assume that the data structure for pixels in the scan line matches the following:

```
typedef {
    I32   Z;
    I32   x;
    U32   r;
    U32   g;
    U32   b;
    U32   a;
}SCAN_LINE_DATA;
```

Note that the data structure has no *y* value since all pixels in the scan line have the same *y* value. Figure 12.12 shows how Z-buffer comparisons and pixel updates to the memory can be combined and done efficiently using the group conditional execution capability of Intel Wireless MMX technology.

```
@ r1 points to current Z-buffer
@ r0 points to array of pixels for processing
@ r2 points to framebuffer
@ r4 = number of pixels in the frame buffer.

Outer_Loop : @ For each position in the frame buffer

wldrd   wR1, [r0], #8      @ wR1 = B1 Z1
wldrw   wR0, [r1], #4      @ wR0 =  0 Z_current
wldrd   wR6, [r0], #8      @ wR6 = R2 G2
@ r3 = number of pixels to compare
Inner_Loop : @ loops over all the pixels to compare

wcmpgtuw wR2, wR1, wR0     @ wR2 = XXXX Mask for Z
textrcw  R15, #1           @ Extracts flag word 0
wmaxuw   wR4, wR1, wR0     @ Chooses higher Z
                           @ Pre-fetching next cache line
                           @ can be done at this point
wstrne   wR4, [r1],#4      @ Updating Z buffer value

wshufh   wR0, wR0, 0x4E    @ wR0 = Z B
wstrwne  wR0, [r2]         @ Conditional store B
wldrd    wR0, [r1], #4     @ wR0 = NEXT PIXEL B Z
wstrwne  wR6, [r2,#4]      @ Conditional store G
wshufh   wR6, wR6, 0x4E    @ wR6 = G R
wstrwne  wR6, [r2,#8]      @ Conditional store R

wldrd    wR6, [r0],#8      @ wR6 = NEXT PIXEL R and G
wldrd    wR7, [r0],#8      @ wR7 = NEXT PIXEL A and B
subs     r3, r3, #1
bne Inner_Loop:

add      r2, r2, #8        @ Update address for frame buff
subs     r4, r4, #1
bne Outer_Loop:
```

Figure 12.12 Z-Buffering Algorithm Implementation

This implementation demonstrates group-conditional execution techniques of Intel Wireless MMX technology. It also points out how and where pre-fetching can be done. The Z-buffering algorithm alone is not an attractive algorithm for SIMD acceleration. Typically, Z-buffering is done with other pixel processing operations, such as shading and texturing, which all use the coprocessor register file. The example shows how Z-buffer comparisons can be performed without having to transfer data back to the processor.

Texture Mapping

Texturing is essentially a mapping between the texture space and the polygon. This operation requires generating a texture map coordinate on the pixel coordinate and looking up the texture value from the texture map. When the pixel coordinates do not map directly to the texture coordinates, an interpolation scheme needs to be used. This mapping is accomplished by using the color of an image at the location indicated by a fragment's coordinates to modify the fragment's color. Texturing is specified only for RGBA mode; its use in color index mode is undefined. In the simplest case, you are mapping one rectangular space into another as shown in Figure 12.13. In general however, mapping must be performed on a general quadrilateral. Following the figure, a point P in the primitive is represented as a vectored sum of the edge vectors.

Any point in the quadrilateral can be expressed in terms of the edge vectors as:

$$\overline{p} = \alpha\overline{a} + \beta\overline{e}$$
$$\overline{e} = \overline{b} + \alpha\overline{(c - b)}$$
$$\overline{p} = \alpha\overline{a} + \beta\overline{b} + \alpha\beta(\overline{c} - \overline{b})$$

Here

$$0 \le \alpha \le 1, 0 \le \beta \le 1$$

However, b = c can be assumed for simplicity.

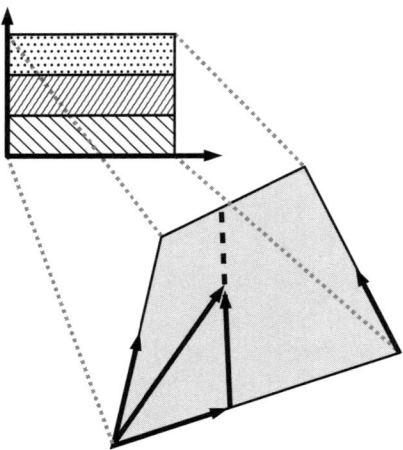

Figure 12.13   Texturing Polygons

For a point p, the texture lookup result is [α,β]. However, [α,β] might not be an existing defined point in the texture map or it might not be an integer. Therefore, bilinear interpolation would be used to estimate the exact texture value for [α,β]. Thus, the texture for that particular pixel is generated by the following formula, as illustrated by Figure 12.14:

$$T_{out}(\alpha,\beta) = T(i,j)(1-x)(1-y) + T(i+1,j)x(1-y) + T(i,j+1)(1-x)y + T(i+1,j+1)xy$$
$$x = \alpha - \lfloor \alpha \rfloor$$
$$y = \beta - \lfloor \beta \rfloor$$

While implementing bilinear interpolation, texture elements, called *texels* for short, can be presented in three different ways. Horizontal interpolation is done between two adjacent pixels where β is an integer. Vertical interpolation is done between texels from two different lines where α is an integer in the texture maps. The last type, bidirectional interpolation, performs interpolation between four different pixels.

For superior quality and photorealism in graphics, higher quality textures are necessary. Impressive textures may improve the perceived quality of an image without having to use as many triangles. However, handheld applications are constrained by memory space, so the number of textures is often restricted. A likely approach is to store textures in a packed fashion and generate other textures through texture filtering or interpolation. Texture mapping is typically done on a pixel-by-pixel basis along the scan line. Texture map values are used to modulate the color values of the shaded pixel.

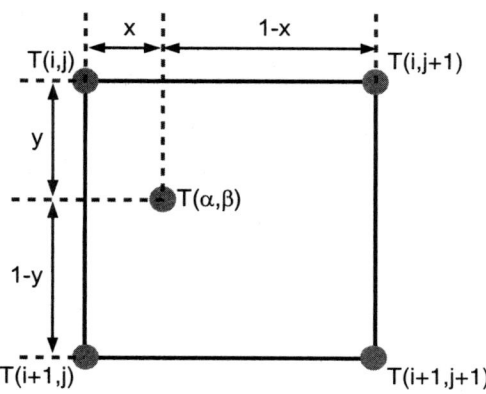

Figure 12.14 Texture Interpolation from a Texture Lattice

Typically, texture values are 16 bits wide. The following code shows how typical texture maps are stored.

```
Typedef struct {
    U16 * m_pTexBuffer;
    U16 m_width;
    U16 m_height;
}Texture_Map
```

The vertex and scan-line edge points usually refer to a texture index of 32-bit precision. During the scan-line operations, the index is also interpolated. Typical vertex primitives with texture indexes may appear as follows:

```
Typedef struct {
    I32    x;
    I32    w;
    U16    r;
    U16    g;
    U16    b;
    U16    a;
    U32    tu;
    U32    tv
}Vertex_with_Texture
```

For two end points of the scan line, *tu* and *tv*, the index into the texture map, are calculated from the vertices of the primitive. Then, for each point on the scan line, the indices are interpolated from the index values of the end points. The following example shows how interpolating derives the texture value.

```
@ du = step-size on the texture in u direction
@ dv = step-size on the texture in v direction
@ du,dv,x,tu,tv all have 32 bit precision
@ r4 holds del_u
@ r5 holds del_v
@ r6 holds current_x;
@ r7 holds edge_x
@ r8 holds edge_tu
@ r9 holds edge_tv
@ r10 = 0
@ r11 = current_y for the scanline

sub    r6, r6, r7      @ r6 distance from the edge
tmcrr  wR0, r8, r10    @ wR0 = edge_tu 0
tmia   wR0, r6, r4     @ wR0=edge_tu+
                       @ del_u *(current_x - edge_x)
tmcrr  wR1,  r9, r10   @ wR1 = edge_tv 0
tmia   wR1, r11,   r5  @ wR1=edge_tv+
                       @ del_v *(current_y - edge_y)

@ wR0,wR1 contains address of the texture map
@ wR0,wR1 is not necessarily integer.
tmcr   wR15, r4
mov    r1, 0xFFFF
tbcsth wR14, r1
         @wR14= 0xFFFF 0xFFFF 0xFFFF 0xFFFF

Loop :
textrmuw  r0, wR0       @ r0 has the pointer to tu
textrmuw  r1, wR1       @ r1 has the pointer to tv
@ from r1 and r0 we need to derive
@ r0 = address of the texel
@ r1 = address of the texel in the next line

wunpckilw wR3, wR1, wR0 @ wR3 = u   v
wsubh     wR4, wR14, wR3 @ wR4 = 1- (u) 1- (v)
wpackhus  wR4, wR4, wR3 @ wR4 = u    v  (1-u)(1-v)
wshufh    wR5, wR4,0x5F @ wR5 = u    u  (1-u)(1-u)
wshufh    wR6, wR4 0x22 @ wR6 = v (1-v)    v (1-v)
wldrd     wR7, [r0]  @ wR7 = [T(i,j+3) T(i,j+2)
                     @        T(i,j+1) T(i,j)]
wldrd     wR8, [r1]
                  @ wR8 = [T(i+1,j+3) T(i+1,j+2)
```

```
                      @          T(i+1,j+1) T(i+1,j)]
wunpckihh wR11, wR7, wR8
                      @ wR10 = [T(i+1,j+1) T(i,j+1)
                      @         T(i,j+1) T(i,j)]
wmulum wR8, wR5, wR6
                      @ wR8 = MSB [uv u(1-v)
                      @           (1-u)v (1-u)(1-v)]
wmulul wR9, wR5, wR6
                      @ wR9 = LSB [uv u(1-v)
                      @           (1-u)v (1-u)(1-v)]
wsrag wR9, #15
waddh wR8, wR8, WR9
                      @ wR8 = round[uv u(1-v)
                      @            (1-u)v (1-u)(1-v)]

wmacuz wR0, wR8, wR10
@ wR0 = (1-u)(1-v)T(i,j)+ (1-u)v T(i,j+1)+
@       u(1-v)T(i+1,j)+ uvT(i+1,j+1)
...
@ wR0 can be packed to reduce precision
@ and now can be used for modulating the
@ color value

... @ update loop condition
bne Loop
@ Looping back for the next pixel
```

This example demonstrates how features of Intel Wireless MMX technology can be easily used to perform bilinear filtering. The code also demonstrates how to perform multiple 16×16 multiply operations in parallel with a rounding mode; in this case, round to nearest. Rounding modes for coefficients may be important for certain algorithms. However, for many gaming applications, a bit of imprecision can be tolerated and rounding may not be necessary, which is more beneficial from a performance point of view.

Texture-mapping operations are one of the highest bandwidth consumers as well. This class of operations is also highly sensitive to memory latency. Pre-fetching should be used as a technique for hiding latency. However, calculating the region to be pre-fetched might not be simple because, depending on the orientation of the primitive, the addresses to the texture maps could be striding in a nonlinear fashion or could even be random for all practical purposes. This possibility can be partially addressed by having smaller texture maps so that a tile of the texture can be pre-loaded into the cache and intermediate points can be generated following the above interpolation scheme.

The following section extends the current implementation to a trilinear interpolation algorithm.

Trilinear Interpolation

Bilinear interpolation is used for data samples over a 2D domain and can be used for regular texture generation. For texture generation from different texture maps, trilinear interpolation is used. Trilinear interpolation is like bilinear interpolation, but it is used for samples on a 3D domain. It is a three-stage process, which needs a total of seven linear interpolation steps; four in the first direction, then two and one as with bilinear interpolation.

Trilinear interpolation is the name given to the process of linearly interpolating points within a 3D box, given values at the vertices of the box. Perhaps its most common application is interpolating within cells of a volumetric dataset.

Consider a unit cube with the upper-left base vertex at the origin as shown in Figure 12.15. The values at each vertex will be denoted V000, V100, V010,...V111. Thus, the interpolated value:

$$V_{(x,y,z)} = V_{(0,0,0)}(1-x)(1-y)(1-z) + V_{(1,0,0)}x(1-y)(1-z) + V_{(0,1,0)}(1-x)y(1-z)$$
$$+ V_{(0,0,1)}(1-x)(1-y)z + V_{(1,0,1)}x(1-y)z + V_{(0,1,1)}(1-x)yz +$$
$$V_{(1,1,0)}x y(1-z) + V_{(1,1,1)}x yz$$

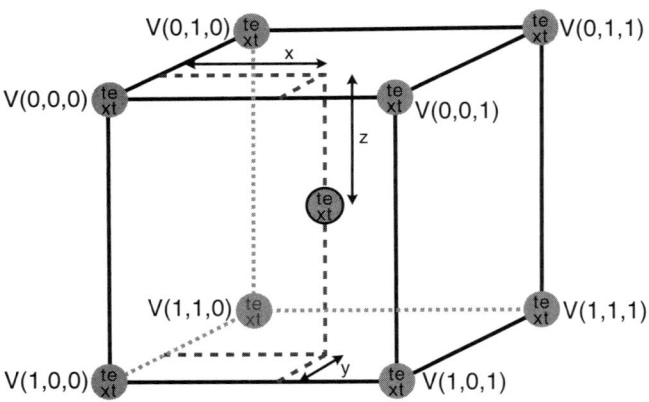

Figure 12.15 Trilinear Filtering

To process the color pixel values in all the vertices requires eight registers. The large register file that supports Intel Wireless MMX technology can be used to hold all the vertex color values while they are being processed, avoiding the overhead of saving and loading. Another challenge in this algorithm is to maintain precision of the three 16-bit-wide coefficients during multiplication. However, some simplification can be made. The trilinear interpolation operation described above can easily be decomposed into two bilinear operations.

$$V_{(x,y,z)} = V_{(0,0,0)}(1-x)(1-y) + V_{(1,0,0)}x(1-y) + V_{(0,1,0)}(1-x)y + V_{(1,1,0)}x\,y$$

$$+ z\begin{pmatrix} V_{(0,0,1)} - V_{(0,0,0)})(1-x)(1-y) + (V_{(1,0,1)} - V_{(1,0,0)})x(1-y) + \\ (V_{(0,1,1)} - V_{(0,1,0)})\,(1-x)y + (V_{(1,1,1)} - V_{(1,1,0)})\,x\,y \end{pmatrix}$$

Assume that the vertex data structures are organized as follows:

```
typedef {
    I16  x;
    I16  y;
    I16  z;
}Tri_linear_DATA;

I32 plane_0[][];
I32 plane_1[][];
```

An implementation of the trilinear interpolation can be done in the following way:

```
@ wR0 - v(0,1,0) v(0,0,0)
@ wR1 - v(0,1,1) v(0,0,1)
@ wR2 - v(1,1,0) v(1,0,0)
@ wR3 - v(1,1,1) v(1,0,1)

wunpckilw wR4, wR1, wR0 @organizing vertex texel values
wunpckilw wR5, wR3, wR2

@ Perform bilinear interpolation on
@ wR4, wR5
@ Store the result in wR6
@ Refer to previous example
@ wR6 contains the 1st Bilinear Interpolation Result

wsubh wR7, wR2, wR0
@ wR7 = [V(0,1,1)-V(0,1,0) V(0,0,1)-V(0,0,0)]
wsubh wR8, wR3, wR1
@ wR8 = [V(1,1,1)-V(1,1,0) V(1,0,1)-V(1,0,0)]
```

```
@Now perform biliear interpolation on wR7, wR8
@Store restult in wR9
@wR9 contains 2ⁿᵈ Bilinear Interpolation Result

wzero wR10
wpackwus wR9,wR10,wR9 @ packing result of BLT-2
textrmuw wR9, r5       @ extracting result into XScale

@ let r4 = z value
tmia wR10, r5, r4
@ Multiplying with z and Bilinear interpolation -II

waddw wR10, wR6
@ adding two bilinear result
wzero wR11
wpackwus wR11, wR11, wR10
@ wR11 - contains the final result
```

This example builds on top of the previous bilinear example. Algorithmic simplification has been made to expedite processing, and care has been taken not to sacrifice the accuracy of the coefficient by excessive truncation.

Alpha Blending and Fogging

Fogging and alpha blending are performed to create special effects such as mist and reflection in a scene. Fogging is used to hide the artifacts introduced by clipping and by the lack of details of a graphics object in a distant plane. In fogging, the algorithm blends a fog color with a fragment color using a blending factor f. Fogging factor f is a number between 0 and 1. As the object moves further away from the eye, f reaches 0; as it moves closer to the eye, the fogging factor f reaches 1.

$$C_{out} = C_{pixel} . f + (1 - f) . C_{fog}$$

Note that the fog color is typically a constant that produces the effect of fading into distant dark or distant white; thus, the fogging operation is simply one multiply operation and one add for each channel and each pixel.

Another similar algorithm is alpha blending, which is used to blend two objects, if one of the objects is semitransparent. This algorithm is used for creating clouds, reflections, and so on. The alpha blending operation is as follows:

$$C_{out} = C_1 . \alpha_1 + \alpha_2 . C_2$$

For most cases

$$\alpha_1 + \alpha_2 = 1$$

The following code example shows a typical implementation of alpha blending. This code can be further optimized by loop unrolling and re-scheduling using techniques from Chapters 9 and 10. The code example is meant to illustrate ease of implementation with Intel Wireless MMX technology. The implementation takes advantage of the Intel Wireless MMX WMADD instruction.

```
@Let us assume color format as RGB
@r0 contains the desired alpha values
@r1 points to input_1 pixel array
@r2 points to input_2 pixel array
@r3 points to output pixel array
@r4 contains 0xFFFF

mov r4, #0xff
mov r4, r4, lsl #8
mov r5, #0xff
orr r4, r4, r5
tbcsth wR0, r0              @ wR0 = [a a a a]
tbcsth wR1, r4              @ wR1 = [1 1 1 1]
wsubh wR2,wR1,wR0          @wR2=[(1-a) (1-a) (1-a) (1-a)]
wunpckilh wR15, wR0, wR1 @wR15=[a (1-a) a (1-a)]
mov r4, #0x80
mov r4, r4, lsl #8
tbcstw wR14, r4            @ wR1 = [1 1 1 1]
mov r4, #16
tmcr wCGR0, r4
ldr r5, =NUM_PIXELS
ldr r5, [r5]

Loop_start:
wldrd wR3,[r1], #8        @ [Rx' Bx Gx Rx]
wldrd wR4,[r2], #8        @ [Ry' By Gy Ry]

@Alignment may be required
wunpckilh wR5, wR3, wR4 @ wR5 = [Gx Gy Rx Ry]
wunpckihh wR6, wR3, wR4 @ wR6 = [Rx'Ry'Bx By]
wmaddu wR0, wR5, wR15

@wR0=[aGx +(1-a)Gy   aRx +(1-a)Ry]
waddwus wR0, wR0, wR14
wsrlwg wR0,wR0, wCGR0
wmaddu wR1, wR6, wR15
```

```
@wR1=[aRx'+(1-a)Ry'   aBx +(1-a)By]
waddwus wR1, wR1, wR14
wsrlwg wR1,wR1, wCGR0
wpackwus wR2, wR0,wR1
subs r5, r5, #1

@wR2 = [Rz' Bz Gz Rz]
wstrd wR2, [r3], #8
bne Loop_start
```

The example has covered a very commonly used class of algorithm. The input data is assumed as an array of structures; however, during processing, it was converted partially to a structure of array. While the current implementation processes two pixels per loop, its efficient use of WMADD saved additional WUNPACK operations that would have been needed for converting fully from AOS to SOA. This example underlines the need for judicial choice and manipulation of the data formats to make best use of the architecture.

Anti-Aliasing

Anti-aliasing is performed to eliminate the jagged artifacts introduced by the discrete nature of the display and the digital world in general. This effect is pronounced for a straight line at a slope or on a sharp curve. Two common approaches for performing anti-aliasing are super-sampling and low-pass filtering. Super-sampling assigns a pixel value based on how much of the actual line or primitive would have been in the pixel space if the image were super-sampled. However, the low-pass filtering scheme is easier to perform. Each pixel is replaced with the average of itself and its eight neighbors. Usually, this replacement is not done since it can destroy much of the edge information. Instead, a weighted average is taken, with the central pixel weighted the highest. The most common way to do so uses the following equation:

$$O(x, y) = I(x-1, y-1) \times \frac{1}{36} + I(x, y-1) \times \frac{1}{9} + I(x+1, y-1) \times \frac{1}{36}$$

$$+ I(x-1, y) \times \frac{1}{9} + I(x, y) \times \frac{4}{9} + I(x+1, y) \times \frac{1}{9}$$

$$+ (x-1, y+1) \times \frac{1}{36} + I(x, y+1) \times \frac{1}{9} + I(x+1, y+1) \times \frac{1}{36}$$

Analyzing the equation reveals that this operation is a matrix multiplication. The multiplicand matrix can be simplified to make it a separable—decompose into x and y functions—and also to simplify the algorithm so that many multiplications can be reduced to mere adds and shifts.

$$\begin{bmatrix} \dfrac{1}{36} & \dfrac{1}{9} & \dfrac{1}{36} \\[2mm] \dfrac{1}{9} & \dfrac{4}{9} & \dfrac{1}{9} \\[2mm] \dfrac{1}{36} & \dfrac{1}{9} & \dfrac{1}{36} \end{bmatrix} = 1/9 \begin{bmatrix} \dfrac{1}{4} & 1 & \dfrac{1}{4} \\[2mm] 1 & 4 & 1 \\[2mm] \dfrac{1}{4} & 1 & \dfrac{1}{4} \end{bmatrix} = \dfrac{1}{9} \begin{bmatrix} \dfrac{1}{2} & 2 & \dfrac{1}{2} \end{bmatrix}^{T} \begin{bmatrix} \dfrac{1}{2} & 2 & \dfrac{1}{2} \end{bmatrix}$$

Following the simplification, anti-aliasing can be implemented as follows:

```
@ Pixel formats are in RGBA or [ABGR]
@ wR0,wR1,wR2 contains pixel(0,0)(1,0)(2,0)
@ wR2,wR3,wR4 contains pixel(0,1)(1,1)(2,1)
@ wR5,wR6,wR7 contains pixel(0,2)(1,2)(2,2)

wunpckilh wR8, wR0, wR2
   @ wR8 = [G(2,0) G(0,0) R(2,0) R(0,0)]
wunpckihh wR9, wR0, wR2
   @ wR9 = [A(2,0) A(0,0) B(2,0) B(0,0)]
wunpckilh wR10, wR5, wR7
   @ wR10 = [G(2,2) G(0,2) R(2,2) R(0,2)]
wunpckihh wR11, wR5, wR7
   @ wR11 = [A(2,2) A(0,2) B(2,2) B(0,2)]

wunpckilh wR12,wR8,wR10
   @wR12 = [R(2,2) R(2,0) R(0,2) R(0,0)]
wunpckilh wR13,wR8,wR10
   @wR13 = [B(2,2) B(2,0) B(0,2) B(0,0)]
wunpckilh wR14,wR9,wR11
   @wR14 = [G(2,2) G(2,0) G(0,2) G(0,0)]

wacch wR12, wR12
wsrah wR12, #2
@ wR12 = (R(2,2)+R(2,0)+R(0,2)+R(0,0))/4
wacch wR13, wR13
wsrah wR13, #2
@ wR13 = (B(2,2)+B(2,0)+B(0,2)+B(0,0))/4
wacch wR14, wR14
wsrah wR14, #2
@ wR14 = (G(2,2)+G(2,0)+G(0,2)+G(0,0))/4

@ Convert AOS to SOA for wR1,wR2,wR4,wR6
@      [(1,0)(0,1)(2,1)(1,2)]
```

```
@ into wR8  = [R(2,1) R(1,2) R(1,0) R(0,1)]
@      wR9  = [G(2,1) G(1,2) G(1,0) G(0,1)]
@      wR10 =[B(2,1) B(1,2) B(1,0) B(0,1)]
wacch wR8, wR8
@      wR8  = [R(2,1)+R(1,2)+R(1,0)+R(0,1)]
wacch wR9, wR9
@      wR9  = [G(2,1)+G(1,2)+G(1,0)+G(0,1)]
wacch wR10, wR10
@      wR10 =[B(2,1)+B(1,2)+B(1,0)+B(0,1)]

waddw wR10, wR10, wR13   @ B-channel
waddw wR8, wR8, wR12     @ R-Channel
waddw wR9, wR9, wR14     @ G-Channel
... @ save the values
```

You can see use of WAVG2 has reduced the need for many multiplications. In addition, no AOS to SOA conversions were needed. The in-place computation makes the anti-aliasing algorithm attractive in many circumstances. One other aspect to note here is the selection of a simplified coefficient. By choosing simplified kernels, the computation could be made simpler. Further simplification of the algorithm, such as using a one-dimensional kernel for line-draw, can yield better performance.

ROP Codes, or Raster Operations

For many text-oriented applications, such as word processing, the image blocks are preprocessed in memory and then they are simply blended or combined with other images for on-screen display. Different fonts, application icons, application backgrounds, and desktops are created using this technique. These operations are called raster operations. There are 256 raster operations that are used commonly in graphics software libraries and in dedicated graphics hardware. These operations perform logical operations on two or three blocks of data. Intel Wireless MMX technology allows 64-bit-wide logical operations. The large coprocessor register files can hold a complete block. Here is an example of a raster operation:

```
@ Raster Operation 14
@ D = NOT (D or (NOT (S1 XOR S0)))
@ r0 = 0xFFFF FFFF
@ r1 = [S0], r2 = [S1], r3 = [D0]
outerloop : @ for each row
... @ loop set up

innerloop : @ for each 64 bit

wldrd  wR0, [r1]
```

```
addne   r1, r1, #8
wldrd   wR1, [r2]
addne   r1, r1, #8
wldrd   wR2, [r3]
addne   r1, r1, #8
wxor    wR0, wR1            @wR0 = S1 XOR S0
tbcstw  wR3, r0
wxor    wR0, wR0, wR3       @wR0 = NOT(S1 XOR S0)
wor     wR0, wR2, wR0       @wR0 = (D OR (NOT(S1 XOR S0)))
wxor    wR0, wR3, wR0       @wR0=NOT(D OR(NOT(S1 XOR S0)))
wstrd   wR0
... @ compare terminating condition
bne innerloop
... @ increment address by stride amount
... @ compare terminating condition
bne outerloop
```

ROP codes typically are performed on a block of data. By choosing block size as 8×8 bytes, maximum throughput can be achieved. Operating on blocks that are aligned is preferable. A block that is non-aligned can be broken down into an unaligned block and an aligned block, assuming the block is large enough. The preceding code sample can be used as a guideline and be extended to work on a block of data for ROP operations. With more data to work on, the loop in the previous example can be unrolled and rescheduled using techniques described in Chapters 9 and 10.

Transformation: Rotation and Translation

Most of the rotation and translation is performed in the geometry pipe using floating point; however, fixed-point implementation can be used for non-complex scenes, saving a lot of computational complexity. These operations are performed on vertices. They can be performed by a matrix transformation of the form shown in Figure 12.16. This transformation is simply matrix multiplication. In fixed-point implementation, the required precision is 32 bits on the coefficients and the vertex coordinates. If the transformation matrix is sparse, as it is for translation and scaling, the operations can be processed with ease. WADD can be used for translation. For scaling, two 32-bit multiplications using the TMIA instruction are needed. The following example shows a case for rotation.

$$[x \quad y \quad z \quad 1]\begin{bmatrix} 1 & 0 & 0 & 0 \\ 0 & 1 & 0 & 0 \\ 0 & 0 & 1 & 0 \\ Tx & Ty & Tz & 1 \end{bmatrix} = [x+Tx \quad y+Ty \quad z+Tz \quad 1]$$

$$[x \quad y \quad z \quad 1]\begin{bmatrix} Sx & 0 & 0 & 0 \\ 0 & Sy & 0 & 0 \\ 0 & 0 & Sz & 0 \\ 0 & 0 & 0 & 1 \end{bmatrix} = [x.Sx \quad y.Sy \quad z.Sz \quad 1]$$

$$Rx = \begin{bmatrix} 1 & 0 & 0 & 0 \\ 0 & Cos(\theta) & Sin(\theta) & 0 \\ 0 & -Sin(\theta) & Cos(\theta) & 0 \\ 0 & 0 & 0 & 1 \end{bmatrix} \quad Ry = \begin{bmatrix} Cos(\theta) & 0 & -Sin(\theta) & 0 \\ 0 & 1 & 0 & 0 \\ Sin(\theta) & 0 & Cos(\theta) & 0 \\ 0 & 0 & 0 & 1 \end{bmatrix} \quad Rz = \begin{bmatrix} Cos(\theta) & Sin(\theta) & 0 & 0 \\ -Sin(\theta) & Cos(\theta) & 0 & 0 \\ 0 & 0 & 1 & 0 \\ 0 & 0 & 0 & 1 \end{bmatrix}$$

Figure 12.16 Transformation Matrices

```
@ For rotation around Z axis Rz
@ r0 input_x
@ r1 input_y
@ r2 cos(θ)
@ r3 sin(θ)

wzero wR0
tmia  wR0, r0, r2
@ wZERO and TMIA can be used for a 32-bit mult.
tmia  wR0, r1, r3
@ wR0 = output _x= x cos() + y sin()
rsb   r3,r3
wzero wR1
tmia  wR1, r0, r2
tmia  wR1, r1, r3
@ wR1 = output_y = -x sin() + y cos()
wpackwus wR2, wR0, wR1
@ wR2 = [output_y output_x]
```

The example shows how effectively 32-bit multiplication and accumulation can be performed. Note that accumulation is a 64-bit accumulator; thus, for successive operations, the precision loss is minimal. Also, each of the coprocessor registers can be a target for an accumulation operation, and each can be used as an accumulator. This example shows two coprocessor registers being used concurrently as accumulators. Thus, a set of matrix transformations can be done in parallel. Applying the multisample technique to this example accentuates the advantage of having implicit multiple accumulators.

Buffer Rotation

For cases where the orientation of the viewing buffer is different for the application, an explicit rotation of the final image may be needed. Inefficient rotation can be expensive and can adversely affect the quality of the graphics software. Rotation of a full buffer is a transpose operation. Intel Wireless MMX technology can be used to perform the transpose operation, as shown in Figure 12.17 and the following code example. The example assumes 8-bits per pixel color depth.

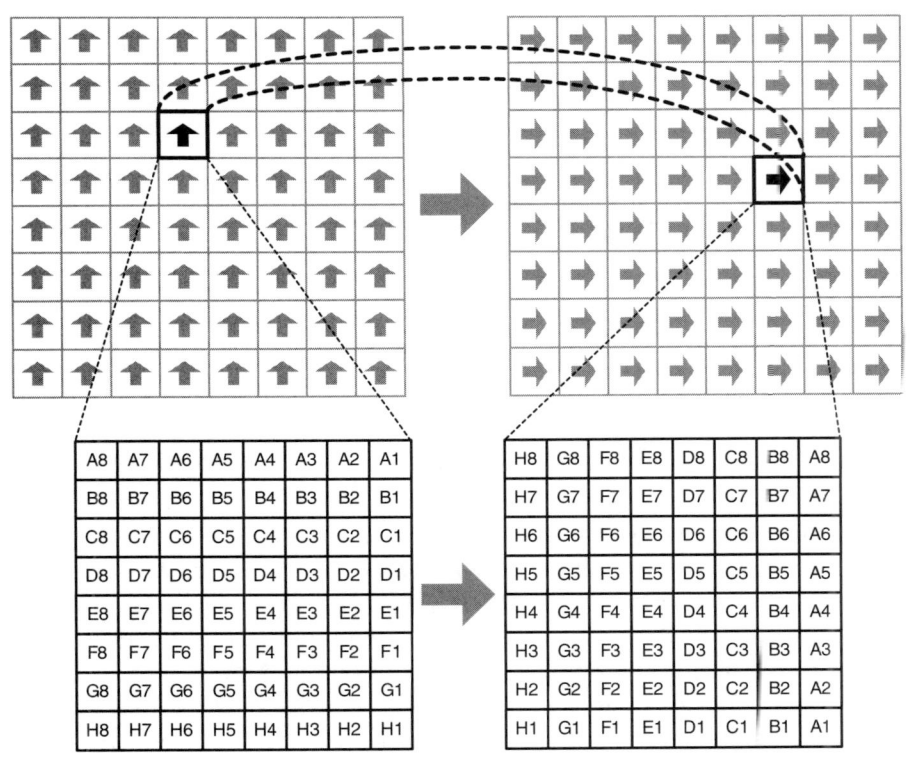

Figure 12.17 Full Screen Rotation

```
@ Transpose can be done on an 8x8 block
@ Let wR0 = row 0 of the block [a8-a1]
@ Let wR1 = row 1 of the block [b8-b1]
@ Let wR2 = row 2 of the block [c8-c1]
@ Let wR3 = row 3 of the block [d8-d1]
@ Let wR4 = row 4 of the block [e8-e1]
@ Let wR5 = row 5 of the block [f8-f1]
@ Let wR6 = row 6 of the block [g8-g1]
@ Let wR7 = row 7 of the block [h8-h1]

wunpckilb wR8, wR1, wR0
@ wR8 = a4 b4 a3 b3 a2 b2 a1 b1

@ similarly, wR9,wR11,wR12 can be done
@ wR9 = c4 d4 c3 d3 c2 d2 c1 d2
@ wR11 = e4 f4 e3 f3 e2 f2 e1 f1
@ wR12 = g4 h4 g3 h3 g2 h2 g1 h1

wunpckilh wR13, wR9, wR8
@ wR13 = a2 b2 c2 d2 a1 b1 c1 d1
wunpckilh wR14, wR12, wR11
@ wR14 = e2 f2 g2 h2 e1 f1 g1 h1
wunpckilw wR10, wR13, wR14
@ wR10 = a1 b1 c1 d1 e1 f1 g1 h1
wunpckihw wR15, wR13, wR14
@ wR15 = a2 b2 c2 d2 e2 f2 g2 h2
@ similarly, we can create
@ wR13 = a4 b4 c4 d4 a3 b3 c3 d3
@ wR14 = e4 f4 g4 h4 e3 f3 g3 h3
@ wR2 = a3 b3 c3 d3 e3 f3 g3 h3
@ wR3 = a4 b4 c4 d4 e4 f4 g4 h4
...
```

The above code assumes that the source block is aligned. Creating two independent routines, one with the aligned case and the other for the un-aligned case, may be the most efficient approach. Also, the above code can be optimized further by appropriate preloading and other operations, as described in Chapter 10. The previous rotation example assumes 8-bit precision per element. Part of the above routine may be used for a 16-bit color (5:6:5) frame buffer. Dividing the rotate task into a series of smaller blocks accelerates the operation and also makes it suitable for different screen sizes. For 16-bit color formats, the working block can be 4×4 instead of 8×8, as shown in the preceding example.

Key Points

Depending on the workload, the approaches described in this chapter offer a varying amount of acceleration. Intel Wireless MMX technology allows you to draw a more pleasing or realistic scene for the same amount of computational power. The key points are:

■ *Algorithmic optimization.* Based on the scene content and human vision, algorithms must be tailored. Better textures may have a higher impact on the user than a greater number of triangles.

■ *Computational optimization.* Correct data organization and data structure selection for storing and retrieving impacts performance. Correct organization and structure also impact the overhead of organizing the data to benefit from Intel Wireless MMX instructions. Pipelining, or operating on more samples concurrently, can offer the highest acceleration.

■ *Memory optimization.* Preloading techniques can be adopted at different levels and offer a great benefit. The footprint can be and needs to be reduced to effectively use caches and perform other operations. Packing textures and using heavy filtering may offer interesting memory and MIPS trade-offs.g306

Chapter 13

Digital Signal Processing

Digital Signal Processing (DSP) has been evolving over the past thirty years, spurred by the rapid advances in computer technology. It has grown into a discipline that makes an impact on almost everyone's daily lives, dominating application areas such as voice and audio, video, radar, telecommunications, and medical instrumentation. Digital filtering refers to the computational process or algorithm in which a digital signal or sequence of numbers is transformed into a second sequence of numbers. This chapter describes a variety of methods for implementing high performance digital filters using Intel® Wireless MMX™ technology. The finite impulse response (FIR), infinite impulse response (IIR), and adaptive FIR least mean squares (LMS) digital filters are developed using several different implementation strategies.

DSP Fundamentals

In many applications, it is necessary to manipulate signals. This manipulation of the signal is intended to change the signal for a variety of purposes. It might be targeted towards manipulation of the frequency spectrum of a signal, the removal of noise and distortion, to provide compression, to sharpen edges in an image, or to minimize interference with other signals in communication systems. This manipulation is often accomplished through the application of digital filters. In general, the digital filtering algorithms are not very complicated; the majority of the functions are implemented with a simple repeated multiply accumulate operation.

The available literature on DSP encompasses many specialized areas. Three of the main subfields of DSP that are particularly well suited to Intel Wireless MMX technology include audio, voice, and image processing. Typical applications of digital signal processing include speech compression and transmission in digital mobile phones, compression and decompression of music, equalization of sound in stereo equipment, weather modeling, economic forecasting, analysis and control of industrial processes, computer-generated animations in movies, and image manipulation. This section provides a brief introduction to some basic terminology.

Digital Signals

A digital signal is the discrete-time representation of an analog, or continuous-time signal, that has been sampled at a fast enough sampling rate and with high enough precision to sufficiently describe it using either fixed point or floating point representations. Figure 13.1 illustrates the analog-to-digital (A/D) signal conversion process.

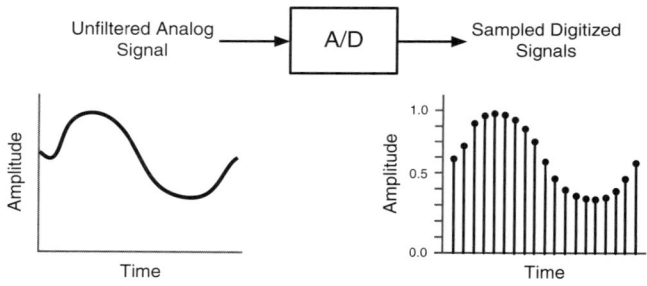

Figure 13.1   Digitizing an Analog Signal

The accuracy of the representation is dependent on a number of parameters. The two most important parameters are the sampling frequency and the number of bits used for the representation of each sampled element. The analog signal is sampled at regular intervals and the value obtained in that interval is represented by a discrete value. The sampling frequency or sampling rate is the rate at which new samples are taken from the continuous signal. The number of bits used for one value of the discrete signal tells you how accurately the signal magnitude is represented. Similarly, the sampling frequency controls the temporal or spatial accuracy of the discrete signal.

In modern lower power DSP architectures, either 16-bit or 32-bit signed operands are used to represent the signal amplitudes at different temporal or spatial locations. The format for the data is often represented in what is known as the *fixed-point format*.

Fixed-Point Format

As discussed in Chapter 7, the Qn fixed-point format provides a standard mechanism for representing fractional values using an integer data type. In this form, the number of fractional bits is represented by n. For example, the Q15 format indicates that the most significant bit is the sign bit followed by an imaginary decimal point, followed by 15 bits of fraction. The $Qm.n$ format is a more explicit representation of fixed-point values. In this format, the integer binary word is partitioned using an imaginary fixed point. The n bits to the right of the imaginary point comprise the fractional portion of the value being represented and these n bits act as weights for negative powers of 2. The m bits to the left of the imaginary point comprise the integer portion of the value being represented, and these m bits act as weights for positive powers of 2, as illustrated in Figure 13.2.

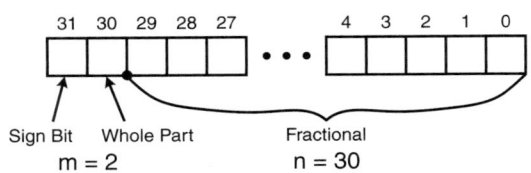

Figure 13.2   The Qm.n Fixed-point Format for Q2.30

The overall Qm.n representation requires a total of $m+n$ bits for both unsigned and signed numbers, however for the signed case the number of bits available to represent the integer portion is reduced by the sign bit. For example, Q2.30 signed representation may have one sign bit and one bit for the integer portion of the value. The conversions from a signed integer to a signed fraction are accomplished by dividing the signed integer by $2^{(n-1)}$, where n represents the number of bits available. The range represented by the fractional value is from -1 to $+1-2^{-(n-1)}$.

Precision Reduction and Biased Rounding

When performing either integer or fractional multiplication operations where the most significant 16 bits or 32 bits of a 32-bit or 64-bit result are needed, two options exist: truncation or rounding. The rounding operation reduces the precision of a number by removing the lower order bits, and possibly modifying the remaining bits to more closely represent the higher precision number. In contrast, when truncation is used, the value is always smaller or equal to the original number.

The simplest implementation of rounding, known as the *round-to-nearest* technique, is to add a constant to the value that is equal to half of the least significant bit of the output, followed by truncation of the lower bits. When performing a 16-bit multiplication with signed integers, adding the constant 0x8000 to the 32-bit result and truncating on bit position 15 produces the desired result. Figure 13.3 illustrates the precision reduction for a 16-bit signed integer multiplication.

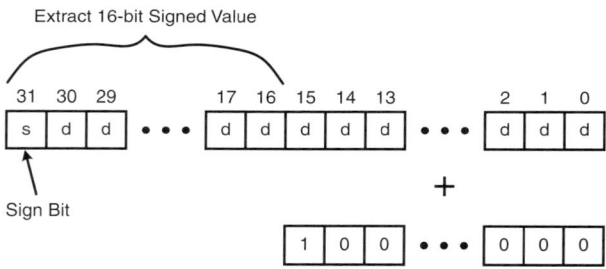

Figure 13.3   Rounding and Left-shift Correction for the Result of a 16×16 Signed Integer Multiplication

In high precision signal processing, a left shift correction is often used for the multiplication of signed fractions. For example, multiplying two signed fractions in a Q1.15 format produces a result which is in a Q2.30 format, that is, 30 fractional bits and two sign bits. In order to eliminate the redundant sign bit, a left shift correction is often introduced prior to rounding the result to a Q1.15 format. Adding the constant 0x4000 to the 32-bit result and truncating on bit position 14 produces the desired result. Figure 13.4 illustrates the precision reduction for a 16-bit signed fraction multiplication.

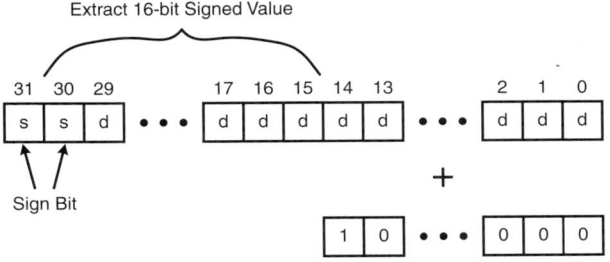

Figure 13.4   Rounding and Left-shift Correction for the Result of a 16×16
Fractional Multiplication

Digital Filters

Digital filters are used to implement a variety of different functions found in almost every area of science and engineering. Digital filters reshape the frequency spectrum of a signal and typically are designed to operate as low pass, high pass, band pass, and band reject filters. Low pass and high pass filters are designed to pass only low and high frequencies respectively. Similarly, filters for band pass and band reject are designed to pass or reject only a certain range of frequencies. Some of these filter types are illustrated in Figure 13.5

Digital filters are specified in terms of desired attenuation and permitted deviations from the desired frequency response. Some of the parameters used in the specification and design of digital filters include the pass band, stop band, and ripple. The hardest part is specifying the desired behavior of the filters and determining how to combine past input values and past output values to get this desired behavior—that is, determining the weights or coefficients. Often, you just punch in numbers to a software package to calculate the relevant coefficients.

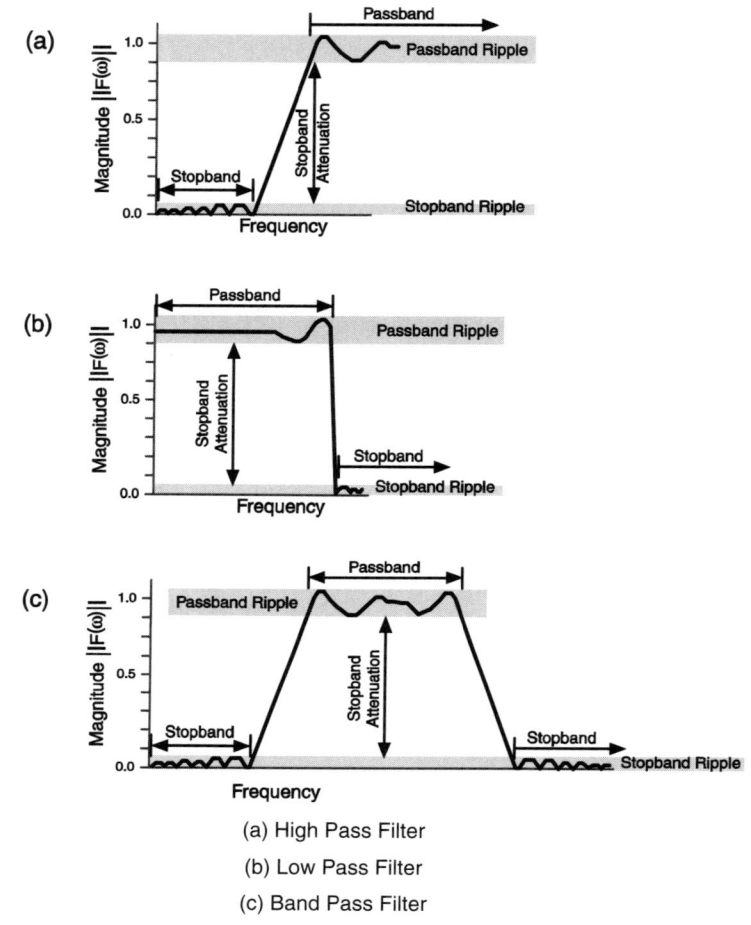

(a) High Pass Filter
(b) Low Pass Filter
(c) Band Pass Filter

Figure 13.5   Examples of High Pass, Low Pass, and Band Pass Filters

FIR Filters

For a number of applications, digital filters are based on the input and output relationship defined by the following linear constant coefficient difference equation.

$$y(n) = \sum_{k=0}^{N-1} a(k) \cdot y(n-k) \; + \; \sum_{k=0}^{M-1} b(k) \cdot x(n-k)$$

If the coefficients *a(k)* are all zero, the output sequence *y(n)* is based on the weighted sum of the present and past inputs, where *M* is the length of the filter. This form of the equation defines a finite impulse response (FIR) filter. If the coefficients *a(k)* are nonzero, the output of the filter is based on a weighted sum of past values of the input to the filter in combination with the output of the filter. This equation defines an infinite impulse response (IIR) filter. The IIR filter will be discussed later.

The FIR filter has all of the coefficients *a(k)* in the equation equal to zero, which reduces the difference equation to the finite convolution:

$$y(n) = \sum_{k=0}^{M-1} b(k) \cdot x(n-k)$$

where *x(n)* is the input sequence and *M* is the length of the filter. Mapping the time domain series into a function of a complex variable allows the cumbersome convolution to be replaced by a simple product. The most widely used transformation is the z-transform, which is associated with the sequence *x(n)* by the following equation in which *z* is a complex valued variable:

$$X(z) = \sum_{n=0}^{M-1} x(n) z^{-n}$$

The z-transform of *y(n)* is *Y(z)*. The transfer function *H(z)* is obtained by dividing *Y(z)* by *X(z)*, which leads us to the following equation:

$$H(z) = \frac{Y(z)}{X(z)} = \sum_{n=0}^{M-1} h(n) \cdot z^{-n}$$

The FIR filter can also be represented using the signal flow graph in Figure 13.6. The Z^1 terms in the network structure represent a delay line. This form of the FIR filter is known as the direct form since the coefficients can be obtained directly from the difference equation.

The coefficients, *b(k)*, of a FIR filter are often referred to as taps. For an N-sample, T-tap filter, the total number of cycles required by an implementation can be represented by a cycle count equation based on these variables. For example, if you were to calculate *N=40* output samples, *y(0)*, *y(1)*, ...*y(N-1)* using *T=16* taps, *b(0)*, *b(1)*, ...*b(T-1)*, the total number of multiply accumulate operations would be simply *NT*.

Supporting operations, such as data loads and loop management, also influence the throughput; however, the *NT* term becomes a key term in the total cycle consumption for the filter.

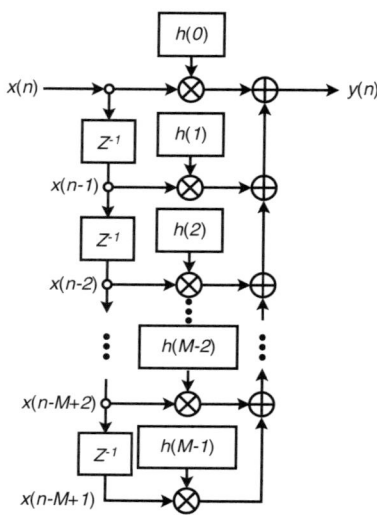

Figure 13.6   Signal Flow Graph for a Finite Impulse Response (FIR) Filter

The Intel Wireless MMX WMAC instruction provides for four parallel 16-bit multiplications with accumulation of the four products. Since the resource latency is two cycles, the best that can be achieved will be NT/2 cycles for the N-sample T-tap filter. This sounds great, however the supporting operations such as data loads and loop management contribute to the cycle count; you would have to do some planning to achieve the best throughput. Now, take a closer look at how to best organize the input samples and coefficients for calculating the FIR filter.

Memory Organization for the FIR Filter

The calculation of the FIR filter requires the coefficient array to be multiplied with an array of input samples. For each output, $y(0)$, $y(1)$, ... $y(N-1)$, the input samples are shifted by one element in relation to the coefficient array, as illustrated in Figure 13.7.

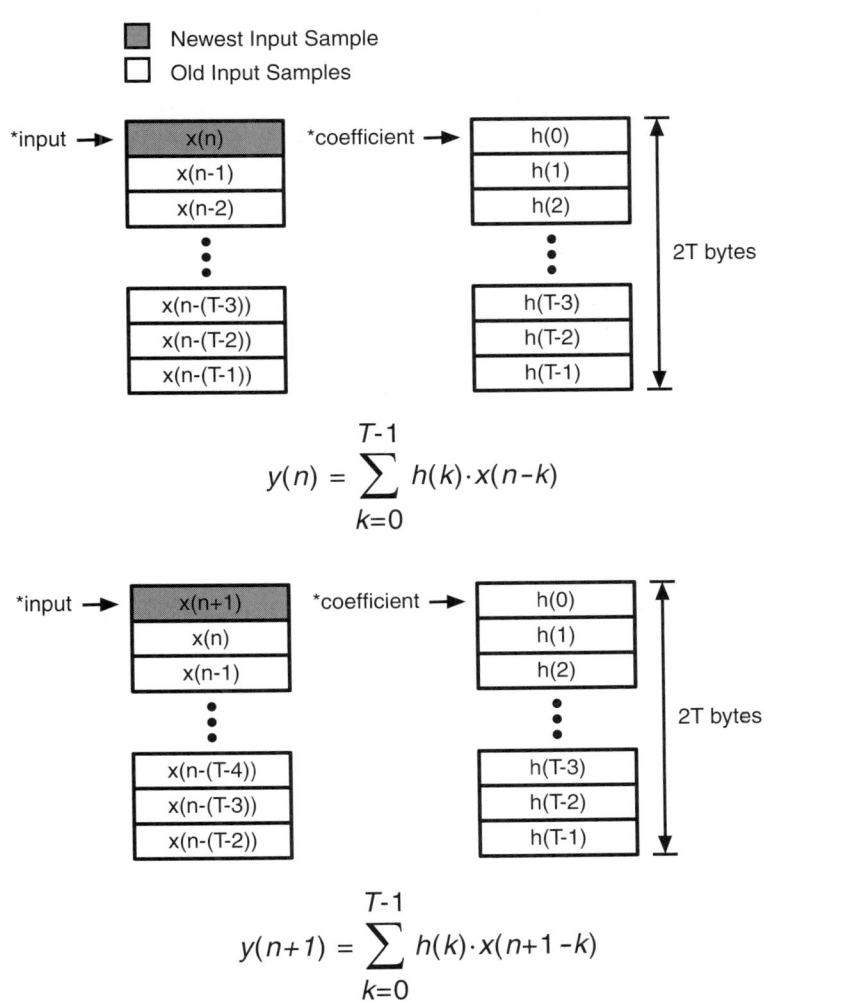

Figure 13.7   Relationship between Input Samples and Coefficients

The coefficient array can always be organized in memory so that it is aligned on a 64-bit boundary, which allows you to use the WLDRD instruction for the coefficient loads. In contrast, the nature of the shift of the array of input samples for each subsequent output means that only every fourth output, $y(n)$, would be accessing the input array on the double-word boundary. So once again, alignment appears to be playing an important role in the calculations.

When implementing the FIR filter, two buffers are required for the coefficients and the inputs, and one buffer is required for the output. The coefficient buffer must always hold a total of T taps, which requires 2T bytes to be allocated in memory. The input sample buffer needs to have at least 2T bytes as well, since each of the samples is applied to the array of coefficients.

Computing the FIR Filter

The computation of the FIR filter is fundamentally based on the multiply accumulate (MAC) operation. Since the FIR filter is based on the MAC operation, the WMACS instruction is the instruction of choice since it provides for the parallel multiplication and subsequent accumulation of four operands.

$$Acc = Acc + \sum_{i=0}^{3} X_i \cdot B_i$$

However, the arithmetic involved is only a portion of the calculation. The management the data streams from three separate data structures requires some careful planning to achieve high throughput. This section takes a look at three possible implementations for the direct form of the FIR filter:

- T-tap single-sample FIR

- N-sample, T-tap multi-sample FIR

- N-sample, 16-tap multi-sample FIR

In the first method, the T-tap single-sample FIR, the amount of memory required for the input buffer is minimized by generating only a single output sample for each application. Since only a single output is generated for each application, you have little opportunity to amortize data and coefficient loads across multiple calculations.

The second method, N-sample T-tap multi-sample FIR, applies the multi-sample technique of Intel Wireless MMX technology, allowing both the data and coefficient loads to be amortized across multiple output calculations. Through careful organization of the calculation, near ideal saturation of the execution resources can be achieved. However, you still have a nested loop structure that can contribute significantly to the overall cycle count, especially when you have a small number of taps.

Finally, the third method illustrates the implementation of the block FIR filter, which makes maximum use of the register file by fixing the number of taps. Often the number of taps is low enough that you can do a preload into the coprocessor register file, allowing the load to be amortized across multiple calculations. The real advantage in the fixed tap implementation is that the outer loop is completely eliminated.

Implementation of the N-Sample, T-Tap Single Output FIR

The single output FIR filter is sometimes referred to as a single-sample filter since it generates only a single output sample for each application. Typically, a single input sample is passed into the routine, and a single output is generated. The C code for the calculation of an N-sample, T-tap single sample FIR filter is shown in Figure 13.8.

```
// ssfir_c.c
//
// T-tap Single Output FIR filter
// Global Project Variables: T,SCALE, and RND

short ssfir_c(short *coef, short *delay_line,
              short *input){
    int i,j,acc;

    delay_line[T-1] = input[i];
    acc = 0;
    for (j = 0; j < T; j++)
        acc += delay_line[j] * coef[j];

    for (j = 0; j < T-1; j++)
        delay_line[j] = delay_line[j+1];

    return (short)((acc + RND) >> SCALE);
}
```

Figure 13.8　Simple C Code for a T-tap Single Sample FIR Filter

In the C code implementation of the filter shown in Figure 13.8, two distinct operations are being performed. The first loop performs the dot product operation generating the output value, and the second loop provides for a shift of the delay line preparing the input buffer for the next application of the filter.

A direct assembly code implementation of the routine illustrated in Figure 13.8 would involve two loops as well. In the first loop, you would perform the dot product, and in the second loop, you would provide an update to the delay line. Reloading the delay line for the alignment following the FIR calculation introduces an undesirable inefficiency that would result in increases in both cycle count and memory bandwidth. Combining the FIR calculation with the delay line update is a far superior approach.

The assembly code routine illustrated in Figure 13.9 folds the delay line update into the calculation of the FIR.

```
@ ss_fir_s.s
@
@ r0 -> pntr to coefficients, r1 -> pntr to delay line
@ r2 -> input sample

    tinsrw wR4,   r2,    #0         @ load input in register
    mov    R6,    #Taps             @ setup loop count.
    wstrh  wR4,   [r1, #2*(16-1)]   @ store input to delay
    wldrd  wR0,   [r1], #8          @ load Last 4 samples
    mov    r9,    #Scale            @ shift value
    wldrd  wR5,   [r0], #8          @ load 4 coefficients
    tmcr   wCGR0, r9                @ transfer shift operand
ssfir_loop:
    wldrd  wR1, [r1], #+8               @ load 4 samples
    wmacs  wR6, wR5, wR0                @ mac  samples
    wldrd  wR5, [r0], #8                @ load coefficients
    subs   R6,  R6,  #8                 @ decrement loop count
    waligni wR7, wR0, wR1, #2           @ align 4 samples
    wldrd  wR0, [r0], #-16              @ load 4 samples
    wmacs  wR6, wR5, wR1                @ mac samples
    wldrd  wR5, [r1], #8                @ load 4 coefficients
    wstrd  wR7, [r0], #+8               @ store to delay line
    waligni wR8, wR1, wR0, #2           @ align 4 samples
    wstrd  wR8, [r0], #+16              @ store to delay line
    bne    ssfir_loop
    wsradg wR6, wR6, wCGR0          @ scale output
    textrmsh r0, wR6, #0            @ return result
    mov    pc, lr                   @ return
```

Figure 13.9 Assembly Code for a T-Tap Single Sample FIR Filter Using
Intel® Wireless MMX™ Technology

The loop has been unrolled to process a total of eight taps per iteration. The loop has a total of 12 instructions that execute in 14 cycles, due to the two-cycle issue latency of the double-word store. The overhead coming into the loop includes the seven instructions and a single load-to-use stall. This sequence of instructions yields a throughput equation of *14*T/8 + 16*. For example, doing a 16-tap filter would take *(14*16)/8 + 16 = 44* cycles. The term *14*T/8 = 1.75*T*, which implies that within the loop the multiplier resources are idle for over three out of every four cycles!

As you can see, the single sample approach to implementing the FIR filter has a serious drawback. Since only one output is calculated for each application of the filter, amortizing the data and coefficient load overhead is not possible. The next implementation illustrates a more efficient approach.

Implementation of the N-Sample, T-Tap Multiple Output FIR

The N-sample T-tap FIR filter performs the same function as the single sample T-tap FIR filter, except now the input buffer is increased to contain more than the minimum T samples. In other words, the array of input samples is set up to contain enough input samples to calculate all N output samples with a single application of a routine. The C code for the calculation of an N-sample T-tap block FIR filter is shown in Figure 13.10.

```
// blockfir1_c.c
//
// N sample T tap Block FIR filter

void blockfir1_c(short *input, short *coeff, short *cout,
                 int N, int T){

int i,j,k,acc;

    for (j=0; j < N ;j++) {
       k = j + T - 1;
       acc = 0;
       for (i=0; i<T; i++) {
          acc += input[k-i] * coeff[i];
       }
       cout[j] = (short) (acc>>15);
    }
}
```

Figure 13.10 Simple C Code for an N-sample T-tap Block FIR Filter

In this implementation of the FIR filter, the first thing to notice is that you have a nested loop. The outer loop executes a total of N times, and for each iteration of the outer loop, the inner loop is executed T times. Within the inner loop, you have the MAC operation, and outside of the inner loop, the pointers are updated and the output stored to memory. The next section covers memory organization in more detail.

Since the WMACS instruction provides the parallel multiplication and subsequent accumulation of four operands, each application of the WMACS instruction processes four taps. The inner loop must be unrolled four times to completely utilize the WMAC instruction. Figure 13.11 shows the C code for the block FIR filter with the inner loop unrolled to process four taps per iteration.

```
// blockfir2_c.c
//
// N sample T tap Block FIR filter

void blockfir2_c(short *input, short *coeff, short *cout,
                 int N, int T){

int i,j,k,acc;

    for (j=0; j < N ;j++) {
        k = j + T - 1;
        acc = 0;
        for (i=0; i< T; i+=4) {
            acc+=input[k-i] * coeff[i];
            acc+=input[k-i-1] * coeff[i+1];
            acc+=input[k-i-2] * coeff[i+2];
            acc+=input[k-i-3] * coeff[i+3];
        }
        cout[j] = (short)(acc>>15);
    }
}
```

Figure 13.11 C Code for an N-sample T-tap Block FIR Filter Unrolled for Four Taps per Inner Loop Iteration

Unrolling the inner loop allows four samples and four coefficients to be processed, but also limits the implementation to multiples of four of four taps. As a result, if the number of taps is not a multiple of four, complications are introduced around edge conditions, which must be handled carefully. In fact, this problem is common when using parallelism, since the number of data elements used by an operation might not be a multiple of two, four, or eight. This result can be handled by having special case code to "finish off" loops; however, such code can be somewhat cumbersome. Padding the arrays with zeros produces a null result that does not affect the computation. Then the code can be written so that the number of data elements it consumes is always a multiple of four.

The decision to pad the arrays with zeroes or to develop some custom code to finish off the calculation should be based on the *NT* metric for the block FIR filter. Before getting into the implementation details, a closer look at the data structures is in order.

Alignment during the calculation of the FIR filter is an important consideration, since the WMAC instruction is not fully utilized unless you are able to provide eight operands. As a result, four alignments occur in the calculation of the FIR filter corresponding to outputs $y(n)$, $y(n+1)$, $y(n+2)$, and $y(n+3)$. Figure 13.12 illustrates the alignments for the four outputs.

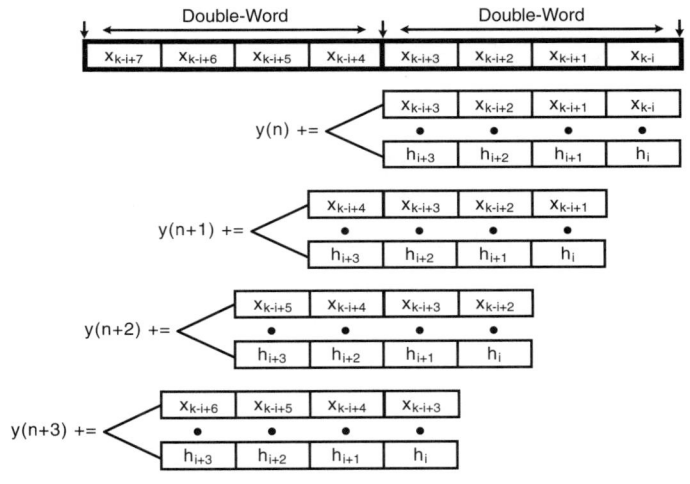

Figure 13.12 The Alignment of Input Samples for $y(n)$, $y(n+1)$, $y(n+2)$, and $y(n+3)$

Two double-word loads are required for obtaining the operands for three out of four of the outputs generated in the execution of the filter. If the Intel XScale® microarchitecture register r0 points to the input sample array, then using the WALIGNI instruction with an immediate value of #2 provides the alignment of operands for the output $y(n+1)$, as follows:

```
wldrd    wR0,[r0],#8   @ load xk-i+3,xk-i+2,xk-i+1,xk-i
wldrd    wR1,[r0],#8   @ load xk-i+7,xk-i+6,xk-i+5,xk-i+4
waligni  wR0,wR1, #2   @ xk-i+4, xk-i+3,xk-i+2,xk-i+1
```

Similarly for the outputs *y(n+2)* and *y(n+3)*, the immediate values of 4 and 6 are used to align the input samples.

```
waligni wR0,wR1, #4  @ xk-i+5, xk-i+4,xk-i+3,xk-i+2
waligni wR0,wR1, #6  @ xk-i+6, xk-i+5,xk-i+4,xk-i+3
```

Because the alignment is so well structured for the FIR filter calculation and the WMAC instructions process four taps, the best implementation of the filter will involve a multi-sample approach. Figure 13.13 shows the C code for the multi-sample FIR, with four taps and four outputs, which is calculated for each inner loop iteration.

```
// blockfir3_c.c
void blockfir3_c(short *input, short *coeff, short *cout,
                 int N, int T){

int i,j,k,acc0, acc1, acc2, acc3;
    for (j=0; j < N ;j++) {
        k = j + T - 1;
        acc0 = acc1 = acc2 = acc3=0;
        for (i=0; i< T; i+=4) {
            acc0+=input[k-i] * coeff[i];
            acc0+=input[k-i-1] * coeff[i+1];
            acc0+=input[k-i-2] * coeff[i+2];
            acc0+=input[k-i-3] * coeff[i+3];

            acc1+=input[k-i+1] * coeff[i];
            acc1+=input[k-i] * coeff[i+1];
            acc1+=input[k-i-1] * coeff[i+2];
            acc1+=input[k-i-2] * coeff[i+3];

            acc2+=input[k-i+2] * coeff[i];
            acc2+=input[k-i+1] * coeff[i+1];
            acc2+=input[k-i] * coeff[i+2];
            acc2+=input[k-i-1] * coeff[i+3];

            acc3+=input[k-i+3] * coeff[i];
            acc3+=input[k-i+2] * coeff[i+1];
            acc3+=input[k-i+1] * coeff[i+2];
            acc3+=input[k-i] * coeff[i+3];
        }
        cout[j]   = (short) (acc0>>15);
        cout[j+1] = (short) (acc1>>15);
        cout[j+2] = (short) (acc2>>15);
        cout[j+3] = (short) (acc3>>15);
    }
}
```

Figure 13.13 C Code for an N-sample T-tap Block FIR Filter Unrolled for Four
Taps per Inner Loop and Four Outputs per Outer Loop Iteration

A total of nine SIMD coprocessor registers and one control register are needed to manage the calculation efficiently:

- Four registers hold the outputs $y(n)$, $y(n+1)$, $y(n+2)$, and $y(n+3)$.

- Two registers hold eight input samples $x(i)$ through $x(i+7)$.

- One register holds the aligned input samples $x_a(i)$, $x_a(i+1)$, $x_a(i+2)$, and $x_a(i+3)$, where x_a indicates that the samples are aligned on byte 2, byte 4, or byte 6 from the two registers holding $x(i)$ through $x(i+7)$.

- Two registers to hold the coefficients, $c(i)$, $c(i+1)$, $c(i+2)$, $c(i+3)$, $c(i+4)$, $c(i+5)$, $c(i+6)$ and $c(i+7)$.

Staying in line with the programming model, several of the core registers are used to manage the pointers and the nested loop structure. Figure 13.14 illustrates one possible configuration of the register file.

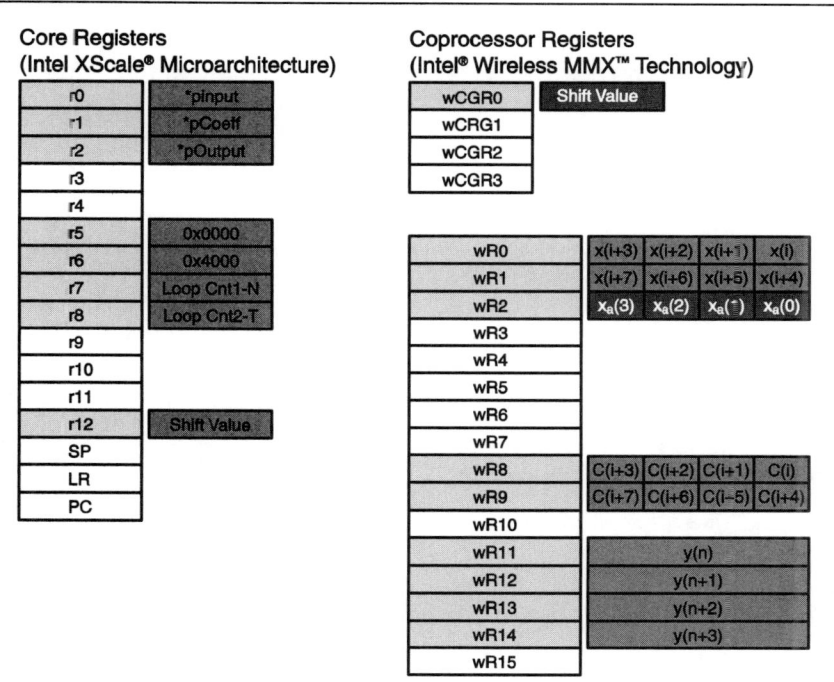

Figure 13.14 Register File Organization for an N-sample T-tap Multi-sample FIR Filter

Planning how to organize the calculation across both the core and coprocessor register files can speed up your development time significantly. Figure 13.15 shows the inner and outer loops for one possible implementation of an N-sample T-tap FIR filter using Intel Wireless MMX assembly code instructions.

```
@ blockfir1_s.s
@ r0,r2 -> input/output pntrs , r1,r3 -> coeff pntrs
@ r7,r8 -> loop counters

OuterLoop:
wldrd    wR0, [r0], #8      @ load four input samples
tmcrr    wR14, r5,r6        @ initialize y(n) for rnd
wldrd    wR1, [r0],#8       @ load four input samples
tmcrr    wR13, r5,r6        @ initialize y(n+1) for rnd
wldrd    wR8, [r1], #8      @ load four coefficients
tmcrr    wR12, r5, r6       @ initialize y(n+2) for rnd
mov      r8,#16             @ setup loop count for Taps
tmcrr    wR11, r5, r6       @ initialize y(n+3) for rnd
InnerLoop:
    wldrd    wR9, [r1], #8      @ load next coefficients
    wmacs    wR11, wR0, wR8     @ y(n) +=
    waligni  wR2, wR0, wR1,#2   @ align input for y(n+1)
    wmacs    wR12, wR2, wR8     @ y(n+1) +=
    waligni  wR2, wR0, wR1,#4   @ align input for y(n+2)
    wmacs    wR13, wR2, wR8     @ y(n+2) +=
    waligni  wR2, wR0, wR1,#6   @ align input for y(n+3)
    wldrd    wR0, [r0], #8      @ load four input samples
    wmacs    wR14, wR2, wR8     @ y(n+3) +=
    subs     r8, r8, #8         @ decrement loop count
    wldrdne  wR8, [r1], #8      @ load next coefficients
    wmacs    wR11, wR1, wR9     @ y(n) +=
    waligni  wR2, wR1, wR0,#2   @ align input for y(n+1)
    wmacs    wR12, wR2, wR9     @ y(n+1) +=
    waligni  wR2, wR1, wR0,#4   @ align input for y(n+2)
    wmacs    wR13, wR2, wR9     @ y(n+2) +=
    waligni  wR2, wR1, wR0,#6   @ align input for y(n+3)
    wmacs    wR14, wR2, wR9     @ y(n+3) +=
    wldrdne   wR1, [r0], #8     @ load four input samples
    bne InnerLoop
wpackdss wR11, wR11,wR12       @ y(n+1) | y(n)
wpackdss wR13, wR13, wR14      @ y(n+3) | y(n+2)
wsrawg   wR11, wR11, wCGR0     @ scale y(n+1),y(n)
wsrawg   wR13, wR13, wCGR0     @ scale y(n+3),y(n+2)
wpackwss wR11, wR11, wR13      @ |y(n+3)|y(n+2|y(n+1)|y(n)|
wstrd    wR11, [r2], #8
subs     r7, r7, #4            @ decrement loop count
mov      r1, r3               @ reset coeff pointer
```

```
sub       r0, r0, #32        @ adjust input pointer
bne       OuterLoop
```

Figure 13.15 Intel® Wireless MMX™ Technology Assembly Instructions for a Multiple Output N-Sample T-Tap Block FIR Filter

The inner loop has been unrolled to process a total of eight taps for each of the four outputs per iteration using a total of 20 instructions, which are executed in 20 cycles. The efficiency of the inner loop is more than twice the efficiency of the single sample example in the "Implementation of the N-Sample, T-Tap Single Output FIR" section. The total number of taps processed per inner loop iteration is 32, leading to a core throughput on the order of $20*NT/32 = 0.625NT$. The outer loop with a total of 19 instructions, plus the two-cycle issue latency for the WSTRD instruction, and a loop fall-through of five cycles, adds another term, $(19+5)*N/4 = 6*N$. Combining the contribution of the inner and outer loops, the approximate throughput equation of $0.625*NT + 6*N$ is achieved. This result looks pretty good, but often the outer loop can be eliminated. Since you have seven of the coprocessor registers still unused, you could store as many as 36 coefficients and eliminate the outer loop completely!

Implementation of the N-Sample, 16-Tap Multiple Output FIR

Eliminating the outer loop when calculating the multi-sample FIR has the potential to reduce the cycle count considerably. For example, if you implement a 40–sample, 16-tap filter using the technique in the previous section, you are looking at a cycle count on the order of, $0.625N*T + 6*N = 640$ cycles. In this example, the outer loop can be eliminated easily since 16 taps would only consume four of the coprocessor registers leaving the rest to manage other aspects of the calculation. This translates into the recovery of nearly 240 cycles. The C code for the calculation of an N-sample, 16-tap block FIR filter is shown in Figure 13.16.

```
// blockfir4_c.c
//
// N sample 16-tap Block FIR filter
// Global Project Variables: N, and SCALE

void blockfir4_c(short *input, short *coeff,
                 short *cout){
    int j, acc0;
    for (j=0; j < N ;j++) {
```

```
acc0 =input[j+15] * coeff[0];
acc0 += input[j+14] * coeff[1];
acc0 += input[j+13] * coeff[2];
acc0 += input[j+12] * coeff[3];
acc0 += input[j+11] * coeff[4];
acc0 += input[j+10] * coeff[5];
acc0 += input[j+9] * coeff[6];
acc0 += input[j+8] * coeff[7];
acc0 += input[j+7] * coeff[8];
acc0 += input[j+6] * coeff[9];
acc0 += input[j+5] * coeff[10];
acc0 += input[j+4] * coeff[11];
acc0 += input[j+3] * coeff[12];
acc0 += input[j+2] * coeff[13];
acc0 += input[j+1] * coeff[14];
acc0 += input[j] * coeff[15];
cout[j] = (short)(acc0>>SCALE);
    }
}
```

Figure 13.16   Simple C Code for an N-sample 16-tap Block FIR Filter

In this implementation of the block FIR filter, the inner loop has been eliminated completely. To have the coefficients available, four coprocessor registers must be allocated to hold the sixteen taps. This allocation still leaves enough registers for performing a multiple sample calculation, as shown with the previous two examples. If you allocate wR0, wR1, wR2, and wR3 to hold the coefficients, and wR11, wR12, wR13, and wR14 to hold the outputs $y(n)$, $y(n+1)$, $y(n+2)$, and $y(n+3)$, eight registers are still available for performing load operations and alignments. The assembly code for a possible implementation of the 16-tap FIR filter is shown in Figure 13.17.

```
@ blockfir2_s.s

_Innerloop:
  wmacsz    wR11, wR3,  wR4       @ y(n) =
  waligni   wR4,  wR4,  wR5, #2 @ align for y(n+1)
  wmacs     wR11, wR2,  wR5       @ y(n) +=
  wlaigni   wR5,  wR5,  wR6, #2 @ align for y(n+1)
  wmacs     wR11, wR1,  wR6       @ y(n) +=
  waligni   wR6,  wR6,  wR7, #2 @ align for y(n+1)
  wmacs     wR11, wR0,  wR7       @ y(n) +=
  wldrd     wR8,  [r0], #8       @ load the next 4 inputs
  wmacsz    wR12, wR3,  wR4       @ y(n+1) =
  waligni   wR4,  wR4,  wR5, #2 @ align for y(n+2)
```

```
wmacs      wR12, wR2,   wR5       @ y(n+1) +=
waligni    wR9,  wR7,   wR8, #2   @ align for y(n+1)
wmacs      wR12, wR1,   wR6       @ y(n+1) +=
waligni    wR5,  wR5,   wR6, #2   @ align for y(n+2)
wmacs      wR12, wR0,   wR9       @ y(n+1) ++
waligni    wR6,  wR6,   wR9, #2   @ align for y(n+2)
wmacsz     wR13, wR3,   wR4       @ y(n+2) +=
waligni    wR10, wR7,   wR8, #4   @ align for y(n+2)
wmacs      wR13, wR2,   wR5       @ y(n+2) +=
waligni    wR4,  wR4,   wR5, #2   @ align for y(n+3)
wmacs      wR13, wR1,   wR6       @ y(n+2) +=
waligni    wR5,  wR5,   wR6, #2   @ align for y(n+3)
wmacs      wR13, wR0,   wR10      @ y(n+2) +=
waligni    wR6,  wR6,   wR10,#2   @ align for y(n+3)
wmacsz     wR14, wR3,   wR4       @ y(n+3) +=
waligni    wR15, wR7,   wR8, #6   @ align for y(n+3)
wmacs      wR14, wR2,   wR5       @ y(n+3) +=
waligni    wR4,  wR4,   wR5, #2   @ align for next iteration
wmacs      wR14, wR1,   wR6       @ y(n+3) +=
waligni    wR5,  wR5,   wR6, #2   @ align for next iteration
wmacs      wR14, wR0,   wR15      @ y(n+3) +=
waligni    wR6,  wR6,   wR15,#2   @ align for next iteration
wpackdss   wR11, wR11,  wR12      @ y(n+1) | y(n)
subs       r5,   r5,    #4
wpackdss   wR13, wR13,  wR14      @ y(n+3) | y(n+2)
wsrawg     wR11, wR11,  wCGR3
wsrawg     wR13, wR13,  wCGR3
wpackwss   wR11, wR11,  wR13      @ y(n+3)|y(n+2|y(n+1)|y(n)
wmov       wR7,  wR8              @ copy for next iteration
wstrd      wR11, [r2],  #8
bgt        _InnerLoop
```

Figure 13.17 Assembly Code Sequence for an N-sample 16-tap Block FIR Filter using Intel® Wireless MMX™ Technology

In this example, only one double-word load is required within the loop and only one is required prior to entering into the loop. Thus, you incur almost no overhead for load-and-store operations. Due to the 2-cycle latency for the WSTRD instruction, 41 instructions execute in 42 cycles. A total of 16 taps are processed to generate each of the four outputs, resulting in a total of 64 taps being processed for each iteration of the loop. This efficiency leads us to a core throughput on the order of $42*NT/64 = 0.656NT$. Since the outer loop has been eliminated completely, the $6*N$ term from the previous example does not contribute to the cycle count, and nearly 240 cycles have been eliminated for a 16-tap implementation.

IIR Filters

The IIR filter also may be used to approximate the same desired response as the FIR filter and selecting one or the other depends on many design parameters. The choice of using an IIR vs. a FIR depends on implementation details, including the execution resources and the desired magnitude and phase characteristics of the filter. The advantage in using the IIR is that it often can be used to achieve the desired behavior with a relatively low order. This practice translates into lower complexity implementations, however the phase response is never linear and the noise characteristics could become an issue when implementing fixed-point solutions, since round-off noise can be amplified due to the feedback loops. The z-transform for the IIR filter has at least one nonzero coefficient, $a(k)$, resulting in the transfer function indicated in the following equation:

$$H(z) = \frac{Y(z)}{X(z)} = \frac{\sum_{k=0}^{M-1} b(k) \cdot z^{-k}}{1 - \sum_{k=1}^{N-1} a(k) \cdot z^{-k}}$$

The linear difference equation can be represented by the network structure shown in Figure 13.18.

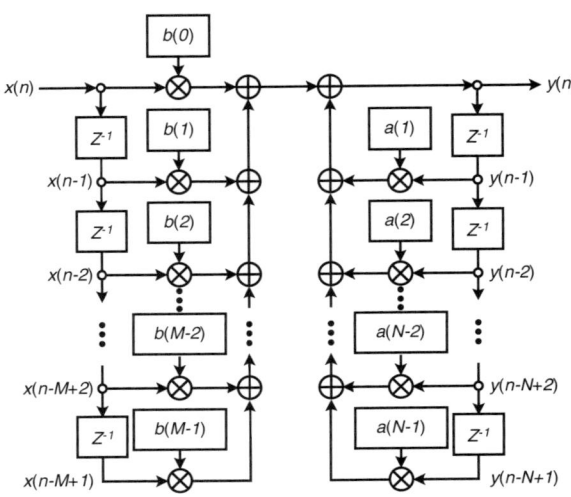

Figure 13.18 Signal Flow Graph for a Direct Form I IIR Filter

This network is referred to as the direct form realization of the Nth order difference equation. An equivalent structure, the direct form II structure, which minimizes the number of delay elements, can also be realized. A second-order direct form II FIR is illustrated in Figure 13.19.

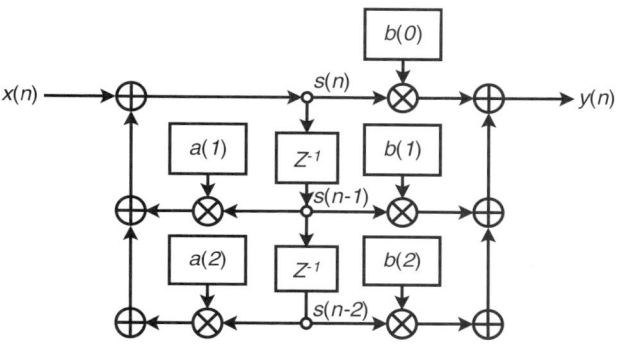

Figure 13.19 Signal Flow Graph for a Second-order Direct Form II IIR Filter

The difference equation for the second-order direct form II filter is:

$$s(n) = x(n) + a_1 \cdot s(n-1) + a_2 \cdot s(n-2)$$
$$y(n) = b_0 \cdot s(n) + b_1 \cdot s(n-1) + b_2 \cdot s(n-2)$$

where *s(n)* corresponds to the different values at the delay nodes, and a_k, and b_k correspond to the coefficients. The second order IIR filter is one of the most common filter forms and is known as the *biquad*. The biquad filter has high enough order to be useful as a basic building block for more complex filters, accommodating the coefficient sensitivities of higher order filters. The z-transform of an IIR filter may also be realized as a series of biquads.

$$H(z) = \sum_{k=1}^{N/2} \frac{b_{0k} + b_{1k} \cdot z^{-1} + b_{2k} \cdot z^{-1}}{1 - a_{1k} \cdot z^{-1} - a_{2k} \cdot z^{-1}}$$

The signal flow graph for a fourth-order IIR filter formed by cascading two biquads with $b_0 = 1$ is illustrated in Figure 13.20.

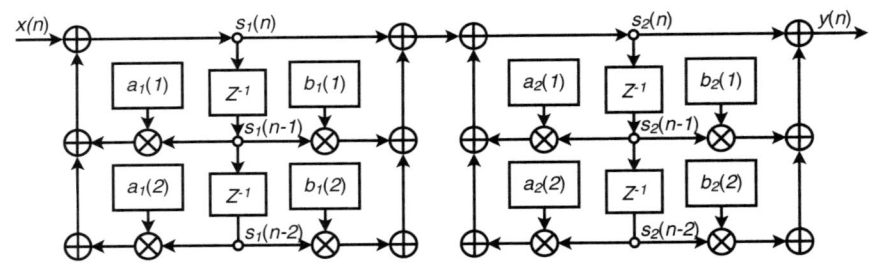

Figure 13.20 Signal Flow Graph for a Fourth-order Cascade Direct Form II IIR Filter

The fourth order filter shown in Figure 13.20 has a total of eight coefficients that are combined with the delayed values represented at each of the four nodes. For each input sample, $x(n)$, a single output, $y(n)$, is calculated. Although the total number of calculations is relatively low, you face several challenges to providing an efficient implementation using Intel Wireless MMX technology.

Computing the Biquad IIR Filter

Implementing an efficient assembly code routine for the cascaded biquad requires careful planning, and before the optimum solution is achieved, you might have to go through multiple iterations. A good place to start is by taking a look at a simple implementation in C. The C code for the fourth-order filter of Figure 13.8 is illustrated in Figure 13.21.

```
// iir_c.c
//
// Fourth-order Cascaded Biquad IIR Filter
// Global Project Variables: SCALE

short iir_c(short *coef, short *delay, short input) {
    int y1, s0, y2, s2;

    s0 = input << SCALE;
    s0 += coef[2]*delay[0] + coef[3]*delay[1];
    y1 = s0 + coef[1]*delay[0] + coef[0]*delay[1];
    s2 = y1 + coef[6]*delay[2] + coef[7]*delay[3];
    y2 = s2 + coef[4]*delay[2] + coef[5]*delay[3];
    delay[1] = delay[0];
    delay[3] = delay[2];
    delay[0] = (short)(s0 >> SCALE);
```

```
        delay[2] = (short)(s2 >> SCALE);
        return (short)(y2 >> SCALE);
}
```

Figure 13.21   C Code for the Fourth-order Cascade Form IIR Filter

This implementation delivers a single output for each call and requires the eight coefficients and four-element delay line to be passed into it. In addition to delivering the output of the filter, an updated delay line is prepared for the next call.

The filter has two basic parts: the arithmetic portion and the delay line update. The arithmetic portion involves a total of eight multiplications and eight additions, so the WMAC instruction with its four-way SIMD could be useful in the calculation. The only problem is that a dependency exists as you proceed through the calculation. Since the new states for each of the biquads, s0 and s2, represent updates to the delay-node values for the filter, they must be calculated independent of the output. One possible implementation is to calculate s0 and y1 using two multiplications, and to calculate s2 using four multiplications. You can do so by folding the calculation of the output of the first biquad stage, y1, into the calculation of the second stage new delay state. s2. In this fashion, a running MAC operation can be used to calculate the output of the filter, y2.

```
S0 = input + coeff[2]*delay[0] + coeff [3]*delay[1];
tmp = s0;
s2 = s0    + coef[1]*delay[0] + coef[0]*delay[1]
           + coef[6]*delay[2] + coef[7]*delay[3];
tmp1 = s2;
y2 = t1    + coef[4]*delay[2] + coef[5]*delay[3];
```

This approach requires some planning around the organization of the coefficients in memory that you might not find obvious at first. Although the WMAC instruction is not fully utilized for the calculation of s0 and y2, it is fully utilized for the delay node value s2. So, the coefficient array can be padded with zeroes at the beginning and end to facilitate the use of double-word loads and multiplication with the delay line variables as packed 16-bit elements. A reorganization of the coefficients to support this implementation scheme is shown in Figure 13.22.

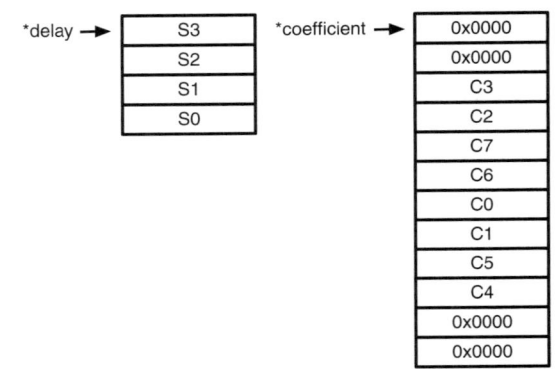

Figure 13.22 Relationship Between Input Samples and Coefficients

The arithmetic portion of the filter may now be executed with three WMAC instructions. Since so few WMAC instructions are required, and each of the outputs of the routine must be scaled, some careful scheduling is needed. For instance, we can calculate s0 with a single application of the WMAC instruction with the coefficients 0, 0, C3, C2, and the delay values, but this value now has to be scaled and stored to update the delay values for the next iteration. The value is also needed for the next calculation. One approach is to create a copy of s0 and continue the calculation, which allows you to update the delay values at a more convenient time. If wR1 and wR3 contains the coefficients and wR2 contains the current delay values, the following sequence can be implemented.

```
wmacs    wR0, wR1, wR2    @ calculate s0
wmov     wR6, wR0         @ copy s0
wmacs    wR0, wR3, wR2    @ calculate y1
```

Although this instruction sequence incurs a four-cycle latency for the writeback following the WMAC operation, several additional operations can be interleaved, and you are now able to continue with the calculations with a copy of s0 in wR6. The assembly code for the fourth-order IIR filter using the coefficient ordering illustrated in Figure 13.22 is provided in Figure 13.23.

```
@ IIR_s.s
@
@ r0 -> coef, r1 -> delay, r2 -> input/output

tinsrw    wR0, r2, #0              @ load input in register
mov       r3,  #14                 @ setup shift operand
tmcr      wCGR0, r3                @ transfer shift operand
wldrd     wR2, [r1]                @ load delay line
wldrw     wR1, [r0], #8            @ load C3,C2
wslldg    wR0, wR0, wCGR0          @ scale the input
waligni   wR7, wR0, wR2, #6        @ shift delay line
wmacs     wR0, wR1, wR2            @ calculate s0
wldrd     wR3, [r0], #8            @ load C7, C6, C1, C0
wstrd     wR7, [r1]                @ store delay line
wmov      wR6, wR0                 @ copy s0
wmacs     wR0, wR3, wR2            @ caluclate y1
wsradg    wR8, wR6, wCGR0          @ scale s0
wldrd     wR4, [r0]                @ load C5,C4,0,0
wstrh     wR8, [r1], #4            @ store s1 to delay line
wsradg    wR9, wR0, wCGR0          @ sclae s2
wmacs     wR0, wR4, wR2            @ calulate y2
wstrh     wR9, [r1]                @ store s2 to delay line
wsradg    wR0, wR0, wCGR0          @ scale y2
wstrh     wR0, [r4]                @ store result
textrmsh  r0, wR0, #0             @ return result
```

Figure 13.23 Intel® Wireless MMX™ Instructions for the Fourth-order IIR Filter

The code sequence has a total of 20 instructions, but the cycle count is 25! One of the extra cycles is due to the two-cycle issue latency of the WSTRD instruction. The remaining five cycles are due to stalls that occur as a result of three factors: following a WLDRD instruction with another memory transaction, the three-cycle latency of the TMCR instruction, and the four-cycle latency to get the final output value out of the multiply pipeline and into the shifter for the final precision reduction.

Adaptive Filtering

Adaptive filters are filters that can adjust themselves in response to a changing environment. They are used in systems that require the filter characteristics to be modified in response to variations in the input signal. Some examples include both voice- and audio-processing algorithms that are used for echo-cancellation, interference canceling, and system identification. A general adaptive filter is illustrated in Figure 13.24.

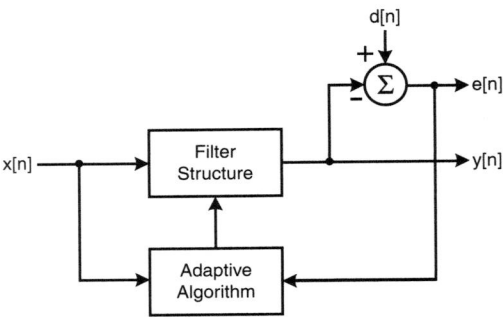

Figure 13.24 General Adaptive Filter

The adaptive filter has two inputs: the input signal, *x(n)*, and the desired output, *d(n)*. The filter output *y(n)* may be expressed with the same difference equation that is used to define the behavior of the FIR and IIR filters discussed in the previous sections, except that now the coefficients are adapted so that the error sequence is as close to zero as possible.

$$y(n) = \sum_{k=0}^{N-1} a_k(n) \cdot x(n-k) + \sum_{k=0}^{M-1} b_k(n) \cdot y(n-k)$$

To provide for the modification of the coefficients $a_k(n)$ and $b_k(n)$, a number of filter update algorithms may be implemented. The Least Mean Squares (LMS) algorithm is one of the most widely used due to its robustness and computational efficiency.

FIR-LMS Algorithm

The FIR-LMS algorithm uses the same finite convolution equation for generating the output values, except that now, for each time index the coefficients are altered. The discrete convolution equation used for representing the filter is similar to the FIR, except now a weight vector represents the coefficients:

$$y(n) = \sum_{k=0}^{N-1} w_k(n) \cdot x(n-k)$$

The LMS algorithm defines the modification of the tap weights according to the simple relationship:

$$w_k(n+1) = w_k(n) + \mu \cdot e(n) \cdot x(n)$$

where,

$w_k(n+1) = $ new taps for the filter

$w_k(n) = $ current taps for the filter

$\mu = $ adaptation parameter

$e(n) = $ error output

$x(n) = $ input samples

The same techniques discussed in earlier sections can also be applied to the FIR-LMS adaptive filter; however, the complexity is increased significantly. Whether the decision is to use the single sample, multi-sample, or the fixed tap approach you must perform the following steps:

1. Perform the FIR filter generating $y(n)$.
2. Calculate the new coefficients $w_k(n+1)$.
3. Calculate the new error e(n).
4. Update the delay line $x(n+1) = x(n)$.

The network structure of the FIR-LMS adaptive filter looks a lot like the structure for the FIR filter, except now, a coefficient update section is added. The network structure for the FIR-LMS filter is illustrated in Figure 13.25.

The structure shown in Figure 13.25 has a total of T coefficients, which are combined with the a delay line of input samples to produce the output $y(n)$. For each output generated, the error between the desired output is calculated, then it is used to modify the coefficient array. The implementation of an efficient assembly code sequence for the IIR can be challenging and several options exist.

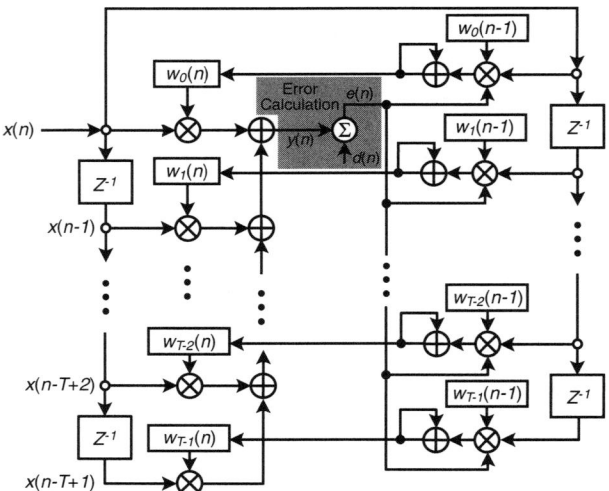

Figure 13.25 The Single Sample T-tap FIR-LMS Algorithm

Computing the Single Sample FIR-LMS Filter

Of the four components of the LMS algorithm, the calculation of the adaptation error requires the least effort because it is a scalar operation that occurs only once, either before or after the FIR calculation and coefficient update.

```
error = d[n] - y[n];
adaptErr = adaptRate*error
```

The remaining three components—the FIR calculation, the coefficient update, and the delay line update—may all be implemented on multiple elements simultaneously. This potential for simultaneous execution makes these components well suited for implementation using Intel Wireless MMX technology. The FIR portion of the calculation is just a repeated multiply accumulate operation.

```
acc = 0;
for(j = 0; j < T; j++)
    acc += coeff[j]*delay[j];
```

The delay line update is a simple shift of the input samples by one element in the buffer, with the first element being initialized to the current input value.

```
for(j = 0; j > T; j++)
    delay[j+1] = delay[j];
delay[0] = in;
```

The coefficient update is more complex since you must perform a multiplication with a reduction in precision from 32 bits to 16 bits in the result, followed by an addition. In addition, the performance of the filter is very sensitive to errors that could occur with this step, so a rounding operation is required, as follows:

```
for(j = 0; j < T; j++)
    coeff[j] = coeff[j]+(adaptErr*delay[j]+0x4000)>>15;}
```

Since the best performance is always achieved by doing as many operations as possible through amortization of load and store overhead, you would want to look for methods to fold the FIR calculation, the delay line update, and the coefficient update into a single assembly code loop. Let's take a closer look at how to best organize the calculation.

Organizing the FIR-LMS Calculation

The implementation of the FIR-LMS filter can provide for the coefficient update either before or after the calculation of the output sample. In addition, it can also be folded into the same loop in a manner similar to the delay line update in the single sample FIR filter example. The C code illustrated in Figure 13.26 shows one possible implementation of the filter where the coefficient update, delay line update, and the FIR filter are performed in the same loop.

```
// lms_c.c
//
// T tap LMS-FIR filter
// Global Variables: T -> Number of taps

void lms_c( short in, short lmsdes, short *coeff,
           short *delay, short *adapterror,
           short *result, short *error){
    int i,j, acc;

    acc = 0x4000;
    for (j = T-1; j >= 0 ; j--) {
        coeff[j] +=(short)(((*adapterror)*delay[j]
                     +0x4000)>>15);
        if( j < T-1 ){
            delay[j+1] = delay[j];
```

```
                 acc += delay[j+1]*coeff[j+1];
             }
         }
    delay[0] = in;
    acc += delay[0]*coeff[0];
    *result = (short)(acc >> 15);
    *error = lmsdes - *result;
    *(adapterror+1) =(short)(adaptrate*(*error) >>15);
}
```

Figure 13.26 Simple C Code for an N-sample T-tap Single Sample FIR Filter

This example serves as a good starting point, since you want to do as much work as possible using the same load and store operations and the same loop overhead. To implement all of the components of the filter in the same loop, you want an organization that allows you to ping-pong your loads and stores. If r3 holds the pointer to the delay line, one approach is to organize the calculations as follows:

```
Loop: wldrd    wR0, [r3], #8      @ load state

      @ update the coefficients using wR0
      waligni   wR2,wR1,wR0,#6     @ align delay line
      wstrd     wR2,[r3, #-8]      @ store delay line

      @ perform the FIR filter using wR2
      wldrd     wR1, [r3], #8      @ load state

      @ update the coeffcients using wR1
      waligni   wR3,wR0,wR1,#6     @ align delay lin
      wstrd     wR3,[r3, #-8]      @ store delay line

      @ perform the FIR filter using wR3
      bne Loop
```

Using this basic structure provides a good foundation for the assembly code implementation. The FIR calculation and the delay line update use the same basic sequence that we used with the single sample FIR example. The next step is to identify the instruction sequence for adaptation of the coefficients.

Adapting the Coefficients

The single sample FIR-LMS filter is very similar to the single sample FIR that has been discussed in previous sections, with the finite convolution and delay line update. The coefficient adaptation is the primary goal of an adaptive algorithm and is often very sensitive to errors, so you need to preserve as much precision in the calculation as possible. Assuming the coefficient and input samples are in a Q1.15 format, the coefficient update would proceed as follows:

1. Multiply the 16-bit adaptation error with the 16-bit input sample x[n] producing a 32-bit result:

   Q1.15*Q1.15 → Q2.30 (two sign bits)

2. Round the lower bits into the upper bits of the product and truncate:

   (Q2.30 + 0x4000) >> 15 → Q1.15

3. Add the adaptation term to the old coefficient value:

   Q1.15 + Q1.15 → Q1.15

The WMULS instruction provides for the parallel multiplication of four 16-bit signed operand pairs, with the ability to select either the upper or lower halves of the resulting 32-bit product. The WUNPCKIHH and WUNPCKILH instructions are used to form the 32-bit words from following the application of the multiplication instructions. Finally, the rounding term can be added, and to get the error term back into a Q1.15 form, use a shift–by–15 instruction followed by the WPACKWSS instruction. Now this value can be added to the old values of the coefficients to provide the adaptation. The TBCST instruction is used to construct the two 32-bit rounding terms as well as the four 16-bit copies of the adaptation value. If r4 holds the adaptation rate and r5 holds the rounding term 0x4000, the following sequence can be used to broadcast the values to wR13 and wR14.

```
TBCSTH      wR13, r4
TBCSTW      wR14, r5
```

Using wR0 to hold four input samples from the delay line, the following sequence can be used to generate the adaptation term.

```
wmulsm      wR5,wR0,wR13    @ high 16-bits u*e[n]*x[n]
wmulsl      wR7,wR0,wR13    @ low 16-bits u*e[n]*x[n]
wunpckihh   wR8,wR7,wR5     @ interleave to get Q2.30
wunpckilh   wR9,wR7,wR5     @ interleave to get Q2.30
waddw       wR8,wR8,wR14    @ add 0x4000 for rounding
waddw       wR9,wR9,wR14    @ add 0x4000 for rounding
wsrawg      wR8,wR8,wCGR0   @ shift by 15 to get Q1.15
wsrawg      wR9,wR9,wCGR0   @ shift by 15 to get Q1.15
wpackwss    wR8,wR9,wR8     @ pack
```

Finally, this sequence can be interleaved with additional operations associated with the FIR calculation and the delay line update. The inner loop for the assembly code implementation of the FIR-LMS filter using this approach is illustrated in Figure 13.27.

```
@ lms_s.s
@
@ r3 -> delay line , r2 -> coefficients
@ r4 -> output , r7 -> adpaterror

_LMSloop:
    wmulsm      wR5,wR0,wR13    @ multiply to get upper
    wldrd       wR4, [r2]       @ load coefficients
    wmulsl      wR7,wR0,wR13    @ multiply to get lower
    subs        r5, r5, #8      @ decrement loop count
    waligni     wR2,wR1,wR0,#6  @ align delay line
    wstrd       wR2,[r3, #-8]   @ store delay line
    wunpckihh   wR8,wR7,wR5     @ compose 32-bit result
    wunpckilh   wR9,wR7,wR5     @ compose 32-bit result
    waddw       wR8,wR8, wR14   @ add 0x4000 for rounding
    waddw       wR9,wR9,wR14    @ add 0x4000 for rounding
    wsrawg      wR8,wR8,wCGR0   @ provide shift by 15
    wsrawg      wR9,wR9,wCGR0   @ provide shift by 15
    wpackwss    wR8,wR9,wR8     @ pack adaptation term
    wldrd       wR1,[r3],#8     @ load next four inputs
    waddh       wR6,wR4,wR8     @ w(n)+u*e[n]*x[n]
    wstrd       wR6,[r2],#8     @ store w(n+1)
    wmulsm      wR5,wR1,wR13    @ get high 16-bits u*e[n]*x[n]
    wldrd       wR4,[r2]        @ load next four coeff.
    wmulsl      wR7,wR1,wR13    @ get low 16-bits u*e[n]*x[n]
    waligni     wR3,wR0,wR1,#6  @ align delay line
    wstrd       wR3,[r3,#-8]    @ store delay line
    wunpckihh   wR8,wR7,wR5     @ u*e[n]*x[n]
    wmacs       wR12,wR2,wR6    @ y[n]+=
    wunpckilh   wR9,wR7,wR5     @ u*e[n]*x[n]
    waddw       wR8,wR8,wR14    @ add 0x4000 for rounding
    waddw       wR9,wR9,wR14    @ add 0x4000 for rounding
    wsrawg      wR8,wR8,wCGR0   @ provide shift by 15
    wsrawg      wR9,wR9,wCGR0   @ provide shift by 15
    wpackwss    wR8,wR9,wR8     @ pack adaptation term
    wldrd       wR1,[r3],#8     @ load next four inputs
    waddh       wR6,wR4,wR8     @ w(n)+u*e[n]*x[n]
    wstrd       wR6,[r2],#8     @ store w(n+1)
    bne         _LMSloop
```

Figure 13.27 Intel® Wireless MMX™ Instructions for the Single Sample FIR-LMS

The implementation shown in Figure 13.27 processes a total of eight samples per iteration. The inner loop uses a total of 33 instructions and consumes 36 cycles due to the two-cycle issue latency of the WSTRD instruction. The rounding of the adaptation term that is used for the coefficient update consumes over half of the entire cycle count.

Key Points

This chapter has shown you how to apply Intel Wireless MMX technology to some of the most widely used digital filtering algorithms:

- Finite impulse response (FIR) filters
  - Single sample implementation
  - Multi-sample implementation
  - Fixed tap implementation
- Infinite impulse response (IIR) filters
- FIR-LMS adaptive filter

The implementation of these filters illustrates some important general strategies for implementing and optimizing Intel Wireless MMX technology code.

- Calculating multiple outputs within the same routine designed to amortize load and store traffic is an important technique. This practice was demonstrated in the multi-sample technique developed for the block FIR.

- Maintaining nested loops often is unnecessary when using Intel Wireless MMX technology, because for some of the more common filters sizes, the number of taps is often low enough that they can be accommodated by the large register file, leaving plenty of registers for calculating multiple output samples and managing the load and store traffic.

- Sometimes the best implementation might not be obvious at first. By padding with zeroes and reorganizing the data, a higher throughput solution can often be realized. In the example for the IIR filter, the coefficient reordering and padding with zeros allowed a higher throughput solution to be realized.

Chapter 14

Digital Image Processing

Advances in digital processing technologies have sparked an explosion in imaging-based applications by making it possible to perform complex operations on multidimensional signals. From digital cameras, camera phones, and digital TV to the Internet, gaming, and medical imaging, almost everyone enjoys the benefits of digital imaging. With the recent proliferation of digital cameras, some of the basic concepts that are associated with image capture and enhancement are becoming more commonly understood by the layman. A color image is captured from a digital camera, processed in its raw state, and then displayed in a form suitable for human consumption using a variety of display and print media. Image processing is a broad discipline that has several specialized application areas. In this chapter, our focus is on some of the key color image processing algorithms required for mobile image capture systems. The chapter examines the use of Intel® Wireless MMX™ technology in spatial filtering, color correction, and color synthesis.

Image Processing Fundamentals

Image processing is based on the manipulation of two-dimensional (2D) arrays of image data. The same concepts used in the manipulation of one-dimensional arrays are simply extended in a second dimension. Application of filters in two dimensions may alter the intensity and spatial frequency response as a function of two dimensions, x and y. In a digital image, the variables x and y describe the spatial coordinates represented by the intersection of the rows and columns. The point of intersection of the rows and columns, *(x,y)*, is referred to as a *pixel*, or picture element.

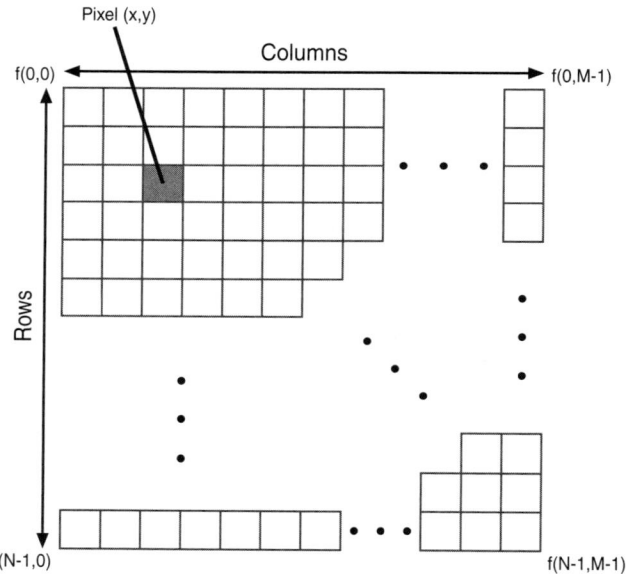

Figure 14.1 Illustration of the Rows and Columns in a 2D Pixel Array

A pixel may be represented in a variety of forms depending on the intended purpose. One application may only require a single variable for each spatial location where other applications may require three or more.

Many resources are available illustrating both general and specialized topics in digital imaging. In this section, some of the basic terminology for general image processing and color image capture systems is introduced.

Digital Images

Digital images are electronic representations acquired through cameras, frame grabbers, or an optical scanning process. In human vision, the world is imaged by the lens of the eye onto the retina, which is populated with photoreceptor cells that respond to wavelengths of light from around 400 nanometers to 700 nanometers. In digital imaging, a camera, a lens, and an array of photosensitive structures mimic our perception of the world through vision. The array of photosensitive structures is referred to as an image sensor pixel array, and these devices are available today in a number of resolutions using CCD or CMOS imaging technologies. The CCD or CMOS image array is sequenced uniformly to form scan lines. The scanned lines are in turn sequenced in time throughout each frame interval to form image frames. When captured in sequence, the image frames form a video sequence, and when captured individually, the image is referred to as a still picture.

By creating a binary representation of the tone or brightness at discrete spatial locations in a 2D grid, photographs, artwork, manuscripts, and printed text can be described. The process of creating a digital image is based on the division of a continuous image, $f(x,y)$, into N rows and M columns.

$$f(x, y) \;=\; \begin{bmatrix} f(0,0) & f(0,1) & . \;\; . \;\; . & f(0,M-1) \\ f(1,0) & f(1,1) & . \;\; . \;\; . & f(1,M-1) \\ . & . & & . \\ . & . & & . \\ . & . & & . \\ f(N-1,0) & f(N-1,1) & . \;\; . \;\; . & f(N-1,M-1) \end{bmatrix}$$

The values at each coordinate position in the grid represent the brightness, amplitude, or spectral response of a sampled signal. In most cases, this representation relates to a physical signal that impinges on the face of a sensor at a particular wavelength. In color imaging, three components represent the primary colors red, green, and blue. One way to visualize a color image is to think of the N×M digital image as three separate arrays, one array for each of the components, $f_R(x,y)$, $f_G(x,y)$, and $f_B(x,y)$.

Image Size

The size of a digital image is described through the product of the rows and the columns. This value represents the total number of pixels. A 1536×2048 pixel image has 3,145,728 pixels, or 3.1 megapixels, and a 1024×1280 has 1,310,720, or 1.3 megapixels. Some common sizes for digital images are provided in Table 14.1.

Table 14.1   Common Image Sizes Used in Digital Imaging

Image Size	Rows × Columns	Total No. Pixels
QXGA	1536 × 2048	3,145,728
UXGA	1200 × 1600	1,920,000
SXGA	1024 × 1280	1,310,720
XGA	768 × 1280	983,040
SVGA	600 × 800	480,000
VGA	480 × 640	307,200
QVGA	240 × 320	76,800

The size of the image tells how many pixels are included, and the spatial resolution indicates the ability to represent detail. The number of pixels in an image is chosen to represent the scene or object of interest at a chosen distance and field of view (FOV).

Bit Depth and Bits per Pixel

Bit depth and bits per pixel (bpp) are determined by the number of bits used to describe each pixel. Bit depth is the total number of bits that are used for the representation of a pixel or an element of a pixel in color imaging. The bits per pixel measurement refers to the total number of bits use to represent the pixel. For example, a 24-bit RGB format is a 24 bpp format that has bit depth of eight for each component R, G, and B. Some common formats are illustrated in Table 14.2.

Table 14.2 Bit Depth and Bits per Pixel for Some Common Formats

Pixel Type	Bit Depth	Bits per Pixel (bpp)
Monochrome	8 bits	8 bpp
RAW8[1]	R,G,B → 8 bits	2.67 bpp
RAW10[1]	R,G,B → 10 bits	3.33 bpp
RGB444	R,G,B→ 4 bits	12 bpp
RGB565	R,B→ 5 bits; G→6 bits	16 bpp
RGB888	R,G,B → 8 bits	24 bpp

Note: (1) The raw formats are an interleaved mosaic of R, G, and B.

The monochrome, or "grey" level, image is a black and white representation a total of 256 possible shades between black and white. The bit depth of eight bits and the 8 bpp imply that each pixel has only one channel and eight bits are used to represent the value.

The RAW8 and RAW10 formats represent the 8-bit or 10-bit pixel depth obtained from modern color image sensors. By using a mosaic of red, green, and providing a synthesis for missing components, the effective bit depth is much lower.

The most popular representation for processed color images is 24 bits per pixel. This representation allows 16,777,216 possible colors to be represented; however, both lower and higher component bit depths are used in various application scenarios.

Color Space

Representing color in images requires more than just one sample at each spatiotemporal location. Actually, several alternative systems for representing color exist. These systems are known as *color spaces*. For use with Intel Wireless MMX technology, you are likely to focus on the two most common color spaces for representing digital images: red, green, blue (RGB) and luminance, chrominance blue, chrominance red (YCbCr).

The RGB color space provides a scheme for three numbers representing the relative proportions of red, green, and blue at each pixel location. When combined, these three additive primary colors can be used to produce any other color. The RGB color space is used for both the capture and display of image data since the varying proportions can be combined easily. However, the human visual system is more sensitive to the luminance, or brightness of the scene, than to the color, so you can realize a reduction in data in the compression process by taking advantage of this characteristic.

The separation of the luminance from the color information is accomplished through the color space transformation of RGB to YCbCr. In this transformation, the luminance, Y, is the weighted average of the R, G, and B components; each chrominance sample, Cb and Cr, is the weighted difference between the luminance and the B and R components, respectively.

The RGB and YCbCr formats are illustrated in Figure 14.2, where each pixel location has three components. Using eight bits for each component, you have a total of 24 bpp for both of the formats before and after the conversion.

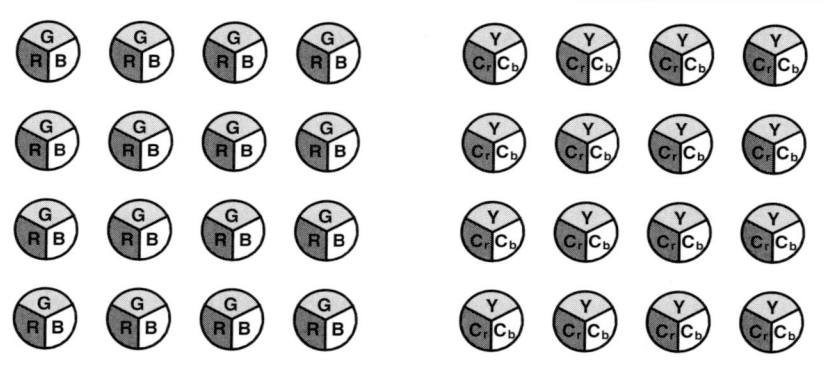

Figure 14.2   RGB and YCbCr Image Formats

The key advantage of using the YCbCr color space is that you can use a lower spatial resolution when compressing or storing the images since the visual system is less sensitive to the color than luminance. The two most popular formats for YCbCr color space use the 4:2:2 and 4:2:0 sampling patterns. The notation a:b:c indicates the sampling frequency of each of the channels. The first digit represents the horizontal sampling frequency of the luminance and the other two digits represent the horizontal subsampling of the chrominance components, Cb and Cr. In the 4:2:2 format, the chrominance samples are subsampled or averaged across two horizontal spatial locations, whereas the 4:2:0 format subsamples or averages them across four sample locations, both horizontal and vertical. The 4:2:2 and 4:2:0 sampling formats are illustrated in Figure 14.3.

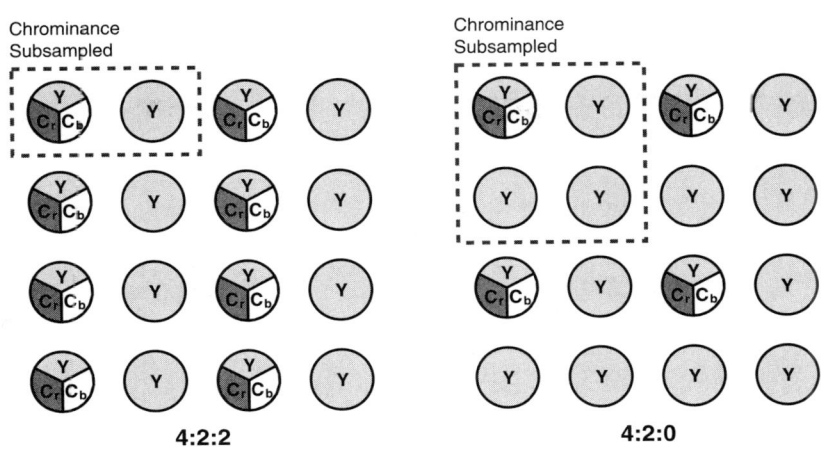

Figure 14.3   Chrominance Subsampling Patterns for the YCbCr 4:2 2 and YCbCr 4:2:0 Formats

The focus of this chapter is primarily 24 bit-per-pixel RGB formats. When working this format, memory organization is an important aspect for parallel processing.

24-Bit-per-Pixel Color Images

The memory organization for color images may be in several different formats. The array of image data may have each of the color components interleaved into a byte packed data structure or each of the color components may be in a three different packed arrays. To complicate things further, the image processing algorithms often need 16 bits of precision, so half-word packed arrays or sparsely packed arrays could occur as well. Figure 14.4 illustrates the packed and the planar formats for 24-bit-per-pixel RGB.

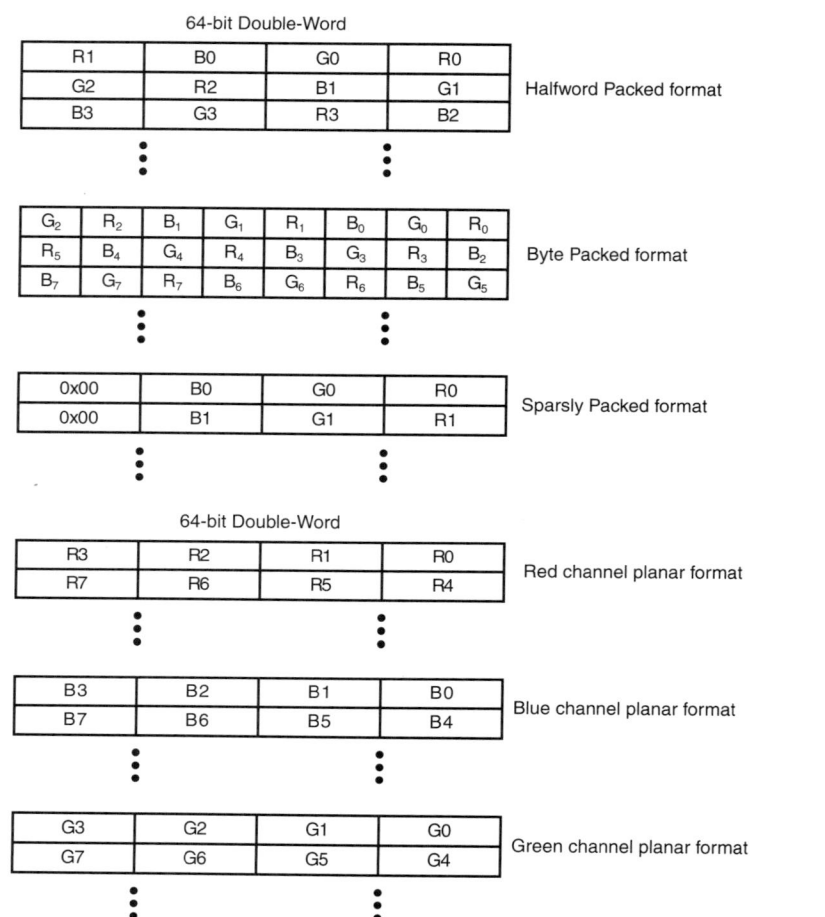

Figure 14.4 Memory Organization for the Packed Byte, Half-word, and Sparse Half-word RGB24 Image Formats

Digital Cameras

The digital camera is the recording medium for modern digital imaging applications. The components of a digital camera include optics, image sensor, and some capability to process the measured data into a form suitable for display, storage, or printing. A simplified view of a camera image capture system is illustrated in Figure 14.5.

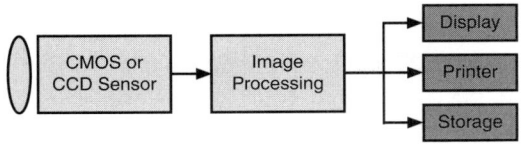

Figure 14.5 Simplified View of Camera Image Capture System

Color cameras and color image sensors are available in many different price ranges and formats. The wide adaptation of color imaging devices is primarily due to the development of low cost image sensors that can provide spectral discrimination.

Color Image Acquisition

The color sensitivity for modern image sensors is provided by a *color filter array* (CFA) applied over an array of photo detectors. The detectors convert the light that passes through the CFA material into a signal that is measured and digitized. You can find a lot of variation between manufacturers of color image sensors when it comes to the implementations of CFAs. The filter array material is usually applied in an interleaved fashion. The pattern can be in stripes or in a structured mosaic. The component filter material is designed to pass the wavelengths of the primary colors red, green, and blue, or of the secondary colors cyan, yellow, and magenta. A mosaic pattern for R, G, B and C, Y, M, G color filters is illustrated in Figure 14.6.

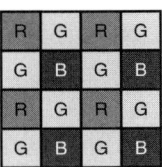

Red, Green, Blue
Mosaic Pattern

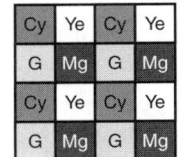

Cyan, Yellow, Magenta, Green
Mosaic Pattern

Figure 14.6 R, G, B and C, M, Y, G Mosaic Patterns

The R, G, B mosaic pattern is the popular Bayer pattern, which uses alternating red-green and blue-green filters for the rows in an image. With only half of the pixels green, one quarter of the pixels red, and one quarter of the pixels blue, a full 24 bits for each pixel can be synthesized through a variety of "de-mosaicing" techniques.

Color Image Processing

The color image processing in a digital camera is used to construct an image that can be displayed on some media with color rendered as close as possible to what the human eye perceives. The basic color processing steps in a color image capture system are illustrated in Figure 14.7.

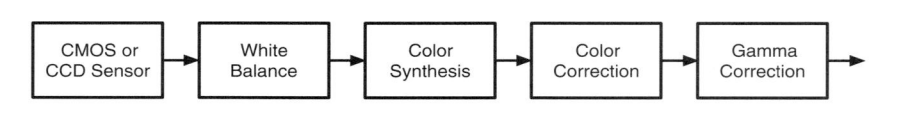

Figure 14.7   Color Processing Steps in Color Image Capture

The white balance operation provides for adjustment of the gain for each of the component channels according to the spectral distribution of the illuminant. The operation is often provided in analog within the sensor itself. The color synthesis is used to generate the missing pixel color components when a CFA mosaic pattern is used. A number of algorithms have been developed to perform this function, and they vary significantly both in complexity and quality. Color correction is used to transform the R, G, and B triads from the camera color space to the color space of the display or to one of several standard color spaces. Gamma correction is used to correct for nonlinearity in the display.

The most computationally demanding components of the color algorithm sequence include the color synthesis and color correction operations. The following sections explore the application of Intel Wireless MMX technology to these algorithms.

Image Filtering

Filtering operations are just as important in 2D signal processing as in 1D processing. Application of spatial filters is often used to enhance visual quality by suppressing noise or sharpening edges. The spatial filter works by manipulating the image data and can either extract, enhance, or preserve some aspect. For example, images are resized by applying a low-pass filter prior to decimation, and edges are enhanced by applying a high-pass filter. Spatial convolution allows you to perform these types of operations, and it is considered central to image processing applications.

Spatial Convolution

To convolve an image, a 2D filter kernel of finite dimensions is aligned with an equal sized subset of the image and then scanned across the image in multiple steps. At each step in the convolution, a different group of pixels are aligned with the kernel. Each of the corresponding overlapping elements is multiplied with the elements of the kernel. The resulting products of the element multiplications are accumulated, scaled if necessary, and then stored to an output image array. The convolution operation can be written as the finite sum in the following equation:

$$c(m,n) = \sum_{j=0}^{N-1}\sum_{k=0}^{M-1} a(j,k) \cdot h(m-j, n-k)$$

where $c(m,n)$, $a(j,k)$, and $h(m-j,n-k)$ represent the output image, input image, and the convolution kernel respectively.

Several issues occur with applying the convolution kernel to images. If you examine the previous equation, it becomes apparent that centering the kernel around the edges of the image requires values of $a(j,k)$ that are outside of the boundaries. Several approaches can handle the non-existent values of the image for $j < 0$, $j >= M$, $k < 0$, and $k >= N$. The simplest method is to extend the image using extra rows and columns around the border. The extra elements can be zero, mirrored values, or a constant. Figure 14.8 illustrates the application of a 3×3 kernel within an image array.

The convolution kernel can be of any size; however, practical implementations often use a 3×3 or 5×5. Convolution is usually done with separate input and output images so the outputs of each convolution steps doesn't affect the neighboring calculations. Low-pass and high-pass filters are usually a basis for most spatial filtering operations.

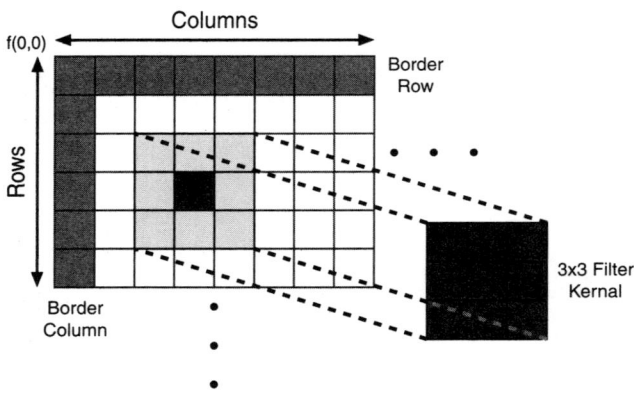

Figure 14.8   Illustration of 2D Convolution with a 3×3 Kernel

Low-pass Filters

Low-pass filtering is applied to images to attenuate high frequency content. It is applied in many image processing applications to either smooth or soften an image enhancing the characteristics of low-frequency objects. Noise that is primarily composed of high-frequency detail can also be eliminated through application of spatial low-pass filters. Often the low-pass spatial filter is applied prior to implementing scaling operations to reduce the aliasing effects that occur with image decimation.

The simplest filter kernel is the *box filter*, or the spatial averaging filter. The filter kernel assigns to all of the coefficients a value of 1, and the constant 1/9 is multiplied times the result to normalize the calculation. This normalization maintains the same brightness in the image. The 3×3 and 5×5 box filters have 9 and 25 coefficients respectively.

$$h_{LP(3x3)}[j,k] = \frac{1}{9}\begin{bmatrix} 1 & 1 & 1 \\ 1 & 1 & 1 \\ 1 & 1 & 1 \end{bmatrix}, \qquad h_{LP(5x5)}[j,k] = \frac{1}{25}\begin{bmatrix} 1 & 1 & 1 & 1 & 1 \\ 1 & 1 & 1 & 1 & 1 \\ 1 & 1 & 1 & 1 & 1 \\ 1 & 1 & 1 & 1 & 1 \\ 1 & 1 & 1 & 1 & 1 \end{bmatrix}$$

When implementing the filter, the scaling value is often multiplied by the coefficients to eliminate the need to do a division following each application. For example, the 3×3 box filter can be implemented by multiplying each of the coefficients by 1/9:

$$h_{LP(3x3)}[j,k] = \begin{bmatrix} \frac{1}{9} & \frac{1}{9} & \frac{1}{9} \\ \frac{1}{9} & \frac{1}{9} & \frac{1}{9} \\ \frac{1}{9} & \frac{1}{9} & \frac{1}{9} \end{bmatrix}$$

Application of the 3×3 kernel in this equation is illustrated in Figure 14.9.

 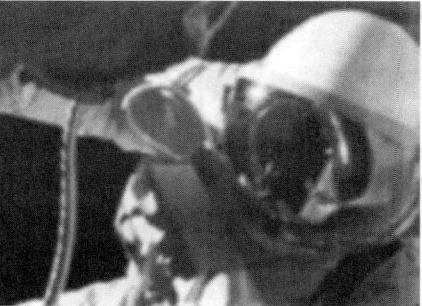

(a) Original Grey Scale Image   (b) Low Pass Filtered Image

Photo Credit: NASA

Figure 14.9   The Low-pass Filter Using the 3×3 Box Filter $h_{LP(3x3)}[j,k]$

High-pass Filters

The high-pass filter amplifies the high frequency content and has an opposite effect to the low-pass filter. The effect of applying the filter is to sharpen the image and is often applied to enhance the details in an image. Typically, the filter is designed with a large positive coefficient in the center of the kernel surrounded by smaller negative coefficients.

A couple of popular high pass 3×3 and 5×5 filter kernels are as follows:

$$h_{HP(3x3)}[j,k] = \begin{bmatrix} -1 & -1 & -1 \\ -1 & 9 & -1 \\ -1 & -1 & -1 \end{bmatrix}, \quad h_{HP(5x5)}[j,k] = \begin{bmatrix} 0 & -1 & -1 & -1 & 0 \\ -1 & 2 & -4 & 2 & -1 \\ -1 & -4 & 13 & -4 & -1 \\ -1 & 2 & -4 & 2 & -1 \\ 0 & -1 & -1 & -1 & 0 \end{bmatrix}$$

The sum of all of the coefficients in these kernels is equal to one, which eliminates the need to have a fractional representation for the coefficients. Another thing to note is that if all of the pixels in the local region are equal, the result of the convolution returns the same pixel value. This result is what you would expect since low-frequency components should be unaffected. Application of the 3×3 kernel in this equation is illustrated in Figure 14.10.

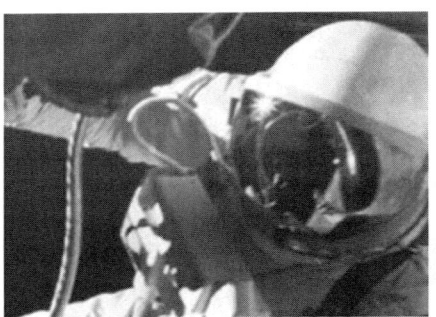

(a) Original Grey Scale Image   (b) High Pass Filtered Image

Photo Credit: NASA

Figure 14.10   The High-pass Filter Using the 3×3 Kernel $h_{HP(3x3)}[j,k]$

Separable Filters

The total number of operations required to perform 2D convolution is high. With an image that is $N \times N$ in size and a kernel that is $K \times K$, the total number of multiply and add operations is $N^2 K^2$. In many cases, it is possible to develop a more efficient implementation if the filter can be decomposed into a row and column filter.

$$c(m,n) = \sum_{j=0}^{N-1} \left\{ \sum_{k=0}^{M-1} a(m-j,n-k) \cdot h_{row}(k) \right\} h_{column}(k)$$

Thus, it is possible to apply two one-dimensional filters, first along the rows and then along the columns. This approach reduces the total number of operations to a total of N^2K. The 1,2,1 and 1,2,2,2,1 low-pass filters display the property of separability and in general most linear filters are separable.

$$h_{LPI(3x3)}[j,k] = \frac{1}{16}\begin{bmatrix} 1 & 2 & 1 \\ 2 & 4 & 2 \\ 1 & 2 & 1 \end{bmatrix}, \quad h_{LPI(5x5)}[j,k] = \frac{1}{32}\begin{bmatrix} 1 & 2 & 2 & 2 & 1 \\ 2 & 2 & 4 & 2 & 2 \\ 2 & 4 & 4 & 4 & 2 \\ 2 & 2 & 4 & 2 & 2 \\ 1 & 2 & 2 & 2 & 1 \end{bmatrix}$$

The equivalent kernel for these filters can be implemented by a row and column filtering operation:

$$h_{LPI(1x3)}[j,k] = hcol[j] \otimes hrow[k] = \begin{bmatrix} 1 \\ 2 \\ 1 \end{bmatrix} \otimes \begin{bmatrix} 1 & 2 & 2 \end{bmatrix} = \begin{bmatrix} 1 & 2 & 1 \\ 2 & 4 & 2 \\ 1 & 2 & 1 \end{bmatrix},$$

Separable filters are quite popular for fast implementations and can provide very good throughput and performance. In the following sections, an implementation using Intel Wireless MMX technology is discussed.

Filtering with Non-separable Kernels

One of the biggest challenges with implementing spatial filtering algorithms is that image data is often represented in linear memory organization. The image is usually in row-major or column-major form. In these forms, the pixels to be multiplied with the 2D kernel are not necessarily stored as neighboring pixels in memory.

To expose the full potential of SIMD operations using Intel Wireless MMX technology, decisions need to be made on how to best implement a 2D access pattern as uniformly as possible. By implementing a well-planned approach, near ideal throughput can be achieved in the parallel execution. The overlap between applications of the kernel to the image pixels provides an opportunity to amortize load overhead across many calculations using the multi-sample approach introduced in Chapter 13.

The separable kernel is the easiest to implement since it removes the need to have a 2D access pattern. However, sometimes the desired effect cannot be achieved with this approach. First, how can you best implement the 3×3 kernel?

Spatial filtering is based on the multiplication and summation of a 2D kernel applied to different locations within an image that is to be filtered. The spatial filtering operation is not unlike the algorithms you see in 1D filtering; however, the management of the data streams from a 2D structure requires careful planning to achieve high throughput. Analyzing the C code for the 2D convolution using a 3×3 kernel is a good place to start. The C code for the implementation of a 2D convolution is provided in Figure 14.11.

```
// CONV2D_3x3_c.c
// 2D convolution using 3x3 kernel
// Global Project Variables: HEIGHT, WIDTH, SCALE, Cij

void CONV2D_3x3_c(unsigned short *input, FRAME *output){
    int  i, j, acc, prow0,prow1,prow2;

    for ( j = 1; j < (HEIGHT-1); j++){
        prow0 = (j-1)*WIDTH;
        prow1 = j*WIDTH;
        prow2 = (j+1)*WIDTH;
        for ( i = 0 ; i < (WIDTH-1); i++){
            acc = C00*input[prow0-1+i];
            acc+= C01*input[prow0+i];
            acc+= C02*input[prow0+1+i];
            acc+= C10*input[prow1-1+i];
            acc+= C11*input[prow1+i];
            acc+= C12*input[prow1+1+i];
            acc+= C20*input[prow2-1+i];
            acc+= C21*input[prow2+i];
            acc+= C22*input[prow2+1+i];
            output -> plane[j*WIDTH+i]=acc>>SCALE;
        }
    }
}
```

Figure 14.11   C Code for a 3×3 Nonseparable Kernel Convolution with an NxM Image

In the C code in Figure 14.11, you are moving across the image along the rows in the image with the nested loop structure. To have the image pixels available for multiplication with the three rows of the kernel requires access to the three rows of the image. In the inner loop, the multiply accumulate operation is performed.

The implementation using Intel Wireless MMX technology also uses a nested loop and some number of multiply accumulate operations. Since the WMAC instruction provides for four 16-bit parallel multiplications with accumulation, it seems to be well suited to the calculation. Images generally are in 8-bit format so an unpacking operation is used to get the data into a 16-bit format. The WUNPCKEL and WUNPCKEH instructions can be used to convert the pixels into a half-word format.

The coefficients of the 3×3 kernel can be preloaded into three SIMD registers as 16-bit operands. One of the half-words is zeroed to facilitate application of the four-way WMAC instruction.

wR0 → 0x00, C02, C01, C00

wR1 → 0x00, C12, C11, C10

wR2 → 0x00, C22, C11, C10

The 2D nature of the calculation requires a 2D approach to addressing the input operands. The core register file can be used to act as an address generator in addition to maintaining the nested loop. One approach is to use three pointers that each point to adjacent rows in the image.

r0 → input image

r2 → input image row (n+1)

r3 → input image row (n+2)

r1 → output image

r9 → inner loop count (number of columns)

r10 → outer loop count (number of rows)

Implementing the addressing scheme is the trickiest part of the calculation. How many columns do you process to maximize the throughput and make the best use of the loaded pixel data? The simplest approach is to run the kernel across all of the columns in the image in a repeated scan. Think of the NxM image as image stripes that are 3xM in size. This method allows good amortization, but does require redundant load operations. Another technique that makes better use of loaded data is to run the kernel down a group of columns in the image. However, significantly lower data cache locality can occur unless the column width is equal to the cache line width, which has the effect of increasing the complexity of the routine, especially around the cache line boundaries.

The design of a routine which scans the kernel across the rows is relatively simple and also has a straightforward implementation. With three of the registers used for holding the coefficients, 13 registers are still available to support the calculation. However, you also need to manage the load stream from the three rows as well. A good approach is to calculate four outputs at a time, *c(m,n)*, *c(m,n+1)*, *c(m,n+2)*, and *c(m,n+3)*. This practice leaves eight registers for loading and aligning pixels from each row. A portion of the assembly code for performing a 3×3 convolution using Intel Wireless MMX technology is provided in Figure 14.12.

```
@ CONV2D_3x3_s.s@

@ r0 -> input image , r2 -> output image
@ wR0-> 0x00,C02,C01,C00; wR1-> 0x00,C12,C11,C10;
@ wR2-> 0x00,C22,C21,C20
outer_loop:
    wldrd     wR3, [r0], #8    @ load 4 pixels row(n)
    mov       r11, r9          @ setup inner loop count
    wldrd     wR4, [r0], #8    @ load 4 pixels row(n)
    wldrd     wR5, [r2], #8    @ load 4 pixels row(n+1)
    wldrd     wR6, [r2], #8    @ load 4 pixels row(n+1)
    wldrd     wR7, [r3], #8    @ load 4 pixels row(n+2)
    wldrd     wR8, [r3], #8    @ load 4 pixels row(n+2)
inner_loop:
    @ Row 1 of kernel
    wmacsz    wR12, wR0,  wR3        @ out(m,n)+=
    waligni   wR9,  wR3,  wR4,#2     @ align inputs
    wmacsz    wR13, wR9,  wR0        @ out(m,n+1)+=
    waligni   wR9,  wR3,  wR4,#4     @ align inputs
    wmacsz    wR14, wR9,  wR0        @ out(m,n+2)+=
    waligni   wR9,  wR3,  wR4,#6     @ align inputs
    wmacsz    wR15, wR9,  wR0        @ Row(m,n+3)+=
    @ Row 2 of kernel
    wmacs     wR12, wR1,  wR5        @ out(m,n)+=
    waligni   wR9,  wR5,  wR6,#2     @ align inputs
    wmacs     wR13, wR9,  wR1        @ out(m,n+1)+=
    waligni   wR9,  wR5,  wR6,#4     @ align inputs
    wmacs     wR14, wR9,  wR1        @ out(m,n+2)+=
    waligni   wR9,  wR5,  wR6,#6     @ align inputs
    wmacs     wR15, wR9,  wR1        @ Row(m,n+3)+=
    @ Row 3 of kernel
```

```
wmacs     wR12,  wR2,   wR7      @ out(m,n)+=
waligni   wR9,   wR7,   wR8,#2   @ align inputs
wmacs     wR13,  wR9,   wR2      @ out(m,n+1)+=
waligni   wR9,   wR7,   wR8,#4   @ align inputs
wmacs     wR14,  wR9,   wR2      @ out(m,n+2)+=
waligni   wR9,   wR7,   wR8,#6   @ align inputs
wmacs     wR15,  wR9,   wR2      @ Row(m,n+3)+=
@ scale four outputs
wsrlwg    wR12,  wR12,  wCGR0    @ scale
wsrlwg    wR13,  wR13,  wCGR0    @ scale
wsrlwg    wR14,  wR14,  wCGR0    @ scale
wsrlwg    wR15,  wR15,  wCGR0    @ scale
@ pack four outputs
wpackdss  wR13,  wR12,  wR13     @ pack 64bits -> 32-bits
wpackdss  wR15,  wR14,  wR15     @ pack 64bits -> 32-bits
wpackwss  wR13,  wR13,  wR15     @ pack 32bits -> 16-bits
wstrd     wR13,  [r1],  #8       @ store four outputs
```

Figure 14.12 Intel® Wireless MMX™ Assembly Instructions for a 3×3 Nonseparable Filter

The inner loop is unrolled to process eight outputs per iteration. The total instruction count is 65, with two stalls associated with the double-word stores, resulting in 67 cycles for preparing eight pixels in the output image. The result is about eight cycles for every pixel produced. The contribution of each of the instructions for this implementation is shown in Table 14.3.

Table 14.3 Instruction Breakdown for the Inner Loop for the 3×3 Convolution

Instruction	Cycles	Description
WMACS	24	Filter calculations
WLDRD	6	Load the input pixels
WALIGNI	18	Align the input pixels
WPACK	6	Pack the output pixels
WSRL	8	Scale the output pixels
WSTRD	4	Store output pixels
BNE	1	Branch

Implementing a column-based approach has the advantage of allowing the both the WLDRD and the WALIGNI to be amortized significantly during the calculation; however, the implementation details increase development time. On the other hand, the separable filter allows both a reduction in complexity for the column-based approach as well as a reduction in cycle count. Let's take a closer look at filtering with separable kernels.

Filtering with Separable Kernels

The separable kernel is much easier to implement since some of the difficulties with the 2D access pattern are eliminated. In addition to a simpler memory access pattern, the total number of multiply accumulate operations are reduced, allowing higher throughput to be achieved. The implementation of the separable filters is often described as two distinct steps. The input image is first convolved across each of the rows generating a row-filtered image. The row-filtered image is transposed and then used as input for a column filtering operation. The final output image is again transposed to regain its original orientation.

In → Row Filter → Transpose → Column Filter → Transpose → Out

Although the transpose operation can be done as a separate step, that method introduces unnecessary memory traffic and cycle consumption. The best implementation does not transpose the image at all. Instead, two different routines are applied. The first routine performs the row transform and overwrites the input buffer without performing the transpose operation. The second routine performs the column transform on the row-transformed data using a column-based approach. In effect, the transpose operation is folded into the column filtering routine. Using this approach, you only require a single image buffer, allowing the entire filter sequence to be implemented in place.

The C code for the row transform for a filter length of 3 where the output image is not transposed is shown in Figure 14.13.

```
// CONV1D_3tap_c.c
// 1D convolution using 3-tap kernel
// Global Project Variables: HEIGHT, WIDTH, SCALE, Cij

void CONV1D_3tap_c(unsigned short *input, FRAME *output){
    int   i, j, acc, prow;

    for ( j = 0; j < HEIGHT; j++){
        prow = j*WIDTH;
        for ( i = 1 ; i < (WIDTH-1); i++){
            acc = C00*input[prow-1+i];
            acc+= C01*input[prow+i];
            acc+= C02*input[prow+1+i];
            output -> plane[prow+i] = acc>>SCALE;
        }
    }
}
```

Figure 14.13 C Code for a 3-tap Kernel Convolution with an N×M Image

This implementation assumes that the data is in a 16-bit format for both the input and output arrays. The assembly code implementation of the row transform using Intel Wireless MMX instructions can achieve good throughput by amortizing the loads in the same manner as the FIR filter examples discussed in Chapter 13. The Intel Wireless MMX assembly instructions for the loop of a three-tap filter with the output written in the same orientation as the input are shown in Figure 14.14.

```
@ CONV1D_3tap_s.s
@ r0 -> input image , r2 -> output image
@ wR0-> 0x00,C02,C01,C00

   wldrd     wR4,[r0],#8       @ load four 16-bit pixels
   smulbb    r11, r8, r9       @ row*height
   wldrd     wR5, [r0], #8     @ load next four pixels
inner_loop:
   wmacsz    wR12, wR0,  wR4       @ out(m,n)+=
   waligni   wR6,  wR4,  wR5,#2    @ align inputs
   wmacsz    wR13, wR6,  wR0       @ out(m,n+1)+=
   waligni   wR6,  wR4,  wR5,#4    @ align inputs
   wmacsz    wR14, wR6,  wR0       @ out(m,n+2)+=
   waligni   wR6,  wR4,  wR5,#6    @ align inputs
   wmacsz    wR15, wR6,  wR0       @ Row(m,n+3)+=
   wldrd     wR4,  [r0], #8       @ load next four inputs
   wpackdss  wR13, wR12, wR13     @ pack 64bits -> 32-bits
   wpackdss  wR15, wR14, wR15     @ pack 64bits -> 32-bits
```

```
wpackwss  wR13,  wR13,  wR15      @ pack 32bits -> 16-bits
wsrlhg    wR13,  wR13,  wCGR0     @ scale by 4
wstrd     wR13,  [r1],  #8        @ store four outputs
wmacsz    wR12,  wR0,   wR5       @ out(m,n+4)+=
waligni   wR6,   wR5,   wR4,#2    @ align inputs
wmacsz    wR13,  wR6,   wR0       @ out(m,n+6)+=
waligni   wR6,   wR5,   wR4,#4    @ align inputs
wmacsz    wR14,  wR6,   wR0       @ out(m,n+7)+=
waligni   wR6,   wR5,   wR4,#6    @ align inputs
wmacsz    wR15,  wR6,   wR0       @ out(m,n+8)+=
wldrd     wR5,   [r0],  #8        @ load next four inputs
wpackdss  wR13,  wR12,  wR13      @ pack 64bits -> 32-bits
wpackdss  wR15,  wR14,  wR15      @ pack 64bits -> 32-bits
wpackwss  wR13,  wR13,  wR15      @ pack 32bits -> 16-bits
wsrlhg    wR13,  wR13,  wCGR0     @ scale result
wstrd     wR13,  [r1],  #8        @ store four outputs
subs      r11,   r11,   #8        @ decrement loop count
bne       inner_loop
```

Figure 14.14 Intel® Wireless MMX™ Assembly Instructions for the Row
Transform of a Three-tap Separable 2D Convolution

The inner loop uses a total of 28 instructions to process eight pixels, and with the two-cycle latency of the WSTRD, the total cycle consumption is 30 cycles per iteration, which translates into a throughput of about 3.75 cycles per pixel just to perform the row transform alone. The breakdown of the instructions from the routine in Figure 14.14 is illustrated in Table 14.4

Table 14.4 Instruction Breakdown for the Inner Loop for the Row Transform Three-Tap Separable Filter

Instruction	Cycles	Description
WMACS	8	Filter calculations
WLDRD	2	Load the input pixels
WALIGNI	6	Align the input pixels
WPACK	6	Pack the output pixels
WSRLHG	2	Scale the output pixels
WSTRD	4	store output pixels
SUBS	1	loop count adjustment
BNE	1	Branch

The next step is to implement the column transform on the row-transformed image provided by the routine in Figure 14.14. The output from the routine was oriented the same way as the input, so it is now necessary to run the three-tap filter down the columns. A good approach is to use the WMUL instruction in combination with the WADDH instruction to perform the calculations. If the core registers r6, r7, and r8 hold the coefficients C0, C1, and C2, the TBCSTH instruction can be used to preload the coefficients into the four half-word fields of three coprocessor registers.

```
tbcsth   wR0, r6        @ C0, C0, C0, C0
tbcsth   wR1, r7        @ C1, C1, C1, C1
tbcsth   wR2, r8        @ C2, C2, C2, C2
```

Using this setup, you can now apply the WMUL and WADDH instruction pair to perform the filtering operation on four pixels at a time using a column-based approach.

Color Synthesis

Modern color CCD and CMOS image sensors use a mosaic of CFA material over a 2D array of photo detectors. This material allows measurement of visible light that is centered around the wavelengths associated with the visible light that humans perceive as red, green, and blue. Instead of three separate $N \times M$ arrays for each of the colors, a single array with a mosaic pattern of CFA materials is used. Some positions in the array measure the green signal, and others measure the red and blue. For each position (x,y) in the array, two of the three components needed for a 24-bit RGB pixel are missing. The Bayer pattern and synthesized 24-bit color are illustrated in Figure 14.15.

Color synthesis algorithms are designed to generate the missing red, green, and blue components of a color image. This method effectively allows three $N \times M$ arrays to be generated from a single $N \times M$ input array. The Bayer pattern CFA is a one of the most popular formats for digital color imaging. A green filter material is applied to half of the array by interleaving it with red and blue material. For an array size of $N \times M$, the total number of green elements is $N \times M/2$, and $N \times M/4$ is the total elements each for the red and blue channels. The synthesis of the missing color components at each position in the array can be accomplished using both standard and proprietary techniques. In general, the algorithms display varying degrees of complexity and visual quality. Depending on the intended purpose, both low and high complexity algorithms may be used in an image capture system.

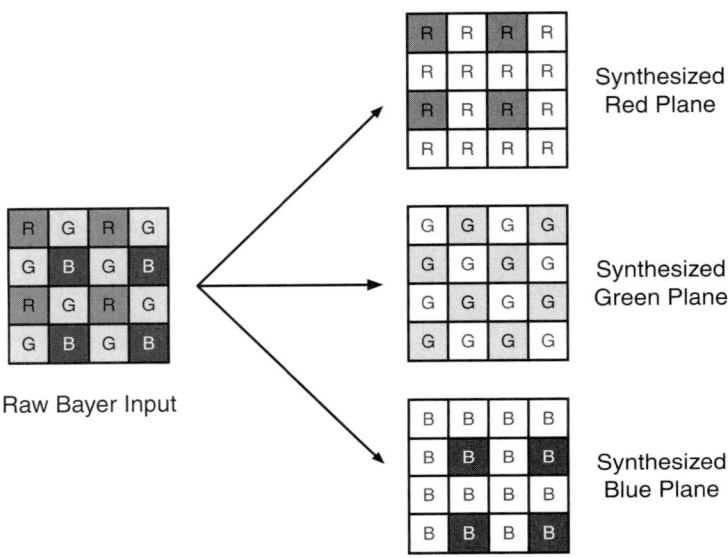

Figure 14.15 Bayer Pattern and Synthesized Color

In a digital camera application, a low resolution digital viewfinder is used instead of optics. The viewfinder is used to compose the scene prior to a higher resolution still capture. Low complexity algorithms are well-suited to the digital viewfinder task in a digital camera; however, more complex algorithms are usually preferred for still images. This is a result of the fact that artifacts are often better tolerated when viewing video sequences due to temporal averaging.

The simplest algorithms display a well-structured sequence of operations using a fixed access or filtering pattern for every pixel. The more complex algorithms often include an adaptation scheme based on some measured image parameter. Since artifacts tend to occur more often around edges, edge-based adaptation is fairly common and can yield drastic improvements in visual quality. However, using edge strength for adaptive control can require significant computational overhead.

This section examines how to apply Intel Wireless MMX technology to one of the most basic color synthesis schemes, the nearest neighbor replication algorithm.

Nearest Neighbor Replication

The nearest neighbor replication (NNR) algorithm is used to generate a 24-bit RGB image from the raw Bayer pattern. The algorithm is very straightforward and just replicates the nearest neighbor at each location in the array by copying the nearest pixel. The Bayer pattern has two different types of rows; the odd rows have red and green interleaved, and the even rows have green and blue interleaved. The nearest neighbor for the red or green pixels within an *RGRG* row is either the left or right nearest pixel element of that color. Similarly, within the GBGB rows, either a left or a right neighbor can be used. However, the *RGRG* rows contain no measured blue pixels and the *GBGB* rows contain no measured red pixels. In these cases, elements from either the upper or the lower rows may be used.

Missing Green Pixels

Half of the locations within the raw Bayer image require you to provide an estimate of the green component for the final 24-bit color image. In Figure 14.16, the replication of adjacent pixels is illustrated for the green channel; the nearest left neighbor is used to fill in the missing locations for the even rows and the nearest right replication for the odd rows.

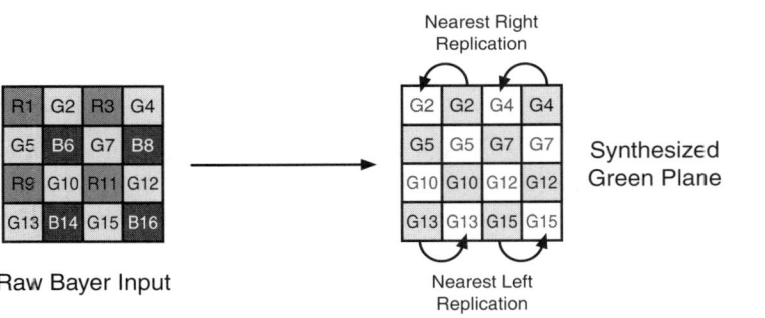

Figure 14.16 Alternating Left/Right Nearest Neighbor Replication for the Green Plane

The Bayer pattern has rows of alternating red/green and green/blue pixels. Generation of the missing green pixels is a straightforward replication of left or right neighbors. The red and blue pixels require a modified approach, since measured values exist on alternating rows.

Missing Blue Pixels

Only one-fourth of the blue pixels needed to compose the blue plane for the RGB image actually exist as measured values. Therefore, 75 percent of the blue channel must be generated using a replication scheme. One way to think about the operation is in 2×2 blocks. A 2×2 block is scanned across the image in steps of two pixels at a time. For each step, a measured blue pixel is replicated in three of the four locations. One way to perform the replication is to use a nearest right neighbor replication for the even rows, GBGB..., and duplicate the elements for the previous odd rows. Figure 14.17 illustrates a possible replication scheme for the blue plane.

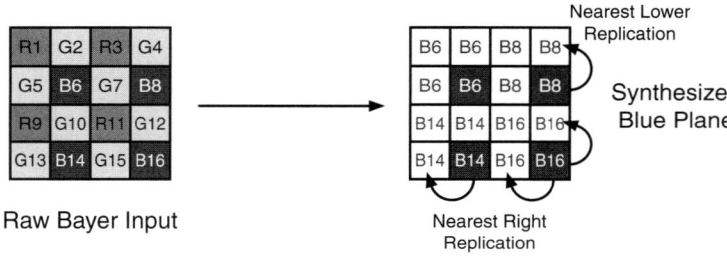

Figure 14.17　Right/Lower Nearest Neighbor Replication for the Blue Plane

Missing Red Pixels

The measured red pixels are only one-fourth the total needed to compose the red plane for a 24-bits-per-pixel RGB image. A similar approach to replication for the blue plane can also be applied to the red plane. Figure 14.16 illustrates a possible replication scheme for the red pixels.

The only difference is that the red pixels are shifted by one element with respect to the blue pixels within the matrix, making it easier to perform a nearest right neighbor replication followed by row duplication for the next row.

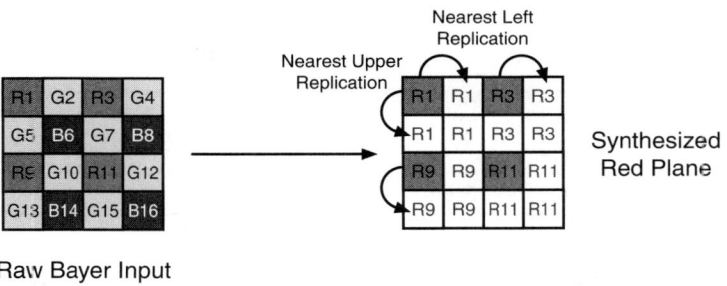

Raw Bayer Input

Figure 14.18 Left/Upper Nearest Neighbor Replication for the Red Plane

Color Synthesis Using NNR

An efficient NNR scheme should minimize the number of instructions issued. Every pixel load always requires three store operations. Therefore, restricting the implementation to work in multiples of eight is a good start, since you can use double-word load and store operations exclusively. This choice is important because load-store traffic is a major contributor to the overall cycle consumption. The real challenge lies in minimizing the data formatting operations.

The NNR algorithm can be developed using a global replication scheme. That is, if red is being generated by a nearest left replication, the blue and green are also replicated in this fashion. This scheme allows a simple C code implementation, but can result in cumbersome assembly code. The application of the same left or right replacement scheme for all of the rows in the raw Bayer image introduces unnecessary operations. These operations occur as a result of boundary pixels either on the borders of the array or within a double word that do not have a nearest left or right neighbor. A more efficient approach for an implementation using Intel Wireless MMX technology is to alternate left and right replications. Table 14.5 provides a summary of the replication scheme.

Table 14.5   Summary of Nearest Neighbor Replacement Scheme

Pixel Type	Odd Rows (RGRG...)	Even Rows (GBGB...)
R	Nearest Left	Previous row
B	Next row	Nearest Right
G	Nearest Right	Nearest Left

Applying this approach has two advantages: alternating between left and right replications helps to reduce the blocking artifact, and the entire algorithm can be performed without having to align any data elements across a double-word boundary.

The input Bayer pattern pixels and the replicated values need to be interleaved. Therefore, your first step is to isolate the color components from each group of eight pixels. Using two different masks that alternate 0x00 with 0xFF enables you to zero out every other pixel in a double word by applying the WAND instruction. One mask is used to isolate the even elements, and the other is used to isolate the odd elements. Using the TBCSTH instruction these masks can be easily constructed in wR15 and wR14 as follows:

```
mov    r6, #0x00FF     @ setup byte mask
tbcsth wR15, r6        @ wR15 -> 0x00FF00FF00FF00FF
mov    r6, #0xFF00     @ setup byte mask
tbcsth wR14, r6        @ wR14 -> 0xFF00FF00FF00FF00
```

With these two masks available, the output arrays can be prepared using a sequence of shift and logical operations. The shift operations align the eight elements within a double word left or right by one byte. A control register is preloaded with the immediate value #8 using the TMCR instruction to support the operation.

```
mov    r6, #8          @ shift operand
tmcr   wCGR0, r6
```

With the mask setup and shift operand in one of the control registers, the formatting operations can now be performed using WSRR/WSLL, WAND, and a WOR instruction group. For example, if wR0 is loaded with eight elements from an odd row, the following sequence can be used to construct eight pixels for the green plane and 16 pixels for the red plane.

```
wand    wR5,wR0,wR15   @ isolate green G,0,G,0..
wand    wR6,wR0,wR14   @ isolate red 0,R,0,R...
wsrahg  wR7,wR5,wCGR0  @ shift green 0,G,0,G,..
wsllhg  wR8,wR6,wCGR0  @ shift red R,0,R,0...
wor     wR7,wR5,wR7    @ pack odd row green
wor     wR8,wR6,wR8    @ pack odd/even row
```

The next step is to decide how to best address the input and output image arrays. You have measured green pixels on each row and measured red/blue pixels on every other row. For each left- or right-replicated group of eight pixels for red and blue, the same data must be stored on adjacent rows in the output. Clearly, you need to be working on two rows at a time using even and odd pointers to the input array and the red, green, and blue output planes. Therefore, you need to manage a total of eight pointers during the calculation and manage a nested loop. Fortunately, the core register file of the Intel XScale® microarchitecture is large enough to support complex 2D addressing schemes by acting as an address generator in addition to performing loop management functions. One possible assignment of the core registers is the following.

r0, r3 → input image even and odd row pointers

r1, r4 → output image red plane even/odd row pointers

r5, r6 → output image green plane even/odd row pointers

r7, r8 → output image blue plane even/odd row pointers

r9, r10 → outer/inner loop counter (row/column count)

Assembly code for this approach using Intel Wireless MMX technology is illustrated in Figure 14.19.

```
@ NNRcolorSyn_s.s
@
@ r0,r3 -> input odd/even row pntr
@ r1,r4 -> output red odd/even row pntr
@ r5,r6 -> output green odd/even row pntr
@ r7,r8 -> output blue odd/even row pntr

outer_loop:
  wldrd    wR0,[r0],#8   @ load odd row GBGBGBGB.
  mov      r9, #COLUMNS  @ setup inner loop count
  wldrd    wR1,[r3],#8   @ load even row ..
  inner_loop:
    wand      wR5, wR0, wR14   @ isolate green G0G0G0G0
    wand      wR6, wR0, wR15   @ isolate blue 0B0B0B0B
```

```
        wsrldg    wR7, wR5, wCGR0    @ shift green 0G0G0G0G.
        wslldg    wR8, wR6, wCGR0    @ shift blue B0B0B0B0
        wor       wR7, wR5, wR7      @ pack odd row green
        wstrd     wR7, [r5], #8      @ store odd green pixels
        wor       wR8, wR6, wR8      @ pack odd row blue
        wstrd     wR8, [r1], #8      @ store odd blue pixels
        wstrd     wR8, [r4], #8      @ store even red pixels
        wand      wR5, wR1, wR15     @ isolate green 0,G,0,G,0
        subs      r9,  r9,  #8       @ inner loop count
        wldrdne   wR0, [r0], #8      @ load odd row RGRG...
        wand      wR6, wR1, wR14     @ isolate red 0R0R0R0R
        wslldg    wR7, wR5, wCGR0    @ shift green G,0,G,0,...
        wsrldg    wR8, wR6, wCGR0    @ shift blue 0,B,0,B,...
        wor       wR7, wR5, wR7      @ pack even row green
        wstrd     wR7, [r6], #8      @ store even green pixels
        wor       wR8, wR6, wR8      @ pack odd row blue
        wstrd     wR8, [r7], #8      @ store odd red pixels
        wstrd     wR8, [r8], #8      @ store even red pixels
        wldrdne   wR1, [r3], #8      @ load even row GBGB...
        bne       inner_loop
    subs    r10, r10, #2       @ outer loop count
    add     r0,  r0,  r11      @ update input odd pntr
    add     r3,  r3,  r11      @ update input even pntr
    add     r1,  r1,  r11      @ update output red odd pntr
    add     r4,  r4,  r11      @ update output red even pntr
    add     r5,  r5,  r11      @ update output green odd pntr
    add     r6,  r6,  r11      @ update output even green pntr
    add     r7,  r7,  r11      @ update output odd blue pntr
    add     r8,  r8,  r11      @ update output even blue pntr
    bne     outer_loop
```

Figure 14.19 Assembly Code for NNR Color Synthesis using Intel® Wireless MMX™ Technology

The inner loop consists of 22 instructions, with six stalls associated with the double-word stores, resulting in a total contribution of 28 cycles for preparing 16 pixels of each color. This total translates into 1.75 cycles for every 24-bit RGB triad. A 640×480 capture stream at 30 frames per second would consume about 16 megahertz for this function.

The benefits in terms of computational efficiency are obvious since no arithmetic is involved and the entire operation can be accomplished by shifts and logical operations. The simplicity of the implementation has drawbacks and image quality can be impacted by introduction of block and edge artifacts. For this reason, the algorithm is unacceptable for still images, for the most part. However, for video preview at high frame rates, most of the problems can be averaged away.

Color Correction

Often, errors in color rendition within an image capture system are due to variations in lighting conditions and the spectral response of filter materials used in image sensors. The R, G, and B spectral response is generated by stimulating the image sensor with different wavelengths of light and then measuring the output. A hypothetical RGB response curve is illustrated in Figure 14.20.

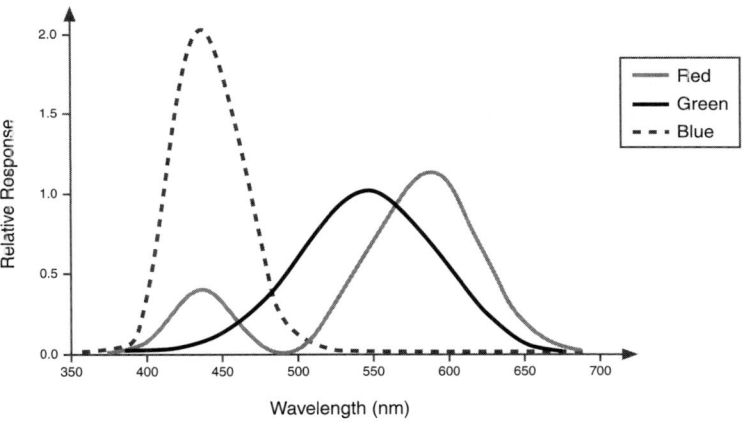

Figure 14.20 Spectral Response Curve of a Sensor with RGB CFA

Because photo detectors and filter material do not in general provide perfect color representation, a color correction step is required. Typically, this step is applied as a 3×3 matrix operation following color synthesis.

$$\begin{bmatrix} R_{correct} \\ G_{correct} \\ B_{correct} \end{bmatrix} = \begin{bmatrix} K_{0,0} & K_{0,1} & K_{0,2} \\ K_{1,0} & K_{1,1} & K_{1,2} \\ K_{2,0} & K_{2,1} & K_{2,2} \end{bmatrix} \bullet \begin{bmatrix} R_{synth} \\ G_{synth} \\ B_{synth} \end{bmatrix}$$

The coefficients, $K_{i,j}$, used for color correction often are supplied by the image sensor manufacturers so system developers can avoid the complexities involved in generating the values. Coefficients are precalculated and converted into a fixed-point format.

Using two bits for the integer portion and eight bits for the fractional portion is more than sufficient for most applications. However, a great deal of variation exists in defining the precision among vendors. The only real requirement for choosing coefficients is that row sum is unity. That is:

$$K_{0,0} + K_{0,1} + K_{0,2} = K_{1,0} + K_{1,1} + K_{1,2} = K_{2,0} + K_{2,1} + K_{2,2} = 1$$

Color Correcting the RGB Image

The color correction of the RGB image is a 3×3 matrix operation. For each RGB pixel, you must perform a total of nine multiplications, six additions, and three scaling operations. Although it sounds simple, complications lurk in the details of managing the data for application to the Intel Wireless MMX SIMD instructions. Let's start by looking at the C code for the 3×3 matrix multiplication illustrated in Figure 14.21.

```
// ColorCorrect_c.c
// Color Correction Routine
// Global Project Variables: NPIXELS,SCALE, Ki,j

void ColorCorrect_c(unsigned short *in,
                    unsigned short *out){
   int j, R,G,B;

   for (j=0; j< NPIXELS; j++){
      R = (in[j]*K00 + in[j+NPIXELS]*K01 +
           in[j+2*NPIXELS]*K02)>>SCALE;

      G = (in[j]*K10 + in[j+NPIXELS]*K11 +
           in[j+2*NPIXELS]*K12)>>SCALE;

      B = (in[j]*K20 + in[j+NPIXELS]*K21 +
           in[j+2*NPIXELS]*K22)>>SCALE;

      out[j] = (unsigned short) R;
      out[j+NPIXELS] = (unsigned short) G;
      out[j+2*NPIXELS] = (unsigned short) B;
   }
}
```

Figure 14.21 C Code for the 3×3 Matrix Multiplication Used in RGB Color Correction

This implementation assumes the 3×3 matrix operation is based on multiplies and additions using 16-bit arithmetic. The WMAC instruction or a combination of the WMUL and WADD instructions can be used for the calculation. If you use the WMAC approach, the benefit of having the addition folded into the instruction is that supporting operations like loads and shifts can be hidden; the coefficients would be prepared in much the same way as for the nonseparable 3×3 spatial filtering kernel. Ideally, this method would work on the R, G, and B components in a sparse 16-bit packed format. This approach is not the best since both memory bandwidth and cycle consumption are increased. The input to the color correction routine is the output RGB data from the color synthesis. The previous section illustrated the generation of the data in a packed byte planar format for each of the channels. This method was the most efficient implementation; it minimized the number of cycles consumed as well as the memory bandwidth. Sometimes the best throughput for a sequence of routines is not obvious.

The decision to work with packed planar data from the color synthesis routine also means that to use the WMAC instruction you would not only have to unpack the data, but also have to interleave the components. So using the WMUL and WADD instruction pair is the best approach.

If the coefficients are duplicated and preloaded into nine of the SIMD coprocessor registers, four outputs can be calculated simultaneously. The TBCSTH instruction is applied in the same manner as illustrated with the three-tap separable filter. The registers wR0 through wR8 can be preloaded with coefficients formatted as follows:

wR0 → K00, K00, K00, K00

wR1 → K01, K01, K01, K02

wR2 → K02, K02, K02, K02

wR3 → K10, K10, K10, K10

wR4 → K11, K11, K11, K11

wR5 → K12, K12, K12, K12

wR6 → K20, K20, K20, K20

wR7 → K21, K21, K21, K21

wR8 → K22, K22, K22, K22

The real work can now be performed using the WMUL and WADDH instruction. If you allocated wR9, wR10, and wR11 to hold four elements from the red, green, and blue planes, you still have four registers available to manage the calculation. Before implementing the routine, you need to do one last thing: define the fractional representation of the coefficients.

The image pixel data is in a 16-bit unsigned format; however, the values are constrained in the range from 0 to 255 for 24-bit RGB color.

Image Pixels → Unsigned half-word
                    Bits[15:8] = 0
                    Bits[7:0]   = pixel value from 0 to 255

The coefficients are in a signed 16-bit fractional format that was introduced in Chapter 13. Since you only need one sign bit, two integer bits, and a maximum of eight fractional bits for the coefficients, you have some flexibility in the way you construct the data within the half-word. This decision is important because the WMULSL and WMULSM instructions can only generate either the upper or the lower half of the 32-bit product, and managing the decimal point can provide you with a higher throughput solution. For example, if you use two bits to represent the integer portion and eight bits to represent the fractional portion, you can construct the coefficients within the half-word using a Q3.13 format as follows:

Q3.13 Coefficients → Signed half-word
                    Bit[15]   = sign bit
                    Bits[14:13] = integer portion
                    Bits[12:5] = fractional portion
                    Bits[4:0]   = 0

To use the WMULSM instruction to perform the calculation, the image pixels must be converted to a Q13.3 format. The assembly code for performing the color correction step using this format for the coefficients is illustrated in Figure 14.22.

```
@ ColorCorrect_s.s
@
@ r0,r1 -> red input\output pntrs
@ r2,r3 -> green input output pntrs
@ r4,r5 -> blue input\output pntrs

    wldrd    wR9,   [r0],  #8    @ load 4 red pixels
    add      r3,    r1, r11      @ green output pntr
    wldrd    wR10,  [r2],  #8    @ load 4 green pixels
    add      r5,    r3, r11      @ blue output pntr
    wldrd    wR11,  [r4],  #8    @ load 4 blue pixels
Loop:
    wmulsm   wR12,  wR9 ,  wR0   @ Rr->R(n)->R(n+3)*K00
    wmulsm   wR13,  wR10,  wR1   @ Rg->G(n)->G(n+3)*K01
    wmulsm   wR14,  wR11,  wR2   @ Rb->B(n)->B(n+3)*K02
    subs     r11,   r11,   #4    @ decrement loop count
    waddh    WR13,  wR13,  wR12  @ Rr+Rg
    wmulsm   wR15,  wR10,  wR4   @ Gg->G(n)->G(n+3)*K11
    waddh    WR13,  wR13,  wR14  @ R'=Rr+Rg+Rb
    wmulsm   wR12,  wR9,   wR3   @ Gr->R(n)->R(n+3)*K10
    wstrd    wR13,  [r1],  #8    @ store R'(n)->R'(n+3)
    wmulsm   wR14,  wR11,  wR5   @ Gb->B(n)->B(n+3)*K12
    waddh    WR15,  wR15,  wR12  @ Gr+Gg
    waddh    WR15,  wR15,  wR14  @ G'=Gr+Gg+Gb
    wmulsm   wR12,  wR9,   wR6   @ Br->R(n)->R(n+3)*K20
    wstrd    wR15,  [r3],  #8    @ store G'(n)->G'(n+3)
    wmulsm   wR13,  wR10,  wR7   @ Bg->G(n)->G(n+3)*K21
    wldrd    wR9,   [r0],  #8    @ load 4 red pixels
    wmulsm   wR14,  wR11,  wR8   @ Bb->B(n)->B(n+3)*K22
    wldrd    wR10,  [r2],  #8    @ load 4 green pixels
    waddh    WR13,  wR13,  wR12  @ Br+Bg
    wldrd    wR11,  [r4],  #8    @ load 4 blue pixels
    waddh    WR13,  wR13,  wR14  @ B'=Br+Bg+Bb
    wstrd    wR13,  [r5],  #8    @ store B'(n)->B'(n+3)
    bne Loop
```

Figure 14.22 Assembly Code for Color Correction using Intel® Wireless MMX™ Technology

The inner loop uses a total of 23 instructions to process four RGB pixels. The total number of cycles for each iteration of the loop is 28, due to the two-cycle issue latency of the WSTRD instructions and two cycles associated with the resource latency of the WMULSM when beginning the loop. This cycle count translates into a throughput of about seven cycles per pixel. The breakdown of the instructions from the routine in Figure 14.22 is illustrated in Table 14.4

Table 14.4   Instruction Breakdown for the Loop in the Color Correction Routine

Instruction	Cycles	Description
WMULSM	9	Multiply pixels by K i j
WADDH	6	Sum the components
WLDRD	3	Load the input pixels
WSTRD	6	Store the output pixels
SUBS	1	Loop count adjustment
BNE	1	Branch

The color correction step is one of the more demanding algorithms used in RAW image capture systems, so developing an efficient implementation is an important step in developing your mobile video and image capture devices.

Key Points

Digital image processing applications can often dominate the available memory and execution resources due to the volume of data involved. The ability to execute these algorithms efficiently can provide a major advantage in the development of image capture and processing systems. Efficiency usually is obtained at the expense of flexibility, and many image-processing architectures are designed accepting this consequence. Performing image processing functions with Intel Wireless MMX technology provides a good balance between flexibility and efficiency delivering adequate throughput for many of today's scenarios.

In this chapter, several algorithms are implemented using Intel Wireless MMX technology:

■ Spatial convolution using a 3×3 nonseparable kernel implementation

■ Spatial convolution using a 1×3 separable kernel implementation

■ Color synthesis using nearest neighbor replication

■ Color correction using fractional arithmetic

The implementation of these algorithms illustrates some important strategies for developing and optimizing with Intel Wireless MMX technology in the area of color image processing. The following points summarize the strategies:

- Image processing is an exercise in both arithmetic execution and efficient management of 2D data structures. Sometimes the best approach is not obvious, and the core register file facilitates the management of many more pointers than typically are available.

- Using a column major approach, as opposed to a row major approach, could deliver a significantly different throughput. This point was demonstrated in the 3×3 nonseparable and 1×3 separable filter examples.

- Knowing the sequence of algorithms and how they are best implemented with the various packed and planar formats allows efficient application development. This point was demonstrated with the color correction and the color synthesis routines.

Chapter 15

H.264 and MPEG-4 Video Compression

Standards are always out of date. That is what makes them standards.

—Alan Bennett

The video encoder is one of the more demanding application domains targeting both the desktop and mobile platforms of today. Over the years, a number of advancements have created options for software developers to improve both quality and compression efficiency. Users' perceived quality parameters are advancing at least as fast as the technology. This chapter covers the basic algorithms used in MPEG-4/H.264 video compression and explains how these algorithms can best be implemented using Intel Wireless® MMX™ technology. After some explanation of the critical algorithms that display parallelism, those algorithms are developed as case studies to show you a methodology for writing optimized code for video processing that uses the techniques introduced in previous chapters.

Video Fundamentals

The representation of video images in digital form generates data. A single frame of image data at a VGA resolution in 24-bit RGB color requires 900 kilobytes of data, and with many of these frames required per second, the effort of resource management grows quickly. Consider that with full motion video around 30 of these VGA frames must be displayed every second. Therefore, 26 megabytes is required for a single second, and a two-hour movie would require 92,000 megabytes!

A video sequence is composed of multiple still images that are usually captured in rapid succession. At some point in the process, a camera generates the still images and they are converted to a standard color space to prepare them for either preview or compression.

Macroblocks

In block-based video encoding schemes, video frames are made up of a 2D array of pixels. The frames are segmented into a number of smaller blocks, called *macroblocks* (MB). The macroblocks are then segmented into a number of smaller blocks of various dimensions. The symmetric block sizes of 16×16 and 8×8 pixels have been standardized in the popular coding standards—for example, H.261, H.263, MPEG-1, MPEG-2, and MPEG-4 —with the 4×4 block size recently introduced in H.264. Figure 15.1 illustrates the symmetric block sizes.

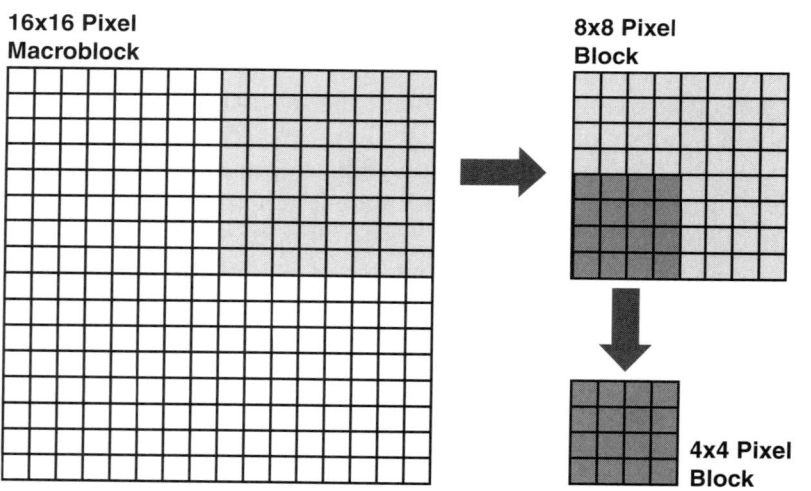

Figure 15.1   Symmetric Block Sizes in Popular Coding Standards

The selection of the block size is based on the scene's structure and amount of detail. The smaller block sizes provide better results if the area contains fine detail, and the larger block sizes work better for homogeneous regions. The concept of matching the block size to the scene structure is extended further with the H.264 standard, and several asymmetric block sizes are introduced, as illustrated in Figure 15.2.

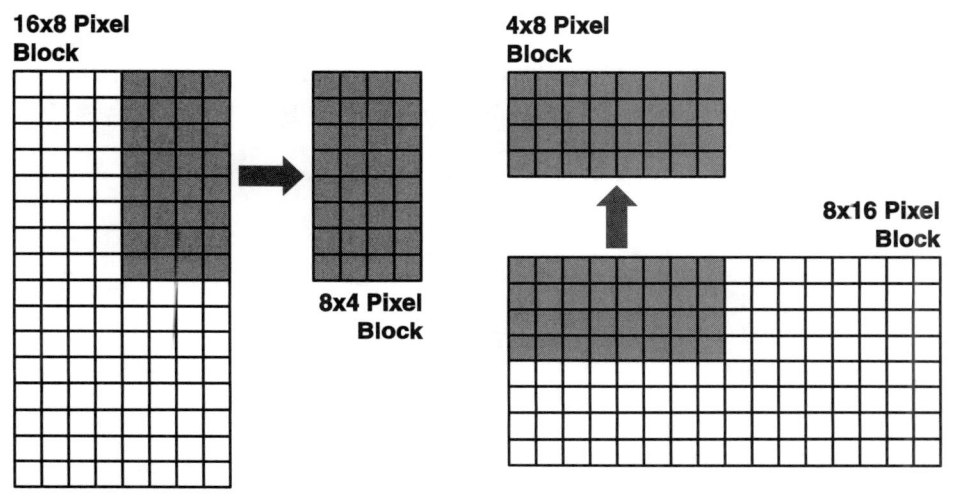

16x8 Pixel Block

8x4 Pixel Block

4x8 Pixel Block

8x16 Pixel Block

Figure 15.2 Asymmetric Block Sizes in H.264

MPEG Video Compression

The compression of digital video is a process that reduces the amount of data to be stored or transmitted. This reduction is accomplished by exploiting both spatial and temporal redundancy that often exists within a sequence of video frames. The MPEG and ITU compression standards describe a hybrid DCT-based motion-compensated encoding scheme that has gained wide adaptation within the industry. These standards define the decoding process and syntax. While no standard defines the sequence of algorithms that provide the steps needed for the encoding of the video frames, the encoder must generate sequences that a compliant decoder can support.

Video Codec

Intel Wireless MMX technology is suited particularly well to algorithms that display a high degree of parallelism and that display the qualities of repetitive calculation and structured data access. In contrast, Intel XScale® technology is suited well to algorithms that are more control-centric. Figure 15.3 shows the basic components of a video encoder/decoder pair.

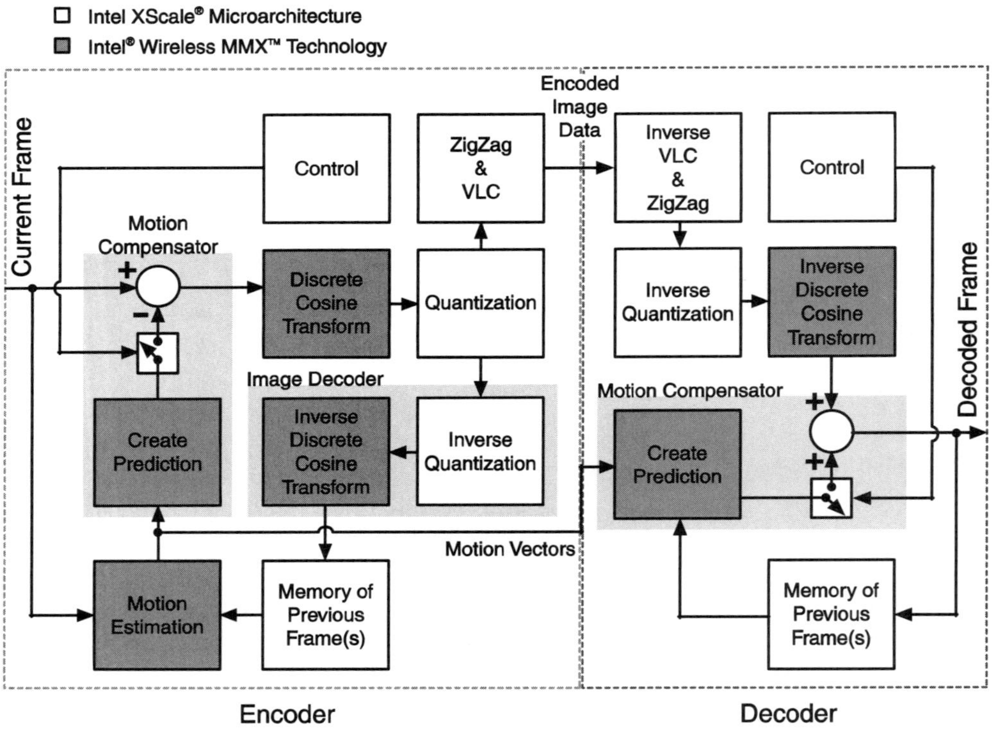

Figure 15.3 Block Diagram of an MPEG Video Encoder/Decoder (Codec)

The shaded blocks in Figure15.3 indicate the component algorithms of the video encoder/decoder to which Intel Wireless MMX technology is best applied and the clear blocks to which the Intel XScale technology is best applied. The optimal partitioning of algorithms between Intel Wireless MMX and Intel XScale technologies is not always distinct, since an application often shares tasks between the two. In other words, you use Intel Wireless MMX technology to handle the repetitive data processing functions and Intel XScale technology to manage the data flow and program sequencing.

Before jumping into the details of the component algorithms, you might want to know exactly what is going on with the video codec at a higher level.

Spatial and Temporal Compression

The video encoder performs both spatial and temporal compression. Spatial compression is accomplished by transforming image data from the spatial domain to the generalized frequency domain, where the data is quantized and encoded. This spatial compression is applied to all image data during the encoding process by applying a 2D Discrete Cosine Transform (DCT) followed by quantization and Huffman encoding. The temporal compression is a bit more complicated and uses motion compensation to remove redundant data within a sequence of images by exploiting similarities between sequential frames. Motion compensation consists of two main functions, prediction and compensation. The prediction of a current frame is based on one or more previously transmitted frames, and the compensation is created by subtracting the prediction from the current frame to produce a *residual frame*. This residual frame is then processed using the spatial encoding sequence. The key to this approach is the prediction. If the prediction is accurate, the residual frame contains less data and is compressed to a very small size.

The video decoder reverses the operations that have occurred at the encoder. The first image to be processed by the decoder is always self-contained and uses spatial compression alone. This singularity is important since this first image is used as the reference for reproducing the temporally compressed frames. The decompression sequence always involves entropy decoding followed by inverse quantization and the inverse DCT. When subsequent images are predicted, the decoding sequence uses the previously decoded frame and the current decoded residual to form the predicted picture.

The compression process used in video encoding is lossy. The term *lossy* describes compression that results in a loss of information between an encoder and decoder. For the video codec, the term applies to the difference between image data seen at the encoder and the decoder. When the image data is compressed spatially, the difference is isolated, and the quality is roughly equivalent to a *JPEG* compression sequence. When the image data is temporally encoded, earlier or later frames become references for generating predicted frames. Thus, a key frame, or *reference frame* as it is called, exists at some point in time prior to the generation of predicted frames. Since a reference is required for predicted frames, the residual calculated at the encoder should use the same reproduced reference frames expected at the decoder. By implementing the decode sequence within the encoder, both the encoder and decoder use the same reconstructed frame to form the prediction for the next coded frame and error build-up is avoided.

The use of terminology like predicted frames, temporal, and spatial encoding is bound to sound complicated and confusing. Fortunately, the standards bodies have defined different picture types to describe the different coding methods. Generally speaking, a frame that is compressed using only spatial compression is described as an *Intra* frame, and a frame that uses motion compensation is described as an *Inter*, or *predicted*, frame.

Picture Coding Types

As mentioned previously, each frame of video data is encoded to form a compressed picture. A video sequence is then partitioned into a group of pictures containing frames that are both *intra* and *inter* coded. The intra-coded pictures provide for spatial compression only, and the inter-coded pictures are a combination of both spatial and temporal compression techniques.

When an image is intra-coded, it is coded as a still image without reference to images captured at different times. Pictures encoded in this fashion are used as a reference for predicted pictures, so they are called *I-type pictures*. When images are strongly correlated, higher compression efficiency can be obtained by coding only the difference between a frame and a reference. The method of motion-compensated prediction is applied to produce either *P-type pictures* or *B-type pictures*. The *P-type pictures* are inter-coded using motion-compensated prediction from a single reference picture that occurred at an earlier point in time. The *B-type pictures* are similarly predicted, using two pictures that occurred at both an earlier and later point in time. Figure15.4 illustrates a typical series of I, P, and B pictures.

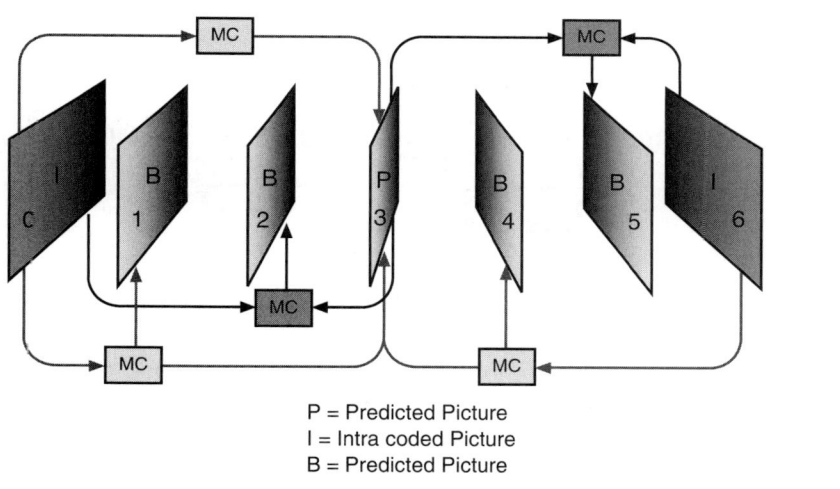

P = Predicted Picture
I = Intra coded Picture
B = Predicted Picture

Figure 15.4   Order of Encoding B and P Pictures in MPEG Compression

Motion Estimation and Compensation

When performing predictive coding, component blocks of sequential video frames are compared at displaced positions, which represent candidate motion vectors in the horizontal and vertical directions. The task of calculating displacement values, *motion estimation*, involves comparing each MB in the current frame to MBs that are in a search region in a previously constructed frame. The size of the search region and the method of comparing the blocks are user-defined. The displacement vector between the best match of the MBs in the two frames is the motion vector (MV) which is represented by horizontal and vertical components. Figure 15.5 illustrates the relationship between the motion estimation and the motion compensation during the encode process.

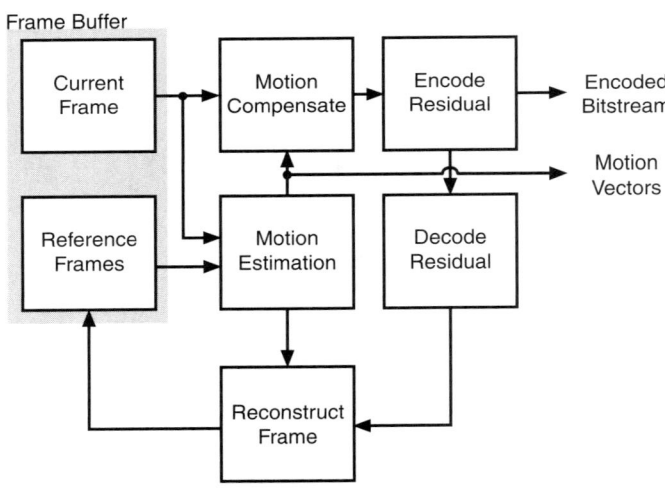

Figure 15.5   Encoder Motion Estimation and Compensation Block Diagram

Motion Estimation

Often, sequential frames of video exhibit a great deal of similarity. Objects moving across the field of view might not change between frames; they just move to different positions. In addition, portions of the scene, such as background, might not change or move at all. The exploitation of this correlation between frames is central to the temporal compression that is provided in the digital motion video standards, and it also places the highest burden on the execution resources. Instead of transmitting the same object or region for each frame, the object or region is transmitted once, and the displacement values are transmitted for each sequential frame. The displacements values, or *motion vectors*, are used to redraw the object in its new position. The task of calculating displacement values—this task is the motion estimation explained earlier—involves creating a model of the current frame based on data in previously encoded frames. The block matching process between a current and a previous frame is shown in Figure 15.6.

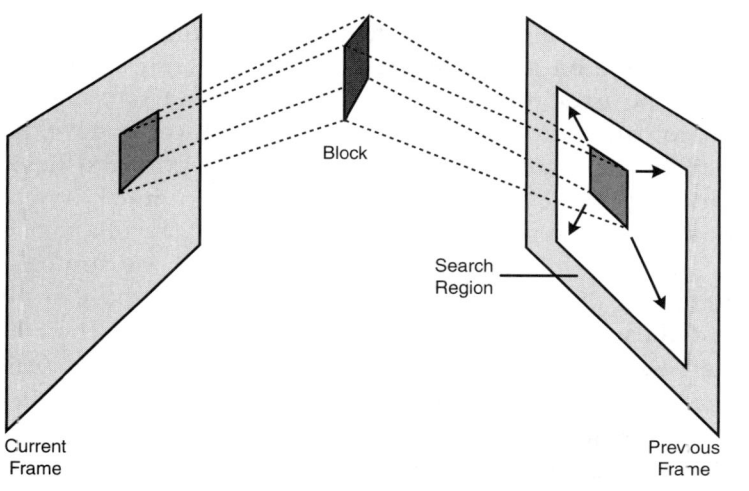

Figure 15.6   Block Matching Used in Motion Estimation

Employing a brute force approach to the motion search would require the system to compute and to compare each row and column displacement within the search window. The block-matching operation could be any error measure, such as the sum of absolute differences (SAD) and the sum of squared difference (SSD).

$$SAD = \sum_{i=0}^{N-1}\sum_{j=0}^{M-1}\left|a(i,j)-b(i,j)\right|$$

$$SSD = \sum_{i=0}^{N-1}\sum_{j=0}^{M-1}\left(a(i,j)-b(i,j)\right)^2$$

Although the SSD can provide better results than the SAD, most video coding implementations use the SAD since it is easier to accomplish in hardware and computing its value is less expensive in software than SSD. The cost of performing the motion search can be reduced by increasing pixel throughput per cycle and employing methods for a faster search or for an early exit.

Fast Motion Search Algorithms

The implementation of a full search algorithm requires the application to evaluate each candidate integer motion vector position within a search area. Displacements for each row and column within the search window are computed and compared. The full search algorithms quickly dominate the execution resources, as the frame rate and resolution of the video data increases. This burden has led to the development of a number of fast search algorithms. For battery-powered devices in real time video applications, such methods become critical; however the reduced complexity causes loss of visual quality and irregularities in data flow.

The fast motion search algorithms often use strategies based on sub-sampling the search region or sub-sampling the distortion calculation, and these strategies are very effective at reducing the computational burden associated with the motion search. The number of SAD calculations made when performing motion search is related directly to the type of motion search algorithm selected. The following sections provide a selection of some of the better known search strategies.

Three-Step Search (TSS)

The Three-Step Search (TSS) algorithm provides good results and has been widely used for the motion estimation step in the video encoding process. In this method, eight positions around a center in a reference region are compared to a block in the source frame. The eight positions around the center correspond to regular displacements in the rows and columns of the reference region. For the first step, the displacement is either four or three pixels, followed by a displacement of two for the second, and finally one for the third. For the center (x,y) and displacement D, the SAD at these each of these positions are calculated, as follows:

SAD(x-D, y-D)	SAD(x, y-D)	SAD(x+D, y-D)
SAD(x-D, y)	SAD(x, y)	SAD(x+D, y)
SAD(x-D, y+D)	SAD(x, y+D)	SAD(x+D, y+D)

Using an initial displacement of three, a maximum displacement of ±6 pixels from the center of the first nine-point grid can result. The TSS algorithm is shown in Figure 15.7.

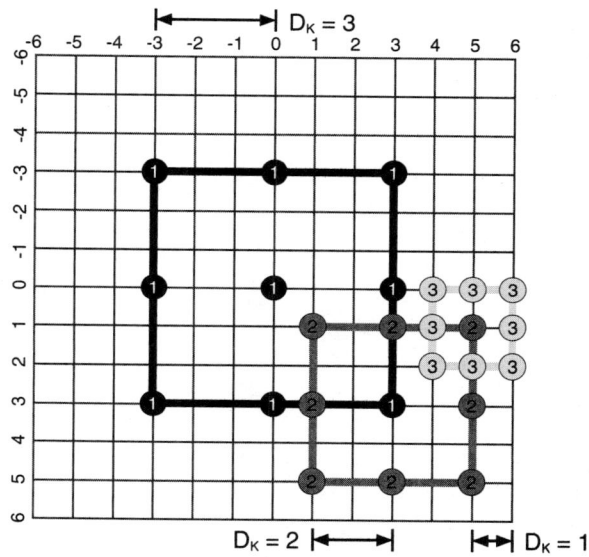

Figure 15.7   Illustration of the Three-Step Search (TSS) Algorithm

Logarithmic and Cross Search Algorithms

The logarithmic and cross search algorithms use a different sampling pattern than the TSS algorithm. The positions around the center again correspond to regular displacements in the rows and columns of the reference region. For the center (x,y) and displacement D, the SAD at these each of these positions is calculated as shown in Figure 15.8.

The logarithmic search uses a diamond grid, which is evaluated with a spacing of four between the block SADs repetitively until the center of the pattern produces the minimum distortion. After this condition occurs, the spacing is decreased and the search is repeated until the minimum is again located at the center. For the last step, an eight-point grid is evaluated. The total number of block SAD calculations is a variable that is determined as the search proceeds.

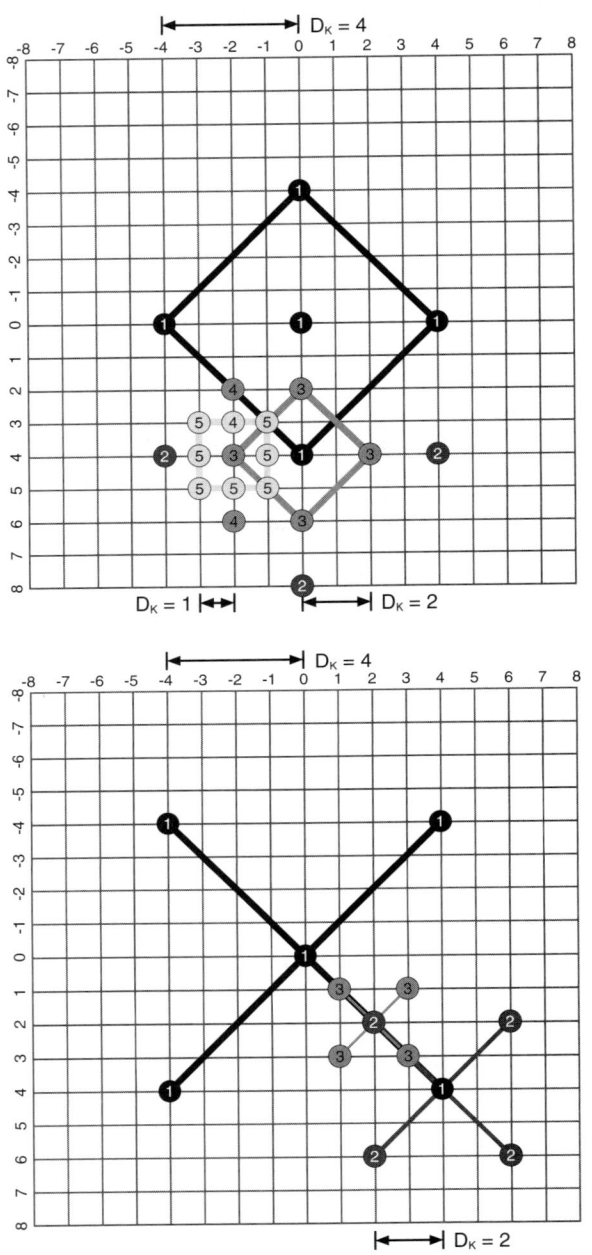

Figure 15.8   Illustration of the Logarithmic and Cross Search Patterns

The cross search algorithm is significantly easier to implement and requires the calculation of a total of 13 block SADs, 5 for step one and 4 each for steps two and three. In this method, four positions around a center in a reference region are compared to a block in the source frame.

The horizontal and vertical distance between search positions can be described through an inter-SAD spacing, $D_{h,i}$ and $D_{v,i}$, for the horizontal and vertical displacements respectively. For many algorithms, the vertical and horizontal inter-SAD spacing is equal and can be represented by a single variable, Dk.

$$D_{h,i} = D_{v,i} = Dk$$

The number of load operations for performing a fixed pattern search may be minimized by taking advantage of the overlapping nature of reference blocks within a search region.

Fractional Motion Estimation

The techniques described so far have involved search techniques applied to integer locations within the search region. In many cases, a better match can be obtained by searching the region at noninteger or fractional locations. In fact, the standards have been evolving with this optimization in mind, so the half-pixel interpolations are becoming common and higher levels of interpolation are used in the recent H.264 standard. The half-pixel prediction implies that a half-pixel motion search is applied after the MV of full pixel accuracy has been performed. To extend the search algorithm, the application interpolates between the samples in the search area to form a higher resolution interpolated region. The half-pixel interpolation is usually performed with the bilinear interpolation algorithm, although H.264 introduces a six-tap separable filter that is applied prior to decimation. The bilinear interpolation algorithm is illustrated in Figure15.9.

The bilinear interpolation for the fractional motion estimation step can be accomplished before or after the integer search. The disadvantage of performing it before the integer search is that the final location for the fractional search is not known ahead of time, and the entire search region must be interpolated. The optimum method is to interpolate only when the data is needed.

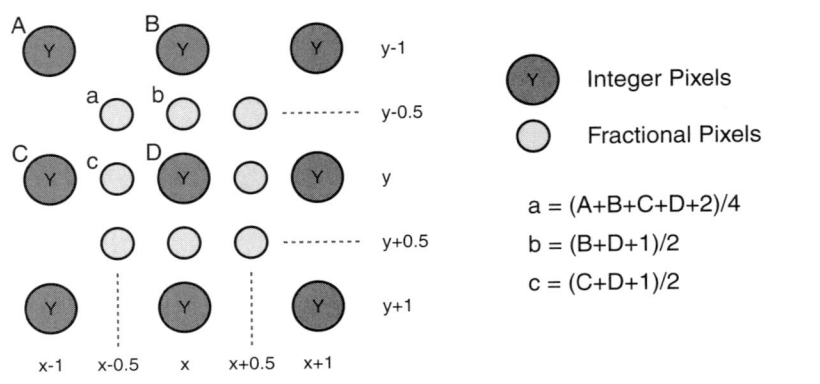

Figure 15.9 Illustration of Half-Pixel Bilinear Interpolation

2D Discrete Cosine Transforms (DCT)

The 2D Discrete Cosine Transform (DCT) is a mathematical operation that is used to transform a block of pixels into the spatial frequency components. The transform is a version of the Discrete Fourier Transform (DFT), in which the sine terms are made to cancel, leaving only the cosine terms. This simplification explains why the term "cosine" is used to describe the transform.

The DCT is performed on 8×8 blocks of image data with the H.261, H.263, MPEG1, MPEG2, and MPEG4. In H.264 an integer transform that roughly approximates a DCT is applied to 4×4 blocks. The transform results in 64 or 16 DCT coefficients for these block sizes. The transform itself does not provide for compression; however, it does define most of a block's information in the lower spatial frequencies and many of the higher spatial frequencies are zero. The remapping of the information in this fashion provides for significant compression potential through quantization and entropy encoding.

8×8 Discrete Cosine Transform (DCT)

The 2D DCT, as with the 2D DFT, is a separable transform: The 2D transformation of a block can be accomplished by applying 1D transforms along the rows and columns of the block in two separate steps. The general equation for the 8×8 2D DCT is expressed by the following equations:

$$F(u,v)=\frac{1}{4}C(u)C(v)\sum_{x=0}^{7}\sum_{y=0}^{7}f(x,y)cos\left[\frac{\pi(2x+1)u}{16}\right]cos\left[\frac{\pi(2y+1)v}{16}\right]$$

where

$$C(u)=\begin{cases}\dfrac{1}{\sqrt{2}} & for\ u=0\\[2ex]1 & otherwise\end{cases}$$

4×4 Discrete Cosine Transform

The basic unit with H.264 is the macroblock, as in the previous standards. However, the basic sub-unit is the 4×4 block rather than the 8×8 block. Following the motion estimation, the residual data within each 4×4 block is transformed based on a 4×4 integer transform that approximates a 4x4 DCT.

$$Y=AXB^{T}=\begin{bmatrix}a & a & a & a\\b & c & -c & -b\\a & -a & -a & a\\c & -b & b & -c\end{bmatrix}[X]\begin{bmatrix}a & b & a & c\\a & c & -a & -b\\a & -c & -a & b\\a & -b & a & -c\end{bmatrix}$$

where

$$a=\frac{1}{2}$$

$$b=\sqrt{\frac{1}{2}}\cos\left(\frac{\pi}{8}\right)$$

$$c=\sqrt{\frac{1}{2}}\cos\left(\frac{3\pi}{8}\right)$$

Quantization

The quantization step is the most important step in the encode process since it affects not only the perceived quality but the bit rate, too. Following the DCT transformation of the residual data, the DCT coefficients are quantized. The quantization process restricts the data to a set of discrete levels and acts to remove components of the transformed data that are less important to the visual appearance of the image while preserving the more important components.

Entropy Encoding

Following the transform coding and quantization, the image data often contain only a few components that are significant, along with a large number zero components. The data within the quantized block are compressed further using statistical techniques.

The nonzero components within a block usually are clustered around the upper left corner, and they can be grouped together by reordering the data using one of the zigzag scanning sequences. The standard zigzag scanning sequence is illustrated in Figure 15.10.

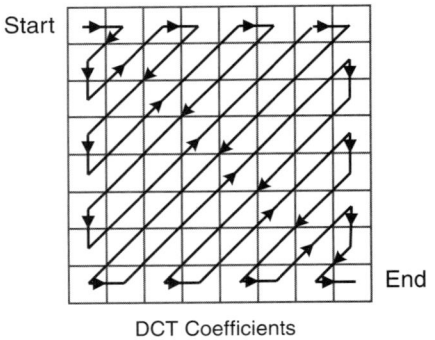

Figure 15.10 Illustration of the Zigzag Scanning Order for Entropy Encoding

Intel® Wireless MMX™ in Motion Estimation and Compensation

The architecture supporting Intel Wireless MMX technology is particularly suitable for the task of video motion estimation. This section is a discussion of the mechanics of the calculation and the architectural features that are available to support the task. The following key points are covered:

- Instruction support for SAD calculation
- Alignment support
- Organization of the register file

The WSADB instruction provides the parallel calculation of the absolute value for the difference of eight pixel pairs with accumulation. For each application of the WSADB instruction, one row in an 8×8 block or half of a row in a 16×16 block can be processed. The instruction needs to be applied only eight times to produce the SAD for an 8×8 block or 32 times for a 16×16 block. Although this economy sounds great, the additional operations required to prepare the operands and manage the calculation have a significant impact on throughput. To maximize the throughput, you must look for opportunities to amortize these supporting operations across as many calculations as possible.

The WSADB instruction does not restrict the choice of 16 SIMD coprocessor registers to be used as the accumulators. Thus, you can consider the calculation of more than one SAD when working within a search region. So, how many SAD calculations can your implementation reasonably support? The register file must also hold both reference and source block pixels. Take a closer look at how Intel Wireless MMX technology can be best applied to motion estimation.

Computing the Block SAD

Block-matching algorithms are based on the arithmetic computation of the block SAD. However, the arithmetic involved is only a portion of the calculation, and the management of two data streams from two separate 2D data structures requires some careful planning to achieve high throughput. Analyzing the C code for the calculation of an N×M block SAD, as shown in Figure 15.11, is a good starting point.

```
// SAD8x8_c.c

// NxM Block SAD Calculation

short SAD8x8_c(unsigned char *pSrc, unsigned char *pRef,
               short stride, short N, short M){
    int i, j, acc = 0;

    for (i = 0; i < N; i++){
        for (j = 0; j < M; j++)
            acc += abs(pSrc[j] - pRef[j]);
        pRef += stride;
        pSrc += stride;
    }
    return (short) (acc);
}
```

Figure 15.11   C Code for an NxM Block SAD Calculation

In this C code, you have two data structures containing the source and reference pixels, an inner loop that calculates the M-pixel row SAD, an outer loop that adjusts the pointers to account for the image width, and sequences for the each of the rows in the block. The optimized assembly code routine involves the basic structure seen with the C code with additional details around the management of load traffic and block sizes.

Instruction Support for the SAD

Because the WSADB instruction is designed to process eight pixel pairs, a straightforward application constrains the inner loop to working in multiples of eight. By providing this constraint, additional formatting steps are not necessary for most of the block sizes of interest, 16×16, 8×8, 16×8, 8×16, and 4×8. If the core registers r0 and r1 hold the pointers to a double-word aligned source block and reference block respectively, a three-instruction sequence performs the sum of absolute difference for the eight pixels and accumulates the result with the contents of wR15, as follows:

```
wldrd wR0, [r0], #8
wldrd wR1, [r1], #8
wsadb wR15, wR0, wR1
```

The number of times that the WSADB instruction is applied for an NxM block is simply NxM/8. For example, when calculating the 16×8 block SAD, the instruction is applied 16 times. The smaller block sizes that are only four pixels wide, the 4×4 and the 8×4, can also use the WSADB instruction by loading the operands as 32-bit words:

```
wldrw      wR2, [r0], #4
wldrw      wR3, [r0], #8
wsadb      wR15, wR2, wR3
```

Since the block sizes vary, an application must have specialized routines to handle these cases, as explained in greater detail in the following sections.

Alignment of Reference Blocks

Two data streams are required to support the block SAD calculation. The source block is the easiest to handle because it is obtained by dividing the current frame of image data into a well-defined grid. The position of the source block can be forced to align within the 2D data structure at a known boundary. Depending on the size of the block, either a 32-bit or a 64-bit boundary may be used. Table 15.1 lists the source block alignments for the different block sizes.

Table 15.1   Alignments for Various Source Block Sizes

Block Type	Source Block Alignment
16×16	64-bit
16×8	64-bit
8×16	64-bit
8×8	64-bit
4×8	64-bit
8×4	32-bit
4×4	32-bit

With the reference block, alignment generally is unknown until the search is executing. This dependency results in the eight possible alignments of the pixels within memory. Figure15.12 illustrates the eight possible alignments of eight pixels within two double words.

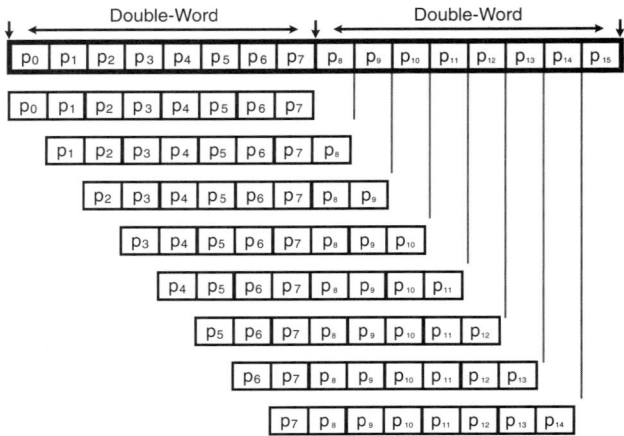

Figure 15.12 Eight Possible Byte Alignments for Eight Reference Pixels

The Intel Wireless MMX load instructions must be aligned on a 64-bit boundary for the double word and on a 32-bit boundary for the word. If this requirement is not followed, an exception is generated, which can severely impact performance. Fortunately, Intel Wireless MMX technology has been designed to support algorithms that naturally operate on byte boundaries, such as motion estimation.

The three least-significant bits (LSBs) of the pointer to the array are used to indicate the alignment. For example, if r1 is pointing to a block in memory and the bits r1[2:0] = 3, the code must align on byte 3, as illustrated in Figure 15.12. Alignment of the block is handled by transferring the three LSBs of the pointer into one of the general-purpose registers then clearing the bits so that the pointer can be used without generating an exception. The following sequence illustrates one way to set up the control register and clear the LSBs of the pointer:

```
and    r3, r1, #7   @ isolate the 3 LSBs into r3
tmcr   wCGR0, r3    @ transfer r3 to control reg
bic    r1,r1,#77    @ clear the 3 LSBs of the ptr
```

In the previous sequence, the core register r1 holds the pointer to the reference block and r3 is used to hold the three LSBs of the pointer. The byte alignment of the pixels is then transferred to the general-purpose register wCGR0 using the TMCR instruction. By transferring the LSBs of the pointer to a general-purpose register and clearing the LSBs of the pointer, you can align each row of the reference block with two double-word loads and application of the WALIGNR instruction.

```
wldrd     wR0,[r0],#8  @ load 8 pixels
wldrd     wR1,[r0],#8  @ load next 8 pixels
walignr0  wR2,wR0, wR1 @ extract 8 pixels based on wCGR0
```

With three instructions required for preparing just eight pixels of reference data, alignment clearly is a going to be big part of the block SAD calculation.

Calculating the Independent Block SAD

Figure 15.13 shows the assembly code sequence using Intel Wireless MMX instructions. The code supports the concepts that were introduced in the previous sections for the calculation of the 8×8 Block SAD.

```
@ SAD8x8_s.s
@ r0 -> previous frame, r1 -> current frame
@ r2 -> imagewidth
@ wCGR0 -> reference block alignment

wldrd    wR0,   [r1]          @ load 8 source pixels
and      r7,    r0,   #7      @ r7 = 3LSBs of *pSrc
bic      r0,    r0,   #7      @ r0 64-bit aligned
wldrd    wR1,   [r0]          @ load 8 reference pixels
tmcr     wCGR0, r7            @ alignment to wCGR0
wldrd    wR2,   [r0]          @ load eight reference pixels
wzero    wR15                 @ zero accumulator
wldrd    wR2,   [r0, #8]      @ load 8 reference pixels
add      r0,    r0,   r2      @ *pSrc += imagewidth
add      r1,    r1,   r2      @ *pRef += imagewidth
mov      r6,#4                @ setup loop count

SAD8x8_loop:
    walignr0 wR3, wR1,   wR2    @ align reference row
    wldrd    wR1, [r0]          @ load ref. pixels
    wsadb    wR15, wR0,  wR3    @ SAD odd rows
    wldrd    wR2, [r0, #8]      @ load next ref. pixels
    add      r0,  r0,    r2     @ *pRef += imagewidth
    wldrd    wR0, [r1]          @ load source pixels
```

```
add       r1,   r1,   r2   @ *pSrc += imagewidth
subs      r6,   r6,   #1   @ decrement loop count
walignr0  wR3,  wR1,  wR2  @ align refernce row
wldrdne   wR1,  [r0]       @ load next ref. pixels
wsadb     wR15, wR0,  wR3  @ SAD even rows
wldrdne   wR2,  [r0,  #8]  @ load next ref. pixels
add       r0,   r0,   r2   @ *pRef += imagewidth
wldrdne   wR0,  [r1]       @ load source pixels
add       r1,   r1,   r2   @ *pSrc += imagewidth
bne SAD8x8_loop
textrmsh  r0, wR15, #0  @ return result
```

Figure 15.13 Intel® Wireless MMX™ Assembly Code Instructions for an 8×8
Block SAD Calculation

The inner loop has been unrolled to process two rows per iteration, resulting in a total throughput of 80 cycles for this implementation. The first thing to notice is that the WSADB instruction only consumes 10 percent of the total, with all of the supporting operations taking up the other 90 percent. Looking at a breakdown of the instruction mix in Table 15.2 helps to identify optimization potentials.

Table 15.2 Instruction Breakdown for the 8×8 Block SAD

Instruction	Cycles	Description
AND	1	Isolate LSBs of pointer
BIC	1	Clear LSBs of pointer
TMCR	1	transfer alignment
MOV	1	setup LSB mask and loop count
WZERO	1	zero accumulator
WSADB	8	sum-of-absolute difference
WLDRD	27	load src and ref block pixels
WALIGNR	8	alignment of reference pixels
ADD	19	adjust pointers for image width
SUBS	4	decrementing the loop counter
BNE	9	Branching to loop start + fall through
TEXTRMSH	1	Transfer result back to r0

The biggest hitter for the independent block SAD calculation is the double-word load operation, with pointer adjustments to support those loads coming in a close second. So, it looks like 46 out of the 81 cycles—over half of the entire cycles—are dealing with management of the data streams.

Unfortunately, you can't do a whole lot to reduce the cycle count for the independent block SAD. The key to success is finding techniques to amortize the load overhead across multiple block calculations.

Fixed Pattern Motion Estimation

When designing algorithms for use with Intel Wireless MMX instructions, you always have options, as discussed in previous chapters. Often, the best approach is based on amortizing the load traffic across as many calculations as possible. For the task of motion estimation, you have another opportunity for optimization due to the difference between attributes of the two data streams during the calculation.

The basic steps involved in the multistep fixed-search pattern algorithms are illustrated in Figure 15.14 for three steps plus a final half-pixel step. The TSS algorithm samples the region more densely with nine block SAD calculations in the first step, followed by eight in the subsequent steps.

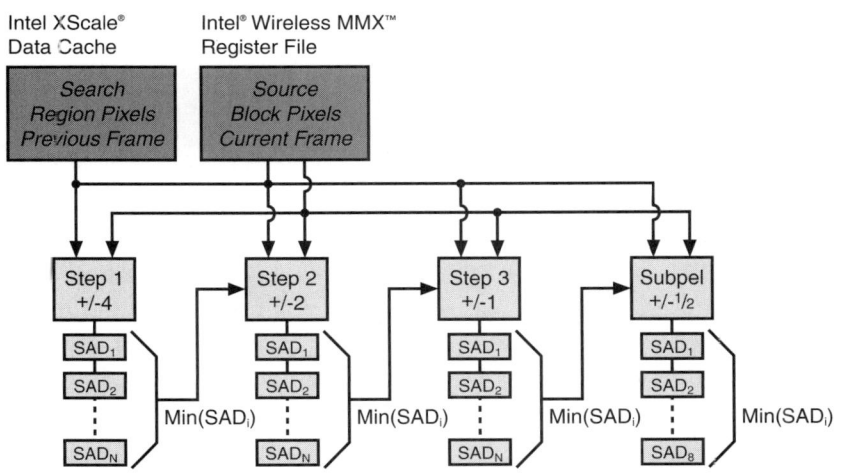

Figure 15.14 Multistep Search Algorithms

The fixed-pattern search algorithms have a similar sequence of events. For each step, a group of block SADs is calculated at different positions within the search region. Following the calculation, the position of the minimum SAD in the group is identified. Once found, this location is used to start the search pattern for the next step. For each step, the motion vector is being refined, and on the final step, the motion vector has been found.

It is useful to think of the motion vector calculation as three distinct steps.

1. Calculate N Block SADs using a sampling pattern in the search grid.
2. Determine the minimum block SAD of the group and its position.
3. Calculate the pointers for the next step.

Even with the use of the fast search algorithms, motion estimation is still one of the most computationally intensive operations in the video encoding process, so it is important to find ways of speeding up the calculation. Designing hand-optimized assembly code routines to optimize the search is the best approach and often results in better performance. Three optimization techniques offer a clear path for speeding up the process: loop unrolling, amortization of source pixel loads, and amortization of reference pixel loads.

Loop Unrolling

You can use loop unrolling to reduce or eliminate the overhead associated with incrementing the loop counter, testing, and branching. More lines of code are required, but significantly better performance can be achieved in many cases. For example, the independent 8×8 block SAD shown in Figure 15.13, two rows are calculated per inner loop iteration. For each iteration, the code performed a loop counter adjustment and a branch operation. In addition, a number of the instructions used did not contribute to the calculation, but served only to maintain the loop structure. Table 15.3 shows a more detailed breakdown of the instructions used in the 8×8 block SAD calculation.

Table 15.3 Detailed Instruction Breakdown for the 8×8 Block SAD

Instruction	Cycles	Description
AND	1	Isolate LSBs of pointer
BIC	1	Clear LSBs of pointer
TMCR	1	transfer alignment
MOV	1	setup LSB mask and loop count
MOV	*1	setup loop count
WZERO	1	zero accumulator
WSADB	8	sum-of-absolute difference
WLDRD	8	load source block pixels
WLDRD	16	load reference block pixels
WLDRDNE	*1	Conditional load for source pixels
WLDRDNE	*2	Conditional load for reference pixels
WALIGNR	8	alignment of reference pixels
ADD	7	adjust pointer for reference stride
ADD	7	adjust pointer for source stride
ADD	*2	unnecessary reference pointer adjust
ADD	*2	unnecessary source pointer adjust
SUBS	*4	decrementing the loop counter
BNE	*9	Branching to loop start + fall through
TEXTRMSH	1	Transfer result back to r0

* Instruction cycles associated with maintaining the loop

In Table 15.3, the instructions associated with implementing the calculation with a loop in the assembly code routine are indicated. Eliminating these instructions allows the recovery of 21 cycles, or about 26 percent improvement in cycle consumption.

Amortize Source Block Data Load Operations

The source block data is applied repetitively to a number of different reference blocks during the execution of a search algorithm. By loading the source block only once for the entire search, you can amortize the load overhead across many calculations. For example, the TSS algorithm requires a total of 25 block SADs to be calculated. If the block SAD was loaded only once, the effective overhead for the entire search would be eight WLDRD instructions to load the 8×8 block and an additional seven

ADD instructions for providing the pointer updates. Amortizing this search across a total of 25 block SAD calculations translates into an effective overhead 15/15= 0.6 cycles for the source block load overhead per SAD when performing the search. In effect, the amortization reduces our 8×8 block SAD calculation by another 27 percent. The 8×8, 4×8, 8×4, and 4×4 block sizes easily fit in the register file, leaving enough registers free to handle other aspects of the calculation. For the 16×16, 16×8, and 8×16, you must consider a partial calculation.

Amortize Reference Block Data Load Operations

The reference block data may be on any byte boundary in memory, which usually requires the application to load an extra eight pixels per row. That is, you incur two 64-bit loads to make sure the program has the required pixels, and you must use the WALIGNR instruction to extract the desired group of eight adjacent pixels for presentation to the WSADB instruction. A number of the motion search algorithms have inter-SAD, Dk, spacing of one or just a few pixels. For example, the TSS starts with an inter-SAD spacing of three or four (D4 or D3) for the first step, is reduced to two (D2) for the second step, and finally drops to one (D1) for the final step. If you found a way to provide for a multi-sample calculation for adjacent SADs, potentially you could amortize the reference pixel data loads across multiple calculations. For example, what if the interSAD spacing is just one pixel and the alignment of the first reference block is between byte 0 and byte 6? The program can load the reference pixels for three adjacent block SADs with the same number of wldrd instructions you had for the single 8×8 block SAD example. The overhead for the load operation for the reference block data could be amortized across three calculations effectively giving us 24/3 = 8 cycles contributed per block SAD. This change would reduce your block SAD calculation by another 38 percent!

This optimization effort is starting to look promising: eliminating loop overhead yields 26 percent, amortizing the source block across multiple calculations another 27 percent, and amortizing reference pixel loads, 38 percent!

The loop unrolling is a straightforward technique that doesn't require much thought. The initial sequence of instructions is copied over several times and you are pretty much done. Preloading the source block is a bit more complicated since doing so uses up some of the available register space, and you also want to minimize reference block loads. The minimization of reference block loads is based on the premise of doing multiple block calculations, in which the inter-SAD spacing is small enough that pixels overlap.

Let's start with taking a look at how the register file should be organized for a fast search algorithm.

Organizing the Register File for the Fixed Pattern Search

Several aspects of the fixed pattern search must be managed. The data streams providing source and reference pixels to the coprocessor execution resources need pointer adjustments and operand alignment. The calculated SADs also must have registers available to hold the results of the comparisons.

The overhead for loading the source data is best amortized across as many block comparisons as possible. For the 4×4, 8×8, 8×4, and 4×8 block sizes, only half, or less than half, of the sixteen 64-bit registers are needed for the preload, which leaves enough registers to handle other aspects of the calculation. For the 16×16, 16×8, and 8×16 block sizes, all registers must be reserved for holding the source block, and in the case of the 16×16 block, they could hold only half of the block. To maintain enough registers to manage the calculation, you can restrict the number of source pixels that are preloaded for a search to 64 pixels. The larger block sizes use the partial SAD calculation described in the following sections with a 64-pixel grouping.

You can use the four general-purpose registers, wCGR0–wCGR3, to provide four different alignments for four different candidate vectors. Since four alignments are possible, you need four registers available for holding the SADs being calculated. Allocating a couple of registers to handle the loads and the aligned data and using the core registers to manage the pointers leads you to the register file organization illustrated in Figure 15.15.

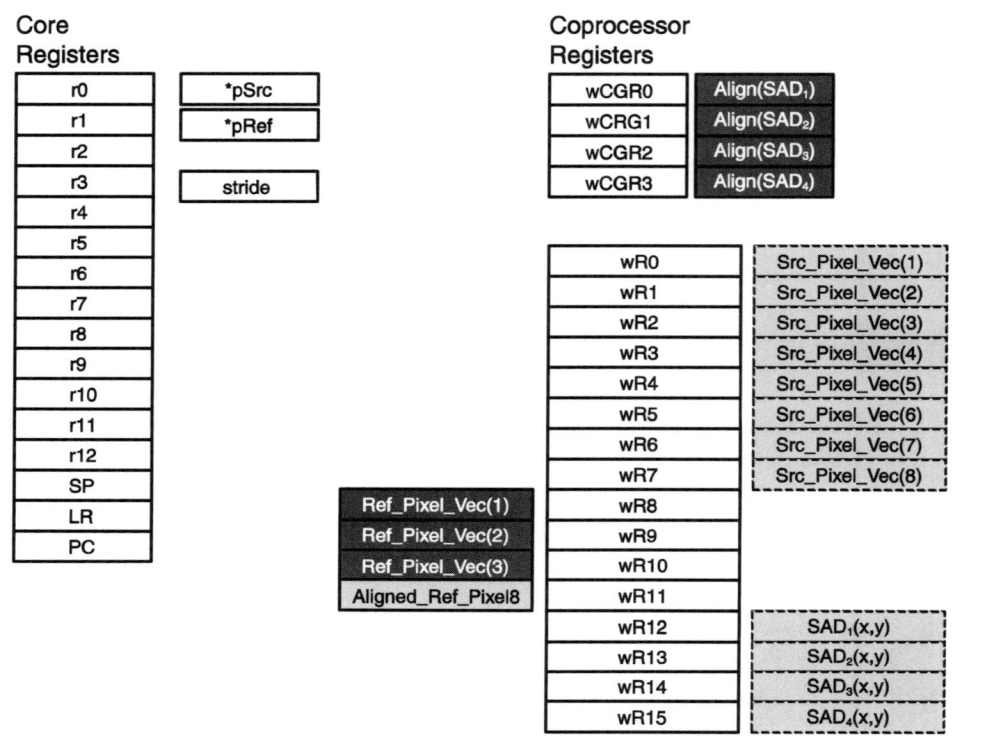

Figure 15.15 Register File Organization for Fixed Pattern Search

This organization of the register file provides most of the features required to design an efficient motion search engine:

Source 64 pixels cached → wR0–wR7

Alignment for reference stream → wCGR0–wCGR3

Execution stream with four running SADs → wR12–wR15

Load stream 24 pixels of reference pixels → wR8–wR10

Aligned groups of eight reference pixels → wR11

The next step is to build the motion estimation engine with Intel Wireless MMX instructions, but first you have to do a little more planning of the sampling patterns and the reference blocks grouping.

Fixed Search Pattern Clusters

The sampling structure of the fixed pattern search algorithms displays a particularly important quality. The blocks of reference pixels to be compared to the source block are adjacent and overlapping within the search region. The inter-SAD spacing (Dk) describes the block displacement where k is the number of pixels separating the blocks. For example, the TSS starts with a displacement of four or three for the first step, followed by two for the second, and finally one for the third.

The eight-point and nine-point sampling grid can be divided up into smaller groups of adjacent and overlapping reference blocks in several fashions. Some options for grouping the calculations are illustrated in Figure 15.16.

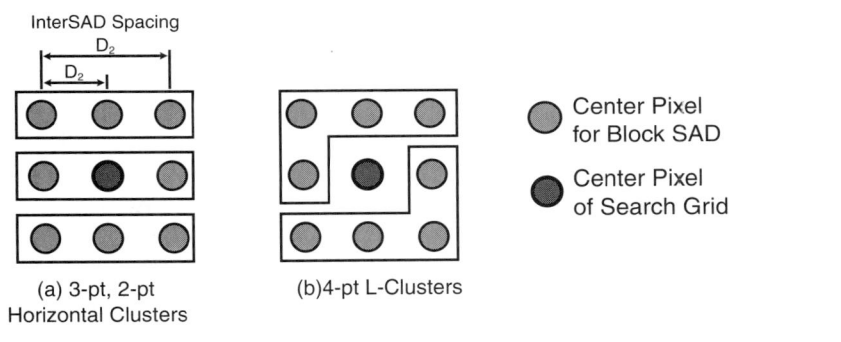

Figure 15.16 Adjacent and Overlapping Clustered SADs

In Figure 15.16(a), the nine-point rectangular sampling grid is grouped as three horizontal clusters containing three adjacent reference blocks each. One possible alternative grouping in (b) illustrates grouping the eight-point sampling grid as two L-shaped clusters. The introduction of block and annular clustering approaches makes additional groupings possible.

The TSS search algorithm can be implemented using a combination of these clustering strategies. For example, during the first step in the search, three groups of adjacent SADs can be calculated using the three-point horizontal clustering routine. Once the first step is performed, the center SAD is known, so you can apply two versions of the four-point L-clustering. The application of the three-point horizontal and four-point L-clusters for the TSS algorithm is provided in Table 15.4.

Table 15.4 Steps and Groupings for Clustering Strategies

Step in the TSS	Dk	No. of SADs	Grouping
Step 1	Dk = 4	9 total	(3) 3-pt Horizontal
Step 2	Dk = 2	8 total	(2) 4-pt L-Cluster
Step 3	Dk = 1	8 total	(2) 4-pt L-Cluster
Step 4	Dk = 0.5	8 total	(2) 4-pt L-Cluster

As you will see in the following sections, the three-point cluster has a very straightforward implementation, and the L-cluster requires only a minor modification of the three-point cluster code.

Alignment of Adjacent and Overlapping Reference Blocks

The alignment of the reference pixels for adjacent SAD calculations is also based on the three LSBs of the pointer to the search grid. Depending on the initial alignment and the desired interSAD spacing, adjacent groups of pixels may cross more than one double-word boundary.

For the D1 spacing, the pixels from rows of two SADs always lie within two double words. If the interSAD spacing is greater than one, two adjacent SADs could cross three boundaries. Using the 8×8 block as an example, the program must always provide two double-word loads for each row if the spacing is D1, and depending on the initial alignment, it might have to provide a third double-word load for higher spacing. The alignment for a D1 and D4 interSAD spacing is illustrated in Figure 15.17, for the cases where the alignment of the first SAD is on a 64-bit boundary and on byte 7 within the double word, too.

Since some alignment or inter-SAD spacing combinations result in an additional double-word load, defining ranges where boundary crossings occur helps in the development of optimized code and avoids wasted cycles. This definition is even more important for three adjacent SADs.

Define the alignment of the first reference block in a cluster to be A1 and the adjacent reference blocks to be A2, A3, and so on. The alignment for the adjacent blocks is determined from *An-1* by adding the interSAD spacing Dk. For example, if A1 = 0, the rows of the first block are on a double-word boundary. An interSAD spacing of D1 indicates that the rows of the second block start on the first byte in the double word, as follows:

$A2 = A1+D1 = 0+1=1$

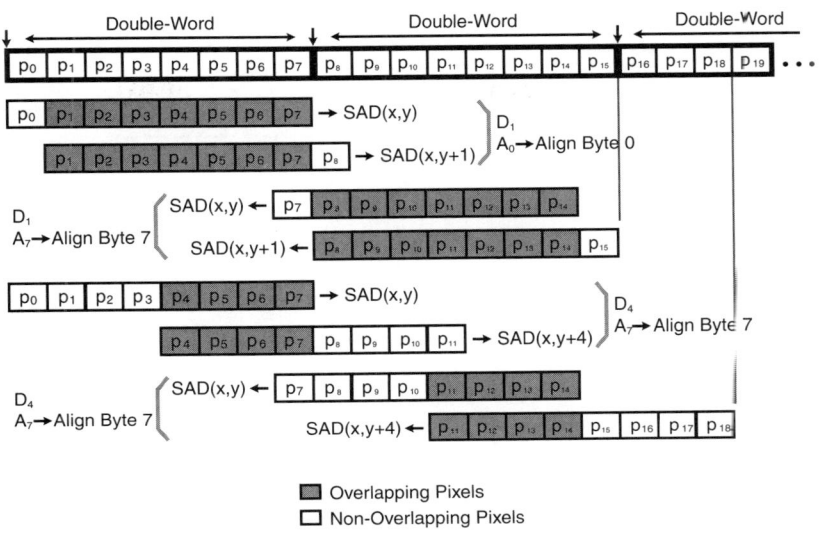

Figure 15.17 D1 and D4 InterSAD Spacing Byte Alignments for Reference Pixels

Similarly, if A1 = 3, the spacing of D1 indicates that the second and third blocks start on the fourth and fifth bytes, respectively.

$$A2 = A1+D1 = 3+1 = 4$$

$$A3 = A2+D1 = 4+1 = 5$$

The following equation generalizes the alignment required of adjacent SADs:

$$An = (An-1 + Dk) \bmod (8)$$

The modulo arithmetic reflects the fact that Intel Wireless MMX technology works with 64-bit double words. You can calculate the number of double words N_{dw} required to support n adjacent SAD calculations using the following equation:

$$N_{dw} = (A1 + n*D1 +8)/8$$

Understanding alignment is the key to making maximum use of reference pixel data loaded into the coprocessor register file. Table 15.5 summarizes the alignment for three adjacent 8×8 reference blocks for various alignments and inter-SAD spacing, and it shows the number of double-word loads.

Table 15.5 Alignment and Number of Double-Word Loads for Three Adjacent SADs

A1 alignment	Adjacent block alignments			
	D1	D2	D3	D4
0	A2=1, A3=2, N_{dw}=2	A2=2 A3=4 N_{dw}=2	A2=3 A3=6 N_{dw}=2	A2=4 A3=0 N_{dw}=2
1	A2=2 A3=3 N_{dw}=2	A2=3 A3=5 N_{dw}=2	A2=4 A3=7 N_{dw}=2	A2=5 A3=1 N_{dw}=3
2	A2=3 A3=4 N_{dw}=2	A2=4 A3=6 N_{dw}=2	A2=5 A3=0 N_{dw}=2	A2=6 A3=2 N_{dw}=3
3	A2=4 A3=5 N_{dw}=2	A2=5 A3=7 N_{dw}=2	A2=6 A3=1 N_{dw}=3	A2=7 A3=3 N_{dw}=3
4	A2=5 A3=6 N_{dw}=2	A2=6 A3=0 N_{dw}=2	A2=7 A3=2 N_{dw}=3	A2=0 A3=4 N_{dw}=3
5	A2=6 A3=7 N_{dw}=2	A2=7 A3=1 N_{dw}=3	A2=0 A3=3 N_{dw}=3	A2=1 A3=5 N_{dw}=3
6	A2=7 A3=0 N_{dw}=2	A2=0 A3=2 N_{dw}=3	A2=1 A3=4 N_{dw}=3	A2=2 A3=6 N_{dw}=3
7	A2=0 A3=1 N_{dw}=3	A2=1 A3=3 N_{dw}=3	A2=2 A3=5 N_{dw}=3	A2=3 A3=7 N_{dw}=3

[ ] Boundary requires either two loads or three loads for each row in the reference region.
[ ] Second alignment operation crosses from the first double word into the second and third.

The lighter gray shaded cells indicate the boundary where the initial alignment combined with the interSAD spacing requires either two loads or three loads for each row in the reference region. The darker gray shaded cells indicate where the second alignment operation crosses from the first double word into the second and third. To develop optimized code, you must consider three separate sequences: one for the three loads per row, one for the two loads per row, and another for the crossing group.

Three-Point Horizontal Adjacent Clusters

Whether the program requires two or three loads to process each row in any three Mx8 block SADs is an important consideration. The method of sequencing the alignment operations must reflect both the boundary crossing into the third double word for SAD_2 and SAD_3.

The alignment setup is identical to the method used for the independent block SAD, except that now three alignments are calculated and transferred to the control registers. If the interSAD spacing is in r4, you would use an eight-instruction sequence to setup the alignments, as shown in Figure 15.18.

```
@ SAD8x8_3ptCluster_s.s

@ setup alignment for adjacent blocks

mov     r5, #7        @ setup the mask for 0b111
and     r3, r0, r5    @ isolate the 3 LSBs into r3
tmcr    wCGR0,  r3    @ transfer alignment for SAD1
add     r5, r3, r4    @ add InterSAD spacing Dk
tmcr    wCGR1,  r5    @ transfer alignment for SAD2
add     r5, r5, r4    @ add InterSAD spacing Dk
tmcr    wCGR2,  r5    @ transfer alignment for SAD3
```

Figure 15.18 Setup for 3-pt Horizontal Adjacent Clusters

The pixels for the rows of the first reference block in the cluster are always contained at least partially in the first double-word load. The second reference block is extracted from either the first and second double word loaded or from the second and third. Similarly, the third double word also may cross the same boundaries.

The three cases can be detected by evaluating the alignment A1, the number of double words, N_{dw}, and the interSAD spacing as follows.

```
if (Ndw == 3){
    if (A1+Dk == 7){
        3ptHcluster_8x8case1();
    else
        3ptHcluster_8x8case2();
else
    3ptHcluster_8x8case3();
```

The first case has three loads and an alignment sequence, reflecting the fact that the first and second reference blocks cross the double-word boundary between the first and second double words. The sequence for processing a row for the three adjacent SADs is provided in Figure 15.19.

```
@ SAD8x8_3ptCluster_s.s

@ Calculate 1ˢᵗ row of 3 8x8 adjacent SADs
@ wR8  -> Ref_Pixel_Vec(0)
@ wR9  -> Ref_Pixel_Vec(1)
@ wR10 -> Ref_Pixel_Vec(2)

add      r0, r0, r13    @ pRef+=stride
walignr0 wR11, wR8, wR9   @ Align_Back_Ref_Pixel8
wsadb    wR12, wR11, wR0  @ SAD(x,y)+=
walignr1 wR11, wR8, wR9   @ Align+1_Back_Ref_Pixel8
wsadb    wR13, wR11, wR0  @ SAD(x+1,y)+= row1 absdiff
walignr2 wR11, wR9, wR10  @ Align+2
wsadb    wR14, wR11, wR0  @ SAD(x+2,y)+= row1 absdiff
```

Figure 15.19 Code Sequence for a Row of Three Adjacent 8×8 SADs for Case 1

The second case still has three loads, but the boundary crossing differs in the ordering of registers for the second WALIGNR instruction. The code sequence in Figure 15.20 illustrates the calculation of the first row for the three 8×8 block SADs.

```
@ SAD8x8_3ptCluster_s.s

@ Calculate 1st row of 3 8x8 adjacent SADs
@ wR8  -> Ref_Pixel_Vec(0)
@ wR9  -> Ref_Pixel_Vec(1)
@ wR10 -> Ref_Pixel_Vec(2)

add      r0, r0, r3     @ pRef+=stride
walignr0 wR11, wR8, wR9   @ Align_Back_Ref_Pixel8
wsadb    wR12, wR11, wR0  @ SAD(x,y)+=
walignr1 wR11, wR9, wR10  @ Align+1_Back_Ref_Pixel8
wsadb    wR13, wR11, wR0  @ SAD(x+1,y)+= row1 absdiff
walignr2 wR11, wR9, wR10  @ Align+2
wsadb    wR14, wR11, wR0  @ SAD(x+2,y)+= row1 absdiff
```

Figure 15.20 Code Sequence for a Row of Three Adjacent 8×8 SADs for Case 2

For the final case, all three reference-block rows are contained in two double words, as shown in Figure 15.21.

```
@ SAD8x8_3ptCluster_s.s

@ Calculate 1st row of 3 adjacent SADs
@ wR8 -> Ref_Pixel_Vec(0)
@ wR9 -> Ref_Pixel_Vec(1)

add       r0, r0, r3      @ pRef+=stride
walignr1  wR11, wR8, wR9  @ Align_Back_Ref_Pixel8
wsadb     wR12, wR11, wR0 @ SAD(x,y)+=
walignr2  wR11, wR8, wR9  @ Align+1_Back_Ref_Pixel8
wsadb     wR13, wR11, wR0 @ SAD(x+1,y)+= row1 absdiff
walignr3  wR11, wR8, wR9  @ Align+2
wsadb     wR14, wR11, wR0 @ SAD(x+2,y)+= row1 absdiff
```

Figure 15.21 Code Sequence for a Row of Three Adjacent 8×8 SADs for Case 3

The throughput is nearly identical for all three cases, with case three requiring one less load per row. Table 15.6 shows the comparative differences.

Table 15.6 Effective Cycle Count for Adjacent Overlapping 8×8 Block SADs

Routine	Cycles	Cycles/SAD
3ptHcluster_8x8case3.s	80	27
3ptHcluster_8x8case2.s	88	29
3ptHcluster_8x8case1.s	88	29

Partial-SAD Approach

You can perform the calculations for SADs with larger block sizes (16×16, 16×8, and 8×16) by dividing the larger block sizes into two or more pieces and performing the calculations with smaller block sizes. As discussed in the previous sections, working with 64-pixel block sizes leaves enough registers free to support calculation of N_{dw}=3 four SADs, and even more if you introduce an additional formatting step, within region and still manage the load traffic.

The method of partial-SAD allows the reference data to be loaded only once and provides good performance in terms of pixel throughput. The calculation consists of two phases: partitioning the larger block SAD calculation into smaller block sizes and the performing a summation of the partial SADs. The resultant SAD for the 16×16 block is calculated by the summation of the partial SADs.

$$SAD_{16x16}(dx, dy) = pSAD_{4x16,1} + pSAD_{4x16,2} + pSAD_{4x16,3} + pSAD_{4x16,4}$$

The advantage of using 4×16 block sizes over 8×8 block sizes when segmenting the 16×16 block is realized through minimizing redundant load operations. This is because reference data is loaded only once as adjacent block SADs are calculated and retired as the search algorithm proceeds.

Determining the Minimum SAD

After a search pattern has been executed, you need to find the minimum of the calculated SADs and retain the corresponding index. The index is used to determine the start point for the next level of a multistep search or, for the last step, to calculate the motion vector. Identifying the index is accomplished better through use of the conditional instructions and the core register file. The textrm instruction can be used to transfer the results:

```
textrm   r3, wR15   @ SAD(i,j)
textrm   r4, wR14   @ SAD(i,j+Dk)
textrm   r5, wR13   @ SAD(i,j+2Dk)
```

The next step is to compare the three SADs and identify the index. The following sequence illustrates the comparison operation using a core instruction sequence.

```
mov     r9, #1     @ initialize the index
mov     r8, r2     @ copy SAD1 to r8 -minSAD
cmp     r8, r3     @ compare SAD1 to SAD2
movlt   r8, r3     @ cond. move new minSAD to r8
movlt   r9, #2     @ conditionally update pointer
cmp     r8, r4     @ compare min(SAD1,SAD2) to SAD3
movlt   r8, r3     @ cond. Move new minSAD to r8
movlt   r9, #3     @ conditionally update pointer
```

In the preceding code sequence, r8 is used to hold the minimum SAD value and r9 the index.

Fractional SAD Calculations

The last step in the motion estimation process involves a half-pixel or quarter-pixel search around the final position that was indicated by the integer search. The steps involved for the half-pixel search are best developed as an extension of the integer search algorithm:

1. Complete the integer search and generate minimum SAD final displacement.

2. Interpolate between samples to generate the fractional pixels.

3. Calculate the minimum SAD for the eight-point grid formed by the interpolation.

4. Update the motion vector with the fractional information

$$MV_i(dx, dy) = MV_i(dx, dy) + MV_{1/2}(dx, dy)$$

The fractional motion search step is illustrated in Figure 15.22.

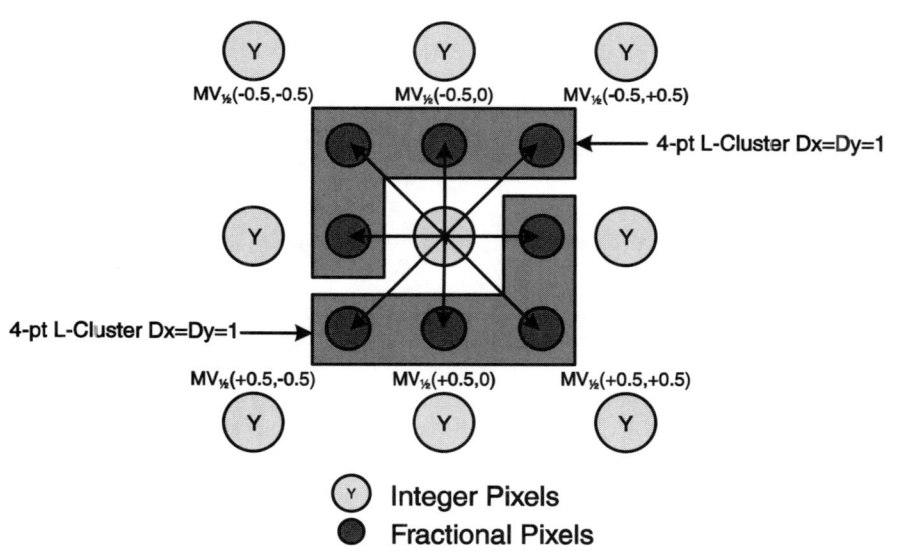

Figure 15.22 Illustration of the Fractional Motion Search Step Using L-Clusters

The keys to achieving the best throughput for the fractional motion search step are again amortization of load overhead and reuse of calculated data. The interpolation operations use similar code sequences as the motion compensation.

Motion Compensation with Intel Wireless MMX Technology

Motion compensation is an important component of video compression that is performed in decoders and encoders. As with motion estimation, the computational load is high enough to warrant acceleration both through specialized routines and tailored code sequences.

Several variations in the operations are performed. They can consist of a simple move of a block of pixels from one data structure to the next or the block move could involve a spatial interpolation. The type of spatial interpolation is indicated by the motion vector that is chosen during encoder motion estimation. The pixels for a block can be present within a single frame, as with the P-type picture, or they can be in two separate frames, as with the B-type picture.

P-Type Pictures

The P-type picture involves forward prediction. In forward prediction, a new picture is created from either a previously decoded I-type picture or a previously created P-type picture. The motion vector indicates whether a block within the picture simply can be relocated or whether the pixels in the block must be averaged before being moved. The forward prediction for the P-type picture is illustrated in Figure 15.23.

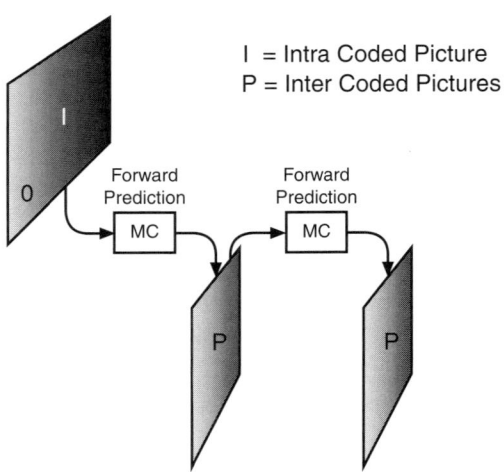

Figure 15.23 Forward and Backward Prediction for P-Type Picture

The P-type motion vector can indicate one of three possible interpolations when using a half-pixel motion vector and one of fifteen when using a quarter-pixel. For the half-pixel motion vector, the interpolations may either be horizontal, 1/2X, vertical, 1/2Y, or diagonal, 1/2XY. The integer motion vector describes the simple block move.

Because the motion vector generated during the motion estimation process can indicate any pixel location within the frame, alignment plays an important role in generating the predicted frame. The same approach used in the previous sections is used for masking the LSBs of the pointer Let's take a look at how best to implement some of the P-type motion compensation operations with Intel Wireless MMX technology.

P-type Integer MV

The integer motion vector is generated when the fractional search does not yield a better match than the final integer location. With the integer MV, you only need to move a block of pixels from one frame to another. The operation is relatively simple, with some complexity around handling the alignment. Two data structures must be accessed. A block from the previous frame is transferred to the current or predicted frame. The C-code in Figure 15.24 illustrates the block move for the integer MV.

```
// MC_PtypeI_c.c

// NXM P-Picture Integer type block prediction

void MC_PtypeI_c( unsigned char *pSrc,
                  unsigned char *pDst,
                  int stride, int N, int M){
int i, j;

for( i = 0; i < N; i++ ){
   for( j = 0; j < M; j++ )
      pDst[j] = pSrc[j];
   pSrc += stride;
   pDst += stride;
   }
}
```

Figure 15.24 C Code for an NxM P-type Motion Compensation

In the C code of Figure 15.24, you again have to deal with two data structures. The nested loop provides for the relocation of the block from the previous frame to the current frame that is being predicted. The inner loop provides the block move and the outer loop adjusts the pointers to account for the image width. The optimized assembly code for moving an 8×8 P-type block is shown in Figure 15.25.

```
@ MC_PtypeI_s.s

@ r0 -> (MV0) previous frame, r1 -> current frame
@ r3 -> imagewidth
@ wCGR0 -> MV0 alignment

and      r7,    r0, #7      @ r7 = 3LSBs of *pSrc
bic      r0,    r0, #7      @ r0 64-bit aligned
wldrd    wR0,   [r0]        @ Ref_Pixel_Vec(0)
tmcr     wCGR0, r7          @ alignment in wCGR0
wldrd    wR1,   [r0,#8]     @ Ref_Pixel_Vec(1)
mov      r12,   #8          @ loop counter
add      r0,    r0,  r2     @ pSrc+=stride

Ptype_Integer_Loop:
    wldrd     wR2,   [r0]        @ Ref_Pixel_Vec(2)
    walignr0  wR12,  wR0, wR1    @ Align_Ref_Pixel8
    wldrd     wR3,   [r0,#8]     @ Ref_Pixel_Vec(3)
    add       r0,    r0,  r2     @ pSrc += stride
    wstrd     wR12,  [r1]        @ store 8 pixels
    add       r1,    r1,  r2     @ pDst+=stride
    subs      r12,   r12, #2     @ decrement loop count
    wldrdne   wR0,   [r0]        @ Pixel_Vec(0)
    walignr0  wR12,  wR2, wR3    @ Align_Ref_Pixel
    wstrd     wR12,  [r1]        @ store 8 pixels
    wldrdne   wR1,   [r0,#8]     @ Ref_Pixel_Vec(1)
    add       r0,    r0,  r2     @ pDst+=stride
    add       r1,    r1,  r2     @ pDst+=stride
    bne Ptype_Integer_Loop
```

Figure 15.25 Assembly Code for 8×8 Block P-type Motion Compensation

In the 8×8 block move routine, you have an instruction mix composed primarily of double-word load/store and alignment operations. The loop has been unrolled to provide for two rows of the 8×8 block to be aligned and moved from the previous I-type or P-type picture to the current predicted picture. In addition to the unrolling, load pipelining has also been used to avoid potential load-to-use stalls. Table 15.7 provides a summary of the instructions.

Table 15.7 Instruction Breakdown for the P-Type 8×8 Block Integer MC

Instruction	Cycles	Description
AND	1	Isolate LSBs of pointer
BIC	1	Clear LSBs of pointer
TMCR	1	transfer alignment
MOV	1	setup LSB mask and loop count
WLDRDNE	*2	last iteration conditional loads
WALIGNR	8	alignment of previous block pixels
WSTRD	16	double-word stores at 2cycles each
ADD	7	adjust pntr for previous frame stride
ADD	7	adjust pntr for current frame stride
ADD	*3	Last pntr adjustment not used
SUBS	*4	decrementing the loop counter
BNE	*9	Branching to loop start + fall through

* Instruction cycles associated with maintaining the loop

The alignment and loop setup for the previous block consumes four instructions, bringing the total cycle consumption for the operation to 76 cycles. You can use a couple of methods to help speed up the operation: loop unrolling for general cases and testing for the special case of the previous block being on a 64-bit boundary. Applying loop unrolling alone removes 20 cycles from the routine, a 26-percent improvement. If you also tested for the special case, you could develop a tailored routine that would eliminate an additional 19 cycles. However, this routine would require additional testing for the LSBs of the pointer and a branch operation to the tailored routine.

The integer motion vector example shows how the loop-unrolling technique can impact performance. With the non-integer displacements, you would like to achieve this quick performance boost. In addition, you need to find out whether any additional gain through data reuse is possible, and to consider the development of specialized routines.

P-type 1/2X MV

The 1/2X fractional motion vector is generated when the fractional search in the horizontal direction yields a better match than both the vertical and diagonal directions in addition to the final integer location. The 1/2X MV is a more complicated than the integer, since now you need to provide an averaging operation before performing the block move. Figure 15.26 shows the C-code for an 8×8 block P-type 1/2X interpolation.

```
// MC_PtypeH_c.c

// NXM P-Picture Half X type block prediction

void MC_PtypeH_c( unsigned char *pSrc,
                  unsigned char *pDst,
                  int stride, int N, int M){
    int    i, j;

    for (i = 0; i < N; i++){
      for (j = 0; j < M; j++)
        pDst[j]=(unsigned char)((pSrc[j]+pSrc[j+1]+1)>>1);
      pSrc += stride;
      pDst += stride;
    }
}
```

Figure 15.26 C Code for an NxM P-type Motion Compensation

The C-code in Figure 15.26 is very similar to the routine for the integer MV. The only difference is that now you will perform an average of adjacent pixels within the block from the previous frame prior to relocation into the current predicted frame. The alignment again becomes an important consideration. For example, the 1/2X interpolation for an 8×8 block performs the following steps for each row:

1. Load two double words.
2. Align row of eight pixels.
3. Align +1 row of eight pixels.
4. Perform the average operation on the two groups.
5. Store the eight resulting pixels in the current frame.

One of the first things you should notice is that two alignments are performed for each row in the 8×8 block. The first is aligned on the integer portion of the MV, and the second is aligned by incrementing this alignment by one. These alignments provide two groups of eight pixels that can be presented to the WAVG2B instruction for averaging. Applying two alignment operations sounds pretty straightforward, but what do you do if the LSBs of MV are all ones? The first group of eight pixels will be aligned properly, but the second group will have the wrong alignment! The eight possible alignments for the 1/2X interpolation are illustrated in Figure 15.27.

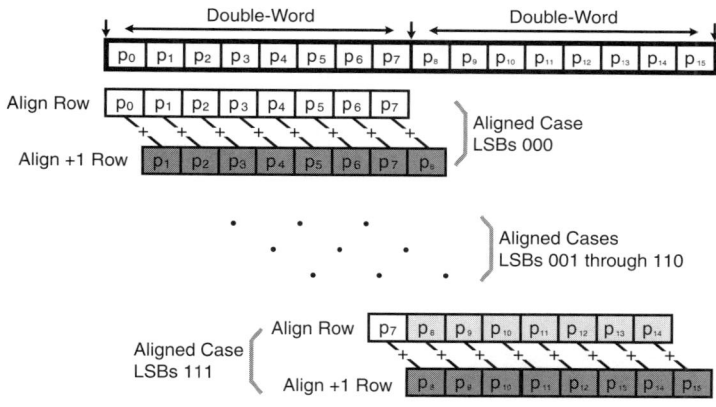

Figure 15.27 Illustration of Half-X Interpolation Alignment Cases

For the case where the alignment indicates byte seven lies within the first double word, you treat alignment as a special case in order to provide the proper operands to the WAVG2B instruction. If you first test the LSBs of the integer portion of the MV, you can branch to a routine that provides a slightly different alignment sequence than you need for the other seven possibilities.

```
if (LSBs == 7)
   MC_PtypeH_case1();  // 1/2X-byte 7 alignment
else
   MC_PtypeH_case2();  // 1/2X-byte 0-6 alignment
```

The routine tailored for the special case would have half the total number of alignment instructions that are required for the other cases, because the second group of eight pixels already is aligned on a double-word boundary. The effort required to develop the second routine is minimal, and the routine can be a duplicate of the general case with half of the alignments deleted. The optimized assembly code for the general cases is shown in Figure 15.28.

```
@ MC_PtypeH_s.s

@ Alignment case 1 thru 6
@ r0 -> previous frame, r1 -> current frame
@ r3 -> imagewidth
@ wCGR0 -> MV alignement
@ wCGR1 -> MV alignment + 1

and     r7,     r0, #7      @ r7 = 3LSBs of *pSrc
bic     r0,     r0, #7      @ r0 64-bit aligned
wldrd   wR0,    [r0]        @ Ref_Pixel_Vec(0)
tmcr    wCGR1,  r7          @ alignment in wCGR0
add     r7, r7, #1          @ alignment+1
wldrd   wR1,    [r0,#8]     @ Ref_Pixel_Vec(1)
tmcr    wCGR2,  r7          @ alignment in wCGR1
mov     r12,    #8          @ loop count

Ptype_HalfX_Loop:
    add     r0,  r0,  r2    @ *pSrc += stride
    walignr1 wR4, wR0, wR1  @ Align_Ref_Pixel
    walignr2 wR5, wR0, wR1  @ Align+1_Ref_Pixel
    wldrd   wR0, [r0]       @ Ref_Pixel_Vec(0)
    wavg2br wR6, wR4, wR5   @ average 8 pixels
    wldrd   wR1, [r0,#8]    @ Ref_Pixel_Vec(1)
    add     r0,  r0,  r2    @ *pSrc += stride
    wstrd   wR6, [r1]       @ store 8 pixels
    subs    r12, r12, #2    @ decrement loop count
    walignr1 wR4, wR0, wR1  @ Align_Ref_Pixel
    walignr2 wR5, wR0, wR1  @ Align+1_Ref_Pixel
    wldrdne wR0, [r0]       @ Ref_Pixel_Vec(0)
    wavg2br wR6, wR4, wR5   @ average 8 pixels
    wldrdne wR1, [r0, #8]   @ Ref_Pixel_Vec(1)
    add     r1,  r1,  r2    @ *pDst += stride
    wstrd   wR6, [r1]       @ store 8 pixels
    add     r1,  r1,  r2    @ *pDst += stride
    bne Ptype_HalfX_Loop
```

Figure 15.28 Assembly Code for an 8×8 block P-type Half-X Motion Compensation

The instruction mix for the 1/2X routine is dominated primarily by double-word load/store and alignment operations again. The loop has been unrolled so that two rows of the 8×8 block can be aligned and averaged. Again, this level of unrolling allows us to avoid any load-to-use stalls, but still has some drawbacks. Table 15.8 is a summary of the instructions for the half-X interpolation routines.

Table 15.8 Instruction Breakdown for the P-Type 8×8 Block Half-X MC

Instruction	Cycles	Description
AND	1	Isolate LSBs of pointer
BIC	1	Clear LSBs of pointer
TMCR	2	transfer alignments
MOV	1	setup LSB mask and loop count
WLDRD	16	load pixel data
WLDRDNE	*2	last iteration conditional loads
WALIGNR	16	alignment of previous block pixels
WAVG2BR	8	perform vector average of 8 pixels
WSTRD	16	double-word stores at 2 cycles each
ADD	14	adjust ptrs for image width
ADD	*3	last ptr adjustment not used
SUBS	*4	decrementing the loop counter
BNE	*9	branching to loop start + fall through

* Instruction cycles associated with maintaining the loop

The alignment and loop setup consumes five cycles, bringing the total cycle consumption for the code sequence to 93 cycles. As with the previous routines, loop unrolling is a good first step toward improving throughput and yields 20-percent improvement.

B-Type Pictures

The B-type pictures are predicted bidirectionally by averaging the motion compensated elements from past and future frames. Using the B-type provides a substantial gain in compression efficiency compared to coding with I-type and P-type pictures alone. The fundamental operation of interpolation is still performed, as it was with the P-type pictures, except that now two pictures are used as a reference, so two motion vectors are required, MV0 and MV1. The computational complexity is more than double that of a P-type picture since the program must evaluate both of the motion vectors and perform the indicated interpolations. The bidirectional prediction for B-type pictures is illustrated in Figure 15.29.

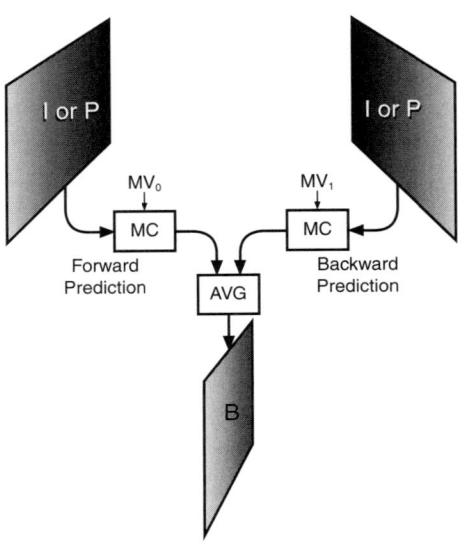

Figure 15.29   Bidirectional Prediction for a B-Type Picture

The simplest method to approach the B-type picture coding mode is to reuse the P-type picture interpolation routines and apply them to both the forward and reverse predictions. The result of each of the predictions must be averaged using a separate routine. You encounter one problem with this approach: an undesirable, and unnecessary, increase in cycle count when you combine the call/return overhead with reloading the previously interpolated pixels to perform the final average operation. Once again, the solution is to fold as many operations as possible into the routine and optimize specialized routines targeting the different possible motion vector pairs.

With the B-type picture, each of two motion vectors can indicate one of the four possible fractional locations when a half-pixel motion vector is used. Therefore, a total of 16 cases must be considered for the development of optimum code sequences. Table 15.9 illustrates the possible combinations for the motion vector pairs.

Table 15.9   Sixteen Possible Cases for a B-Type Picture Prediction

Case	Forward MV	Backward MV
1	MV_0 – Integer,	MV_1-Integer
2	MV_0 – Integer,	MV_1- ½ X
3	MV_0 – Integer,	MV_1- ½ Y
4	MV_0 – Integer,	MV_1- ½ XY
5	MV_0 – ½ X,	MV_1-Integer
6	MV_0 – ½ X,	MV_1- ½ X
7	MV_0 – ½ X,	MV_1- ½ Y
8	MV_0 – ½ X,	MV_1- ½ XY
9	MV_0 – ½ Y,	MV_1- Integer
10	MV_0 – ½ Y,	MV_1- ½ X
11	MV_0 – ½ Y,	MV_1- ½ Y
12	MV_0 – ½ Y,	MV_1- ½ XY
13	MV_0 – ½ XY,	MV_1- Integer
14	MV_0 – ½ XY,	MV_1- ½ X
15	MV_0 – ½ XY,	MV_1- ½ Y
16	MV_0 – ½ XY,	MV_1- ½ XY

Developing 16 individual routines might seem like a daunting task at first, but once you think it through, most of the code easily can be copied from one routine to the next. To see how that works, take a look at the development of optimized code using Intel Wireless MMX instructions for a couple of the 16 cases for the B-type picture.

B-type Integer-Integer MVs

The most straightforward case is when both motion vectors indicate integer displacements. Both of the future and past image blocks must be read and the pixels within each block must be averaged. The C code in Figure 15.30 illustrates the calculation.

```
// MC_BtypeII_c.c

// NXM B-Picture type block prediction
// MV0-Integer, MV1-Integer

void MC_BtypeII_c( unsigned char *pSrc0,
                   unsigned char *pSrc1,
                   unsigned char *pDst,
                   short stride, int N, int M){
    int i, j;

    for (i = 0; i < N; i++){
        for (j = 0; j < M; j++)
            pDst[j]=(unsigned char)((pSrc0[j]+pSrc1[j])>>1);
        pSrc0 += stride;
        pSrc1 += stride;
        pDst += stride;
    }
}
```

Figure 15.30 C Code for an NxM B-picture Type with MV0 and MV1 Indicating
Integer Location

In the previous code sample, three data structures must be accessed.
The forward and backward prediction vectors could be aligned on any
byte boundary and the predicted frame, which is still to be generated, is
known to be aligned on a double-word boundary. You could develop
four optimized routines to handle the four possible cases of having an
MV0 and an MV1 on double-word and byte boundaries, however the testing and branching for each increases the complexity and the performance of the end result is likely to be marginal at best. So let's keep things
simple and develop a routine to handle two arbitrary alignments.

The code in Figure 15.31 is for the integer, integer B-type picture motion compensation.

```
@ MC_BtypeII_s.s

@ r0 -> previous frame, r1 -> current frame
@ r2 -> future frame,   r3 -> imagewidth
@ wCGR0 -> MV0 alignment
@ wCGR1 -> MV1 alignment

wldrd    wR0,    [r0]        @ Forward_Ref_Vec(0)
mov      r12,    #8          @ loop counter
wldrd    wR1,    [r0,#8]     @ Forward_Ref_Vec(1)
```

```
Btype_IntInt_Loop:
    add      r0,   r0,   r3      @ pSrc0+=stride
    wldrd    wR2,  [r2]          @ Forward_Ref Vec(0)
    subs     r12,  r12,  #1      @ Decrement loop count
    wldrd    wR3,  [r2,#8]       @ Forward_Ref_Vec(1)
    walignr0 wR6,  wR0,  wR1     @ Align_Back_Ref_
    wldrdne  wR0,  [r0]          @ Back_Ref Vec(0)
    add      r2,   r2,   r3      @ pSrc1+=stride
    wldrdne  wR1,  [r0,#8]       @ Back_Ref_Vec(1)
    walignr1 wR7,  wR2,  wR3     @ Align_Forward_Ref
    wavg2br  wR8,  wR6,  wR7     @ Back_1/2X_inter
    wstrd    wR8,  [r1]          @ Store pixels
    add      r1,   r1,   r3      @ pDst+=stride
    bne      Btype_IntInt_Loop
```

Figure 15.31 Assembly Code for an 8×8 Block B-type Integer/Integer Motion Compensation

The assembly code routine in Figure 15.31 provides eight-pixel output for the predicted block per loop iteration. The alignment for the blocks from the past and future frames is isolated in the same way that such blocks were described in previous sections, and alignment tasks are transferred to the control registers wCGR0 and wCGR1. The instruction breakdown for the sequence in Figure 15.32 is shown in Table 15.10.

Table 15.10 Instruction Breakdown for the B-Type 8×8 Block Integer-Integer MC

Instruction	Cycles	Description
WLDRD	32	Load source block pixels
MOV	1	Setup loop count
WLDRDNE	*2	Last iteration conditional loads
WALIGNR	16	alignment of block pixels
WAVG2BR	8	average the pixels
WSTRD	16	double-word stores at 2cycles each
ADD	14	adjust pntr for prev. and future frame
ADD	7	adjust pntr for output frame
ADD	*3	last pntr adjustment not used
SUBS	*8	decrementing the loop counter
BNE	*13	branching to loop start + fall through

* Instruction cycles associated with maintaining the loop

The complete routine executes in 126 cycles and is heavily dominated by alignment, double-word loads, and pointer updates. The loop-unrolling technique can be applied to recover 26 of these cycles, delivering a 20-percent improvement.

B-type 1/2X-1/2X MVs

The 1/2X-1/2X case is more complicated than the integer-integer case. Now you must perform the 1/2X interpolation on two blocks and average the results. The C code in Figure 15.32 illustrates the calculation.

```c
// MC_BtypeHH_c.c

// NXM B-Picture type block prediction
// MV0-1/2X , MV1-1/2X ***

void MC_BtypeHH_c(unsigned char *pSrc0,
                  unsigned char *pSrc1,
                  unsigned char *pDst,
                  int stride, int N, int M){

    int i, j, tmp0, tmp1;

    for (i = 0; i < N; i++){
        for (j = 0; j < M; j++ ){
            tmp0 = (pSrc0[j]+pSrc0[j+1]+1)>>1;
            tmp1 = (pSrc1[j]+pSrc1[j+1]+1)>>1;
            pDst[j] = (unsigned char)(tmp0+tmp1)>>1;
        }
        pSrc0 += stride;
        pSrc1 += stride;
        pDst += stride;
    }
}
```

Figure 15.32   C Code for an NxM B-Type Picture with both MV0 and MV1 Indicating 1/2X Locations

The 1/2X-1/2X compensation for the B-type picture requires the code to perform two independent 1/2X interpolations in addition to the average of these results. The same issues with alignment occur around the special case of the vector indicating byte 7 with a double word. As a result, the code must test both vectors and branch to one of four possible routines. Figure 15.33 shows a possible organization of the register file. The control registers wCGR0 and wCGR1 hold the alignment of the block from the past frame. The control registers wCGR2 and wCGR3 hold the alignment of the block from the future frame.

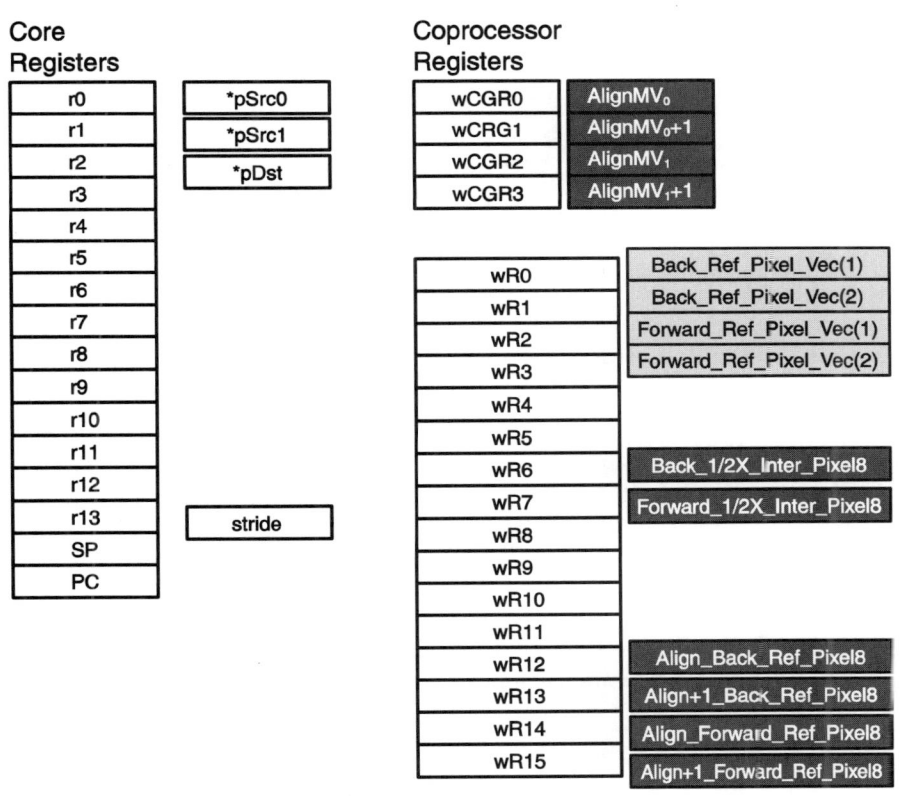

Figure 15.33 Register File Allocation for B-Type Picture 1/2X-1/2X Interpolations

The sample code in Figure 15.34 is for the 1/2X, 1/2X B-picture type motion compensation.

```
@ MC_PtypeHH_s.s

@ r0 -> previous frame, r1 -> current frame
@ r2 -> future frame,   r3 -> imagewidth
@ wCGR0 -> MV0 alignement
@ wCGR1 -> MV0 alignment + 1
@ wCGR2 -> MV1 alignment
@ wCGR3 -> MV1 alignment +1

wldrd      wR0,    [r0]        @ Back_Ref_Pixel_Vec(0)
mov        r12,    #8          @ loop count
wldrd      wR1,    [r0,#8]     @ Back_Ref_Pixel_Vec(1)
Btype_HH_Loop:
    add        r0,    r0,    r3     @ pSrc0+=stride
    wldrd      wR2,   [r2]           @ Forward_Ref_Vec(0)
    subs       r12,   r12,   #1     @ decrement loop count
    wldrd      wR3,   [r2,#8]        @ Forward_Ref_Vec(1)
    walignr0 wR12,  wR0,   wR1     @ Align_Back_Ref_
    walignr1 wR13,  wR0,   wR1     @ Align+1_Back_Ref
    wldrdne    wR0,   [r0]           @ Back_Ref_Vec(0)
    add        r2,    r2,    r3     @ pSrc1+=stride
    wldrdne    wR1,   [r0,#8]        @ Back_Ref_Vec(1)
    walignr2 wR14,  wR2,   wR3     @ Align_Forward_Ref_
    walignr3 wR15,  wR2,   wR3     @ Align+1_Forward_Ref_
    wavg2br    wR6,   wR12,  wR13   @ Back_1/2X_inter_pix8
    wavg2br    wR7,   wR14,  wR15   @ Forward_1/2X_inter
    wavg2br    wR8,   wR6,   wR7    @ Back_1/2X_inter_
    wstrd      wR8,   [r1]           @ B_type_Pixel8
    add        r1,    r1,    r3     @ pDst+=stride
    BNE   Btype_HH_Loop
```

Figure 15.34 Assembly Code for an 8×8 Block B-type 1/2X-1/2X Motion Compensation

The code sequence illustrated in Figure 15.34 executes in 144 cycles with the loop providing 8-pixel output for each iteration. The sequence is dominated by double-word load and stores operations in addition to alignment operations. The instruction breakdown is illustrated in Table 15.11.

Table 15.11 Instruction Breakdown for the B-Type 8×8 Block 1/2X-1/2X MC

Instruction	Cycles	Description
WLDRD	32	Load source block pixels
MOV	*1	Setup loop count
WLDRDNE	*2	Last iteration conditional loads
WALIGNR	32	alignment of block pixels
WAVG2BR	24	average the pixel data
WSTRD	16	double-word stores at 2 cycles each
ADD	21	adjust ptr for prev. and future frame
ADD	*3	last ptr adjustment not used
SUBS	*8	decrementing the loop counter
BNE	*13	branching to loop start + fall through

* Instruction cycles associated with maintaining the loop

The complete routine executes in 161 cycles and is heavily dominated by alignment, double-word loads and pointer updates. The loop-unrolling technique can be applied to recover 27 of these cycles delivering a 16-percent improvement.

Key Points

Video compression is one of the more demanding applications being migrated to modern mobile communication devices. As resolution and frame rate increase, the memory and execution resources of the application processor easily can become saturated. To address these performance demands, Intel Wireless MMX technology serves as a coprocessor to the Intel XScale microarchitecture. Intel Wireless MMX technology provides several architectural features that improve performance and power efficiency for video compression algorithms. These features include a large register file, specialized instruction support for performing multiple SAD calculations, and alignment support for the pixel stream. Understanding the best way to use these features has been the primary subject of this chapter.

This chapter has shown you how to apply Intel Wireless MMX technology to video fast motion search algorithms and motion compensation. The key learning's from this chapter are:

■ The large coprocessor register file available with Wireless MMX technology allows a programmer to reduce load bandwidth significantly when executing multimedia algorithms. For motion estimation, the pixels from a source block need to be loaded only once for multiple comparison, leaving enough registers to manage other aspects of the calculation. These aspects include management of the reference block pixel loads, alignment the collection of clustered block SADs.

■ For many algorithms, misaligned data occurs naturally. Since alignment is important for achieving high performance, alignment using the WALIGN instruction is an important technique. The WALIGNR instruction is designed to enhance the performance for both motion estimation and motion compensation.

■ Loop unrolling is a powerful technique for improving performance. This technique has been demonstrated with the block-based calculations performed in motion estimation and compensation.

■ Developing specialized code sequences is often the best approach for obtaining the maximum throughput. The 1/2X motion compensation and the clustered SAD techniques illustrate that creating specialized code sequences often can be achieved through a simple copy of a basic code sequence and that the effort involved is low.

References

Bik, Aart J.C. 2004. *The Software Vectorization Handbook: Applying Multimedia Extensions for Maximum Performance,* Hillsboro, OR: Intel Press.

Intel Corporation. 2004. *Intel XScale® Core Developer's Manual.* Santa Clara, CA: Intel Corporation. A copy is included on the CD-ROM and you can find it at http://www.intel.com/design/intelxscale/273473.htm

Intel Corporation. 2004. VTune™ Performance Analyzer Web site at http://developer.intel.com/software/products/vtune/

Intel Corporation. 2004. Intel® PCA Developer Network Web site at http://developer.intel.com/pca/

Intel Corporation. 2004. Intel® Integrated Performance Primitives Web site at http://developer.intel.com/software/products/ipp/

Intel Corporation. 2003. Intel® Software Development Tools for Intel XScale® Microarchitecture, Santa Clara, CA: Intel Corporation. Available at http://www.intel.com/software/products/compilers/cevc/

Intel Corporation. 2003. Intel Assembler for Intel XScale® Microarchitecture, rev 1.17, Santa Clara, CA: Intel Corporation. Intel order number: 278586-006.

Intel Corporation. 2003. Intel® C++ Compiler, rev 2.0, Santa Clara, CA: Intel Corporation. Intel order number: 278496-006

Intel Corporation. 2003. Intel® Linker, rev 2.0, Santa Clara, CA: Intel Corporation. Intel order number: 278467-005

Intel Corporation. 2003. Intel® Library Manager, rev 1.3, Santa Clara, CA: Intel Corporation. Intel order number: 278468-002

Reinders, James. 2004. *Using the VTune™ Performance Analyzer: Measurement and Tuning Techniques for Software Developers*, Hillsboro, OR: Intel Press.

Taylor, Stewart. 2004. *Intel® Integrated Performance Primitives: How to Optimize Software Applications Using Intel® IPP*, Hillsboro, OR: Intel Press.

Index

66 As the pace of technology introduction increases, it's difficult to keep up. Intel Press has established an impressive portfolio. The breadth of topics is a reflection of both Intel's diversity as well as our commitment to serve a broad technical community.

I hope you will take advantage of these products to further your technical education. 99

Patrick Gelsinger
Senior Vice President and Chief Technology Officer
Intel Corporation

**Turn the page to learn about titles
from Intel Press for system developers**

Practical Advice for Writing Faster, More Efficient Code

Intel® Integrated Performance Primitives
How to Optimize Software Applications Using Intel® IPP
By Stewart Taylor
ISBN 0-9717861-3-5

Intel® Integrated Performance Primitives (Intel® IPP) is a software library for application developers that increases performance from Intel's latest microprocessors. Incorporating these functions into your code provides time-to-market advantages while reducing the overall cost of development. The lead developer of Intel IPP explains how this library gives you access to advanced processor features without having to write processor-specific code.

Introducing the many uses of Intel IPP, this book explores the range of possible applications, from audio processing to graphics and video. Extensive examples written in C++ show you how to solve common imaging, audio/video, and graphics problems.

You will learn how to:
- Become proficient using the Intel IPP library and application programming interface
- Apply Intel IPP to improve performance and speed development of your applications
- Use Intel IPP to solve common application problems

66 *Filled with comprehensive real-world examples. I'm recommending this book to my entire software team.* **99**

Davis W. Frank,
Software Program Manager,
palmOne, Inc.

● VTune™ Performance Analyzer Essentials
Measurement and Tuning Techniques for Software Developers
By James Reinders
ISBN 0-9743649-5-9

Intel® VTune™ performance tools "illuminate" your system and everything running on it. If you are a software application developer, software architect, quality assurance tester, or system integrator, this definitive book on the VTune™ Performance Analyzer gives you information that is otherwise not available in one place. The book shows the analyzer in action, providing numerous examples and step-by-step techniques.

COMING FALL 2004

Take the guesswork out of software tuning

● The Software Vectorization Handbook
Applying Multimedia Extensions for Maximum Performance
By Aart J.C. Bik
ISBN 0-9743649-2-4

The growing popularity of multimedia extensions has renewed an interest in vectorizing compilers. *The Software Vectorization Handbook* provides a detailed overview of compiler optimizations that convert sequential code into a form that exploits multimedia extensions. Compiler engineers and programmers of scientific, engineering, and multimedia applications will learn the latest techniques for improving software performance. The primary focus is on the C programming language and multimedia extensions to the Intel® Architecture, although most conversion methods are easily generalized to other imperative programming languages and multimedia instruction sets.

❝ Rarely have I seen a book of such a great value to compiler writers and applications developers alike... ❞

*Robert van Engelen,
Assistant Professor,
Florida State University*

Please go to this Web site

www.intel.com/intelpress/bookbundles.htm

for complete information about
our popular book bundles.
Each bundle is designed to
ensure that you read important
complementary topics together,
while enjoying a total purchase
price that is far less than the
combined prices of the
individual books.

About Intel Press

Intel Press is the authoritative source of timely, highly relevant, and innovative books to help software and hardware developers speed up their development process. We collaborate only with leading industry experts to deliver reliable, first-to-market information about the latest technologies, processes, and strategies.

Our products are planned with the help of many people in the developer community and we encourage you to consider becoming a customer advisor. If you would like to help us and gain additional advance insight to the latest technologies, we encourage you to consider the Intel Press Customer Advisor Program. You can **register** here:

www.intel.com/intelpress/register.htm

For information about bulk orders or corporate sales, please send email to
bulkbooksales@intel.com

Other Developer Resources from Intel

At these Web sites you can also find valuable technical information and resources for developers:

developer.intel.com	general information for developers
www.intel.com/IDS	content, tools, training, and the Early Access Program for software developers
www.intel.com/software/products	programming tools to help you develop high-performance applications
www.intel.com/idf	world-wide technical conference, the Intel Developer Forum

INTEL
PRESS